MARTIN BUBER'S
LIFE AND WORK

MARTIN BUBER'S

LIFE AND WORK

The Early Years, 1878-1923

Maurice Friedman

Wayne State University Press   Detroit   1988

92   91   90   89   88   5   4   3   2   1

Library of Congress Cataloging-in-Publication Data

Friedman, Maurice S.
  Martin Buber's life and work.

  Originally published: New York: Dutton, c1981–c1983.
  Includes bibliographies and indexes.
  Contents: [1] The early years, 1878–1923 — [2] The middle years, 1923–1945 — [3] The later years, 1945–1965.
  1. Buber, Martin, 1878–1965. 2. Philosophers, Jewish —Germany—Biography. 3. Philosophers—Germany—Biography. 4. Zionists—Germany—Biography. 5. Jews—Germany—Biography. 6. Jews, German—Israel—Biography. I. Title.
B3213.B84F727   1988   296.3'092'4   87–25415
ISBN 0–8143–1944–0 (pbk. : v. 1 : alk. paper)

Designed by Barbara Huntley.

Erratum

The pages from the original printing by E. P. Dutton, Inc. were used in producing this reprint. Miscellaneous errors were corrected with the exception of a repeated spelling error. Dag Hammarskjöld is spelled consistently as Hammarskjøld.

To Hal Scharlatt,
Who Urged Me to Bake This Bread,
and to Grete Schaeder,
Who Helped Me to Leaven It

The way in this world is like a knife edge.
There is an abyss on either side, and the
way of life lies in between.
—RABBI MOSHE LEIB OF SASOV

Contents

Preface

WHEN I PUBLISHED *Martin Buber: The Life of Dialogue* at the end of 1955, it was the first systematic and comprehensive book on Buber's thought in any language. In addition to tracing the development of Buber's thought and organizing his mature work around the problem of evil and its redemption, I devoted separate chapters to the significance of Buber's thought for theory of knowledge, education, psychotherapy, ethics, social philosophy, symbol, myth, and history, biblical faith, Judaism, and Christianity. Buber called this book the "classic study of my thought," helped me find an English publisher, and tried very hard to find publishers for a German and for a Hebrew translation of the book. During the more than a quarter of a century that I have devoted to the study, interpretation, and translation of Buber's works I have followed the life-thread of the questions that opened for me in one sphere after another — philosophy, religion, ethics, education, drama, psychotherapy, and social change. Now, at the end of this work, I have completed the most difficult task of all — *Martin Buber's Life and*

Work. In contrast to *The Life of Dialogue* — a systematic, analytical, and comparative work — *Martin Buber's Life and Work,* to coin a term, is a "dialography," an attempt to show Buber's thought and work as his active personal response to the events and meetings of his life. This means a change of emphasis from philosophical anthropology as an abstract analysis of the human condition to the concrete, historical, and unique. It means pointing to Buber not merely as a thinker but as an image of meaningful personal and social human existence, as he himself pointed to the Yehudi in his Hasidic chronicle-novel *For the Sake of Heaven* and to the Hasidic masters in *Tales of the Hasidim.*

However barbarous the neologism, I mean "dialography" seriously as a replacement, for *this* book at least, for the category of "biography." In the course of a dozen years of work on *Martin Buber's Life and Work,* I have become convinced of the fundamental falsification that is introduced by the evolutionary, developmental, or process approach to biography. This struck me particularly vividly when I read Dag Hammarskjøld's *Markings* in preparation for my chapter on Buber and Hammarskjøld. To understand the meeting and the continuing dialogue between Buber and Hammarskjøld, I would need to understand what most biographers necessarily leave out of account: the uniqueness of Hammarskjøld, the uniqueness of Buber, and the unique, present meeting between them that can never be grasped as merely a sum of their two uniquenesses. In any case, I could never regard Hammarskjøld merely as an event within the flow of Buber's becoming. Biography leads us to see events as clustered about a life — as if the event were contained in the life rather than, as is actually the case, the *life* in the events. To see the event — the meeting with other persons and situations — as merely part of a life process or development is necessarily to see it one-sidedly. To see the life in the event is to begin to glimpse the profound two-sidedness of every event.

In one of Martin Buber's tales of the Hasidim, Rabbi Leib, son of Sarah, says that he came to see the great preacher, the Maggid of Mezritch, not to hear him say Torah but to see the way in which he laced and unlaced his felt boots. The title that Martin Buber gave to this little tale is "Not to Say Torah but to Be Torah." This is not, as it might seem, a contrast between what a person is and what a person says. Rather, it is the basic way in which we speak to one another — through what we are. The whole person, who has brought his or her inner contradictions into some meaningful personal direction, communicates "Torah" — instruction and guidance on the way — even by his or her most casual and unintentional acts. All gestures, utterances, and actions bear the stamp of the unique person that he or she is. This person will also teach in words, but what he or she *is* is the guarantor of what he or she *says*. In another tale the same Rabbi Leib contrasts apparent speaking — mere words — and real speaking — with or without words:

> This is what Rabbi Leib, son of Sarah, used to say about those rabbis who expound the Torah: "What does it amount to — that they expound the Torah! A man should see to it that all his actions are a Torah and that he himself becomes so entirely a Torah that one can learn from his habits and his motions and his motionless clinging to God. . . ."

The words of an intellectual, even those of a genius, can exist detached from the man himself. The words of a wise man cannot. When the teachings of sages are transformed into objective doctrine divorced from the persons themselves, their real meaning is lost. All true teaching derives from and points back to the concrete life of the persons who have shown others the way. However much this life may be transformed and embellished by legend, there remains a historical core which the legend itself communicates, the core that witnesses to the encounter between this person and the persons of his or her time.

Martin Buber was a great philosopher, a consummate poet, a world-famous scholar of the Bible and of Hasidism — the popular Jewish mysticism that he almost single-handedly made part of the heritage of the Western world. He was one of the most learned men of his time, a universal scholar with an amazing command of languages and disciplines of knowledge. He was a genius with an inexhaustible store of creativity that produced a treasury of books, essays, poems, stories, a novel, and a play. But above all he was a wise man. "It is not true that wisdom comes of itself," Buber said. "It begins in learning and fulfills itself in true teaching." A true teacher is one who points the way. In Buber this pointing took place through his personal response to each situation, and his words were the product and expression of his response. That is why Buber's friend Abraham Joshua Heschel said, after Buber's death, that the man was greater than his writings. The writings are great indeed, but their true greatness can be grasped only in relation to the person who wrote them. The seriousness and responsibility with which Buber uttered each word, and their full significance, can never be comprehended through the words alone.

The way to true dialogue and the way to true communication are the same: not to simplify and popularize, turning difficult concepts into easy stereotypes, but to grasp what you are concerned with so wholly and concretely that you can communicate it directly and simply without being unfaithful to its integrity. The true mediator is the person who practices what Buber called "obedient listening": to listen so faithfully and respond so fully as to make alive for others the truth that has been made one's own.

I have tried in this book to help other people enter into my own dialogue with Martin Buber — a dialogue for over thirty years with the words of Martin Buber and for fifteen years with Buber himself — so that they too can understand and respond to his image and his word which have spoken so powerfully to modern man. A biography usually purports to *explain* a life, to make it understandable, by taking a series of discrete and present events and turning them into a stream of past-and-future, a connected process in time. However, despite my friendship and work with Buber over many years — even, perhaps, because of it — I could not presume to capture his life in some developmental scheme or re-create fully the concrete details and texture of an enormously rich and variegated life span of nearly ninety years. I have tried rather to center this book around "events and meetings" in Buber's life and thought. Through this I hope to do what Buber himself did in his "Autobiographical Fragments" — to show the concrete event as the real matrix of his philosophy. Such events are not just illustrations of universal and self-sufficient concepts. They are the living reality out of which all true concepts arise and in the fire of which they must constantly refine and test themselves. Thus my concern in this book is neither Buber's thought nor his life taken separately, but the meeting of the two in the situation and the event. It is in Buber's encounter with the persons and situations of his time that his active presence is revealed, and it is to this presence, above all, that I should like to point. In its human significance it transcends his worldwide influence and illuminates his writings. "There are some men," Buber has written, "who without intending to do so transform men's image of God." For many this is just what Martin Buber has done. Through his personal presence as well as through his teachings Buber has taught me and countless others that the biblical God is neither harsh and wrathful nor all-forgiving and understanding but a God whose presence means a demand — a demand that is at once judgment and love because it asks of the one who is addressed that he respond with his whole being.

Martin Buber was the philosopher of dialogue only because in the first instance he lived the *life* of dialogue. This does not mean that Buber was by nature a man of dialogue. In his youth he was more drawn to books than to men, and even the closest friends of his maturity — Hugo Bergmann and Ernst Simon — testified that dialogue did not come to him spontaneously. Neither does it mean that he was a man who lived his ideals. Buber was not an idealist, but, as he himself said of Albert Schweitzer, "a realist of the spirit." He did not think it possible or even desirable to live continually in dialogue. But he certainly lived dialogue as a direction of movement, as a constant opening of himself to the claim of the hour and responding from the depths of his own person, from "here where one stands" — in joyful and creative situations as well as tragic and bitter ones.

Martin Buber's Life and Work emphasizes the meetings on the narrow ridge of history and personal life out of which grew Buber's thought, his image of the human, and his great interpretations. "Worte an die Zeit" — Words to the Time — thus Buber called two small pamphlets that he wrote in 1919 in response to the crisis of postwar Europe. In the deepest sense of the term, the whole of his works, even his translation of the Hebrew Bible and his retelling of Hasidic tales, may be understood as words addressed to the time: they grew out of situations and speak to situations. To understand the encounters on the narrow ridge which produced these works is to understand more fully the works themselves. It is also to understand, as Arnold Jacob Wolf put it at the New York Buber Centennial Conference, that "More than anyone else writing in the first half of our century, perhaps, Buber addresses our own situation."

Insofar as possible, I have ordered the parts and chapters of this book chronologically; however, the central subject around which I have focused each particular chapter and part has made some overlapping necessary. *The Early Years* describes the road to *I and Thou* because *I and Thou* is the classic work which Buber himself saw as the first fully mature expression of his thought. This is not just a matter of intellectual and philosophical development but of events and meetings in many different spheres of life. Buber's loss of his mother as a child, the threat of the infinite he experienced at fourteen, his early poetry, his activity in the Jewish Renaissance movement and in cultural and political Zionism, his encounter with mysticism and his discovery of Hasidism, his "Speeches on Judaism," the impact on him of the First World War, his editorship of *Der Jude,* the murder of his friend Gustav Landauer, his work in postwar education, community, and politics, and his maturing from the "easy word" to the "hard word" — all these were necessary steps and roads toward Buber's in–depth understanding of all *real* living as meeting. Through them he reached not merely the *philosophy* but also the *life* of dialogue, the "I-Thou relationship."

I have made full use of letters from and to Buber in the three volumes of the *Briefwechsel* and wherever else I could find them in order to give a sense of Buber the person. I have translated them myself, as everything else in this book that was in German and was not yet or not adequately translated into English. An abridged version of the *Briefwechsel* will be published by Schocken Books in English translation. My references are in every case to the German original.

I have followed a suggestion of my friend Richard Hewitt and eliminated all footnotes and even footnote numbers from the text, including the Preface. Instead I have placed at the back of each volume the sources for the chapters in this volume. This should greatly increase the readability of the book, which is my prime objective. Even where I have not been able to break the sources down into subheadings, it should be possible for the scholar to trace the sources for specific passages without too much difficulty. That an enormous amount of scholarship has gone into this book will be evident from the sources, but I do not want scholarship to get between the story and the reader.

When Martin Buber was a university student, he became intensely interested in the German socialist Ferdinand Lassalle. Ignoring everything that was problematic about him, he formed from the rest a hero after the model of Carlyle. Asked to lecture to a socialist club, he chose this subject. When he was through, an old tailor came up to him with eyes gleaming. "I was in Lassalle's most intimate circle," he told the young Buber, grasping his hand. "As you have portrayed him, so he was, so he was!"

"How good it is to be confirmed thus!" Buber thought to himself. But the next moment all his pleasure left him. "No, it is *I* who have been confirming a lying idol," he realized. In an instant all that was vain and contradictory in Lassalle's character became present to him. In the weeks to come he tried in vain to recapture some image of Lassalle through psychological analysis. All the simplifications by which he attempted to grasp Lassalle's life in the end proved illegitimate. "Slowly, waveringly, grew the insight into the problematic reality of human existence and into the fragile possibility of doing justice to it."

In writing this book, I too have been aware of "the problematic reality of human existence" — of our time in particular and of a man whose life, even more than that of most great men, defies adequate comprehension. I have been all too conscious, indeed, of "the fragile possibility of doing justice" to Buber as a person, as a presence, as an active force for almost a century of contemporary history. Yet I have had to write this book as a witness to one who has shown us "the way of man" in a time when both our personal uniqueness and our humanity are in jeopardy. Martin Buber's significance for us is not that he was a saint or a *zaddik* or even one to whom the life of dialogue came easily, but rather that he was a person who embodied the contradictions and ambiguities of modern existence and yet was able again and again to reach personal wholeness and integrity in faithful response to the persons and situations of his time.

MAURICE FRIEDMAN

Solana Beach, California
December, 1979

Acknowledgments

IN 1965 soon after Hal Scharlatt left his career as a brilliant young lawyer to become an editor for McGraw-Hill, he approached Arthur Cohen about writing a "critical biography" of Martin Buber. Arthur Cohen responded that he could not do it, and that only I could. I agreed on the condition that the phrase "critical biography" not appear in the contract, since I was determined to write the unique book that I felt that I could write and did not want to be constrained by stereotyped conceptions of biography, or even "critical biography." After eight editors and three editors in chief I followed the suggestion of my literary agent Georges Borchardt and took *Martin Buber's Life and Work* to Dutton, where Hal Scharlatt had meanwhile become the editor in chief. Hal really believed in this book, despite its slow progress (by 1969 I had completed only one volume) and said that it would long outlast both of us (he was ten years younger than I). In 1974 I received a warm letter from him with a long article from the London *Times Literary Supplement* suggesting that a Buber renaissance might indeed be in the offing. After I had read his letter I opened one from his secretary Miranda Knickerbocker telling me that he had died of a heart attack the very night after he wrote me. Added to my shock and grief for the loss of a great editor and a friend was a crushing sense of existential guilt. Why had I not succeeded in ten years in completing this book that he had spurred me on to write so that he might have seen it while he was still alive? I dedicate this book to him and to his memory.

In 1969 I went to Israel for a third time, and there I shared with Grete Schaeder, the author of the distinguished study *The Hebrew Humanism of Martin Buber,* what I had written of the first volume together with the suggestions for cutting that had been generously made by the patient and loving effort of my friend and future colleague Christine Downing. Grete Schaeder was at that time hard at work on what is certainly the most impressive single piece of Buber scholarship, the editing of three-volume *Buber Briefwechsel,* the exchange of letters between Buber and a host of other persons over seven decades. She liked what I had written, but she thought it might be well for me not to publish *The Road to I and Thou* (the title of the first volume) until I had the letters she was bringing out for the comparable period of time. Though my book covered the essential milestones in Buber's life, the letters would help to "leaven" it, she said. I followed her advice and found the 1,500 letters she had selected out of 45,000 so representative and helpful that I cannot do less than dedicate this book to her too for a colossal labor of love.

Elie Wiesel has been a faithful friend throughout in relation to this book. After three exhausting lectures in Los Angeles and one in San Diego, he stayed up all night to read a thousand pages of the manuscript of the second volume before taking a plane at seven o'clock in the morning! When he had finished reading, Elie exclaimed, "Buber has been done an injustice," referring, I believe, to the way Buber is regarded in Israel. Elie's encouragement has helped me keep in mind the unique book that I have wanted to write. I have already expressed my gratitude to Grete Schaeder and Chris Downing. I am also deeply indebted to my old friend and former editor Richard Huett, who, as a freelance editor, undertook the formidable task of helping to cut this book, "playing hammer and anvil" in a dialogue with me to make the book both clearer and more readable. The patience, understanding, encouragement, and help of Bill Whitehead, senior editor at Dutton, have contributed much to making this book possible in its present form. For many months my friend and student Judy Stoup has given all of her spare time to type more than a thousand pages of this book, without which I could never have made my part of the deadline, and has made many helpful suggestions in the process. Myrtle Keeny typed most of the first, smaller volume during the years I was living in Swarthmore. I am also indebted to Winifred Strupp, who worked for a year as my assistant at Manhattanville College of the Sacred Heart, and Professor Jonathan Woocher of Carleton College, who, as my Ph.D. student and research assistant at Temple University, worked for two years to help me organize the materials for the second volume. My friend Professor Richard Hycner, formerly my Ph.D. student at the California School of Professional Psychology, San Diego, read many of the chapters of the second volume and made helpful suggestions for cutting. Sylvia Davis, my student at International College, has helped me by careful proofreading of much of the manuscript for the second volume. My friend Susan Richards has done more than any other single person to help me complete the second volume. Her unstinting work has taken off of my shoulders many burdens that were making real progress impossible! In addition to that she has helped to proofread the second volume and made many valuable suggestions concerning it. She has believed in this book and has given fully of herself for it. I am also grateful to my friend Virginia Lewis Shabatay for a careful reading and editing of the first volume which produced a great many needed changes.

When I was in Jerusalem in 1966 Ernst Simon talked personally with me, as did Hugo Bergmann and a great many others whom I list in the sources, and gave me many helpful suggestions. Simon made it clear from the outset that he had not time to read my book, and he has requested me not to acknowledge him in such a way that he might be held responsible for any possible inaccuracies in it. Nonetheless, I must express my gratitude to him for the many helpful and insightful essays that he has written on Buber in German and Hebrew, of which I have made use in this book.

I should like to acknowledge my indebtedness to the Gustav Wurzweiler Foundation and the Memorial Foundation for Jewish Culture of New York City, to the Philosophical Society of Philadelphia, and to Temple and San Diego State Universities for grants and "assigned time" that helped me in the writing of this book. I am also indebted to Ernst Simon and Rafael Buber for permission to use those of Buber's letters that are not in the *Briefwechsel* and are not directed to me personally. (The nearly three hundred letters that Buber wrote to me personally have been an invaluable source of material for the last part of the second volume of this book.) I am grateful to the Weizmann Institute in Rehovot, Israel, the Central Zionist Archives in Jerusalem, and the Leo Baeck Foundation in New York City for making those letters available to me. I must also express my indebtedness to the Martin Buber Archives and the Hebrew and National University Library of Jerusalem for making available to me a roomful of Buber materials, a room in which to work, a table on which to type, and a dozen letters.

I should like to thank my colleague Professor Ernest M. Wolf of San Diego State University for checking over the numerous German quotations in the text of both volumes.

I am greatly indebted to Rafael Buber and to the Martin Buber Archives of the Jewish and National University Library at the Hebrew University, Jerusalem, for permission to use the photographs that appear in this volume of *Martin Buber's Life and Work*.

PART I

Beginnings

(1878-1901)

CHAPTER 1

Meeting and "Mismeeting": Buber's Childhood and Youth

MORDECAI MARTIN BUBER was born in Vienna in 1878. He lived with his parents in a house over the Danube River, and he watched the moving canal with so intense an enjoyment that even toward the end of his life he could close his eyes and still see it flowing. Bound up with that experience was the certainty that nothing could happen to him. It is striking that it is in a chapter entitled "The World of Security" that the Austrian-Jewish writer Stefan Zweig described the Vienna in which he and Martin Buber, who was three years older, spent their early childhood:

> Growing slowly through the centuries, organically developing outward from inner circles, it was sufficiently populous, with its two millions, to yield all the luxury and all the diversity of a metropolis, and yet it was not so oversized as to be cut off from nature, like London or New York. The last houses of the city mirrored themselves in the mighty Danube or looked out over the wide plains, or dissolved themselves in gardens and fields, or climbed in gradual rises the last green wooded foothills of the Alps. One hardly sensed where nature began and where the

city: one melted into the other without opposition, without contradiction. Within, however, one felt that the city had grown like a tree that adds ring upon ring, and instead of the old fortification walls the Ringstrasse encircled the treasured core with its splendid houses. Within, the old palaces of the court and the nobility spoke history in stone. . . . In the midst of all this, the new architecture reared itself proudly and grandly with glittering avenues and sparkling shops. But the old quarrelled as little with the new as the chiselled stone with untouched nature. It was wonderful to live here, and in this city which hospitably took up everything foreign and gave itself so gladly; and in its light air, as in Paris, it was a simple matter to enjoy life.

But the certainty was soon shattered. Martin Buber's mother literally disappeared without leaving a trace, and the home of his childhood was broken up. This had a depressing effect on all the family, and particularly on the young Martin, who, even though he never spoke of it, bore signs of mourning and bereavement throughout his youth. The three-year-old child was sent to live with his paternal grandparents while his father later remarried with the permission of the high rabbinic court of Lvov. Only later was it discovered that Buber's mother had gone to Russia and had remarried there.

Martin Buber's grandfather Solomon Buber and his grandmother Adele lived on a large estate near Lvov (Lemberg), then the capital city of the Austrian "crownland," Galicia. Buber describes his grandparents as people of high rank, "noble persons in the exact sense of the term and, in a special manner, suited to and supplementing each other." This nobility of character placed an indelible stamp on the life of the child; for his grandparents became both parents and teachers to him. However, the effect on him was to intensify his sense of isolation and abandonment. They were not people who talked over their personal affairs even with each other, much less before the child. They said nothing in his presence about the separation of his parents. Nor did they prepare him in any way for what he might hope to expect in the future. Since no one told him that his mother had disappeared, he assumed that he would see her again soon. But in the atmosphere of his grandparents' house, he did not dare even to ask if this were so. His unasked question did receive an answer, nonetheless, from an altogether unexpected source.

The house in which his grandparents lived had a great rectangular courtyard surrounded by a wooden balcony extending to the roof on which one could walk around the building at each floor. Once when he was not yet four, the child stood on this balcony with a girl several years older, the daughter of a neighbor whom his grandmother had asked to look after him. They both leaned on the railing, and here there took place the dialogue which had not taken place with his grandparents. "I cannot remember that I spoke of my mother to my older comrade," Buber related. "But I still hear how the big girl said to me: 'No, she will never come back.' " He remained silent, but he had no doubt that she had spoken the truth.

This was the decisive experience of Martin Buber's life, the one without which neither his early seeking for unity nor his later focus on dialogue and on the meeting with the "eternal Thou" is understandable. The fact that he could accept unquestioningly what this diminutive authority had said did not lay his problem to rest. On the contrary, it marked its true beginning. It was realism but not resignation. It moved him into a new situation which was to be the touchstone and testing point of every other situation into which he entered. The words "She will *never* come back" remained with him and with the passing years became indelibly fixed. After more than ten years, he began to perceive what had happened to him — unusual though it was — as something that concerned not only him but everyone. In connection with this experience he later coined the word *Vergegnung* — mismeeting — to designate the failure of a real meeting (*Begegnung*) between men.

> When after another twenty years I again saw my mother, who had come from a distance to visit me, my wife and my children, I could not gaze into her still astonishingly beautiful eyes without hearing from somewhere the word *"Vergegnung"* as a word spoken to me.

Anyone who has looked at a picture of Martin Buber's mother as a young woman will not think his reference to her "astonishingly beautiful eyes" the product of sentimentality or nostalgia. It would have been more than understandable if he had clung throughout his life to the dream image of the mother he had known, as Marcel Proust clung to his mother and Franz Kafka to his father. The remarkable thing is that, for all the strength of his longing, he did not. "I suspect," Buber concluded this autobiographical fragment, "that all that I have learned in the course of my life about genuine meeting had its first origin in that hour on the balcony."

The corollary of Martin's "mismeeting" with his mother was his meeting, in the deepest sense of the term, with his grandparents, and in particular with his grandmother Adele. According to Buber's childhood friend Chaim Bloch, Adele Buber was the daughter of the rich Mr. Wizer, the owner of a paper factory in Sasov, near Zlotchov. Sasov was the home and last resting place of Rabbi Moshe Leib, disciple of the Hasidic rabbi Shmelke of Nikolsburg and himself one of the most beloved of *zaddikim,* or Hasidic leaders. Among the Jews in this small Galician town where Buber's grandmother grew up, the reading of "alien" literature was proscribed. The education of girls was still more limited. For them all literature, with the exception of edifying popular books, was held unseemly. When she was fifteen years old, Adele Wizer set up for herself in the storehouse a hiding place in which stood volumes of Schiller's periodical *Die Horen,* Jean-Paul's book on education, *Levana,* and other German books which she had secretly and thoroughly read. When she was seventeen years old, she brought these books with her to her marriage and, with them, the custom of concentrated reading. She was one of those Jewesses of that period who, in order to create freedom and leisure for their husbands to study the Torah, managed their businesses for them. Yet this remarkable woman embodied the wisdom behind Rabbi Moshe Leib's saying: "A human being who has not a single hour for his own every day is no human being." In addition to rearing her two sons and keeping the accounts for her husband, she managed to find time for herself. Each day she recorded income and expenditures in large-size, similarly bound copybooks. But each day too, in between these entries, she registered, after she had spoken them half aloud to herself, the passages which had become important to her out of her reading. She would also set down her own comments, as her part in her dialogue with these great spirits.

With her, Buber tells us, immediate experiencing and reflecting on experience were not two stages but two sides of the same process. Both in her speech and in her writings, the thoughts she communicated seemed like something perceived.

> When she looked at the street, she had at times the profile of someone meditating on a problem, and when I found her all alone in meditation, it seemed to me at times as if she listened. To the glance of the child, however, it was already unmistakable that when she at times addressed someone, she really addressed him.

Adele Buber did not send Martin to school until he was ten years old. Instead she had him taught by private tutors; humanism, with particular stress upon languages, was for her the royal road to education, and the child's own inclinations and talents lay in the same direction.

Martin Buber did not begin to speak until he was three. When he came to live with his father's parents at the age of four, he found himself in an environment in which very different peoples lived next to one another and a great many languages were spoken. In his grandfather's, as in his father's, house the German language predominated, but the language of the street and the school was Polish. "Only the Jewish quarter rustled with the rough and tender Yiddish, and in the synagogue there resounded, alive as ever, the great voice of Hebrew antiquity." But Buber owed his special relation to the German language to his grandmother Adele. She reared her sons, and later Buber himself, to respect the authentic word that cannot be paraphrased, that integral unity of word and thought which this age has lost sight of. Everything she wrote down was in a pithy and firm German, and her oral utterance was the same. Buber's grandfather was a true philologist, a "lover of the word," but his grandmother's love for the genuine word affected the child even more strongly: because this love was so direct and so devoted.

Buber saw the wonderful variety of human languages as the prism in which the white light of human speech at once fragmented and preserved itself. But already in his boyhood he realized that this variety came at a price. Time after time he followed an individual word or even structure of words from one language to another, and in the tracing found that something had been lost that apparently existed only in a single one of all the languages. What was lost was not merely nuances of meaning but the meaning itself. This precocious and undoubtedly very isolated and lonely little boy devised for himself dual-language conversations between a German and a Frenchman, later between a Hebrew and an ancient Roman. Through these conversations he came "half in play and yet at times with beating heart," to feel the tension between what was heard by the one person thinking in one language and what was heard by the other person thinking in another. "That had a deep influence on me," Buber testified, "and has issued in a long life into ever clearer insight." Indeed, it is here that one can find the essence of dialogical understanding not as precise definition, technical communication, or subjective empathy, but as "inclusion" — experiencing the other side of the relationship while not losing the awareness of one's own and of the polar tension between one's own and the other.

Why then did this essential insight, central to Buber's developing philosophy of dialogue, disquiet him? The answer is known by anyone who has ever tried to translate from one language into another: the difficulty of remaining faithful to the original while literally re-creating the meaning in the second language. Buber's knowledge of languages as a boy of fourteen or so made it possible for him at times to provide his grandfather Solomon Buber, whom he went to visit daily from his father's house, with a little help at his work on the Midrashim. Occasionally it happened that in reading "Rashi," the great Bible and Talmud exegete of the eleventh century, Solomon Buber found a text explained through a reference to a French turn of speech and asked young Martin how this was to be understood. At times Martin had to deduce from the Hebrew transcription the old French wording and then to make this understandable first to himself, then to his grandfather. Later, however, when he sat alone in his room in his father's house, he was oppressed by the question: What does it mean and how does it come about that one "explains" something that was written in one language through something that one is accustomed to say in another language? The world of the Logos and of the Logoi — the world of the word and the world of words — opened itself to him, darkened, brightened, darkened again.

Buber's favorite language as a child was Greek, and his philosophical education was established in particular on a thorough reading of Plato in Greek. When Buber took his *Abitur* — the examination given on leaving his gymnasium — the instructor questioned him about a speech of the chorus in Sophocles. Buber recited the passage from memory and thereby ended the examination.

Buber spoke German, Hebrew, Yiddish, Polish, English, French, and Italian and read, in addition to these, Spanish, Latin, Greek, Dutch, and other languages. This polyglot background was of importance for Buber not only as a translator, but also, as Hans Fischer-Barnicol has pointed out, as a predominantly German author. Even in conversation he knew how to express differences of meaning simply and surprisingly, not because he used individual words in unusual senses or coined new words, but because he employed long-familiar turns of speech with especial attentiveness and lent a customary grammatical function a fresh, deeper significance. This entirely unselfconscious quality of attentive listening characterized his writing as well. By comparing the way things were said in German with analogous uses in other languages, he had become particularly aware of the possibilities of expression of the German alone.

French, however, was one language the child Buber learned only with great pains, as he recounted after he had received an honorary doctorate from the University of the Sorbonne in Paris. Buber's grandparents had written for a Frenchman to come to their estate in Galicia; he not only had to teach grammar to young Martin and introduce him to the French classics but also had to be concerned about tutoring him in French conversation suitable for salons. On their walks, the French tutor talked incessantly to the boy. This chatter finally annoyed Martin so much that when the chance presented itself he gave the pedagogue a hefty push at the edge of a fishpond. The poor man landed in the water and finally had to be fished out, drenched to the skin.

More than any other single element in his physical appearance except his gentle but penetrating eyes, it was Buber's beard which gave him the appearance of the "Zaddik [Hasidic rabbi] of Zehlendorf," as he was jokingly called even by his family when he lived in that suburb of Berlin. Still later, it made many speak of him as a biblical prophet. Buber was photogenic, and he knew it, and he was not shy about having his picture taken. His appearance, indeed, was an integral part of the impact he made in his lectures. But Buber did not wear the beard because he wished to appear to be a *zaddik,* still less a prophet. Nor did he wear it out of identification with traditional Jewish forms. The real reason for Buber's beard, which he wore from his youth, was what the poetess Else Lasker-Schüler described as his "Moses mouth." The doctor had to deliver him by the use of forceps, and he thereby received an injury on the right side of his mouth which produced a disfigurement in the otherwise exceptionally handsome youth. This disfigurement he covered by the beard, and though it was not kept a secret, it was known only to relatively few. To those who did know about it, it was inevitable that it should seem somehow fateful or significant. The philosopher Fritz Kaufmann mentioned it in connection with that curious combination of success and failure that characterized Buber's life. Still others saw it as the special mark that is placed upon a man who is empowered and commanded to speak the word. Thus Schalom Ben-Chorin compares Buber in this respect to Isaiah, "a man of unclean lips" until they were purified by the glowing coal of the seraph, and to Moses, of whom the Bible says that he was a man of heavy tongue and lips.

Abraham Joshua Heschel has suggested that Buber's style cannot be really understood without recognizing the great impact of Yiddish on it. Although Buber preferred to speak German rather than Yiddish and spoke a pure, classical German rather than any form of dialect, his early fondness for the color and warmth of Yiddish never left him and did, indeed, influence his style and with it his way of thinking. In 1904 Buber translated, from Yiddish to German, David Pinski's *Eisik Scheftel*, "a Jewish workers' drama in three acts," and published it in the Jüdischer Verlag that he and his friend Berthold Feiwel had established. The man who was to write within the next two years two books on the very highest level of cultural German and who had to work for years until he could simplify and bring down to earth the overly ornate style of his youth was delighted by the popular ethnic qualities that he found in Yiddish. In his Foreword to *Eisik Scheftel,* Buber denied that Yiddish is a "jargon" or even simply a dialect and described it as something *sui generis.* It had developed from a folk idiom to a language of high quality, he claimed, not precisely rich but supple, pliant, less abstract but warmer than the Hebrew by which it is supplemented, full of incomparably gentle and rough, tender and malicious, accents. Here the people itself speaks, and to transpose its words into the syntax of High German would mean to do violence to the essence of what it says. For this reason, Buber left many characteristic words and forms of declension unchanged, and, in fact, wherever it would not injure the understandability of the text, he tried to preserve the Yiddish sentence structure, order, exclamations, interjection, and popular turns of speech. Yiddish did not cease to be of central importance for Buber. Practically all of the Hasidic legends and tales that he worked over for a lifetime and many Hasidic teachings were originally in Yiddish. Almost sixty years later, Buber reaffirmed his statement of 1904: "Yiddish is that spoken idiom of the popular masses of East European Jewry that has continually delighted me as the popular itself become speech." One single difference, indeed, between Buber's early rendition of the legends of the Baal-Shem and the legendary anecdotes that he later developed as the best form of rendering Hasidic tales is that the former tend to be exalted and romantic while the latter retain the rough, humorous, and down-to-earth quality of the Yiddish original. By the same token the former, even when they take the form of long stories, are usually lyrical or epical, while the latter, no matter how short, are invariably dramatic.

Buber's grandfather Solomon was, as Buber himself described

him, the last great scholar of the Haskalah, or the Jewish Enlightenment. He was unusual in his combination of business and scholarship. Although a self-taught man, he learned languages and their interrelationships so well that he is to be thanked for the first, and today, still *the* authoritative, critical editions of the Midrash — a special class of Talmudic literature made up of interpretations of the Bible, wise sayings, and rich saga. In his civil occupations, Solomon Buber was not only a great landowner but also a corn merchant and the owner of phosphorite mines on the Austrian-Russian border. An experienced man with independent judgment, he belonged to the leaders of the Jewish community and to the town's chamber of commerce. He never neglected his honorary offices, but he left much of the management of his business to his wife Adele (she conducted it most capably, although she made no decision without consulting him).

Contrasting his own more modest reputation with the fame of Buber's grandfather and the eminence that marked Martin Buber even in his twenties, Buber's father, Carl, is reported to have gently complained: "I am only the son of my father and the father of my son." Solomon Buber was one of the leading Jews and citizens of Lvov, beloved by and loving his fellowmen. He was also honored near and far by Jews of every branch of Judaism, even by the zealots among the Misnagdim — the opponents of the Hasidim — and by the Hasidim of Belz and Zans. His many articles and his arrangements, introductions, notes, and explanations of the Midrashim led Jewish writers and rabbis from all over the world to enter into correspondence with him and to send him their own works. The most learned Jewish scholars and rabbis of his time honored him and spoke of him with respect, even though in his outlook he saw himself not primarily as a Jew but as "a Pole of the religion of Moses."

Despite the many activities of business and scholarship that absorbed Solomon Buber, he found time to be something of a companion to his gifted grandson. If it was his grandmother Adele who taught him the true love of reading and of language, it was his grandfather who, even after Martin had gone back to live with his father, introduced him to the world of scholarship and, what was more important, to the task of Hebrew translation which was to occupy Martin throughout his life.

While Buber saw his mother only once again, his father reentered his life from his ninth year on. Carl Buber had remarried, and the boy went to join his father and his stepmother every summer on his father's estate. At fourteen he moved from his grandfather's house to his father's townhouse.

Although in his youth Buber's father had strong interests in the issues that Darwin's *Origin of Species* and Renan's *Life of Jesus* had made current, his influence on his son Martin was not an intellectual one. What struck the child, rather, was his father's devotion to agriculture, which made him a phenomenon among the East Galician landed property owners. He was far in advance of those around him in his scientific farming, working for thirty-six years to heighten the productivity of his soils through careful testing of all kinds of implements. Once he even brought with him from the Paris International Exhibition a great packing of breeding eggs of a type of hen still unknown in the east, holding it on his knees the whole long journey to protect it.

What made him still more exemplary was that he combined this mastery of technique with a direct concern for the animals and plants with which he worked. When he stood in the midst of the splendid herd of horses, he greeted one animal after the other, not merely in a friendly fashion but each one individually. When he drove through the ripening fields, he would halt the wagon, descend, and bend over the ears of corn again and again, finally breaking one and carefully tasting the kernels. He was not some English nature poet but a practical farmer: "This wholly unsentimental and wholly unromantic man was concerned about genuine human contact with nature, an active and responsible contact." From accompanying his father at times in his work on the estate, the boy Martin learned something that he could not have learned from any book. In his own person, Carl Buber anticipated one of the most fundamental aspects of his son's later thoughts: that the man who practices immediacy does so in relation to nature just as much as to his fellowman — the "I-Thou" relation to nature is a corollary of the "interhuman."

Carl Buber, his son later reported, took part in the life of all the people who were in one way or another dependent on him — the laborers attached to the estate in their little houses built according to his design that surrounded the estate buildings, the peasants who performed services for him under most favorable conditions, and the tenants. He concerned himself with their family lives, with the upbringing and schooling of the children, with all who became sick or aged. This solicitude was not derived from any principles,

Buber asserted, but was directly personal. This same way of acting in relationship to people carried over into the town. He was fiercely averse to impersonal charity. "He understood no other help than that from person to person, and he practiced it." Even in his old age, he accepted election to the "bread commission" of the Jewish community of Lemberg and fulfilled his responsibilities himself, in direct contact with those in need. He constantly visited these people in order to discover their real wants and necessities.

The last thing that Buber has told of his father is particularly significant for the development of the son. Carl Buber was "an elemental story teller." When he spoke about the people whom he had known, he always reported the simple occurrence without any embroidery — "nothing more than the existence of human creatures and what took place between them." Perhaps the most remarkable achievement of Martin Buber was that, in the course of a long lifetime of retelling Hasidic and other legends, he himself became "an elemental story teller" in just this sense.

If Martin Buber's parents had remained together in Vienna, his education undoubtedly would have been entirely different from what it was. It isn't likely that he would have been kept at home with private tutors studying languages until he was ten. Even when young Martin did go to school (it was called the Franz Joseph's Gymnasium, after the Emperor) it was really in most respects a Polish gymnasium, not an Austrian one. Since the Ruthenians had their own schools, by far the largest number of the pupils in Buber's schools were Poles, with a small Jewish minority. The language of instruction and of social intercourse was Polish, but it was not, of course, a Polish national school. Individually, the pupils got on well with one another, but the two groups as such knew almost nothing about each other.

The classroom included five rooms with six benches apiece at each of which two pupils sat. The farthest bench to the left at the window belonged to Martin and his best friend. For eight years they sat at this same bench, his friend to the left and himself to the right. During the fifteen-minute recesses the whole school used to storm out to the square and play until the signal bell. When the weather was inclement they stayed together in the classroom, usually forming small groups talking with one another.

At this school Buber received his basic instruction in a variety of subjects, the report cards on which can still be seen in the Buber Archives at the National and University Library in Jerusalem. There he learned the excellent command of Polish that remained with him even when he no longer had occasion to use the language and that once enabled him more than fifty years later, as Abraham Heschel has related, to address a group of Poles in perfect Polish. Even when he had gone to the University of Vienna, he kept contact with the Polish student movement, probably in particular with the socialists. His uncle Rafael Buber was himself a prominent Polish socialist. Some months before the outbreak of World War II, Buber went as an emissary to Lodz, Poland, from the Hebrew University.

One of the earliest memories that remained with Martin Buber in his old age was the red riding habit that he wore as a child. But his love of horses was not confined to riding. When he was eleven years of age, spending the summer on his grandfather's estate, now as often as he could do it unobserved, he used to steal into the stable and gently stroke the neck of his darling, a broad dapple-gray horse. This was no casual delight for him, but a great, deeply stirring happening. When he wrote of it many years later, the memory of his hand stroking the horse was still fresh and with it the sense of friendly contact the "the immense otherness of the Other." This otherness did not remain strange for him, like the otherness of the ox and the ram, but rather let him draw near and touch it.

> When I stroked the mighty mane, sometimes marvellously smooth-combed, at other times just as astonishingly wild, and felt the life beneath my hand, it was as though the element of vitality itself bordered on my skin, something that was not I, was certainly not akin to me, palpably the other, not just another, really the Other itself; and yet it let me approach, confided itself to me, placed itself elementally in the relation of *Thou* and *Thou* with me. The horse, even when I had not begun by pouring oats for him into the manger, very gently raised his massive head, ears flicking, then snorted quietly, as a conspirator gives a signal meant to be recognizable only by his fellow conspirator: and I was approved.

If it was experiences such as this that made Buber unwilling to relinquish his concept of an "I-Thou," or direct, open, personal relationship with nature, this particular experience became for him a concrete example of "reflexion," the basic movement of "the life of monologue." As "dialogue" did not mean for Buber two speaking, so "monologue" did not mean one. It meant turning toward oneself and away from the particularity of the other person. In "reflexion" the other is allowed to exist only as "a part" of one-self. Once when young Martin was stroking the horse, it struck him what fun it gave him, and suddenly he became conscious of his hand. The game went on as before, but it was no longer the same. The next day when he gave the horse a rich feed and stroked his mane his friend did not raise his head. Aware of how his relation-ship to the horse had changed, he felt himself judged. Later when he thought back on the incident, he no longer imagined that the horse had noticed his lapse into monologue.

Martin Buber spent his first year of university studies in Vienna, the city of his birth and earliest childhood. "The detached, flat memory images," he wrote of Vienna sixty years later, "appear out of the great corporal context like slides of a magic lantern; also many districts that I could not have seen address me as acquain-tances." The return at this point in his life to Vienna had a pro-found effect upon Buber which, in his own words, established some-thing "that in later years could not be shattered by any of the cri-ses of the age." What this was Buber again described in terms of mutual contact, contact with otherness. "This original home of mine, now foreign, taught me daily, although still in unclear lan-guage, that I had to accept the world and let myself be accepted by it; it was indeed ready to be accepted." In the rich and exciting Vienna of the turn of the century, Buber found a unique culture in which south German, Jewish, and Slavic influences were mixed.

> Nowhere at that time was there so much openness to the cultural contacts of the Scandinavian north and of the Romance literatures as in Vienna, but here all these influences which had arisen in firmer, harder forms, nearer to reality, seemed transformed by a warmer, feminine na-ture.

Stefan Zweig saw Vienna's passionate drive toward cultural ideals as the product of the fact that for centuries Austria had been neither politically ambitious nor militarily successful. Instead, making music, dancing, the theater, conversation, and proper and urbane deportment were cultivated in Vienna as particular arts. Vienna drew into itself the most diverse forces of nationality and culture, loosened, propitiated, and harmonized them. "It was sweet to live here, in this atmosphere of spiritual conciliation, and sub-consciously every citizen became supranational, cosmopolitan, a citizen of the world," wrote Zweig.

> Even in the lower circles, the poorest drew a certain instinct for beauty out of the landscape and out of the merry human sphere into his life; one was not a real Viennese without this love for culture, without this sense, aesthetic and critical at once, of the holiest exuberance of life.

But the Jews in Vienna were the patrons and exponents of culture in a way that in former ages the nobility had been. Writing at the beginning of the 1940s, Zweig claimed that "most, if not all that Europe and America admire today as an expression of a new, rejuvenated Austrian culture, in literature, the theatre, in the arts and crafts, was created by the Viennese Jews."

During his two semesters at the University of Vienna Buber attended lectures that left little impression upon him. Even the significant scholarly lectures did not have the same impact as the seminars into which he had prematurely flung himself. Nor was it the content of the seminar that strongly influenced him but the form, the seminar itself: "The regulated and yet free intercourse between teacher and students, the common interpretations of texts, in which the master at times took part with a rare humility, as if he too were learning something new, and the free exchange of question and answer" — all this disclosed to Buber, more directly than anything that he read in a book, what makes the human spirit actual: the reality *between* person and person.

While Buber was studying at the University of Vienna, he adopted the Viennese style of speaking and writing, particularly of those in the forefront of Vienna culture who were developing a language of great richness and beauty, though often overcultivated and somewhat affected. Overlying his love of Yiddish and his childhood experiences with Polish, German, Greek, and Latin was the impact on the young Buber of his total immersion in the exciting but chaotic artistic and intellectual atmosphere of Vienna at the turn of the century. "The well-to-do student of philosophy and of the history of art and literature loved the playful elegance, the sublime pathos of the new-romantic sensibility and aesthetic," writes Fischer-Barnicol, "the urbane spirit of the coffeehouse intelligence. Soon he became the friend of the poets, Hofmannsthal, Beer-Hofmann, Schnitzler, . . . and, in fact, appeared to want to become 'only' a poet, a member of the literati."

Hugo von Hofmannsthal was the Viennese poet whose work initiated and virtually seduced Martin into availing himself of "the primordial gold of speech" in the Vienna of his day. "Let the heir be a squanderer," so began the "Song of Life," that magic and be-witching poem by Hofmannsthal, which became Martin's siren call. After young Buber had purchased on a Vienna street the issue of *Wiener Rundschau* in which this poem appeared, he sat down on a bench in a public park and read. "A shudder (not of enjoyment, but truly a 'holy shudder') overcame me: this verse there had been written only a short time ago." It was Buber's first penetrating ex-perience of the contemporary, and it remained so vividly present to him that a half century later he chose this poem as one of three that he contributed to an anthology of favorite German verses.

Another Viennese poet whom Buber was drawn to during this period was Richard Beer-Hofmann, for the collected edition of whose works the aged Buber wrote a remarkable introduction, in English in Buber's "Gleanings." Beer-Hofmann too was concerned with the theme of "the heirs" and of the conquering of death through heritage. But in his case, this theme expanded to include the heritage of Israel (Beer-Hofmann was Jewish). In the early *Jewish Almanac* that Buber and Berthold Feiwel edited there ap-peared Beer-Hofmann's classic "Lullaby to Miriam," named for his daughter. Buber saw this poem as Beer-Hofmann's first mature answer to the terror of death and loneliness: our being itself is an inheritance from our forebears that we in turn bequeath to our children. In *Jacob's Dream* and the uncompleted David trilogy to which it is a prelude, this theme became that of Israel, the suffer-ing yet enduring people. If Beer-Hofmann's influence on Buber was not so great as Hofmannsthal's, the friendship between Buber and Beer-Hofmann was even closer and the path these two men took more similar.

Another strong influence on the young Buber, again more im-portant than that of Beer-Hofmann, was the strange and romantic figure of Stefan George. In the early years of this century, George was even more famous and influential than Rainer Maria Rilke, particularly because of the school of followers that George drew around him. At the age of eighteen, Buber became acquainted with George's poetry (a year earlier than Hofmannsthal's), and al-though he never entered into a personal relationship with George, as he did with Hofmannsthal and Beer-Hofmann, Buber continued to think highly of much of George's poetry even during his own later years. "When I read George's poem *Der Tag des Hirten*" (Shep-herd's Day), wrote Buber, "I knew that in this, in my time a poet lived." Five years later, when he was twenty-three, Buber read the prelude to George's book of poems, *The Tapestry of Life*, and learned that poems may be as legitimately united in a series as verses in a poem — "and the series was a dialogue." "These are two events — unforgettable but perhaps uncommunicable — which have influenced my youth," Buber added, and "the second far more powerfully than the first."

Buber's admiration for George never led him to make a cult out of his poetry and personality as so many of George's followers did, nor did he ever associate himself with the George Circle, though he knew and respected among its members such important poets as Friedrich Gundolf, Karl Wolfskehl, and Rudolf Borchardt. Of George himself Buber said that he was problematic as a man, but as a poet he had composed as many as twenty-five beautiful German poems.

It was undoubtedly Hofmannsthal and George who most directly influenced the poetry that Buber wrote in his early years. The young Buber's enthusiasm for the Jewish Renaissance movement produced not only many essays but also quite a number of poems, some of which, years later, Buber quite rightly judged "pathetic little verses," others of which were not quite so bad, but all of which were unmitigatedly romantic. Buber did not see fit to include a single one of these poems in his *Nachlese* — his "gleanings" of what, aside from his collected works, deserved to be preserved of all his writings. But he did include four early poems, two on Elijah (1903 and 1904), intended to be part of a play (hence ancestors of the play *Elijah* which Buber wrote in 1956), and two from a poem cycle entitled *Geist der Herr* (Spirit Is the Lord, 1901). The atmosphere of these two latter poems of Buber's — "The Disciple" and "The Magicians" — seems distinctly that of George.

THE DISCIPLE

The gray hand of the storm lay over both.
The Master's hair bore a black glow.
Enveloped and rocked to sleep in dumb suffering
Was the face of the disciple, pale and kind.

The way was rocky. Lightning and mountain fire
Zigzagged around them like trembling branches
The boy's step grew weak and ever more timid,
The old man walked as always, straight and firmly.

The blue eyes gazed dreaming into his own,

And through the narrow cheeks beat the shame,
The mouth was set as from repressed weeping,
The great longing of a child came.

Then the master spoke: "From much wandering
I took the golden might of the one truth:
If you can be your own, never be another's."
And silently the boy walked in the night.

If "The Disciple" shows the master teaching independence to the disciple, "The Magicians" lays stress not upon proud isolation but upon the need for mutuality and the unsatisfactory character of a power that does not know it. The band of magicians marched by the silent master sitting on his black throne and told of their seeking and the power that they found: one found in the mountain shaft the drive to form, another the force of becoming in the grain of seed. But finally a crowned man came whose speech made every heartbeat die away and the word with it: "Above all power there has remained to me the craving for a person I might love, for all power is dead."

Of the many, many figures that one might mention from classic German literature (the breadth and depth of Buber's reading was phenomenal, and he remembered perfectly what interested him), two must in particular be singled out as early and continuing major influences on his thought and on his style: Goethe and Hĩderlin. The importance of Goethe for Buber can be seen from the fact that it was a verse of Goethe's that Buber placed as a motto at the beginning of *I and Thou*: "So waiting I have won from thee the end/God's presence in each element." In the second part of *I and Thou*, moreover, where Buber gives three examples of those who speak the word "I" truly, in such a way as to share in reality and strengthen the mutuality between I and Thou, it is Goethe whom he selects as the man who speaks the "I" of the I-Thou relationship with nature:

How beautiful and legitimate the full I of Goethe sounds! It is the I of pure intercourse with nature. Nature yields to it and speaks ceaselessly with it; she reveals her mysteries to it and yet does not betray her mystery. It believes in her and says to the rose: "So it is You" — and at once shares the same actuality with the rose. Hence, when it returns to itself, the spirit of actuality stays with it; the vision of the sun clings to the blessed eye that recalls its own likeness to the sun, and the friendship of the elements accompanies man in the calm of dying and rebirth.

It is another element in Goethe, however, that Buber particularly pointed to in selecting for the anthology his favorite Goethe poem, "The Testament of Ancient Persian Faith" from the *West-östlichen Divan.* "From time to time I open the book to these pages," Buber recounted, "but I do not read them for I have, in fact, known it by heart from youth." Although the whole poem — nineteen stanzas of four verses each — was reprinted in Buber's section of the anthology, in his commentary Buber drew attention to only a single verse. This was the third line of the seventh stanza. In an action otherwise unheard of in his poetry, Goethe had this line stressed: *"Schwerer Dienste tägliche Bewahrung"*(Daily achievement of difficult tasks). When Buber looked at this line, he testified, he would remember once again a lonely, painful morning when this verse unexpectedly came into his head. At that moment he recited it aloud, gave the emphasis its full due, and burst into tears. "How good, how mysteriously good it was that he had stressed these words! This emphasis is itself a testament."

> *Und nun sei ein heiliges Vermächtnis*
> *Brüderlichem Wollen und Gedächtnis:*
> Schwerer Dienste tägliche Bewahrung,
> *Sonst bedarf es keiner Offenbarung.*

"And now let there be a holy testament of brotherly willing and memory: *Daily achievement of difficult tasks;* no revelation is needed other than this."

Buber attributed to Goethe his own central concern with man *as man* in "relationship to the Supremely Alive, i.e., to Divine Being," without transgressing the borderline on the other side of which lay "a mystical, timeless view of Being." The true human person, Buber interpreted and proclaimed, is open to the world and achieves true humanity through his helpfulness to others. This openness means acceptance of all ways to the truth, all relationships to the Divine, in the hope for an association of truly human persons, touching and comprehending all others, and thus making mankind a true humanity.

> Any genuine life-relationship to Divine Being — i.e., any such relationship effected with a man's whole being — is a human truth, and man has no other truth. To realize this does not mean to relativize truth. The ultimate truth is one, but it is given to man only as it enters, reflected as in a prism, into the true life-relationships of the human persons. . . . Hu-

man truth is not a conformity between a thing thought and the thing as being; it is participation in Being. It cannot claim universal validity, but it is lived, and it can be lived exemplarily, symbolically.

Hölderlin is a more limited figure than Goethe, but he is also distinctly more modern, and an age that still values Nietzsche and Rilke values Hölderlin too, including even the fact of his insanity and its effect on his poetry. It is Hölderlin's seven-page poem-hymn "Patmos" that Buber selected as his third favorite poem for the anthology of favorite German verse. It is from Hölderlin's "Patmos" that Buber took that verse that occupies such a central place in the third dialogue of *Daniel* and in *I and Thou*: "Where danger is, the delivering power grows too."

When the eighteen-year-old Martin came to Vienna, he discovered a whole world of living theater whereas before "theater" was merely dramas read in books. What affected him most strongly was the great Burgtheater, which was in many ways the central cultural institution in prewar Vienna in a way that was hardly possible in any other city. This Imperial theater was for the Viennese "the brightly-colored reflection in which the city saw itself, the only true corigiano of good taste," as Stefan Zweig described it:

> In the court actor the spectator saw an excellent example of how one ought to dress, how to walk into a room, how to converse, which words one might employ as a man of good taste and which to avoid. The stage, instead of being merely a place of entertainment, was a spoken and plastic guide of good behaviour and correct pronunciation, and a nimbus of respect encircled like a halo everything that had even the faintest connection with the Imperial theatre.

Into the Burgtheater at times, day after day, the young Buber rushed up three flights after several hours of standing in line in order to capture a place in the highest gallery.

> When far below in front of me the curtain went up and I might then look at the events of the dramatic agon as, even if in play, taking place here and now, it was the word, the "rightly" spoken human word that I received into myself, in the most real sense. Speech, here in this world of fiction as fiction, first won its adequacy; certainly it appeared heightened, but heightened to itself.

It was only a matter of time, however, until — as always happened — someone fell for a while into recitation, a "noble" recitation. Then this whole world, mysteriously built out of surprise and law, was shattered for him — until after a while it arose anew with the return of the face-to-face dimension of the play.

What Buber learned here about living, spoken speech, of the speech that "takes place" in the "between," was not and could not be restricted to the artistically detached sphere of the theater alone. It illuminated for him human existence as such, and as such became for him one of the highways leading to *I and Thou*. This reality of speech-as-event was particularly connected for Buber with Vienna. Having learned this in the theater, he could now hear it in the street:

> Since then it has sometimes come to pass, in the midst of the casualness of the everyday, that, while I was sitting in the garden of an inn in the countryside of Vienna, a conversation penetrated to me from a neighboring table (perhaps an argument over falling prices by two market wives taking a rest), in which I perceived living, spoken speech, sound becoming "Each-Other."

In his first year as a student at the University of Vienna, Buber occupied himself with literature, the history of art, and philosophy. In the winter semester 1897/1898 Buber studied at the University of Leipzig, and in the summer of 1899 he studied at the University of Zurich. In Leipzig and Zurich he attended lectures on philosophy, history of art, history of literature, psychiatry, Germanics, classical philosophy, and national economy. His philosophy at that time was particularly oriented to the natural sciences. He attended the lectures of Ernst Mach, Austrian physicist and philosopher, Wilhelm Wundt, German physiologist and ethnopsychologist, and Carl Stumpf, German philosopher and psychologist, and was an enthusiastic student at the psychiatric clinic.

An incomparable portrait of Martin Buber as a university student is given us by the friend of his youth, Ahron Eliasberg. Even before Eliasberg met him, Buber's name was familiar to him. The families of the two youths were related, and Buber's father and stepmother often came to Eliasberg's home city of Pinsk, where they spoke of Martin's rare gifts. As a result, Eliasberg was overjoyed when he heard one day during his first semester at the University of Leipzig that Martin Buber had been invited to dinner along with him at the house of some relatives. Before he actually met Buber, he found his name in the student register and tried unsuccessfully to imitate Buber's already distinguished signature! When the eagerly awaited day finally came, Buber exceeded all his expectations. Martin told of his two semesters as a student at the University of Vienna, of his meetings with writers and scholars, and of the contents of the courses he took there. He expressed a very strong interest in Wundt's ethnopsychology, which he had read for the first time, and recited whole stanzas from the old and the very newest poets. "I saw at once," Eliasberg reports, "that his knowledge was genuine, and I tumbled from admiration to admiration, from enthusiasm to enthusiasm."

From then on, the two youths met frequently and had much to do with each other. It is difficult to express, says Eliasberg, how much instruction, stimulation, even elevation he owed to this youth, only six months his senior, whose many-faceted personality was already at that time essentially formed.

Together they read philosophical and poetic works, among which were the writings of the great sociologist and philosopher Georg Simmel, who was later Buber's teacher at the University of Berlin. The young Buber gave Eliasberg glimpses of his extensive acquaintance with great literary figures. He was an enthusiastic supporter of Peter Altenberg, who at that time was almost unknown in Germany, and Eliasberg was much impressed when in his presence the newest work of the poet arrived with a dedication and an accompanying letter for Buber. The latter had an acute ear for the voices of the time. He was one of the first to notice and recognize Walter Rathenau, later a great German-Jewish statesman and man of letters in the Weimer Republic. Rathenau's antithesis of "not knowing yet creating" expressed Buber's own feeling about life. When with the close of the winter semester, Buber left Leipzig, he sent Eliasberg Schopenhauer's works and inscribed in them:

> *Content yourself with the world as it is — the wise men teach.*
> *But I call to you boldly: Create for yourself a world!**

Shortly after they became acquainted, Eliasberg discovered in a volume of German poetry edited by Karl Emil Franzos a poem of Buber's whose opening stanza expressed a similar joy of life.

---

* *"Mit der gegebenen Welt begnüge dich — lehren die Weisen.*
  Aber ich rufe dir kühn: Schaffe dir selbst eine Welt!"

You torment yourself without cease,
You seek and do not find.
The burden of life is itself for me
Gladness and poetry. *

Buber's tirelessness was stupendous, Eliasberg reports. Once they rode to Berlin — fourth class, of course — in order "to rescue" a Zionist meeting, and they came back the same day. The train left Berlin at one in the morning, and they arrived in Leipzig at dawn. As always in such cases, Buber did not go to bed but went instead to a meeting held that morning. Then back to the house, where he donned a frock coat in order to take part in a banquet which was followed by a ball. Buber, at that time a passionate devotee, danced the whole night through and then proceeded directly from the ballroom to his classes at the university.

In addition to his regular courses at the university, Buber worked in the psychological seminar of Wundt and — as the only nonmedical student — in the physiological institute. He also took part in the activities of the seminar on art history run by August Shmarsov, who, hardly known to the wider public, surrounded himself with an esoteric circle of respectful admirers. Along with this, Buber found time to take part in whatever social and artistic groups Leipzig offered. It goes without saying that he missed none of the premieres of the "Literary Society" founded by Hans von Weber, the evenings with authors, and above all the performance of new theater pieces.

Buber quickly became prominent in Leipzig Jewish society. The rabbi Dr. Porges, whose house he much frequented, called him "a lad of genius," while his wife, who had formed around herself a circle of "beautiful spirits," championed Buber with a vigor that was possible only in a "salon." Through the Porges family Buber joined the "Ethical Culture Society," to whose closeted existence he lent an unaccustomed splendor with his two lectures on Lassalle and "Individualistic and Socialistic Ethics." Buber was at that time captivated by Lassalle and probably felt himself to be destined for a similar life. He prepared himself thoroughly for his first lecture. The effect of the not yet twenty-year-old was staggering — because of the fullness of his research, the independence of his judgments,

---

* *"Ihr zerquält euch ohne Rast, / Sucht und findet nicht,*
  Mir ist selbst des Lebens Last/Frohsinn und Gedicht."

and the force of his delivery. The public was immediately overcome. "I have never again," attests Eliasberg, "so experienced
youth triumphing." It is striking that this was the very lecture
whose success so profoundly shattered Buber by forcing him to
see the problematic aspects of Lassalle that he had formerly chosen to overlook.

CHAPTER 2

The Threat of Infinity and the Promise of Time

WHEN AHRON ELIASBERG and Martin Buber walked home together after their first meeting, Buber called attention at one point to the opposite side of the street. "Beyond good and evil therefore," Eliasberg remarked, and Buber asked, "Have you too read Nietzsche?" "No," answered Eliasberg timidly, "and you?" "Oh, for two or three years I was a passionate Nietzschean," the teenage boy replied, "but now I see in him only just. . . ." Poor Eliasberg was crushed.

Precocious and even affected as these words must seem, Buber was not just throwing sand in his eyes. Though clearly not averse to letting his young friend glimpse his knowledge in order to impress him, his knowledge of Nietzsche was more than superficial. Indeed, before his Nietzsche period he had been deeply influenced by Immanuel Kant, the rationalist philosopher of the Enlightenment, and that when he was only fourteen! Nor was this influence merely an intellectual one; it was deeply involved in the boy's personal existence. Whatever the link may have been between the three-year-old's loss of his mother, and the fourteen-year-old's terror before the infinity of the universe, we have no reason to doubt the authenticity of the crisis through which the boy Buber passed at fourteen nor the seriousness of his relationship to the philosophy that saved him from it. The inner Buber knew none of that easy success and mastery that the admiring Eliasberg reported of the outer.

In his "Autobiographical Fragments" Buber linked this crisis over the infinity of space and time, in which Kant helped him, to his seduction by Nietzsche when he was seventeen. In both cases philosophy encroached directly upon his existence in a way that had nothing to do with his philosophical education. This education in philosophy was grounded in particular in a thorough reading of Plato (Greek was his favorite language), and was a gradual process. His encounters with Kant and Nietzsche, in contrast, "were catastrophic events which broke through the continuity — the presupposition of all genuine educational work."

When Buber related the first of these two events in "What Is Man?" he set it in the context of Pascal's recognition of the uncanniness of man's existence beneath the infinite spaces between the stars. This confrontation with infinity makes man's very existence a casual and questionable one, for it makes of man the essentially vulnerable creature whose knowledge that he is exposed robs him of the sense of being at home in his world. As a result, any concept of space and time, a finite no less than an infinite one, becomes terrifying to man, for both make man conscious that he is no match for the world. The fourteen-year-old Buber — even more precocious in this respect than the young mathematical genius Pascal — experienced this in a way that deeply influenced his whole life:

> A necessity I could not understand swept over me: I had to try again and again to imagine the edge of space, or its edgelessness, time with a beginning and an end or a time without beginning or end, and both were equally impossible, equally hopeless — yet there seemed to be only the choice between the one or the other absurdity. Under an irresistible compulsion I reeled from one to the other, at times so closely threatened with the danger of madness that I seriously thought of avoiding it by suicide.

In his "Autobiographical Fragments," written twenty years after "What Is Man?" Buber told us that the question about time had tormented him far more than that about space. He was irresistibly driven to want to grasp the total world process as actual, and that meant to understand time either as beginning and ending or as without beginning and end, each of which proved equally absurd:

> If I wanted to take the matter seriously (and I was ever again compelled to want just this), I had to transpose myself either to the beginning of time or to the end of time. Thus I came to feel the former like a blow in the neck or the latter like a rap against the forehead — no, there is no beginning and no end! Or I had to let myself be thrown into this or that bottomless abyss, into infinity, and now everything whirled. It happened thus time after time. Mathematical or physical formulae could not help me; what was at stake was the reality of the world in which one had to live and which had taken on the face of the absurd and the uncanny.

Salvation came to the fourteen-year-old through a source which, however philosophically appropriate, can only seem amazing to anyone who is familiar with the text. Although the first sentence of Kant's *Prolegomena to All Future Metaphysics* warns that it is intended not for pupils but for future teachers, the young Buber dared to read it and found in it a philosophical freedom which produced a profoundly quieting effect on him. Through it he came to the view that space and time are not real properties that adhere to things in themselves but mere forms of our sensory perception, the formal conditions by which we grasp the world of phenomena. It further disclosed to him that the concept of the infinity of space and time is as impossible as that of their finiteness. Neither is inherent in our experience. They represent, rather, an irresoluble antinomy of ideas which do not necessarily correspond to any reality of being. A philosophy which produced in Buber's older contemporaries philosophical skepticism, along the lines of Vaihinger's "As If" philosophy, gave the boy philosophical peace.

As a result, the youth for whom philosophical questions had become matters of life and death no longer needed to torment himself by inquiring about an end to time. Time was no longer a sentence hanging over him, for it was his, it was "ours." The question was explained as unanswerable by nature, but at the same time he was liberated from having to ask it. This philosophical peace took on a mystical quality very foreign to the rationalist Kant, who spoke of man as a citizen of two worlds, the noumenal and the phenomenal, but claimed no direct contact with or knowledge of the former. At this moment there appeared to Buber the intuition of eternity, an intuition which even at the end of his life he held to be the most remarkable intellectual achievement of man. Eternity is not endless time. It is rather Being as such, Being which is beyond the reach alike of the finitude and infinity of space and time since it only appears in space and time but does not enter into this appearance. Buber not only gained an inkling of the reality of eternity as quite different from either the infinite or the finite; he also glimpsed the possibility of a connection between himself — a man — and the eternal. Thus, in his uncharacteristic response to Kant, Buber got an inkling not only of the "I-It," or subject-object relation, but also of the "I-Thou."

This insight was dimmed for a period of years by the appearance on his horizon of the star of Nietzsche and in particular of Nietzsche's most impassioned and least philosophical book, *Thus Spake Zarathustra.* This book, characterized by Nietzsche himself as the greatest present that had ever been made to mankind, did not calmly confront the young Buber and liberate him as did Kant's *Prolegomena.* Rather its grandly willed and splendidly expressed philosophy stormed over him and took possession of him, robbing him of his freedom for a long time to come. That this invasion and seduction could take place can be explained only by the fact that the glimpse of the eternity which Kant had afforded him had not become real enough to still within his turbulent soul the problem of time that tormented him. Almost seventy years later a schoolmate of Buber's from the Polish gymnasium wrote him, after reading his *Meetings,* that he remembered his great enthusiasm for Nietzsche's *Zarathustra* and how he always brought it with him to school!

In utmost contrast to the rationalistic Kant, Nietzsche offered a dynamism and a creative flow of life force that held the young Buber in thrall throughout the period of his earliest writings. Nietzsche himself saw the basic conception of *Thus Spake Zarathustra* as an interpretation of *time*, and he added to the Heraclitean emphasis on the flow of time an almost equally Heraclitean emphasis on the "eternal return of the same." Time, for Nietzsche, was not an endless line stretched out into the infinite, such as had tormented Buber when he was two years younger. It was an infinite and essentially circular sequence of finite periods of time, which are like one another in all things so that the end phase of the period goes over into its own beginning. This conception, characterized by Nietzsche as "the most abysmal teaching," was dismissed by the mature Buber as "no teaching at all but the utterance of an ecstatically lived through possibility of thought played over with ever new variations." It is an untransformed Dionysian pathos, produced by the enthusiasm of the modern Dionysian over his own heights and depths. Even the seventeen-year-old could not accept this conception as such, but it produced in his spirit "a negative seduction."

The primal mystery of time — the manifest mystery of the uniqueness of all happening, namely, that each event takes place once and never recurs — was obscured by Nietzsche's pseudo-mystery of the "eternal return of the same." The fascination of *Zarathustra* eclipsed the youth's earlier intuition of that genuine eternity which sends forth time out of itself and sets us in that relationship to it that we call existence. "To him who recognizes this," the mature Buber was to say, "the reality of the world no longer shows an absurd and uncanny face: because eternity is."

If the influence of Kant thus foreshadowed Buber's later dialogue with the "eternal Thou," the influence of Nietzsche set him on the long road that led up to it. That he had not in fact moved beyond Nietzsche in the way that his statement to Eliasberg might suggest was made abundantly evident in the earliest of his German essays (he had written several essays in Polish before this) — "Nietzsche and Life-Values" (1900). What he said there of Nietzsche is so like what he himself became that it brings to mind Hawthorne's story "The Great Stone Face," in which the hero gradually takes on the image of the man whom for years he had admired and looked up to.

There have been persons at all times, wrote Buber, who could not be classified or characterized by any group name, for every label did them violence; one feels that no name expresses the essential in them. They are as great and undefinable as life itself, whose apostles they are. To such belongs Friedrich Nietzsche.

Is he a philosopher? He has not erected any unified and consistent system of thought. Is he a psychologist? His deepest knowing is that about the *future* of souls. Is he a poet? Only if we think of the poets as they someday shall become: "Seers who tell us something of the possible," who enable us "to anticipate future virtues." Is he the founder of a new community? Many arise in his name, but they do not come together, for each finds in Nietzsche a different star to follow "in this night sky full of blessing." Buber did not disregard Nietzsche's personal problematic, as he had Lassalle's, but he saw it as a part of his significance for the age: that the sick man teaches a new health ("stronger, more humorous, more tender, more daring, more lusty"); that the silent thought-poet, devoted to the contemplation of the innermost things, glorifies the will to power and a rebirth of instinctual life. He appears to us like the crystallization of our own tragedy, and we learn to love him like a near and distant friend, the suffering friend who needs broth and medicine like us, the creating friend who always has a completed world to present. In the confused unfruitful busyness of the present he gathers the genuine and the productive. He erects before our eyes the image of the heroic man who creates himself and surpasses himself. To the worshiper of the beyond he teaches the high meaning of the earth and of the human body. In opposition to the ideal of a comfortable and painless life, he sets a life of storm and danger, whose powerful beauty is only pain. In place of the greatest good of the greatest number, he teaches as the goal of mankind the bringing forth of great men and great works. To the Creator God he brings a great opponent: the *becoming* God in whose development we can take part, the dimly glimpsed event of future evolutions. In 1901 Buber wrote: "The creative person finds his watchword not in the past but in the future and receives his law not from the God enthroned of yore but from the becoming God." Buber had not at this time fully worked out for himself the sense in which the creative person is *not* limited to the artist – a question of enormous importance for his own future development, since he might have remained a poet and a writer of poetic prose without becoming, in a deeper sense of the term, a creative *person.*

Buber was so taken with *Thus Spake Zarathustra* at the time that he decided to translate it into Polish and had actually translated the first part. He had just started the second part when he received a letter from a well-known Polish author who had likewise translated several sections of the book and who proposed that they do the work in common. Buber preferred to withdraw in his favor. But the fascination of the book itself he could not renounce. He had to work his way through many stages of thought before he arrived at his criticism of Nietzsche's "will to power" as a "sickness," and of his teaching of the "Superman" and of the value scale of strong-and-weak as "no teaching at all."

For years a distinctly Nietzschean note sounded forth even in Buber's essays on Judaism, Zionism, and the Jewish Renaissance.

The very emphasis in his early essays on the active and productive as opposed to the static and unproductive confronted Buber with the same problem with which Nietzsche wrestled, namely the relationship between dynamism and form — between a "Dionysian" energy which may prove destructive of all form and an "Apollonian" limitation which may destroy all dynamism. Buber was equally opposed to the Dionysian principle when it becomes demonic and destroys form and to the Apollonian principle when it hardens, changing from a living creation to a decaying, life-destroying rigidity. It is with this latter decaying form that the Buber of this period identified the unfruitful, life-denying intellectuality of the ghetto and the overemphasis of official rabbinic Judaism on a rigid ceremonial law. Correspondingly, he described Hasidism as the true bearer of the Jewish formative principle — the unifier of life and the spirit, the consecrator of actions through the intention of inwardness, the creator of a community of love and righteousness.

In "Twofold Future" (1912) Buber spoke in true Nietzschean fashion of an alternation between the forms of culture and the "fruitful chaos" of religion. When a culture disintegrates and loses the strength of its cohesion, there arises that fruitful chaos in which alone the seed of a growing religiousness can develop. Thus Buber identified religiousness with the revolutionary principle which destroys old forms and releases suppressed power. This concern for time and for the dynamic remained with Buber in his later thought.

In 1960 Buber confessed that since reading Kant's *Prolegomena* he had not ceased to reflect on the problem of time and that it always brought him to an impasse in his thinking. The threat of infinity remained for Buber, as with Pascal, a lifelong torment but one that proved to be the occasion for, rather than the obstacle to, existential trust.

PART II

Zionism

(1898-1904)

CHAPTER 3

Zionism and the "Jewish Renaissance"

FOR NIETZSCHE it was the "death of God" that enabled man to recover his alienated freedom, projected onto the "celestial naught," and to express his will to power in the creativity that led upward to "the Superman." For the young Buber, Nietzsche's celebration of creativity soon proved inadequate without those roots that would allow him to feel part of a larger community. "Today," Buber wrote in 1902, "faith lies to life and does violence to its surging meanings." But the "surging meanings" are not enough in themselves. Today the tempter does not lead the creative man to a high mountain to show him all the kingdoms and splendor of the world, as Satan did to Jesus. Instead he tempts him through infinity — to lose himself in the inessential, to roam about in the great confusion in which all human clarity and definiteness has ceased. Thus the threat of infinity which Buber experienced as a fifteen-year-old now takes on new form — the form of formlessness, of the whirl of unmastered possibilities which every young person who goes out into the world experiences, but which Buber himself experienced to an overwhelming degree.

As long as Buber lived with his grandfather, his roots were firm, although many questions and doubts perplexed him. Soon after he left his grandfather's house, and until his twentieth year and even later, his "spirit was in steady and multiple movement, in an alternation of tension and release, . . . taking ever new shape, but without center and without growing substance." He lived, in short, in the "World of Confusion," the modern equivalent of that abode to which Hasidic myth assigns the lost and wandering souls. "Here I lived," wrote Buber in 1918, "in variegated richness of spirit, but without Judaism, without humanity, and without the presence of the divine."

In an age which still values "creativity" and "self-expression" as the highest of intrinsic values, it may be hard to understand why young Buber should not have been happy and fulfilled during this period in which he began to discover and to realize his multiple gifts. But "creativity" can also be an expression of fragmentation rather than of the wholeness of the person. The need to direct that neutral but unchanneled passion which the Talmud calls the "evil urge," which Buber stressed in his Hasidic teaching, the need for "direction," which he intoned in *Daniel*, and the need for decision, which he put at the center of *I and Thou* — all became evident to him for the first time during this painful period of outer dispersion and inner turmoil. The implicit comparison of the creative person with Jesus — the essential and, to Buber at this period, the creative man of his age — is appropriate because Buber too was tempted. But his temptation, though lacking the ironic triviality of Eliot's Prufrock — "I am no prophet — and here's no great matter" — was not the Yes or No that confronted Jesus. In the language of *I and Thou*, it was "the centreless Many" that "plays in the iridescent sameness of its pretensions."

> The fiery stuff of all my ability to will seethes tremendously, all that I might do circles around me, still without actuality in the world, flung together and seemingly inseparable, alluring glimpses of powers flicker from all the uttermost bounds: the universe is my temptation.

At a still later stage Buber identified this whirl of potentialities with the period of puberty, though denying to it a specifically sexual cause. He spoke of the evolving human person as "bowled over by possibility as an infinitude" — again the threat of the infinite!

The plenitude of possibility floods over his small reality and over-whelms it. . . . The soul driven round in the dizzy whirl cannot remain fixed within it; it strives to escape . . . it can clutch at any object, past which the vortex happens to carry it, and cast its passion upon it. . . .

"For him who has lost his God the people can be a first station on his new way," wrote Buber in the same essay as that in which he spoke of the temptation of the creative man. This was exactly Buber's own experience. The first impetus toward his liberation from "the whirl of the age" came from the young movement of Zionism through which he took root anew in the community.

No one needs the saving connection with a people so much as the youth who is seized by spiritual seeking, carried off into the upper at-mosphere by the intellect; but among the youths of this kind and this destiny none so much as the Jewish. . . . The most sparkling wealth of intellectuality, the most luxuriant seeming productivity (only he who is bound can be genuinely productive) cannot compensate the detached man for the holy insignia of humanity — rootedness, binding, wholeness.

Buber's "To Narcissus," published in a Vienna student journal about 1900, is an unmistakably autobiographical picture, written at the very time, of the confusion of his soul and its longing for personal direction and for roots in a tradition. Both the title and the contents suggest the essential futility of a life focused on its own creativity.

> *And every day you dip yourself into life only*
> *To give your soul new jewels,*
> *New song and new play;*
> *And every night you weave yourself*
> *In sweet faery feasts and varicolored dreams.*
> . . . .
> *Your heart glows in the whirling dance of the sparks,*
> *Drunk with the pale wine of dreams.*
>
> *Yes, you think often of the people's glow and longing,*
> *Stunted and confined in the press of day-by-day,*
> *And you lay your forehead in your hands,*
> *Wounded and sick from so much dead beauty,*
> *Yet not like one who with wild dread and tears*
> *Shakes his fist, and thinks in hot oaths.*
> *Like the weary sunset in autumn*
> *The complaint of your painful dream flows on.*
> . . . .

Then you will thirst for the fragrance of the shells,
For anger and hope, pain and desire,
And will despair, when the days roll on
And you are always only aware of your dream,
You will long for command and order,
For a God, who thundering calls: "You must!"
. . . .
Then you will lie once in the night,
And your powers, which you have towered up
Level upon level, and which once conquered victory for you,
Are unused, extinguished like a light.
. . . .

Then you will die — not like him who lives with
All and now goes into the splendor of the whole,
Not like him who now returns to wall himself in his mother's womb,
The most beautiful happiness, the purest prayer of all —
No, you will die, in confused stammering
Like one who no longer understands himself. . . .

What delivered Buber from this narcissism was the new Zionist movement of Theodor Herzl. When the young Eliasberg first made the acquaintance of Buber, the latter was anything but a Zionist. Except for the positive influence of his grandfather, he grew up, says Eliasberg, in the milieu of a superficial salon culture of bourgeoisie who despised everything Jewish from the bottom of their hearts. When Eliasberg got to know him, he would often hear from his lips the expression "really Jewish" used as a form of disparagement. Buber also remained close to Polish socialist circles and gave a much-applauded lecture at a secret conference of Polish students in which delegates from the three realms of the Empire took part. But he was no Polish assimilationist. He read Herzl's journal *Die Welt*, to which Eliasberg was the sole subscriber in Leipzig, and often discussed Zionist questions. He even coined a striking personal formula for his unsureness in Jewish matters: "I will take on myself all the duties of Zionism, yet will enjoy none of its rights." But as important for him as Zionism at this time were the simple Jewish men whom he discovered in Hasidic synagogues.

Buber spent the summer holidays of 1898 on his father's estate in Galicia. From there he wrote to Eliasberg that he had discovered a work that had finally converted him to nationalism and to Zionism. It was Mathias Acher's (Nathan Birnbaum's) *Modern Judaism*. According to Buber in *Israel and Palestine* (1945) this book completed what Moses Hess had begun — the synthesis of the national and the social idea in Judaism. Buber wanted to return to Leipzig in the winter and become politically active for Zionism, and Eliasberg was only too happy to have his friend join him in his cause. Buber carried on his activities with all the zeal of a neophyte. Although completely unschooled in political action, they succeeded in creating a foothold for Zionism in Leipzig and ended by founding a local chapter and a union of Jewish students. Buber, of course, was elected its first president. In the ornaments of his insignia, though still without a beard, "Buber cut the figure of a young Samson."

In March the Leipzig chapter sent Buber as their representative to the Zionist convention in Cologne, at that time the seat of the organization. Buber, who now longed for further study, did not return. As a parting present, Eliasberg sent him Jacob Burckhardt's *History of Greek Culture*, which had appeared shortly before. From Cologne Buber wrote Eliasberg: "I have the book before me and ask myself when *we* shall have such a work, a "History of Jewish Culture." Only after many years did Eliasberg understand the full import of these words.

If Buber's Jewish education had really been so superficial and his antipathy to things Jewish so basic as Eliasberg suggests, he could never have found his way to Zionism. His university years were, to be sure, a period in which he had largely lost his moorings from that thoroughgoing Judaism which dwelt in his grandfather, "without his troubling himself about it." But no "salon culture" could remove the lasting effects of those years between four and fourteen that he spent in his grandfather's home, surrounded by the world of the Midrash in which his grandfather lived "with a wonderful concentration of soul, with a wonderful intensity of work." Speaking of his grandfather, Buber wrote:

> Without having ever appropriated the philological methods of the West, he revised the manuscripts with the reliability of the modern scholar and at the same time with the presence of knowledge of the Talmudic master who has directly at hand for each sentence and each word whatever relates to it in the entire literature — not as material of memory alone, but as an organic possession of the whole person. The spiritual passion which manifested itself in his incessant work was combined with the untouchable, imperturbable childlikeness of a pure human nature and an elementary Jewish being. When he spoke Hebrew (as he frequently did when foreign guests visited him from distant lands), it sounded like the speech of a prince returned home from exile.

The extent to which Solomon Buber continued to be present for Martin as an image of authentic humaneness and authentic Jewishness even in the midst of cultural Zionism is shown by a letter Martin wrote his grandparents in January 1900 on the occasion of his grandfather's birthday:

> Since I have been away from home, I have made the acquaintance of many persons of culture: artists, poets, and men of science. But I have never seen the childlike magical force of the spirit, the might of a strong and simple striving so purely and beautifully embodied as in grandpapa, never has a scholar and worker with ideas seemed to me so worthy of love (I mean: so worthy of the greatest love.) I can seldom hold back my tears — tears of the innermost veneration — when I think of his beloved face. . . . That your loving kindness, dear grandfather, which has so often lent me comfort and joy and steadiness, shall long be preserved for me is the glowing hope of my heart. The tirelessness and singleness of your creation has often led me back to myself when I have scattered myself in many directions. . . . I cannot show my thankfulness and my love to you better than when I — in my spheres — emulate your manner and place my life, like yours, in the service of the Jewish people. You have drawn forth and utilized treasures from the spiritual life of the Jewish past; as a young man who longs still more for the deed than for knowledge, I have in mind working together with and helping to create the Jewish future. But both are ruled over by the spirit of the eternal people and in this sense I can perhaps say that I shall continue your lifework.

On the other hand, Buber's conversion to Zionism did not mean unqualified affirmation of everything Jewish and a complete reversal of his earlier critical attitude. On the contrary, his call for a "Jewish Renaissance" meant precisely the purifying and cutting away of those elements in Galut (exile) Judaism which he considered to be unhealthy degenerations — shallow adaptations to the surrounding culture or fossilized emphasis on hair-splitting commentary and rules of ritual law. In one way this call is a clearly Nietzschean celebration of the noble, the strong, the creative, the pure. But in another, it is obviously a continued identification with the Jews and Judaism which prevented Buber, even when most alienated, from becoming an assimilationist like so many other Jews of that period. Zionism was the first political, secular movement in which Jews of "the better class" dared in polite society to speak the name "Jew" aloud. It is unthinkable that it would have attracted Buber had he really been a "Jewish anti-Semite," as Eliasberg imagined, and still less that Buber would have from the first seen Zionism as a Jewish Renaissance Movement rather than as a purely political antidote to anti-Semitism.

The Zionism of Theodor Herzl, to be sure, was started as a direct reaction to the anti-Semitism that the Dreyfus trial laid bare in France. The French army, state, and church conspired to keep an innocent man — Alfred Dreyfus, a captain in the French army and a Jew — imprisoned for years on Devil's Island until the great French writer Émile Zola won his freedom in a controversial action that shook France to its foundations. Chaim Weizmann also came to Zionism in part through the far more terrible anti-Semitism in Russia, culminating in the pogroms that led thousands upon thousands of Jews to flee to Western Europe and to America. But even this Zionism was by no means simply a negative or defensive movement. It was characterized in its early years by the heroic spirit lent it by Theodor Herzl, who incarnated the Nietzschean vitalism in a Jewish form that did much to assuage Buber's sensitivity to the negative effects of both ghetto Judaism and the Enlightenment.

Although in Germany a pseudo-scientific racial theory had arisen aimed at justifying attacks on the Jews, most Western Jews, as Robert Weltsch has pointed out, ignored or expressly denied the existence of a Jewish problem. It was considered tactless at that time to identify anyone as a Jew, nor did most Jews know any longer what such identification meant. The word "Jew" had lost all positive meaning, whether of religion or a people, and had become a mere term of abuse. Jewish learning was given up in favor of secular culture, and the difference between the image of the Jew held by the larger public and that which the new classes of assimilated Jews held of themselves was simply overlooked.

The Zionist movement which arose in its Western political form with the first Zionist Congress in Basel, Switzerland, in 1897, represented for the first time a Jewish group which did not deny the existence of a Jewish problem but rather recognized it as a basic problem not only of the Jews but of the European world. For the Western Zionist, politics gradually came to replace religion as the focus of Jewish life. Herzl's thesis that the Jews were a single people with national rights like any other exploded on the European stage as an unprecedented political demand. The Emancipation ushered in by the Enlightenment and by Napoleon had liberated the individual Jew but not the Jewish people. The assimilated Jews feared that the Zionist claim would lead to the loss of even these individual rights. (The Nazis later made devastating political capital out of Zionism to precisely this effect.) The Zionists, in contrast, believed that the assimilated Jews would welcome the Jewish national movement as moral reparation for their wounded sensibilities, caused by increasing anti-Semitism, and for the shrinking of their possibilities for development.

Was anti-Semitism a direct or indirect cause of Buber's conversion to Zionism? We have no evidence other than his clear identification with the sufferings of his people and his enthusiastic adherence to the cause. Three years before the 1903 pogroms in Russia, Buber wrote his fiancée Paula with keen sympathy of his encounter with a group of leaderless and lost Russian Jews on their way to America and of his efforts to help them find food and shelter at the railway station in Berlin, where the officials "treated them like animals." Though Buber joined the movement in 1898, a year after the first Congress, and admired its leader as a Jewish hero, his relationship to the movement from the start was very different from that of Herzl. He was, to begin with, one of that group of young men whom Herzl, with his talent for leadership, succeeded in winning to his cause — young men full of enthusiasm and the joy of discovery. What is more, Zionism meant for Buber a return to Jewish roots which Herzl never had and an escape from that very assimilation which, except for his political activity, marked Herzl to the end. If it had not been for Zionism, says Hans Kohn, Buber might have become one of the lonely and tragic literati, fascinated by all the cultures of the world yet without roots in any.

Buber's first letter to Herzl was written from Leipzig in the name of the newly formed group of Zionists over which he presided and to which Eliasberg belonged. Expressing the conviction of this group that Leipzig provided a favorable ground for "agitation in the grand style" and that it could become a center for the movement, Buber invited Herzl to come to Leipzig to speak "if only for an hour" to share with the Jews there that enthusiasm which would awaken in them all that was lacking to make them Zionists: courage and decisiveness. Because of the immigration into Leipzig of Jews from Russia and Galicia, assimilation was not so far along there as in other great German communities. The old fire burns in them, noted Buber, and need only be rekindled by the struggling will to freedom which will give them the courage to acknowledge their longing.

In embracing Zionism Buber found for the first time a channel into which he could concentrate his energies, like his grandfather, and give himself to fruitful and unremitting work. The "Jewish Renaissance" which Buber anticipated in his essays of this period first took place in his own soul. Although Buber in his old age deemed only four of the poems of this period worthy of preservation in his "Gleanings," his other, specifically Zionist poems give us an insight into his inner devotion to the movement that even his flaming and youthful prose does not afford us. The first of these, "Our People's Awakening," was published without Buber's knowledge by the much older Reverend William Hechler, whom Buber had met in a railway carriage in the autumn of 1899. In conversation the two men discovered that, on entirely different bases, they shared a common interest in Zionism. Reverend Hechler held a firm eschatological belief in the living Christ, and he saw the return of the Jewish people to their homeland as the promised precursor for Christ's second coming. He was journeying at that time to the Grand Duke of Baden, whom he had a short time before introduced to Herzl. When Buber showed Hechler his "hymn," the latter was filled with such enthusiasm — "entirely without basis" Buber commented a half century later — that he declared he must read it to the Grand Duke. Not only did he do this, but he shortly afterward published "the questionable little opus" without Buber's knowledge, "after he had furnished it with some, if possible, still more pathetic titles for each of the stanzas."

Another more concise and moving expression of the same feeling is Buber's 1899 poem "Prayer":

> *Lord, Lord, shake my people,*
> *Strike it, bless it, furiously, gently,*
> *Make it burn, make it free,*
> *Heal your child.*
>
> *God, give the lost glow*
> *Back to my weary people,*
> *In wild, intoxicated flames*
> *Bestow on them your happiness.*
>
> *See, only a fever can save it*
> *And raging exuberance,*
> *Awaken it, and, Father, lead the throng*
> *To Jordan's fields.*

Buber at this time wrote a cycle of poems about Elisha ben Abuya, the contemporary of the great Talmudist and martyr Rabbi Akiba. Abuya is commonly known in the Talmud as "Acher," the heretic, and Buber seems to have identified himself both with Acher's rejection of the Jewish law and with his sense of ostracism and exile, an identification which he also carried over at this period to a very different Jewish heretic, the philosopher Spinoza. Although Buber's Zionism was in no real sense religious at this time, he saw the Jewish festivals as celebrations of the resurging life of the people, much in the fashion of the secular Israeli today. His "Purim Prologue," composed for the Purim celebration of the National Jewish Union in Berlin, is not so much the memory of a historical event as the presage of a future liberation.

> *Today slaves, tomorrow we shall be free masters!*
> *This year in narrow, sunless strangeness,*
> *Next year in our fatherland!*

In his prose piece "Feast of Life: A Confession" (1901), Buber reached a still more sustained personal ecstasy over the tie between the Jewish festival and the Jewish Renaissance:

> Festival, sparkling as the morning sun and ardent as the flood, ancient, ever new, immortal, I love you!
>
> Once I turned from you as a child from its mother whom it imagined it had outgrown, tired of familiar forms and longing for new adventures . . . .
>
> Now I return to you, like a child to its mother, whose inexhaustible beauty reveals itself to him in a moment of blessing, like a child to its mother who offers worlds and asks no thanks. . . .

(How different was Buber's experience with his own mother, who was not there for him to return to and who offered him no worlds!)

> Because I know what my people's future will be, because I see the invisible turning of its destiny, I pray to my people for you, as one prays to a God — that it remain alive. . . .
>
> And I know: a people that has no homeland must see the unity of home replaced by a bond of common, meaningful experience if it will remain a people. . . . Organic unity comes only from visible, tangible things that weave themselves deeply into the original sense-life of the people and produce a mood of home, a national being. Thus, only thus do feelings of togetherness, deeds of folk liberation arise. . . .
>
> Therefore, I love you, festival of my people!
>
> Not because a God commands it. I have learned to step respectfully aside when heavenly pronouncements stride by. But I love you because my people must command itself to keep you.

> For in my returning to the old festivals, they have become new. I do not come now to the rigid monuments of protected tradition, but to the fresh, consecrated gardens of a young people. Not to feasts of the dead past, but to feasts of the living future.
>
> This is reserved for my people: to celebrate the year's life of the re-won fruitful earth, the story of the cornfield and the vineyard; festival for the memory of farmers who are not yet born, festival which ties the history of the new land of the Jews to the history of the old, festival which tells the *whole* history of a people's soul.

It is startling how close the young Buber is here to Mordecai Kaplan's Reconstructionist program of deliberately transvaluating Judaism by retaining the old forms while supplying them with new, modern meanings. If the mature Buber resolutely rejected the substitution of Jewish culture and civilization for the directly experienced command of God, this can certainly not be said of the young Buber. Nor is this attitude toward the Jewish festivals merely the corollary of one or two rhapsodic expressions. In his speech at the Third Zionist Congress in Basel in 1899 Buber proposed in all seriousness that Hanukkah (the Feast commemorating the victory of the Maccabees over the Hellenistic influences that were desecrating the Temple) be consciously turned into a Zionist festival celebrating the future, and this suggestion was greeted with wild applause. Zionism had become the new religion.

The connection of this Zionist enthusiasm with the vitalism and creativity of Buber's Nietzschean period is evident. Only now it is focused in a movement. Buber went so far as to claim that everything good and fruitful that took place within Judaism in the last two millennia was in a deeper sense Zionist because it led to life. There are two sorts of criticism, he added. The *analytical* destroys, atomizes, dissolves, negates. Nowhere and never can there arise from it creation and the engendering glow of the great life. In contrast to it is the *synthetic* critique which seeks and values that which persists in its *wholeness* — in order to build what is coming into being. Building is "the one thing that is needful." (This word of Jesus recurs again and again in Buber's early writings.) The truth is not the atom but the whole living thing. From such a standpoint, the young enthusiast attacked the intellectuals and the half-believers, the cold and the lukewarm. The intellectuals know only presuppositions and conclusions. They do not know the wonder that unexpectedly blooms at this place and in this moment. The lukewarm believe, but they generate nothing with their belief; they are ready neither for suffering nor for sacrifice. They cannot attain that fulfillment which comes only to those silent heroes who are ready to commit themselves with all their whole being.

In his essays on the Jewish Renaissance written in this same period, Buber called for a fight against the enemies within their ranks who divide and weaken the Jewish people, for the release of latent energies, and above all for the restoration of the unified, unbroken feeling for life of the Jews so that it might again find natural expression in reality and in art. In place of Goethe's universalism he set a national universalism in which each people would increase the common wealth of mankind out of its own being, a life of mankind impregnated with beauty and benevolence in which each individual and each people would co-create and co-enjoy, each in its own way and according to its own values. Renaissance does not mean return but rebirth: a renewal of the whole person. It will be more difficult for the Jews than for any other people to enter into this renaissance because of the inner *ghetto* and *golus* (exile) which fetter them: the *ghetto* of unfree spirituality and the compulsion of tradition divorced from the life of the senses; and *golus* — the slavery of an uncreative making of money and the hollow-eyed homelessness that destroys all unified will. Deliverance from these fetters can come not through the program of a *party* but through the unwritten program of a *movement.* This movement will cause the Jews again to feel themselves as an organism and to strive for the harmonious unfolding of their powers, to put as much of their souls into walking, singing, and working as into intellectual problems, to call trees, birds, and stars their brothers and sisters.

The Zionist movement must be broadened to include all the factors and movements of spiritual rebirth, and at the same time deepened by leading it from the rigid and empty formalities of superficial activism to an inward, living comprehension of the people's being and the people's work. Zion must be reborn in the soul before it can be created as a tangible reality. When all who belong to the movement make their Zionism active not merely with words but with their whole being, when they regard their whole life as a holy preparation for the new and wonderful time that shall come, when they *live* it as such, with true seriousness and purpose, when such a Zion of the souls exists — then the other, the Palestinian Zion, will not be long in following. For where there is true dedication, there is strength.

The Jewish Renaissance is the goal and meaning of the Jewish movement; the Zionist movement is the consciousness and will that lead to the Renaissance. This consciousness and will are all the more necessary because neither Hasidism nor the Haskalah — the two great movements that arose in the mid-eighteenth century and prepared the way for the Jewish Renaissance — was able to issue into it by itself. Hasidism replaced the old compulsion of the law by the new Jewish mysticism which liberated feeling, purified intention, and set as the goal of the law that man himself should become a law, should freely embody what was formerly an external command. Haskalah, the Jewish Enlightenment, stepping forth in the name of European civilization, liberated thought and led the individual Jew to independence. But neither one alone accomplished the full liberation and activation of the newly awakened forces of the people. The wonder was that these two movements produced what they did and not that the one degenerated and the other left no legacy of immortal works; for the inner liberation in Hasidism and the Haskalah was experienced only by the Jews of the East — the Jews of community — whereas the outer liberation, the emancipation, was enjoyed only by the Jews of the West — the Jews of the dispersion. This essay foreshadows Buber's own great accomplishment of combining and integrating Hasidism and the Haskalah.

The Jew of the era of the Jewish law was a passive hero who courageously endured all the stages of martyrdom without a cry and with pride but whose action and thought had no active impact. The new Jewish type, Buber wrote, is acting freely, acting not according to the law but according to its own convictions, and striving toward creativity. But for this type to come into being, the consciousness of the limitation had to awaken in the national movement and the will to overcome this limitation had to arise in Zionism. Through Zionism the longing is awakened for a new, free, independent life which will bind West with East and produce a specifically Jewish fruitfulness.

In Zurich in the summer semester of 1899 in the Germanics seminar of Professors Albert Bachmann and Adolf Frey, Buber met Paula Winkler, whom he later married. At that time a woman studying in a university was still a rarity. Paula Winkler combined great intellectual gifts with a personality marked by a strong drive toward freedom. Already, before her studies in the university, she had lived outside her parents' house in an artists' colony in Southern Tyrol. Her teacher at that time described her as a "wild elfin being, tough, gifted, unhesitating, uncannily intelligent, and of a commanding will." Her combination of realistic traits with a breath of the romantic anticipated the way in which her literary work wove precise portrayals of reality with myth and mystery. Theodor Herzl called her "a great talent" and was ready to print contributions of hers in the *Neue Freie Presse*, the newspaper in which all the young and unpublished writers of Vienna dreamed of being published. Her first book of stories, *Die unechten Kinder Adams* (The Illegitimate Children of Adam), appeared in 1912.

Paula was almost a year older than the twenty-one-year-old Martin when they met, and she undoubtedly possessed the stronger and more mature personality of the two. "It is impossible," writes Grete Schaeder, "to overestimate the significance of the fact that in his youthful years Buber met a woman who was equal to, indeed superior to him, in poetic gifts and power of expression and understood and spurred on his productivity to the highest degree." Something of the quality of this relationship is conveyed to us by their letters of August 1899. "Sweet one, dear one, you must not be so alarmed when a letter does not reach you," Paula wrote to Martin. "But truly, you will not drive yourself too much? Above all, do not work nights! Dear one, Thou, promise me that! . . . I love your great work — I would never want to injure it. But I would like to slip myself like a sheltering cloud between you and your little daily cares." Buber replied, telling her of his Zionist activities: "I work mostly in silent, brief relationships, awakening slumbering thoughts. . . . For that which *I* have to say the time is not yet present. I do not know whether this Congress will bring it to me. But what I do is fruitful. Perhaps now will come the lightning which will draw forth my innermost powers." The one committee in which he took part, Martin informed Paula, was the Action Committee, "because I like that: to participate in movement." Paula replied with a long letter in which she castigated a friend who wanted to give up the categories Jew and Christian, French and German, man and woman, in favor of "cosmopolitanism." In ridiculing this position, Paula sounded quite a few Nietzschean notes of her own. "Why not intensify the man in man, the woman in woman to high perfection, to a wonderful flowering — in order that they can then stand as human being to human being?"

Cosmopolitanism — nirvana of nationalities! Obliteration of opposites. Obliteration of boundaries! Rest!

Oh no, opposites, movement, life! We do not want to sleep! Oh those lame, rotton, exhausted ones! —

The occasion for this argument was the Zionism which Paula too espoused. "That a people homeless and persecuted for two thousand years should long for its ground, out of which it could again win peace, distinction, and strength, is that something incomprehensible?"

In April 1900 Martin wrote Paula from Berlin of his longing to reach his hand into the streaming and fermenting of the racial essence and tear out and shape the forms that remain unfinished in its "real history." "To complete the great underground history of the people!" In August Martin notified Paula that he was living a part of each day in the world of his "Satu-story," an Egyptian legend of suffering and revenge, the unfinished handwritten manuscript of which still exists in the Buber Archives. "Dearest," Martin added, "the last days that I was together with you this time were so beautiful in their restful light that they gave me a whole new force. You know my way of creating and you will understand what that means to me: I have found my own artistic path." In addition to Satu, he planned to revive Old Indian and Hebraic stories and a narrative of Herodotus and a late Greek love story. "The way from the material to me is not so far as that from the folkbook to [Goethe's] *Faust* and yet, still, it is farther: the unfolding of a hundred generations that stand between my soul and that of the original teller of the saga."

Early in 1901 Max Nordau, Herzl's next-in-command, wrote Buber in appreciation of one of his Zionist manuscripts, a confirmation which did him immeasurable good "in a time of doubt and loneliness." "They were for me the first words of Zionist understanding for my small labors, and they have, therefore, been of unforgettable importance to me." In July 1901 Martin wrote to Paula unburdening all the pathos of his longing for creativity:

> Above all it has become irresistibly clear to me that I must with all my power collect myself in the next months, or rather weeks, must produce something, otherwise I shall lose all that remains of my artistic initiative, and without that all ability is like a bird without the strength to soar; of what use is it that one "can fly"? You know that I have no extensive talent, therefore the hand must be taut. . . . You must understand, dearest, that this is a question of life and death. It concerns simply my art: If I let myself go, I shall go to ruin — that is certain. Then I can

further develop myself as a *Privatdozent* [unsalaried lecturer who receives only students' fees] and in general as a competent person; but that will be the end of creating living things.

At the very time when Buber was immersing himself completely in Zionism and the Jewish Renaissance, he married a woman who was a Munich Catholic by upbringing. This action of Buber's led his old friend Chaim Bloch to break off all connection with him until after the war, since in the circles in which Bloch moved mixed marriages were seen as really a form of apostasy. In Buber's case, intermarriage was in no sense tantamount to assimilation. If anything, it was his wife who assimilated to the Jews. At the cost of a complete and permanent break with her family, Paula Buber formally converted to Judaism before her marriage, including the traditional *mikva,* or ritual bath. She was, to use her own phrase, an ardent "philozionist." Buber's Zionism made a deep impression upon her, and she offered him in turn both understanding and a creative resonance of her own, as Hans Kohn points out:

> The young Jew, who longed at that time for a maturity of Jewish peoplehood in the fullness of living, form illuminated by beauty, found in this young woman, in whose being, as with many Southern Germans, romantic sense-forms and Nordic thoughtfulness were joined, not only understanding for the dreams and strivings of his people, but also the embodiment of that free, beautiful, self-confident humanity that since the Enlightenment many of the best young Jews had found in non-Jewish women.

In October 1901 Paula announced to Martin that she wanted to be active with him on behalf of Zionism. "I have the feeling that I can, I must do something for it." The next day she wrote "Dear Maugli," the pet name they called each other from Rudyard Kipling's *Jungle Book,* that of all the plans for a unified Jewish artistic life that of a Jewish stage, which he proposed, was probably the most difficult. "Are there plays there? And would it not be difficult to write plays for the stage? The idea demands time. You should not pluck any unripe fruit, dear one." "I grow in your cause," she added. "It will be mine and that of our children."

Martin's response to Paula was a powerful confirmation of the fact that Paula's greater maturity was tied up with his need for a mother that had marked Martin's life ever since his own mother left him:

> One thing you cannot understand, that every moment here I guard myself with all my strength against all my unrest, against all my cares, against all my knowing, against all my desires, against whatever would enslave me. Every moment. And that your letters are the only thing that give me strength. Everything else is too interwoven with care and unrest. Your letters are the only thing. Aside from them perhaps the thought that a mother is in you, the belief in that. Now I know: I have always, always sought my mother.

Paula Winkler's "Confessions of a Philozionist," published in *Die Welt*, is part and parcel of the same Zionist enthusiasm which fires Buber's early poetry and prose. It gives concrete details of her own background that are of help in understanding how it was that this brilliant and proud young Catholic could respond with such generous enthusiasm to the movement of a people not her own and could join her life to that of one of its leaders. Her attitude to the Jews was not the ordinary one, she averred, because her mother had lived as a young girl in the neighborhood of a small Jewish settlement and received from its life strong and lasting impressions. Her mother spoke often and with rare warmth of this little place, and this image remained with the child. But beyond all the charm of difference, strange and wonderful words and customs, there lay the dark background of a painfully moving past, a story of cruel suspicion and comfortless flight, a story of heroism and endless sufferings.

Among the people with whom Paula Winkler grew up, Jews were not singled out, and she hardly knew what a Jew was. But when she was twenty-three, she encountered anti-Semitism with frightening clarity while witnessing a gang of children turn on a brown-eyed little boy and torment him with cries of "Jew-child," until his slightly older sister came up with swinging fists and rescued him from his oppressors. Zionism itself was a word that she had hardly heard and whose meaning she did not know, she wrote, until the Third Zionist Congress in Basel in 1899 where Buber's speech evoked in her a lifelong response.

> A human mouth spoke to me with wonderful force. . . . And my heart stood still. . . . And then it was again as if he spoke with iron tongues, and all the bells in the world rang out over men. It was no longer an individual man . . . the uncanny longing, wish, and will of a whole people came pouring forth. . . . It came over me like everything great in life and like life itself — came and carried me with it.

It was as if she saw hovering over every Jewish head a crown of thorns, the very image of the crucifixion that Buber himself used in his poetry of this period. The ancient longing for the old earth will be fulfilled, she prophesied, and the primally deep wounds of this old, sick, noble people healed!

> How I love you, people of affliction! How strong your heart is and how young it has remained! No, you shall not become another, you shall not go under in the confusion of alien peoples. . . . In being different lies all your beauty, all happiness and joy of earth. Remain your own! . . . How I love you, you people of all peoples, how I bless you!

This same call to remain themselves, to remain different, was voiced by Paula Winkler in two articles on "The Jewish Woman" published in *Die Welt* later that same year. In them, she assigned to the Jewish woman a role which we may well imagine she herself played when she wed the young genius who was burning with fervor and still struggling toward his own personal direction through the chaos within and without.

> I believe that in the Zionist movement as in every other there are many young men full of thoughts, full of plans, full of impulses, but unknown and misunderstood. And above all the blossoms of their heart and spirit lies the frost of loneliness and lets them become unfruitful and rotten. Not everyone prevails, and thus so much that is lovable and significant spoils and dies. . . . If such men knew of a house where one listened to them gladly, where one gladly discussed what moved them! Would not they become more courageous and self-confident, would not the movement gain so much thereby?

That the young Paula's enthusiasm did not extend equally to the practical Zionist activities that took her husband away for weeks at a time is shown by the following amusing anecdote which she herself related to Dr. Moritz Spitzer of Jerusalem, Buber's secretary and helper during the Nazi years in Germany. Once when she and Martin were standing at a railway station, a train pulled in, and a man got off. When he and her husband caught sight of each other, they waved their arms in the air, ran to meet each other, and embraced. "Another one of those dreadful Zionists!" she said to herself. A moment later Buber introduced her to a friend from an entirely different sphere — the German poet Hugo von Hofmannsthal.

In October 1902 Martin wrote Paula from Lemberg, where he had gone to visit his family: "Here everything is as confined as in a dungeon. I regard you more than ever as my freedom. One must take the whole world-riddle into one's relationship to one person, otherwise one is badly off." In contrast to the Talmudic warning, Buber asserted that one may "look at all the mysteries." "See them in one human being who is yours, and you lie at the heart of the world." Schaeder quotes a "monstrous document" of 1902 superscribed "For You" in which, as she comments, "a very young man could not distinguish between life and poetry":

> Before you came, I was dream and Golem. But when I found you, I found my soul. You came and gave me my soul. Is not my soul, therefore, your child? So you must love it. . . .

Through Paula Winkler, Buber became more courageous and self-confident, stronger and firmer. This was the decisive relationship of his life.

CHAPTER 4

Political versus Cultural Zionism:
Herzl versus Ahad Ha'am

TOGETHER WITH SOME OLDER FRIENDS, above all Berthold Feiwel and E. M. Lilien, Buber took a leading part in the cultural unfolding of the Jewish Renaissance. They enriched the movement not only with poems and stories but also with translations out of Hebrew and Yiddish. As Hans Kohn points out, the activity of Buber and his circle was not simply an artistic one. It converted the Zionism of the West into a broader and deeper stream and thus brought it closer to the older Jewish movement of the East.

> The Zionism of these young men produced . . . tangible reality, presence, fullness. All later cultural strivings of Zionism are grounded in the activity of this circle of 1900 to 1904, in its tireless devotion and its youthful enthusiasm.

Buber was spokesman for the Agitation Committee at the Third Zionist Congress at Basel in 1899, and his speech was the watchword of the new cultural movement, as opposed to the narrower, purely political conception of Zionism. Zionism is no party matter, Buber said, but a *Weltanschauung* — a world view. "We must win the *whole* people for our cause," he said, and win them not merely by external agitation but through inner transformation. They must not be Zionists as one is a conservative or a liberal, but as one is a man or an artist. This can be accomplished through "inner agitation, through nourishing Jewish culture, . . . the spirit of the people, its national history, and its national literature, through education of the people."

"Herzl had a countenance lit with the glance of the Messiah," Buber recalled in later years. The extent to which Buber looked to Herzl as the charismatic leader by whose mere presence an irresolute group could be transformed into a great movement is shown by the invitation which he sent him in 1900 to come to speak to the Berlin Zionists. Even our adherents, he wrote him, come with a thousand questions, doubts, objections which we cannot overcome with small gatherings. "But if you were to speak here, then everything would be transformed with a single stroke and the movement led to new life." But Buber did not depend simply upon Herzl to spur on the movement. In the winter of 1900/1901 Buber founded a section for Jewish Art and Knowledge in the Berlin Zionist Union.

In 1901 Buber found himself in a position to further his vision of the movement. In that year he succeeded his friend Berthold Feiwel to one of the most important positions in the movement — the editorship of *Die Welt*, the official organ of the Zionist party. Writing Buber that Feiwel had to resign for reasons of health, Herzl invited him to take over the editorship and offered him a free hand in one-third of the paper, to fill it with whatever he wished, including his own editorials and even two pages of stories. Buber answered this call with that warmth and definiteness which already at this early age marked his character. "Your invitation has brought joy to my heart," he wrote, "because it is an indication of trust and because it offers a splendid possibility of work."

> In my opinion the "World" is destined to become the organ and the center of the young Jewish intellectual and artistic movement. We have many young, struggling talents most of whom do not know where they belong. With promotion and direction conscious of the goal it would not be long at all before we could come to Europe with a literary manifesto. This development would parallel our political one.

The enormous activity that the editorship of *Die Welt* released in Buber can be seen from his many contributions to the 1901 volume of the weekly, as well as from his other Zionist writings of 1901 and the years immediately following. This came about in part through his successful insistence that the editor of the paper must represent an independent power in the movement and not be entirely subservient to the Action Committee.

In 1901 at the Fifth Zionist Congress in Basel it was Martin Buber who played the central role in the successful fight that the "Democratic Fraction" waged against Theodor Herzl for official recognition of the decisive importance of cultural Zionism. The one-sided spirituality of the ghetto which regarded nature, the human body, and art as inimical had been replaced in recent times, Buber stated in his speech on Jewish art, by a rebirth of creativity, the activity of the whole organism and the renewal of seeing. A whole and complete Jewish art, like a whole and complete Jewish culture in general, would be possible only on Jewish soil. But the seeds of culture exist, affording a fertile potentiality that ought to be nurtured. Zionism and Jewish art could be a great force for a living beholding and perception of nature, man, and art. Such living beholding and perception is essential; for only whole men can be whole Jews, capable and worthy of creating a homeland for themselves.

At the end of Buber's speech there was prolonged applause and many came up to congratulate him. Thanks principally to his fiery speeches, Martin wrote Paula, they had won an important victory in the ordering of business. "This congress is a turning point. We youth are beginning to take the affairs in hand." Despite the warm reception of Buber's speech, and later motions by Buber and others, Herzl did not allow Buber and Chaim Weizmann to present the resolutions of the Culture Committee until the last day of the Congress. Finally, on the morning of December 30, 1901, Buber was given the floor, and in the name of the Culture Committee, he offered resolutions concerning cultural elevation, a national library in Jerusalem, a Jewish university, and a subsidy for the Jüdischer Verlag. "We do not want culture demonstrations," Buber concluded, "but actual work, work for the rebirth of a Jewish people, the finest expression of which is the development of a new Jewish folk culture."

After allowing Buber to present these resolutions and Weizmann to elaborate on the proposal for a Jewish university, Herzl then gave the floor to two orthodox Russian rabbis who strongly opposed "Jewish culture" as a threat to Jewish religion.

Buber's reaction was immediate and sharp and constituted a questioning of Herzl's leadership such as had probably never before taken place in a Zionist Congress. But Herzl, ascertaining that no fewer than sixty people had indicated from the floor their desire to speak to it, said he could not allow such a discussion to precede the choices for the committees, which he called the "life-needs of the movement." At this point nearly forty delegates (without pre-concerted agreement) rose from their seats and left the hall and decided to make a protest to Herzl for using his influence in this way to secure the rejection of the proposals of the Culture Committee. Herzl promised to repair the situation and begged them to return to the Congress. Berthold Feiwel and Chaim Weizmann resigned their offices, and Feiwel, in the name of thirty-seven delegates, read a sharp protest against the manner in which the presidium had handled the resolutions of the Culture Committee and had influenced the vote on its discussion. Herzl then supported and brought to the vote all the resolutions of the Culture Committee. Only one was voted down, the subsidy of Buber's and Feiwel's Jüdischer Verlag. The rest, including the first official resolution for the establishment of what later became the Hebrew University in Jerusalem, were approved, and the forty victorious delegates returned to their seats. Max Nordau, in an interview, later stated that in the Democratic Fraction lay the Golus, the exile. This view Buber vigorously rejected and with it the conception of a unity which would sacrifice differences of views for the sake of party discipline. This forced unity was precisely what characterized the Golus, Buber asserted, and necessarily so because of the enmity of the outer world. "But now, in the new land of the spirits that we have created for ourselves, we need no such dearly bought conformity. . . . We too want a unity, but one which builds itself upon the harmony of free, full voices."

The issue which Buber raised here was decisive both for the origin and continuation of Zionism and for the future State of Israel. In his autobiography Chaim Weizmann told how, three years before the Fifth Congress, a Zionist society was founded in Switzerland by seven Russian Jewish students in the teeth of the opposition of such leading socialists and communists as Plekhanov, Trotsky, and Lenin, all of whom were in exile there. In still further defiance of this opposition, Weizmann and his friends decided to call a mass meeting of Jewish students for which he brought Buber and Feiwel from Berlin as the main speakers.

> The meeting . . . expanded into a sort of congress, and lasted three
> nights and two days! . . . We scored a tremendous triumph. One hundred
> eighty students enrolled in the Zionist Society. . . . This was the first
> real breach in the ranks of the assimilatory revolutionists in Switzerland.
> I recall that Plekhanov was particularly outraged by our success. He
> came up to me after the close of the meeting and asked me furiously:
> "What do you mean by bringing discord into our ranks?" I answered:
> "But Monsieur Plekhanov, you are not the Czar!"

The Democratic Fraction did not arise out of the Fifth Congress
as a spontaneous protest. On the contrary, it emerged as an organized group from a Young Zionist conference held in preparation
for the Congress. It was this that gave Buber the assurance that he
spoke for the young Zionists and that made possible the spontaneous and unplanned walk-out on the part of so many when their
aims were brushed aside. It was Buber who formulated the slogan
for the Fraction — *"Gegenwartsarbeit"* — work in the present for
building agriculture in Palestine and for cultural and educational
preparation in the exile rather than postponing these until that supposedly near hour when Zionist diplomacy would obtain from the
Turkish sultan the charter giving official permission for settlement
in Palestine.

One of the most important practical activities of the Democratic
Fraction was the founding in 1902 of the Jüdischer Verlag, under
the editorship of Buber and Feiwel. This press produced a Jewish
almanac, books on Jewish art, and collections of Jewish poetry, all
of which Buber contributed to as well as helped to edit. "You are
the only really creative person in our small circle," Berthold Feiwel
told Buber in 1902, "and you must reserve and prepare yourself
for a place among the greatest of our movement." If this work was
seen by Buber as an active contribution to cultural Zionism, it was
also regarded by him as an attack on purely political Zionism. A
second important outgrowth of the Democratic Fraction was the
pamphlet on a Jewish university which Buber, Feiwel, and Weizmann brought out in 1903. This pamphlet was prepared for by a
year of incessant activity. In a letter of November 20, 1902, Weizmann wrote to Buber asking him to collect by Easter an imposing
list of names for Jewish University committees to be established in
Vienna, Berlin, Paris, London, and Brussels. "You and only you
must solve this problem," Weizmann appealed. "You can do it,
dear Martin, if you work energetically at it. . . . I beg you, dear
Martin, do, do. Never yet has the universtiy question seemed to

me so exceedingly important." On December 10, Weizmann's plea changed to a harsh imperative as he chided Buber for not writing:

Dear Martin!

You know that I am a friendly and patient man, but now my patience is really at an end. This is the fourth letter in which I must again repeat all questions, but I must really leave off, for I have received as yet no answer. If you think that I can do something for our cause in this manner when I am treated thus by my closest and best friends, you are decidedly in error. . . .

Weizmann's letter had the desired effect. Buber responded immediately and in eight full pages. At the same time, he vigorously rejected Weizmann's accusation that he was treating him badly. "Really, you do me a great injustice," he wrote and then sketched a picture of his personal situation that gives us a rare glimpse into the price that he paid, and the mental state under which he carried out his many activities and produced his creative writings.

I am suffering from a severe attack of nerves, lie often half the day on the sofa in cramps, can work neither on my dissertation nor on anything else, have had in general to lay aside *all* work, and now you reproach me for not having yet succeeded in bringing the university matter to a first conclusion. . . . But actually the university matter was precisely the *only thing* on which I have worked now — so far as I was physically able to do so.

It is striking how in almost every letter between Buber and Weizmann the need of one or the other or both for money is a subject of discussion and complaint. In one letter Buber wrote Weizmann that he not only could not send him money but was in a desperate position himself. His baby (his second child Eva) was sick, and this necessitated heavy expenditures. "You can hardly imagine this situation," Buber wrote Weizmann, "you who have not yet had to provide for others. I go around in a continual feverish tension, must always and always think about procuring money, and as a result can do no systematic work." "My dear friend," Buber concluded not too consolingly, "I can well imagine that you have financial cares, but believe me, they are child's play compared with what I must go through. Almost every moment I feel the abyss open at my feet. — But enough of that — no other person, not even one's best friend can understand and feel with one in this."

The Buber-Weizmann-Feiwel pamphlet was the first serious proposal in print for a Jewish university and received a warm and widespread welcome from Jews of many lands. Published in Hebrew, German, English, Russian, and Yiddish, it represented the second decisive step toward a goal which was realized only twenty years later, the resolution approved by the Fifth Congress being the first. Chaim Weizmann supplied the statistics about the exclusion of Jewish students from practically all Russian universities and technical high schools, whereas Buber and Feiwel supplied the ideology. The Jewish university was put forward not only on the grounds of providing Jewish students a place where they could study, but also on the assumption that it would be a powerful demonstration of living Jewish nationality, of the creative Jewish spirit, a spiritual center for Jews throughout the world, a preparation for the establishment of a Jewish homeland, and a stimulus to Jewish cultural work and technical development.

Another issue on which the Democratic Fraction cooperated under the leadership of Weizmann, Buber and Feiwel was the opposition to Herzl's plan to establish the Jewish homeland in East Kenya (mistakenly called Uganda), a territory of the British Empire, rather than in Palestine. Although much of Herzl's support came from the *Hovevei Zion*, the Eastern Jews who were drawn to Zionism by their real love of Zion, he himself was not averse to finding a shelter in some other land for the Jews fleeing from Russian pogroms. Herzl saw himself as the founder of "the Jewish state," but he was not really a "lover of Zion" in any deep sense of the term. For the young Zionists, in contrast, Herzl's proposal of Uganda was nothing less than a betrayal of the cause. The climax of this conflict came in the Sixth Congress. Herzl succeeded in winning the support of a majority of the Congress for an expedition to investigate "Uganda." But almost half the delegates walked out in a mood of profound melancholy, weeping and declaring the Basel program betrayed. Almost three hundred delegates voted "yes," but one hundred seventy-seven voted "no" and one hundred abstained. Among those who voted against the investigation were for the most part the Russians, but also those from the Western group: Buber, Feiwel, Lilien, Davis Trietsch, and others of the Democratic Fraction.

In 1903 a flier was distributed announcing the intention of establishing in January 1904 a journal *Der Jude,* to be edited by Martin Buber and Chaim Weizmann. In contrast to *Die Welt, Der Jude* would not be a party organ but "an independent organ for the free and valuable exchange of opinion." *Der Jude* should be a European review which would combine thorough discussion of Jewish problems with an honest and unprejudiced criticism of what was sick or deficient within Judaism. Above all it would be a vehicle for the young generation and for the Jewish Renaissance that they were ushering in.

Buber's personal hopes for this review are of particular importance in light of the fact that in the end, despite his willingness to defer to his friend "Told" (Berthold Feiwel) and put himself at his disposal, it was Buber alone who made the journal a reality — thirteen years later, in the midst of the radically altered situation of the First World War, yet precisely in the spirit that his letter to Weizmann and Feiwel projected in 1903:

> I am for a positive organ: positive knowledge, positive criticism, positive initiative. No rhetoric, no literary affectation, no compromise. Open battle with great viewpoints. Basic . . . work in all spheres: sociological, economic, historical, cultural-psychological. An organ of free discussion for all original and effectively presented opinions, but with editorial emphasis on a radical-social and modern cultural standpoint. . . . In the literary part only *Jewish* productions, and, of course, only original and significant ones. Observations and evaluation of all literary, artistic, scientific, social, etc., manifestations of Jewishness. A living and *synthetic* chronicle of the *inner* correspondence of the whole of Jewry.

Despite the important support of Ahad Ha'am (the pen-name of Asher Ginzberg, founder of cultural Zionism who strove to make Palestine the spiritual center of Judaism), the proposal fell through, and it was left to Buber alone to found the journal during the upsurge brought about by the First World War.

The temporary setback on *Der Jude* by no means overshadowed the specific successes which Buber and Weizmann realized on the support of the national library in Jerusalem, the founding of the Jüdischer Verlag, the acquiring of support for the Jewish university, the defeat of the "Uganda" project, and above all these the general triumph of cultural Zionism and *Gegenwartsarbeit* over the purely political, external positions of Herzl.[*] Despite the apparent reestablishment of unity at the end of the Fifth Congress, it meant, in fact, the separation of Buber and his friends from Herzl. Herzl

---

[*] See Note A in Sources for Chapter 4 at the end of this volume, p. 380.

was not the man to tolerate such an open challenge to his authority, nor did his last-minute support mean a real understanding of the democratic-cultural Zionism for which Buber, Weizmann, Lilien, Feiwel, Trietsch, and others were fighting. According to Hans Kohn, it was only thanks to the circle surrounding the Jüdischer Verlag, particularly Buber and Feiwel, that Zionism in German-speaking Europe not only did not disintegrate with the death of Herzl and the disappointment over the futility of his diplomatic actions, but after 1910 was able to take an upward swing that made it for a time the most active and leading part of the Jewish Renaissance movement.

In 1944 Buber recorded a memory of Herzl from 1901 that throws great light on the difference in approach between the leader of the Zionist movement and his younger followers. "We venerated him, loved him," wrote Buber, "but a great part of his being was alien to our souls. In a word, Herzl the liberal was alien to us." To Herzl cultural work was a mere accessory that added interesting, if slightly exotic, nuances to the Zionist movement but could never form a great and decisive reality in the life of the people. 1901 was the year when Buber was closest to Herzl. Before that he had not been personally near to him, and after that his activity in the opposition led to an alienation of Herzl that the latter overcame only in the last days of his life. In May or June 1901 they met in the Zionist Central Bureau in Vienna to discuss the editorship of *Die Welt.* On the wall of the room where they met hung the new Palestine relief map which had just reached the Bureau. After a brief greeting, Herzl led Buber at once to the map and began to point out to him the economic and technical future of the land. His finger glided over the deserts and there were terraced settlements; it glided over an empty plain and there arose in powerful rows the factories of a hundred industries; it led over the Bay of Haifa and through the force of his words Buber beheld the "future port of Asia." Finally his finger returned to the Jordan River and Herzl recited to him the plan to erect a mighty dam that with its energy would supply the total economic life of the land. And now his finger tapped on a point of the map, and he cried: "How much horsepower has Niagara? Eight million? We shall have ten million!" Buber stood entranced before this magic work. He seemed to feel the Jordan-Niagara Falls spraying over him, and at the same time he had to smile: how remote that was, how unreal! No, it was not for that, thought the young man, that we served; it was not to take part in the Americanization of Asia that we inscribed Zion's name on our banner. God be thanked that this was only a dream!

Only long afterward, many years after Herzl's death, did it become clear to Buber that at that time it was Herzl — and not he — who had meant the real Palestine. For Buber at that time it was "das geliebte und Gelobte" — the beloved and the Promised Land that had to be won anew, the land of the soul and of the message, the land in which the miracle of redemption would reach fulfillment. For Herzl, in contrast, it was a wholly particular land with wholly particular geographical and geological characteristics, and therefore also with clearly determinable technical possibilities which he not only knew but also beheld in his mind's eye.

In 1902 when he had already left the editorship of *Die Welt,* Buber published a statement thanking those who had tried to help him make it a great historical spiritual movement and dissociating himself, as he wrote to Herzl, from the course that he could foresee the paper would take. But he complained to Herzl in this same letter that his intentions had been misunderstood:

> I am accustomed to set forth my views and intentions at every point; but I shall always defend myself against false views and intentions being foisted on me by way of calumny. It would make me very glad if I could make perfectly clear my position toward the Party leadership and the Party organ, and I would be very grateful to you if you would grant me an interview for this purpose. I find it very painful to see myself ever again misunderstood without having the opportunity of ending once and for all these misrepresentations.

The rift between Buber and Herzl that had begun with the Third Congress in 1901 became a decisive break in 1903. This time, however, the controversy was focused on personalities and seemed, to the young Buber, to demand a choice of loyalties between the two men who had been most important to him in his Zionism — Theodor Herzl and Ahad Ha'am. The year before, Herzl had published his novel *Altneuland,* his somewhat utopian picture of how life in the new Jewish state might be. Ahad Ha'am subjected this book to a penetrating criticism of Herzl's view of Zion. "If you will it, this is no fairy-tale," Herzl wrote on the title page, but to Ahad Ha'am it seemed more of a nightmare. Herzl's Zionism was to him nothing short of a new and more effective type of assimilation in which the author went out of his way to credit non-Jews for everything original in the new state and made no mention of Hebrew instruction or Hebrew culture either in its projected education or in its learned academy.

The editor of *Ost und West*, which planned to publish a German translation of Ahad Ha'am's article from *HaShiloah*, extended to Herzl the courtesy of sending him a copy of the translation before publication so that he might have a chance to reply. Herzl, instead, in a shocking breach of good faith, passed the article along to Max Nordau without the editor's knowledge, thus making it possible for Nordau to distribute a "reply" to every important German-language Jewish newspaper and journal on the day before the translation of Ahad Ha'am's article was published in *Ost und West!* Nordau directed a sharp and insulting personal attack against Ahad Ha'am himself. "Ahad Ha'am belongs to the worst enemies of Zionism; for this secular protest rabbi dares to give himself out as a Zionist and to distinguish himself from the real Zionism, the only one that exists, by calling it political Zionism!" Before the German-reading public could even know what he was replying to, Nordau maligned Ahad Ha'am's person, his spiritual and cultural leadership, his very real devotion to a Jewish homeland in Palestine, and that cultural Zionism for which he and his followers in the Democratic Fraction stood.

Buber and some of his friends protested to Herzl against the tone of Nordau's reply. Buber in particular asked Herzl whether the form of Nordau's article and the manner in which it was circulated seemed to him calculated to affect favorably the development of the movement. "Both seem to me so foreign from your own manner that I find it impossible to accept the idea that they had your full and innermost approval. Why is there not room in the party for the expression of the opinion of each party member — each in proper form?"

Herzl in his reply evaded Buber's questions. He called Ahad Ha'am "the stinking enemy that creeps into our ranks," and left unclear whether he had in fact seen and approved of Nordau's article before its publication. As a result Buber, Feiwel, and Weizmann published in the new Hebrew periodical *Hasman* (The Time) a protest declaration which was signed by numerous personalities, including Siegfried Bernfeld, Marcus Ehrenpreis, Alfred Nossig, Davis Trietsch, and Saul Tshernichovsky. Herzl saw in this protest a personal attack against him, and his anger was still further aggravated by an unsigned article (by Benjamin Segal) in *Ost und West*, prefacing Ahad Ha'am's finally published review of *Altneuland*.

Herzl mistakenly believed that Buber himself had inspired this article, and his bitterness, as a result, was particularly directed against him. Herzl finally took explicit responsibility for asking Nordau to write the article against Ahad Ha'am and said that Buber might use that information as he liked. Nordau had penned a crude answer to a malicious attack, which Herzl believed was a threat to the party, and which had to be answered. Then turning the attack on Buber, Herzl asked how it was that he, a friend of free expression of opinion, found no word to say against the anonymous article in *Ost und West,* of which, it was reported to Herzl, Buber had knowledge before its publication.

Less than a week later, in reply to a further communication on the part of Buber, Herzl wrote the letter which decisively alienated Buber and his friends and made any real reconciliation impossible. Herzl accused Buber, in effect, of having left the movement, and this Buber could not forgive. "Without going further into details," Herzl wrote Buber, "I shall not conceal from you my view that the so-called 'Fraction' for reasons unknown to me, has fallen into error. My advice is: Try to find your way back to the movement, which certainly – like everything human – has its errors, but . . . consists for the most part of men of good will. . . ." Reminding Buber of how he made both Feiwel and him editors of the party organ *Die Welt* and of how few restrictions he placed on them, Herzl closed with the wish that their minds would again become clear and that they would realize and actively repent the serious errors that they had committed against Nordau.

In his previous letters Buber had sought to show Herzl that "the idealism that burned in us, incapable as it was of polite expression, . . . was, next to your personal dream and ideal, the single great force in the movement and that only in these two – in your effective energy and our boundless enthusiasm – did the meaning of the people's destiny live." Now Buber wrote Herzl that he and his friends did not need to find their way back to the movement, that they stood as firmly within it as anyone, "and, with all due respects I cannot allow you to pronounce a negative judgment on this question."

We may assume from Buber's own words in his 1944 reminiscence over Herzl and the map of Palestine that Herzl overcame some of his estrangement from Buber at the very end of his life. When Herzl died in July 1904 Martin informed Paula that his death came dreadfully unexpectedly and incomprehensibly.

> For him it was, to be sure, the best possible time to die — before all
> the unavoidable events, disappointment and decline, and at the height.
> What shape the movement will now take cannot yet be foreseen. But
> one can also barely think about that, so deeply is one shattered by the
> personal alone.

Nonetheless, in this decisive and tragic encounter of two men,
"each of whom was as he was," there was a remarkable foreshadowing of the conflict between the Seer and his loyal but independent
disciple the Yehudi in Buber's Hasidic chronicle-novel *For the Sake
of Heaven.* Here too there are not enough resources in the relationship to prevent the differences from crystallizing into a fixed opposition. Buber did not mention that these words of Herzl's were
directed to him personally, but there is enough indignation in the
way he speaks of them to bear out Ernst Simon's statement that it
was many years before Buber could overcome the anger that this
"advice" of Herzl aroused in him.

Buber inserted this incident in the midst of an objective analysis
of "Herzl and History" written in 1904, the year of Herzl's death.
In this analysis he recognized Herzl's greatness but not his Jewishness. Herzl gave form to Zionism which, before him, was an
inchoate mass. "Herzl laid his hand on it with a firm, shaping pres-
sure. A sure, but unheeding hand. How many noble possibilities
were killed!" Herzl was the first man to pursue Jewish politics in
the Exile, and that will never be forgotten. In the name of the
Jewish people he negotiated with the great powers of Europe. Although involved in public affairs and political conflicts, he was,
said Buber, a thoroughly unpublic man who bore within his soul
deep, inescapable inner conflict. Both dreamer and practical man
at once, he was the hero of a time of transition, the lord of a sick
people. His greatest deed was that he gave his people an image —
not the image of a real man, but an ideal image, a heartening, up-
lifting prototype.

For all this, Buber emphasized, it is fundamentally false to cele-
brate him as a *Jewish* personality, as one could celebrate Spinoza,
Israel Baal-Shem (the founder of Hasidism), Heinrich Heine, or
Ferdinand Lassalle. In Herzl there lived nothing of an elemental
Jewish nature.

> Herzl was a Western Jew without Jewish tradition, without Jewish
> childhood impressions, without Jewish knowledge acquired in his youth;
> he grew up in a non-Jewish milieu and never came into contact with the

Jewish masses; no human creature was so alien to him as a Jewish prole-
tarian. . . . He was a whole man, he was not a whole Jew. In these seven
years of Congress Zionism I have admired from the heart his human
image in its beautiful greatness and superiority, in its noble devotion
and power of action, in its unbending faithfulness, even in its humanly
broad errors. As a Jew he always appeared to me incomplete.

He was also incomplete as a Zionist, as Buber understood the term.
He never grasped the movement in its wholeness. He never saw the
Zionist party as only the conscious limb of a greater organism. He
was never truthfully aware of the Jewish Renaissance. Those intellectuals of independent thought who left the party were in Herzl's
eyes renegades, and Ahad Ha'am he saw as an obscure, spiteful
journalist. At this point in logical, if hidden, association with Ahad
Ha'am — the cause of his break with Herzl — Buber told his own
experience — in the third person: " 'Try to find your way back to
the movement,' he wrote once to a representative of the radical-
national wing of the party. To the movement! "

What piqued Buber particularly about this was that Herzl identified the movement with himself. This was in fact, in Buber's eyes,
Herzl's greatest weakness and his greatest strength. Affirmatively, it
gave him his upright, unshakable optimism and his inexhaustible
energy and made him into the most influential man of action of the
new Jewish era. "He believed in himself not as in a person but as in
a cause." But it is to the negative side of Herzl's identification of
cause and person that Buber devoted his most illuminating reminiscence of Herzl and of Herzl's impact on his own development as a
person and a thinker. The occasion was the Sixth Zionist Congress
in 1903, and though the conflict was still between Herzl and the
Democratic Fraction, the specific form of his "fulminating speech
against the opposition" was an attack on Buber's friend and co-
worker Davis Trietsch with no direct personal clash between Buber
and Herzl.

Herzl countered Trietsch's criticism of his policy with a personal
attack on Trietsch's own colonizing activities.[*] After the speech,
Herzl retired to the presidential room, and soon afterward Feiwel
and Buber followed him in order to point out the untenability of
his accusations and to demand an investigating commission. On
the way to the presidential room Buber was deeply disturbed. He
had indeed stood in decisive opposition to Herzl since the previous

---

* See Note B in Sources for Chapter 4, p. 383.

Congress, but that had always been entirely a matter of a difference of position. He had never for a moment ceased to believe in the man himself. But now for the first time his soul revolted — so powerfully that writing about it a quarter of a century later he could still remember it physically. Yet when he entered the room, the sight that met him transformed his excitement in an instant, and the heart that had a moment before been pounding now froze.

In the room were only Herzl and his mother. Madame Jeannette sat on a chair, unmoving, silent, but with eyes from which the most lively sympathy streamed. Herzl paced up and down through the room in great strides; his vest was unbuttoned, his breast heaving and sinking. This "caged lion," whose gestures before were always so mastered and masterly, now breathed wildly. Herzl's pallor struck Buber only later, so burning was his glance.

It had suddenly become compellingly clear to Buber that it was impossible here to remain inwardly the representative of *one* side. Outside was an injured man, his friend and fellow fighter, to whom a public injustice had been done, and here was the man who had done the injustice, who had inflicted the wound, yet a man who, even though misled, was still his leader, sick with zeal, consuming himself for his belief.

"There were great and dreadful moments," Martin wrote Paula.

> The shattering that I experienced is perhaps the greatest of my life. Never have I witnessed thus the cruelty of human nature. Now I am in a court of honor that has to decide about the strangest thing in human history.... One thing dominates me: I want in my life to bring forth unconditional purity and greatness, at any price.

For the twenty-five-year-old this was one of the first times in which he set foot on the soil of tragedy, where all question of being in the right disappeared. "There was one more, still greater thing to learn: how out of the grave of being in the right, the right is resurrected." But this he learned only much later.

Although they carried out their task and pointed out and demanded what they had to, Buber and Feiwel could no longer do so with conviction. What it amounted to was appealing from Herzl, who identified himself with the cause of Zionism, to the cause itself and who could do that? Herzl walked back and forth in the room, and it was impossible to tell whether he listened. Buber looked over at Herzl's mother, and saw that her face had darkened and that there was something in it, he did not know what, that frightened him.

Suddenly Herzl stopped before them and spoke to them in a tone altogether different from what one would have expected — a passionate but smiling tone, although no smile lay on his lips. "I should have taken him to task wholly differently!" he cried. "But there in front of the platform, directly opposite me, a young woman was placed — his fiancée, I have been told — she stood there and her eyes blazed at me — I tell you: a wonderful person! I could not do it!" And now his mouth also smiled, as if liberated. The "charmer 'Told' " smiled in his romantic way, and Buber smiled too — very much, to use his own simile, like a schoolboy to whom it has just occurred that the Latin author he is translating meant real friends and real lovers. On the face of Herzl's mother, which was no longer dark, there also stood a smile.

This was the last time Buber saw Herzl at such close quarters. Later, after Herzl's death, Buber found himself forced again and again to ponder the relation of "cause" and "person." He recognized that most men of action see no sense in discussing principles and methods when what counts in the last instance is the man who is entrusted with carrying them out. As long as a leader like Herzl has "charisma," then one who does not is in no position to judge him. Only a standpoint which Buber reached many years later — that which demands a real dialogical relationship between leader and led — could call this concept into question. Buber's later view of tragedy — where each is as he is and the resources to bridge the gap are lacking — is anticipated here even more powerfully than in his own earlier break with Herzl. With it is anticipated that fundamental principle of the life of dialogue that confirms the opponent even in his opposition because it does not see two *points of view* as opposing each other but two *persons*. It realizes that neither the truth nor the right is an affair of "monologue" that can reside simply in one side to the exclusion of the other. It is this awareness, growing out of this event in which he "set foot on the soil of tragedy," that accounts for that remarkable characteristic in Buber's personality to which Hans Kohn points in this very connection of his conflict with Herzl:

> When Herzl died a short time afterward, Buber found the right words to characterize his personality and his position in the Jewish Renaissance movement. He did not fail to recognize the unique greatness of Herzl.

He paid tribute to him in unforgettable words which were all the greater in that they stemmed from a full awareness of what was problematic and inadequate in Herzl's personality and were spoken by a man whom Herzl held to be his opponent. But this has ever again proved to be a characteristic of Buber's. Without consideration for the position taken not only by his opponents but also by critics who judge him insultingly and from above, though far beneath him in human and spiritual significance, he does full justice to them. In full and unprejudiced knowledge of each man's essence he emphasizes the good and the valuable in him. He feels respect for human significance wherever it confronts him, and speaks of it in a becoming manner. This is today so rare among scholarly and spiritual workers that it deserves to be pointed out.

Buber's readiness to do justice even to those who opposed and insulted him does not mean that he was "objective" in the usual sense of the term, i.e., that he detached his reason from the rest of his person. It means rather that even in involving himself in the situation, he did not lose sight of the side of the other and was ready to pay sincere respect to any quality of greatness that he encountered. Such a confirmation of the other does not mean the exclusion of one's own subjectivity, but it does mean a change in the ordinary manner of subjectivity. Instead of a closed mind that shuts out whatever does not fit into one's views or bolster one's ego, it means an openness to what is really other than oneself.

Such a combination of full involvement and openness to the other is possible only for a relatively whole person, however, and this Buber was just in the painful process of becoming. If he showed an almost uncanny insight into many aspects of his leader's personality, his own relationship to that personality was clearly not worked through — neither in 1904 when he wrote his first essays on Herzl nor even in 1910 when he sought to supplement his earlier judgments. He reaffirmed in 1910, to be sure, his criticism of a purely political, diplomatic action, spurred on to ever more desperate attempts by each new wave of anti-Semitism, leading to the power and then to the soul of a dictator, abjuring the slow, gradual work of building the land. But in 1910, looking back from the vantage point of someone now in his thirties, Buber labeled himself and his friends "lyrical doctrinaires" who asked only about opinions and not about individuals. What Buber wrote six years before, when he had not yet freed himself "from the din of battle, from heroic living on the surfaces," was right but not *essential.* What was essential was that in Herzl's very lack rested his naive, primary, elemental greatness — a greatness which Buber and his friends ("we problematic men") did not possess. Buber knew that the true Jewish question was an inner one because existence itself was a problem to him. "That is the great and tragic Jewish inheritance: the problematic, the Galut form of inner division." To the problematic man, existence is given as an abundance of contradictions. In contrast to him, to Buber himself, stood Herzl, the unproblematic man, the elemental active one who wanted to help others to peace and security and saw only that.

Buber was under no illusion that it was within his power to become such an elementary active man. Yet in 1910 he set up Herzl, the nonproblematic man, as the model for the man who must overcome his inner problematic, and proclaimed that for Judaism in crisis, in transition, what matters above all is not the thinking but the acting life. "Theodor Herzl is a leader to the acting life." One cannot go back to Herzl, but one can swing out over one's inner division into that unity of the forces of the soul that is ready to receive *illumination*, illumination that teaches work and deed. *"There is a transformation through the will."*

There is no mistaking the false note here. Buber's knowledge of the tragic, his full recognition of the problematic, his respect for his own deep searching and probing — all seem to have deserted him here before the desire to reaffirm the lost leader. If he anticipated by a half century the contemporary understanding of the problematic of modern man as residing above all in his inner division, nevertheless he sidestepped the real issue of the problematic — the need to face it and work through it before one can reach any greater wholeness. One reason for this sidestepping may be the overwhelming importance for him of the encounter with death — the dark but no longer nameless messenger. At the beginning of the 1904 essay on "Herzl and History" he wrote:

> For a man who only speaks when he has something to say, it is a difficult decision to share his thoughts at the grave of a revered and great man. The shudder of eternity will not allow words to come, and everything that human speech may give, appears shockingly thin and wretched where the speechless might of death has announced itself.

At the end of the 1910 essay he wrote:

> While I am writing this down, it suddenly strikes me: he would have been fifty years old now.

I did not understand before, as in this moment, this simple and cruel
reality before which the heart must stop and the mouth become dumb.
And now I feel it as I have never yet felt it: how orphaned we are.

Buber's final written evaluation of Herzl, written almost a half
century after his association with him, is more positive than his
1904 statement and more realistic than his 1910 one. Like Leo
Pinsker, the author of *Autoemancipation* — the other great Zionist text of the period — Herzl was frightened out of his security by
anti-Semitism. Yet he did not enter into history and discover the
meaning of being insecure, but broke out in order to make his community secure. Nonetheless, Herzl's utopian Zionist novel, *Altneuland* — the very book that had been the occasion of the decisive
split between Herzl and Nordau, on the one side, and Ahad Ha'am,
Buber, and the Democratic Fraction, on the other — is now praised
by Buber as "a significant document of the inner unification of a
person with a cause." One has not without justice reproached *Altneuland* for lacking national-cultural content, Buber commented
from a summit considerably farther above the battle than any that
he had attained in his earlier evaluations. Nonetheless, it is not an
abstract humanity that emerges from the book; it is the humanity
of the people's common striving toward a true life. Central to the
novel, indeed, is the recognition that Zion is genuinely Zion only
when it realizes the prophetic meaning that once imbued the name,
when its new structure, therefore, is erected on human love. "Here
Herzl's national humanism attained a pure unfolding."

At the same time the guilt that may have lain behind the 1910
essay is faced and the earlier insight into Herzl's tragic contradiction recaptured. Herzl said to his physician that he would die not
only of heart disease but of the Jews. By this, Buber averred, Herzl
meant the passionate and inconsiderate opposition to the "Uganda"
project, which Buber and Weizmann helped to lead, and the painful
experiences with his followers, to which Buber certainly contributed. Yet at a deeper level of his being, wrote Buber at seventy,
Herzl suffered from the contradiction within himself, of which the
antithesis between "Zion" and "Jewish state" was only one manifestation.

Buber had to work through his relation to his two chief images
of the human during this period — Herzl and Ahad Ha'am. In doing
so he made a choice decisive for the rest of his life. This choice
was not a matter of accepting one man and rejecting the other.

Both were important figures for him, and he grew through his relationship to both. Writing in 1917, Buber spoke of the "mild melancholy" of the eyes of Ahad Ha'am and the wrathful melancholy of Herzl's. "I have looked into the eyes of both in decisive moments, moments of test — Herzl raged, Ahad Ha'am understood; naturally my soul was with the raging one, the unjust one — but the other was not a bourgeois!" Buber's personal relationship with Herzl was and remained more important to him than that with Ahad Ha'am. But it was a question of a basic decision for an image of man, a decision which Buber himself later saw as confronting every people and the Jewish people in particular: that between the leader and the true teacher. Ahad Ha'am dared what Herzl, with his devotion to the abstractions of political movement, did not — to bring idea and reality into faithful relationship. It was to him, at that time, despite all differences, that Buber gave his allegiance. It was he who made manifest the true mystery of the perseverance of Israel apart from its biological continuity — the teaching and learning that connect the generations spiritually. His goal for the Jewish people was not merely a guaranteed survival, nor merely an independent life in its own land, nor merely a life in its own culture. All this was insufficient if it did not include a life of genuine responsibility face to face with the truth.

Ahad Ha'am's Zionism was not "smaller" than political Zionism but greater. He too strove for a Jewish communal life in Palestine, not even shying away from the designation of a "Jewish state," and he too saw a great mass settlement as the precondition for this community. But he viewed this mass settlement as the organic center of a great living world Judaism whose existence depended on this organic center. For political Zionism the state was the goal and Zion a "myth" that inflamed the masses. For Ahad Ha'am the state was the way to the goal that is called Zion. If Israel reduced Zion to "a Jewish community in Palestine," even that community would not come into being. That Ahad Ha'am recognized this is not to be ascribed to any idealism but rather to his realism: he took seriously the special conditions of the manner and the history of Israel, saw that a new historical reality had grown out of them, a "way that no one had yet travelled," and he saw Israel at the same time as it is, sick and miserable and incapable of being saved by anything other than the will to completion. What divided Herzl and Ahad Ha'am, wrote Buber, was a difference other than that which is often spoken of between Western Judaism, which is diminished in its *Jewish* substance, and Eastern, which is diminished in its *human* substance. "It is the difference between a transformation of the attitude and a transformation of the whole man, . . . between a slogan and a direction; more clearly still: it is the difference between a teacher and a leader."

> Leading without a teaching attains success: Only what one attains is at times a downright caricature of what, in the ground of one's soul, . . . one wanted to attain. . . . Unhappy, certainly, is the people that has no leader, but three times as unhappy is the people whose leader has no teaching.

To believe that the land and the language will produce everything of themselves was no longer possible to Buber, as in the days of his early romantic enthusiasm over the heroic Nietzschean leader Theodor Herzl. Instead he chose the way of the teacher who lives in responsibility to reality and to truth. If Buber could not in the end become both leader and teacher, he did become in the deepest sense the true teacher for the Jewish people, for modern Zion, and for the world.

PART III

Mysticism

(1898-1917)

CHAPTER 5

Encounter with Mysticism

AS IMPORTANT AS WAS BUBER'S contribution to early Zionism and the Jewish Renaissance movement, it represented in his own life and thought only the first step in his liberation from the aimlessness of the times. In 1918 he recognized what his early essays on the Jewish Renaissance show no inkling of: that becoming part of the Jewish nation does not by itself transform the Jewish man. It gives him roots, to be sure, but he can be just as poor in soul with it as without it. This does not mean that Buber later saw his early nationalistic fervor as entirely invalid. On the contrary, it was an important and essential stage that led to a further transformation. Yet it did so only because it was to him "not a satiating but a soaring, not an entering into the harbor but a setting out on the open sea." But there is a judgment here for all that. If it was a beginning rather than an ending, nonetheless it was "too easy," as he wrote Weizmann, revealing more enthusiasm than substance. "I professed Judaism before I really knew it." Only after blind groping did Buber reach his second step, wanting to know Judaism, and by knowing he did not mean the storing up of knowledge but the biblical knowing of involvement and mutual contact: the immediate, "eye-to-eye knowing of the people in its creative primal hours." It was through such knowing that Buber came to the second important stage on his way, namely, the discovery of Hasidism.

The Hebrew word *Hasid* means a pious man, and Hasidism is commonly identified as a form of communal pietism, the popular Jewish mysticism which arose in Eastern Europe in the eighteenth century and spread like fire among the communities of oppressed and unhappy Jews. Buber spent a lifetime expounding the *uniqueness* of Hasidism. Yet the encounter with Hasidism was both preceded and followed by an encounter with mysticism as such.

Ernst Simon has remarked that Buber is the finest example of Rilke's dictum that fame is the collection of misunderstandings piled around a great name. None of us is quite willing or able to dispense with categories, particularly in the case of a philosopher and thinker. But we can at least escape the trap of labeling Buber a mystic or *not* a mystic by focusing on his *encounter* with mysticism.

One of Buber's earliest encounters with mysticism was within an explicitly social context, the Neue Gemeinschaft, or New Community, founded by the brothers Heinrich and Julius Hart in or near Berlin. The New Community combined an emphasis on divine, boundless swinging upward, as opposed to comfortably settling down, with the aim of a communal settlement which should anticipate the new age in beauty, art, and religious dedication. The New Community was led and taught by the socialist Gustav Landauer. Next to his marriage, Buber's friendship with Landauer, who was eight years older, was probably the decisive relationship of his adult life. Buber met Landauer in 1899 at the time when the latter was almost twenty-nine. Landauer undoubtedly encouraged the switch in Buber's university studies from science and the history of art to Christian mysticism. In 1906, after years of study, Landauer published the first modern edition of the great German mystic Meister Eckhart, a translation which, Hans Kohn points out, bore many resemblances to the basic principles which guided Buber's first attempts to translate Hasidic writings.

During the years 1899 and 1900 Buber was close to the New Community and gave lectures there on the great Lutheran mystic Jacob Boehme and on "Old and New Community." The lecture on Boehme which Buber gave before the New Community undoubtedly formed the basis for the essay on Boehme that he published in 1901 — the most original and impressive of his earliest writings.

Certainly the "wonderful world feeling" of which Buber spoke in this essay is completely consonant with the goals of the New Community. It is more "world feeling" and the relation of the "I" to the world that absorbed Buber than Boehme's ecstatic experience or his elaborate mystical and gnostic theosophy. What Buber said of Boehme was certainly true of his own experience at this period: for all its effect on one, the world still remained eternally distant and strange. "The individual consumes himself in dumb, hopeless solitude." Nonetheless, we have a relation to the world, which is no completed whole compelling us but is a continual process of becoming. We ourselves form and create this process in that at every moment an unconscious existential judgment about things, i.e., about sense impressions, speaks in us: this is. The changes that our creation awakes themselves become a source of numberless new and liberating sense impressions of many kinds. Thus we are not the slaves but rather the lovers of our world. We do not see the things-in-themselves but our sense impressions — thus far Buber looked back to Kant. But we enter into a creating and loving relationship with these very sense impressions through which we have an impact on them and they on us.

It is in this essay that Buber quoted Ludwig Feuerbach's thesis that "man with man — the unity of I and Thou — is God" — only to reject it. "We stand nearer today," wrote Buber, "to the teaching of Boehme than to that of Feuerbach, to the feeling of Saint Francis of Assisi who called the trees, the birds, and the stars his brothers and still nearer to the Vedanta." By the Vedanta, Buber meant that central tradition of Hindu mysticism which in its austerest expressions in the Upanishads affirms that reality is nondual (even the statement that it is one would imply a second) and that the seeming multiplicity of the world is actually *maya*, or the illusion of creation. Buber may have agreed intellectually with the Vedanta at this point, but the prime fact of his experience was the division between the "I" and the world, and the rest of the essay focuses on conflict and love precisely as bridges between *separated* individuals. Things neither exist in rigid separation nor melt into one another, but reciprocally condition one another.

The world is for Boehme a harmony of individual tones fully developed in their individuality yet born from one movement. But Boehme does not content himself with this bridge between the individual and the world, and "it is in this that he most nearly approaches us. It is not enough that the 'I' unites itself with the world. The 'I' is the world. Since God is the unity of all forces, so each individual bears the properties of all things in himself, and what we call his individuality is only a higher grade or development of this property. Heaven and earth and all creatures and even God himself lie in man." In a curious fusion of Renaissance mysticism and turn-of-the-century vitalism, Buber freely adapted images from the Last Supper and the Christian communion: "When I bring a piece of fruit to my mouth, I feel: this is my body. And when I set wine to my lips, I feel: this is my blood."

The title of Buber's dissertation, written for the University of Vienna, is "From the History of the Problem of Individuation (Nicholas of Cusa and Jacob Boehme)." In the Foreword Buber stated that these were two segments from a larger work which would discuss the history of the problem of individuation from Aristotle to Leibniz and the newer philosophy. Buber chose Cusanus and Boehme with the hope of proving that their metaphysical individualism created the base for that ethics of personality that found its most harmonic philosophical expression in the German theologian Schleiermacher and its most far-reaching literary expression in Emerson. Both Cusanus and Boehme expounded a basic concept that characterized the renewal in Renaissance philosophy of Neo-Platonism (the mysticism of the Greek philosopher Plotinus and his followers): the development of the multiplicity of the sense world out of the unity and simplicity of the idea. For Nicholas of Cusa this meant the emanation of relative realities out of the absolute reality; for Boehme, in contrast, the actualization of the absolute possibility. For both, however, individualization was real. It is significant that Buber did *not* turn to mysticism, as so many modern thinkers since him have done, as the negation of the self and of personality.

What drew Buber to mysticism was, first of all, his own personal awareness of the threat of infinity and the sense of aloneness in the face of outer separateness and inner contradiction. But it was also clearly that mechanization and mass culture that Kierkegaard, Nietzsche, and Dostoevsky had protested against in the century that had just concluded. For the medieval mystic the individual was only the bearer of a life experience encompassing the transcendent. Individuation was given only to be renounced and overcome. In contrast to his later interpretation of Meister Eckhart as retaining some independence of the soul from God, Buber here claimed that Eckhart fully identified being with All-being and regarded everything individual as only its negation and as an obstacle on the way to perfection. Although Buber later spoke of Eckhart as the greatest mystic of the Western world, in this early essay he rejected Eckhart's view, or what he supposed it to be, as approaching, in its negation (though only in this), the modern natural sciences. For the natural sciences the individual is also not a specific problem but only in a certain measure the intersection point of several partly known, partly still unknown circles, the point at which the several, more or less investigated, natural laws become operative and are actualized. The world spirit ushered in by the astronomer Laplace would see the individual as only a combination of atoms or of energies in mathematically definable size, manner, and form and their interaction.

Cusanus resumed in modern form, said Buber, the perseverance and the absolute value of the individual in his particularity. But individualism for Buber at this juncture, as for Cusanus, did not mean mere difference. It meant uniqueness — that which makes a person or thing of value in itself, that which is unrepeatable and for which no other value can be substituted, that which is not a matter of usefulness or function but, however much it may exist in relation to others, is an absolute center in itself. This concept of uniqueness — the uniqueness of the person but also the uniqueness of every thing — is the first necessary step on Buber's way to the philosophy of dialogue, the "I-Thou" relationship. It is not a sufficient step, however, and for years it was for Buber himself a block to dialogue. Yet the true meaning of the unique relation of the unique person to the unique reality that he encounters can be neither understood nor approached except by way of this concept. This and the idea of the *coincidentia oppositorum* — the coincidence of opposites which unites them without diminishing their oppositeness — are two of the essential ingredients of the "life of dialogue" that Buber took from Nicholas of Cusa and Renaissance mysticism at the beginning of his way. "The seeing of your eye cannot be the seeing of any other eye," he wrote. "The individual is the center point of an infinite world process."

Each creature is perfect even if in relation to another it appears less than perfect, Buber wrote. Each wants to persist in its own being. Even if this persistence should lead to conflict, this conflict is the source of becoming as well as of destruction. And only through the fact that each unfolds itself with all its powers does the harmony of the world-happening awaken, which figures forth the one

God in the numberless variety. Over against this multiplicity of absolutely different, indeed opposite, things stands the absolute unity and identity of the divine ground of the world. All is God: the undivided origin, the unfolded world, and the goal of the unification of all being. In Him all things, even the opposites, are included without losing their opposition: He is the *complicatio contradictoriorum,* the *coincidentia oppositorum.* The activation and realization of the spiritual power of God is the goal of the creation and of every particular being. The universe is included in each thing, but in each as this particular thing. Everything concrete attains rest in God as in its perfection. Each creature has its line of realization; but God is the point in which all lines of perfection meet. God does not want to abolish the differences of the things in which he reveals Himself but to perfect Himself in them.

In Boehme, Buber found a more modern thinker than Cusanus and one whose influence on him was equally great and lasting. Boehme combined a really modern dynamic with a dialectic of good and evil taken from the Hebrew Kabbala, a dialectic which Buber later encountered anew in another child of the Kabbala — Hasidism. "Each thing longs for the other, for it is determined by the other." Its powers are lured out of it and made actual through its encounter with the other. This process leads again not to the overcoming but to the intensification and spread of individuation. Even "fire," Boehme's "lower ternary" into which everything is drawn and consumed, indirectly serves the "upper ternary" of light. The higher it flames up, the higher is the light.

The Jewish theologian Franz Rosenzweig published one passage from Buber's dissertation as his contribution to a volume of "unknown writings" issued in honor of Buber's fiftieth birthday. The passage in question was a brief side discussion of the teaching of Valentin Weigel, who seemed, to the Buber of that period, to offer a more satisfactory answer to the problem of opposites than Boehme, who treated it historically, as a problem of creation. Boehme oscillates between theism and pantheism, wrote Buber, and never worked his way out of this conflict. Weigel, like Buber himself at this period, points to "the becoming God" — a teaching which Buber many years later rejected categorically. In 1904, however, Buber suggested that Weigel went beyond Boehme precisely in his doctrine that only through the creation of the world does God become God and the doctrine that God comes to that self-knowledge which completes consciousness only in man, i.e., in the evolution of creation, the evolution of God in the world. Rosen-zweig rightly contrasts this statement with Buber's later (1923) condemnation of "the hopelessly perverted conception that God is not but rather becomes — in man or in mankind." Buber himself pointed to it later as something that had been destroyed in him during the First World War:

> Since 1900 I had first been under the influence of German mysti-cism from Meister Eckhart to Angelus Silesius, according to which the primal ground (*Urgrund*) of being, the nameless, impersonal godhead, comes to "birth" in the human soul; then I had been under the influ-ence of the later Kabbala and of Hasidism, according to which man has the power to unite the God who is over the world with his *shekinah* dwelling in the world. In this way there arose in me the thought of a realization of God through man; man appeared to me as the being through whose existence the Absolute, resting in its truth, can gain the character of reality.

It is clear from this confession that Meister Eckhart had more decisive and lasting influence on Buber than his doctoral disserta-tion suggests. The eternal birth of God in the soul, the dialogue between the soul and God in which God laughs at the soul and the soul laughs back at God, the emphasis upon life as more basic than the meaning of life — all entered not only into Buber's early mysticism but into his later existentialism and his philosophy of dialogue. In 1921 Buber was to quote, as a companion saying to the central teaching of Hasidism, one of the propositions of Meister Eckhart condemned by the Pope in 1329: "The noble man is that only-begotten Son of God whom the Father eternally begets."

Buber opened his 1904 article on Landauer's writings with a quotation from Landauer's translation of Meister Eckhart. Through this article we can understand Landauer's impact on Buber and the way in which the dialogue between the two men issued into a fruit-ful dialectic in Buber's own thought. Though none of Buber's own writings even hint at the radical skepticism that underlay Landauer's mysticism as well as his anarchism and his socialism, it is clear that Buber confronted that skepticism and developed his own thinking in response to it. The modern mystic has often, indeed, come to his mysticism by way of radical negation. But Buber extended this insight into a hardly tenable generalization, supposedly true of all mystics and philosophers, and he made Landauer the crowning representative of them all.

. . . That which is the representative meaning of his work, the insight that all true working is rooted in the deepest doubt, all genuine creation rests in the most radical negation, all pure world-affirmation proceeds from the most ultimate despair, philosophers and mystics of all ages have intimated; but none has won this insight for our immediate life feeling and made it as fruitful as he had, with no one has this basic motif taken so far-reaching and manifold forms . . .; he does not exhaust himself in attacking dogmas, making answers questionable, shattering securities, but each time he knows to replace an old dogma by a new world-image, an old answer by a new world-metaphor, and he erects a kingdom of playful, creatively conscious illusion there where all ground has given way under one's feet.

Landauer was above all else a pathbreaker for Buber in his slow and painful progress from soaring enthusiasm to the "lived concrete." Landauer left the New Community after a short while, rejecting as utopian quackery the Hart brothers' suspension of all opposites in a bath of optimistic good will. Landauer recognized the tragic as an essential element of life. As a man of the new age, he demanded, like Buber later, looking reality in the face without fear, affirming its tragedy without sentimentality and working in and through it.

Buber's great personal admiration for Landauer is evident from his comparison of two essays on anarchy that Landauer had written six years apart. The road from one to another is not merely a development, he said, but one of the most beautiful documents of human self-liberation. In the latter Landauer recognized that in his earlier desire to bring freedom to the people he was not an anarchist but a despot. Those are free, Buber commented, who detach themselves from all compulsion of the soul and now devote themselves to erecting a new society in the midst of the old one. Anarchy is, in truth, a basic disposition of every man who wants to form a new being out of himself; he feels that a death must precede every rebirth. It is precisely this insight that one must become nothing in order to reach the really new that Buber adopted two years later in the startlingly different form of the teachings of the Baal-Shem-Tov. Even in this earlier form, the mystical quality is unmistakable. He is freest who is most inwardly bound to the world, Buber proclaimed; for he lets what is most inward in him rule. In him the life of all the generations from which he has come has become a new, unique reality. This statement looks back to "the wonderful world feeling" of Buber's 1901 essay on Boehme and forward to the contrast between inward "blood" and outward "environment" in the first of his "Speeches on Judaism."

That there is a Nietzschean and even a Cartesian element in the skepticism of Landauer as interpreted by Buber is not surprising. Descartes' certainty only of his own existence, reducing all else to the status of unreal phantoms, can be overcome, wrote Buber, only by an act of Nietzschean will that creates the world even when it has no ground to do so — out of the sheer unwillingness to live in a solipsistic hell. If the world that is thus created is mystical, it is a mysticism so frankly subjective as to alienate him who looks to mysticism to supply the meaning which the world has not offered. "This world is mine," asserted Buber, "created by me, with that highest validity that only the act of creating can lend it. The spectre of absolute truth is driven away; only the world-images of the individuals live, and that means comprehending the world not with the detached intellect but with one's whole personal being."

There are no individuals, only communities, Buber paraphrased Landauer. The generations are only the rhythm of the waves of a great stream; in each individual the whole of the world of his ancestors is real and effective, and so much the stronger the more he withdraws from the environment into himself. It was Buber and not Landauer, as Hans Kohn has pointed out, who made this insight of Landauer's a guidepost for his life. Although Buber was never the man simply to adopt another man's ideas, there is no question but that the influence of his friendship with Landauer on his own development was incalculable.

In his earlier writing, Landauer was unwilling and perhaps unable to give finished artistic expression to his personal development in the very process of its becoming. In this respect, the two men could have formed no greater contrast; for Buber's own early works of a year or two hence were all too artistic. Yet Buber paid tribute to the unity of life-experience which Landauer expressed in these works as deeper and greater than "the great mass of smooth and well-rounded productions that are today called literature." One feels, Buber wrote, that here someone has set down his innermost struggles, still trembling with life — pure, undialectical becoming, which he makes no attempt to explain causally. Buber summed up the two main stages of Landauer's development in the two sentences: "We must burst all bonds in order to find ourselves," and "We must bind ourselves in the moment that we have burst all bonds." The freedom of the first is a revolution which is not merely talked about but already formed. Through it the breath of the free mountains blows, and in it we can feel the stretching of unshackled limbs; yet the freedom of the second is greater still: lived rebirth.

In *Ecstatic Confessions* (1909) Buber brought together a large number of personal descriptions of mystic ecstasy from a wide range of times, religions, and cultures which he had spent many years in assembling. In 1903 he shared the plan for this project with Gustav Landauer when he sent him his comments on his unpublished Eckhart manuscript. In 1907 he wrote Eugen Diedrichs, the future publisher, that although he intended to include a number of little-known German Catholic women in his selection, such as Mechtild von Magdeburg, his "Confessions" had as little to do with Catholicism as with Protestantism and was much more concerned with life-affirmation and positive genius than with asceticism and world-flight. He saw these "communications of visionary, dream-endowed persons about their innermost lives" as "a document of the greatest importance for the soul of humanity," but if he did not find the publishers he thought just right for it, he was quite ready to postpone or even abandon the project and keep it for his personal pleasure.

In the introductory essay, "Ecstasy and Confession," Buber presented what he believed to be the essence of those experiences. The ecstatic at the time of ecstasy has achieved true and perfect unity, Buber claimed, in which the world and the "I" are one and all multiplicity has disappeared. Speech is a part of the world of multiplicity and therefore can have no place in the experience of the ecstatic, nor can anything external, whether person or thing. Yet when the ecstatic returns to the meeting with his fellowmen, he cannot help but try to communicate his experience to them. To attempt to express the ineffable is the tension and pathos of the ecstatic — the impossible task which he can neither fulfill nor lay aside.

The important question that we must ask is whether the unity which the mystic experiences in ecstasy was seen by Buber simply as a subjective phenomenon, as he later held it to be, or whether it has metaphysical significance. Not suspecting that their poor individual "I" contains the world "I," asserted Buber, most mystics have connected their experience with God and have made of it a multiform mystery. Only in the primitive world of India is the "I" proclaimed that is one with the All and with the One. The unity which the ecstatic experiences when he has brought all his former multiplicity into oneness is not a relative unity; for the ecstatic man no longer has outside of himself others with whom he has community: it is the absolute, unlimited oneness which includes all others — complete identification.

No sooner had he stated this position of unqualified nondualism, however, than Buber modified it in the direction of the dynamic mysticism of Boehme and Meister Eckhart. The mystic desires to create a lasting memorial of his ineffable experience of ecstasy, and in so doing he brings the timeless into time and changes the unity without multiplicity into the unity of all multiplicity. On the magic wings of communication and the word, Buber glided from mystical ecstasy to the great myths of the One which becomes the many because it wishes to see and be seen, to comprehend itself as many while remaining One. This is the myth of the primeval Self that turns itself into world, that of the "I" that creates a "Thou." Thus the ecstatic experience is only one pole of the movement of the world spirit from the many to the one and the one to the many. "We turn inward and listen — and we do not know which sea's roar it is that we hear."

As I have pointed out in *Touchstones of Reality,* there is a distinction between accepting the validity of mystical experience and the ontological or metaphysical concepts that mystics have inferred from that experience. Even at this early stage, Buber was unwilling to equate the *experience* of nonduality with an unqualified *philosophy* of nonduality. At the same time it is clear that he did not see the mystic experience as the Christian *unio mystica* or as an *encounter* with a power that accosted and seized him, but as a turning inward to some ground of being beneath the individual "I." Forty-five years later, Buber wrote me:

> As far as I understand mysticism, its essential trait is the belief in a (momentous) "union" with the Divine or the absolute, a union not occurring after death but in the course of mortal life, i.e., as interruption. If you read attentively the introduction to *Ekstatiche Konfessionen,* you will see that even then, in my "mystical" period, I did not believe in it, but only in a "mystical" unification of the Self, identifying the depth of the individual self with the Self itself.

In 1910, a year after the publication of *Ecstasy and Confession,* Buber attended the first German conference of sociologists at Frankfurt am Main. In a major address, the eminent German sociologist and historian of religion Ernst Troeltsch proposed that mysticism should be added to church and sect as a sociological category. During the debate which followed, Buber quite properly criticized this attempt to erect a type of religious experience into a social form or group. But he went on to assert that mysticism should be understood as a "religious solipsism," a completely isolated experience of the individual self.

It is, said Buber, simply a psychological category — the most absolute realization of that special quality of self-perception and that intensity of self-enhancement which makes possible an "apperception of God," the founding of a personal relation to a content of the soul experienced as God. Although the social forms of religion are sometimes founded on mysticism, mysticism itself negates community. For it there is only one real relationship, the relationship of the individual to God. The pure type of mystic is completely unconcerned with outer freedom, which has for him neither value nor reality in the face of the inner freedom of his relation with the divine. External unfreedom is even a positive value for him, since it pushes him invariably into isolation and thus disciplines him invariably for his task. Mysticism, "the true content of the religious experience," can have nothing to do with the normalization of the relationships between men.

This statement demonstrates dramatically how Buber's early thought did not grow all of a piece but proceeded forward in one direction while remaining behind in another. It is as if Buber were simultaneously at least four different persons at this point: the interpreter and spokesman for Hasidism — the decidedly *communal* Jewish mysticism; the editor of the series of forty social-psychological monographs of *Die Gesellschaft*, for which he coined the category of *das Zwischenmenschliche* — what is between man and man; the young prophetic voice calling the Jewish people to awareness of themselves as a people; *and* the lonely mystic seeking his isolated relationship with God. A long road still lay ahead to that personal integration in the mature light of which Buber criticized Kierkegaard for the very religious solipsism that he here exalted. What is more, the tendency to relegate all reality, including the religious, to the soul, against which Buber was to warn in the strongest possible terms thirteen years later, clearly triumphed here. The *psychologism* at the heart of his definition of mysticism is unmistakable.

In "The Teaching of the Tao," written in the same year that

this sociological conference was held, Buber took a decisive step forward in integrating his encounter with mysticism into his personal philosophy. This essay focuses not upon mystical experience but upon a central teaching and a central person. The teaching is a simple whole which includes all of one's life. It must be distinguished from science and law — which are concerned only with a part of one's life — and from religion, which, as a degeneration of the teaching, is a collection of parts. The teaching goes beyond "is" and "ought," knowledge and command; it only knows how to say the one thing needful that must be realized in genuine fulfilled life. This realization is no abstract conception, feeling, or act of will, no unity of world, knowledge, God, spirit, or being. Rather it is the unity of *this* human life and *this* human soul. Genuine life is united life. Each thing reveals the Tao through the way of existence, through its life. But the oneness of the world is only the product and reflection of the oneness of the completed human being.

The teaching is realized in genuine life, wrote Buber in 1910, the life of the "central man." The central man adds no new element to teaching. Rather he fulfills it in authentic, unified life, raising the conditioned into the unconditioned. He seeks out and speaks to the simple, his poor brothers in spirit, in the language that they can hear: in parable. When he dies, the memory of his life becomes a parable itself. Parable is the insertion of the absolute into the world of events, myth the insertion of the world of things into the absolute. Parable and myth stand between teaching and religion, leading from the one to the other. They "attach themselves to the central human life in which the teaching has found its purest fulfillment: the parable as the word of this man himself, the myth as the impact of this life on the consciousness of the age."

If the *teaching* must be refracted in the prism of the parable, so the *life* too of the central man is not seen as reflected in a mirror but as refracted in a prism: it is *mythicized.*

> *Myth* does not mean that one brings the stars down to earth and allows them to tread it in human shape; rather in it the bliss-bestowing human shape is elevated to heaven, and moon and sun, Orion and the Pleiades, serve only to adorn it. Myth is not an affair of yonder and of old, but a function of today and of all times, of this city where I write and of all places of man. This is an eternal function of the soul: the insertion of what is experienced . . . into the magic of existence. The stronger the tension and intensity of the experience, the greater the for-

mative power that is experienced. Where the highest shape, the hero and saviour, the sublimest event, the life that he has lived, and the mightiest tension, the profound emotion of the simple, meet, the myth arises which compels all the future.

The great German sociologist Georg Simmel wrote Buber that with the concept of "teaching" he had singled out a very important and autonomous category that hitherto had been obscured amid other tendencies. "What you communicate out of Chinese philosophy is of extraordinary significance. Like the theses of Meister Eckhart, it gives one the feeling of something necessary breaking out of the depths."

The emphasis on realization of unity of life as more important than any philosophical knowledge or religious belief, and the doctrine of the action which is performed with the whole being, play an increasingly significant role in Buber's philosophy from this time forth and enter into his interpretation of Hasidism and Judaism. Yet the teaching of the unity of the central person and the world is still "mystical" in a sense that Buber's mature thought is not.

At this period and immediately after it, Buber was working on his first attempt at a comprehensive and original philosophical statement – *Daniel: Dialogues of Realization.* In *Daniel,* the mystic's demand for a life lived in terms of the highest reality and the existentialist's demand for self-realization and genuine existence meet in spirit. As such it forms an important transition between Buber's early mysticism and his later existentialism of dialogue. It also shows explicitly why Buber had to pass through mysticism in order to reach his own independent relation to being and why he could not simply reject mysticism after he arrived at dialogue as so many of the Protestant theologians who have adopted the "I-Thou" philosophy do. The reason Buber had to turn his back on his earlier mystical philosophy is an existential one. He recognized that through this philosophy he had tried to attain unity at the cost of denying his life-experience. Yet mysticism bequeathed to Buber a glimpse of an essential reality which had to be realized in the fragmentariness of existence. Thus the way of the Vedanta confirmed in him the striving for unity; for what revealed itself to him in detachment and concentration must prove itself true in the scattered totality of his life-experience.

In 1914, the year after the publication of *Daniel,* Buber wrote two separate essays which cast a curiously contrasting light on his relationship to mysticism. In "The Altar" Buber described the famous Issenheim altar, a triptych by the painter Matthias Grünewald, whom Buber called a brother to Meister Eckhart, who preached two centuries before in the same Alsatian cloisters. The traditional Christian figures in the painting emerge in Buber's treatment as the characters in a drama of color pointing to a new sort of mysticism — found within the world of sense rather than apart from it. The glory above color is the spirit of heaven which does not disclose itself to earth. "Our world, the world of colors, is *the* world." Yet we are not condemned to a fragmentary existence. The person who realizes the teaching in a central life becomes one through the strength with which he embraces the world. He rejects none of its colors, yet he receives none of them before it is pure and intensified. Through this the real world, the world of colors, is revealed. This is not the original unity. It is the unified glory achieved out of becoming and out of deed. "He loves the world, but he fights for its unconditionality against all that is conditioned." And we can do the same: "We cannot penetrate behind the manifold to find living unity. But we can create living unity out of the manifold."

This is clearly panentheism in which existence is only potentially holy and needs to be hallowed and not pantheism in which the world is seen as already holy. It is life- and world-affirming rather than life-denying. It is the qualified nondualism of the One becoming the many and the many returning to the One rather than a simple proclamation of the identity of the Self with Being as such. But it is unmistakably mysticism. Therefore, it is with some astonishment that we read in an essay written in the same year, published in the same book, and bearing much of the same feeling about the sense world, that Buber did not consider himself a mystic at this time!

The very opening of the conversation recorded in "With a Monist" is Buber's refusal to allow himself to be labeled a mystic and the consternation that this refusal creates:

> "You are a mystic," said the monist, looking at me more resignedly than reproachfully. It is thus that I would represent to myself an Apollo who disdained to flay a Marsyas. He even omitted the question mark. . . .
> "No, a rationalist," I said.
> He fell out of his splendid composure. "How? . . . I mean . . ." he stammered.

After this, Buber led his partner in dialogue through a variety of positions culminating in what was indeed his own most mature thought: that all comprehensibility of the world is only a footstool of its incomprehensibility, but that this latter — the confronting, shaping, bestowing in things — can be known by the man who embraces the world, humbly and faithfully beholding what comes to meet him. This eloquent confession served only to bring the monist back to his original contention: "So for all that you are a mystic," he said and smiled in the way that a monist must "when a fellow like me, after diffuse dissembling, in the end turns out to be a hopeless reactionary." Buber reiterated his rejection of the label, this time on two grounds: the place he granted to reason and the affirmation of the sense world:

> "No," I answered, and looked at him in a friendly way, "for I still grant to reason a claim that the mystic must deny to it. Beyond this, I lack the mystic's negation. I can negate convictions but never the slightest actual thing. The mystic manages, truly or apparently, to annihilate the entire world, or what he so names — all that his senses present to him in perception and in memory — in order, with new disembodied senses or a wholly supersensory power, to press forward to his God. But I am enormously concerned with *this* world, this painful and precious fullness of all that I see, hear, taste. I cannot wish away any part of its reality. I can only wish that I might heighten this reality. . . . the reality of the experienced world is so much the more powerful the more powerfully I experience it and realize it. . . . And how can I give this reality to my world except by seeing the seen with all the strength of my life, hearing the heard with all the strength of my life, tasting the tasted with all the strength of my life? Except by bending over the experienced thing with fervour and power and by melting the shell of passivity with the fire of my being until the confronting, the shaping, the bestowing side of things springs up to meet me and embraces me so that I know the world in it?"*

This is still "personal mysticism" creating unity out of the manifold. Yet Buber was right, nonetheless, to reject the label. For the ordinary conception of mysticism is indeed one that turns away from the world and denies the life of the senses. For all its fervor, one can hear in these lines the approach of the existentialism of dialogue, the pointing to the "lived concrete" that marked Buber's mature thought. If *Daniel* is a transition from mysticism to existentialism, "With a Monist" is a whole stage further along the same

---

* See Note in Sources to Chapter 5, p. 385.

road. It is only a stage, however, and it is one that comes just before the decisive turning in Buber's life that began, by his own report, with the First World War.

Mysticism gave Buber a new approach to reality, claims Kohn, in which his heart could break through from the mechanization, superficiality, and indirectness of that period to the immediacy of spiritual life. But it also served to remove Buber into an ecstasy in which he no longer heard the call of the immediate hour. What was problematic was not the mystical experience itself but the interpretation of it and the effect of this interpretation on his life.

> Now from my own unforgettable experience I know well that there is a state in which the bonds of the personal nature of life seem to have fallen away from us and we experience undivided unity. But I do not know — what the soul willingly imagines and indeed is bound to imagine (mine too once did) — that in this I had attained to a union with the primal being or the godhead. That is an exaggeration no longer permitted to the responsible understanding.

What *is* permitted to the responsible understanding, Buber asserted, is the recognition of an undifferentiated prepersonal unity hidden beneath all personal change, though even this is not *above* the creaturely situation but *beneath* it. In experiencing this unity of one's own basic self one naturally tends to see it as unity in general; for one is no longer aware of any reality other than oneself. The consequence of this compelling but "irresponsible" interpretation is the duality that rips life asunder into the everyday creaturely life and the "deified" exalted hours. The experience of ecstasy leads the mystic to regard everyday life from then on as an obstacle or at best a mere means to recapturing the moment of ecstasy. It is precisely this "exalted form of being untrue," as Buber later called it, that characterized Buber's own ecstasy and the divided life it produced:

> In my earlier years the "religious" was for me the exception. There were hours that were taken out of the course of things. From somewhere or other the firm crust of everyday was pierced. Then the reliable permanence of appearances broke down; the attack which took place burst its law asunder. "Religious experience" was the experience of an otherness which did not fit into the context of life. It could begin with something customary, with consideration of some familiar object, but which then became unexpectedly mysterious and uncanny, finally lighting a way into the lightning-pierced darkness of the mystery itself. But also,

without any intermediate state, time could be torn apart — first the world's firm structure, then the still firmer self-assurance flew apart and you were delivered to fullness. The "religious" lifted you out. Over there now lay the accustomed existence with its affairs, but here illumination and ecstasy and rapture held, without time or sequence. Thus your own being encompassed a life here and a life beyond, and there was no bond but the actual moment of the transition.

Buber did not attain his ecstasies through the regular practice of "meditation" — quiet sitting and concentration of mind and spirit on some word or image. "I never had anything to do with willed, 'pre-meditated' meditations," Buber wrote me. "As to meditations coming spontaneously, I knew them in earlier days, but never since my thought reached its maturity." Buber reached his mature understanding after he not only gave up the *hours* of mystical exaltation but also the *belief* that accompanied it, namely the belief "in a 'mystical' unification of the Self, identifying the depth of the individual self with the Self itself." "Perhaps the main point in my personal evolution was the rejecting of *this* mysticism too."

How resolutely Buber turned away from such an illegitimate division of life we can only understand in the context of his encounter with the First World War. But Buber's "conversion" did not mean, as some have thought, a rejection of mysticism *in toto*. On the contrary, much of it remained with him and informed his lifetime of work on Hasidism and his own philosophy. Presence, presentness, immediacy, ineffability, a meaning which can be lived and confirmed but cannot be defined, the action that appears like nonaction because it is whole and does not interfere — all these accompanied Buber on the long road ahead.

CHAPTER 6

The Discovery of Hasidism

HASIDISM is the popular mystical movement of East European Jewry. The Hasidic movement arose in Poland in the eighteenth century, and, despite bitter persecution at the hands of traditional Rabbinism, spread rapidly among the Jews of Eastern Europe until it included almost half of them in its ranks. The Hasidim founded real communities, each with its own *rebbe*. The *rebbe*, the leader of the community, was also called the *zaddik*, the righteous or justified man. Each one of these *zaddikim* had his own unique teaching that he gave to his community and that helped bring the people into direct relationship to God. Later, hereditary dynasties of Hasidim arose, the *rebbes* lived in great palaces, surrounded by awe and superstition, and the *zaddik* became more of a mediator between the people and God.

To speak of Martin Buber's "discovery of Hasidism" is not to speak of Hasidism as a world that was unknown to the West before Buber but of a meaningful encounter with it that made it for the first time of major significance to the Western world, both Jewish and non-Jewish. Until the turn of the century, Hasidism was largely regarded by those who knew about it at all in the West as a form of crude popular superstition, perhaps of interest as a revival movement, but of no intrinsic value within the stream of Judaism and positively at odds with the whole spirit of the Haskalah, or Jewish Enlightenment, and of the modern Science of Judaism. Here and there a storyteller such as Yitzhak Leib Peretz had given an insight into this strange world, but otherwise it represented the very things which the Western, Europeanized Jew was most anxious to get away from. The new wave of Jewish nationalism and a romantic impulse to discover the deeper forces at work in the life of the East European Jewish masses led historians and scholars like Simon Dubnow, writers like Samuel A. Horodetzky and Micha Joseph Berdichevsky, and great poets like Isaak Peretz to a discovery of the world of Hasidic legend which, writes Gershom Scholem, "possessed tremendous poetic appeal and marked a new era in Jewish literature, especially that in Hebrew, Yiddish, and German."

Buber first encountered Hasidism when his grandfather took him to Sadagora, the seat of a dynasty of *zaddikim*. There Buber encountered the Hasidic movement, not in its flowering, to be sure — that had passed with the grandfathers — but still in a living organic tradition. The descendant of the great founders could still evoke a shudder of profoundest reverence when he stood in silent prayer or interpreted the mystery of the Torah in hesitant speech at the third Sabbath meal. Even though the later Hasidim for the most part sought out the *rebbe* as a magic mediator, in their souls still glowed the old saying that the world was created for the sake of the completed man (the *zaddik*). "Here was, debased yet essentially intact, the living double kernel of humanity: genuine *community* and genuine *leadership*."

> The palace of the rebbe, in its showy splendor, repelled me. The prayer house of the Hasidim with its enraptured worshippers seemed strange to me. But when I saw the rebbe striding through the rows of the waiting, I felt, "leader," and when I saw the hasidim dance with the Torah, I felt, "community."

Although Solomon Buber was an "enlightened" Jew, a *Maskil*, he liked to pray among the Hasidim and used a prayer book full of mystical directions. He liked to take his grandson Martin to a small Hasidic *Klaus* or synagogue to pray. Buber's father, in contrast, occasionally lured him away from his grandfather to worship in the Temple in Lemberg, a liberal synagogue. This contact with "liberal" religion had so little influence on Buber that once on a Day of Atonement young Martin caused annoyance in the Lemberg Temple by following the Orthodox tradition of bending his knee and prostrating himself.

When he was fourteen and was now living with his father all year round on the estate in Bukovina, Martin ceased to put on *teffillin* (phylacteries). Until that age he was a very observant and fervent Jew, and the high point of his religious experience came only a short while before his full observance ceased. Between his thirteenth and his fourteenth year, he experienced Yom Kippur (the Day of Atonement) with a force by his own account unequaled by any other experience since then. Nor could this experience be dismissed as merely that of a child; for this was near the very age when Martin almost committed suicide over the infinity of time and space. Perhaps, Buber suggested to Franz Rosenzweig when he was already forty-four, he was even less a child at thirteen than more than thirty years later, "and this in a poignant sense."

> At that time I took Space and Time seriously; I did not hold back as I do now. And then, when the sleepless night was heavy upon me and very real, my body, already reacting to the fast, became as important to me as an animal marked for sacrifice. This is what formed me: the night, and the following morning, and the Day itself, with all its hours, not omitting a single moment.

After this, despite sporadic contacts with Hasidism, the vision paled into the boy's unconscious, and only after beginning to find roots again in Zionism and the Jewish Renaissance did he come to a new and deeper encounter with the Hasidic movement. At first, as we have seen, he saw Hasidism as one of the elements, along with the Haskalah, or Jewish Enlightenment, that had to be integrated into the new Judaism in order for the Jewish Renaissance movement to find its way forward. The influence of Ahad Ha'am undoubtedly made itself felt here, since Ahad Ha'am came from a Hasidic background and appreciated what the movement had to offer to the new spiritual center of Judaism that he was trying to create.

For all this, Buber's encounter with Hasidism can be described only as a breakthrough or a conversion, if one uses this latter term in the biblical sense of a total turning of one's existence rather than a leap of faith. After coming back to Judaism through

Zionism and then realizing that he did not really know Judaism, Buber began to return to the Hebrew of his childhood. Although at first repelled by the "brittle, ungainly, unshapely material," so foreign to any of the Western languages that he loved, he gradually overcame the strangeness and beheld with growing devotion what was essential in it. At this point he came upon a little book entitled the testament of Rabbi Israel Baal-Shem, a collection of sayings said to have been uttered by Israel ben Eliezer (1700-1760), the "Good Master of the Name of God," who was the founder of Hasidism. Something of that combination of fire and spirit that Buber much later pointed to as the uniqueness of the "Besht" (as he was called after his initials) must have communicated itself to the soul of the young man in whom spirit and fire, intellect and passion, yearning and will, were also so strong.

It was the Baal-Shem's words about fervor that forever won the young man's soul: "He takes unto himself the quality of fervor. He arises from sleep with fervor, for he is hallowed and become another man and is worthy to create and is become like the Holy One, blessed be He, when He created His world." It is not that fervor had in any sense been lacking in Buber before. But this was fervor with direction, all the awesome power of the "evil urge" taken up into the service of God, Boehme's "ternary of fire" spiraling upward into the "ternary of light" without losing any of its power thereby. A theophany, an epiphany, a revelation, a breakthrough — call it what we will, this was one of the truly decisive moments in Buber's life:

> It was then, that, overpowered in an instant, I experienced the Hasidic soul. The primally Jewish opened to me, flowering to newly conscious expression in the darkness of exile: man's being created in the image of God I grasped as deed, as becoming, as task. And this primally Jewish reality was a primal human reality, the content of human religiousness. . . . The image out of my childhood, the memory of the zaddik and his community, rose upward and illuminated me: I recognized the idea of the perfected man. At the same time I became aware of the summons to proclaim it to the world.*

The combination of summons and sending, of revelation and mission, to which Buber later pointed in *I and Thou,* came for Buber as a single moment of meeting.

---

* See Note A in Sources for Chapter 6, p. 386.

If it had been simply disillusionment with political Zionism that had produced this meeting, one might have expected the already diversely occupied young man to fling himself into still other activities to substitute for those from which he had withdrawn. Instead, at twenty-six, he withdrew himself for five years from action in the Zionist party *and* from writing articles and giving speeches. In order to go forward, he had first to retire into the stillness. "I gathered, not without difficulty, the scattered, partly missing, literature," he wrote, "and I immersed myself in it, discovering mysterious land after mysterious land." The breadth of his early activities was exchanged for a work in depth; his public activity came to a total standstill; and he labored with unremitting energy exploring the new region, making it his own, and giving it new form. Buber emerged from this retirement with a new wholeness which kept in check his tendency toward dispersion. It also gave him a unique personal direction from which, even in the most terrible crises, he was never again deflected.

Buber produced his first two Hasidic books in Florence, where he lived during much of the years 1905 and 1906. What this period in Florence meant to Buber was, first of all, immersion in a city which charmed and engrossed him and at the same time freed him for the intensity of concentration to which he felt called. In a letter from Florence at Christmas 1905, Buber wrote:

> Florence suits me, as all of us, well; we have no contact with other men at all and hardly miss it, for one lives with this city, with its houses, with its monuments, with its former generations. . . . Then I am writing various things about Florence. . . . I hope in this way to accumulate a whole collection of essays, chiefly, however, about partly or totally unnoticed things (destroyed frescoes, street tabernacles, gravestones, Gothic traces, the culture of the streets, lay orders, street songs, sayings, the old Ghetto, etc.), which could be later united into one volume, perhaps under the title: *The Hidden Florence.*

The love for the theater which Vienna had kindled in Buber continued in Florence, and in Florence he wrote his first essays on the theater per se. The first of these was an article on the great actress Eleanora Duse as she appeared in Florence, the second on three different roles played by the actor Ermette Novelli.

Buber began by portraying "the Duse," as he called her, not as a separate individual but as the voice of her Italian ancestors. She transmutes the gestures of the people "as we see them here on the streets, in the market places, in the courtyards and lifts them to the threshold of the aesthetic. She gathers into herself what in everyday life remains fragmentary, troubled, broken, and in her it becomes a work of revelation." There is an immediacy of expression here which cannot be called thought yet has its own form that is determined by the life-experience of many generations. But individuation takes place here too — as it does for every individual who emerges from the security of the familiar into the threat of the infinite, and precisely here lies the dramatic tension. The abyss opens between man and man, and this abyss robs the word of its power. For the word is never something for and in itself but comes to completed reality only through being received. Now the person who has received from the tradition closes over, no longer believes, or recognizes, and the word falls to the ground powerless, profaned. All tradition fades away, and the individual comes into being who can only fight but no longer speak. His word is no longer a communication but a battle. Here the future Buber of the "Speeches on Judaism" with their emphasis on the chain of the generations and the Buber of the threat of infinity and the problem of individuation come together.*

The essay on the actor Novelli begins with a quotation from "the last of the Jewish mystics," Rabbi Nachman of Bratzlav, about whom at that very moment Buber was writing in his first book. There are two kinds of human spirit, said Rabbi Nachman, and they are like backward and forward:

> There is one spirit that man attains in the course of time. But there is another spirit that overwhelms man in great abundance, in great haste, swifter than a moment, for it is beyond time and for this spirit no time is needed.

This distinction between two kinds of spirit Buber applied to the relation of theater to drama. This relation could mean: that the theater realizes (or "interprets") the drama, it says what is to be said, it presents what is to be presented, it is the poetry itself in the form of living movement; or: the theater completes the drama, it makes whole what is desired there, it leads the creative process to its goal; or: the theater recasts the drama, it uses it as stimulus or as material. There are two types of great actors, Buber also

---

* See Note B in Sources for Chapter 6, p. 386.

maintained: those who by means of their remarkable capacity for receiving and imitating unite the movements of expression into a total figure, and those who by means of their ability to live through from within the manner and existence of persons, real or fictitious — "to step into their skins" — produce the kinds of expression characteristic of such persons. The former type belongs to the spirit that is acquired in the fullness of the ages, the latter to the spirit whose wings are like the moment of self-experience.

Putting the two essays together, we can say that the great actor must know both community with the people and the agony of isolation of the person who is aware of the abyss between person and person which kills communication and the word. He must know the tension of this simultaneous distance and relationship from within, as if he had stepped into the skin of the other. He experiences the polarity between the actor and the audience, the actor and the other actors, and the actor and the character that he plays. For this to take place, "putting oneself into the other's shoes" cannot be mere empathy but the act of "inclusion," or "experiencing the other side" without giving up one's own side of the relationship.

It might appear that Florence represented still another temptation to the young Buber to fragment himself, especially since he not only explored it and wrote about it but took part in its cultural life and wrote essays on the theater there. The evidence is all to the contrary. At Christmas 1905 he wrote in a letter from Florence:

> We must give up all that which is only seemingly ours, which does not really nourish and warm us, which does not stir us up and satisfy us, if we are to come to ourselves. I have experienced it. . . . How do I live? As at the beginning of a good path that I do not yet wholly know but that I know is right. . . . I am glad that I have . . . been set free from a false sphere of work; for it is only now that I can again work whole and free. . . . Even my connection with Judaism has deepened; if I enter party activities once again, again say something about this problem of problems, it will certainly be something purer and greater than I once said when I was imprisoned by catchwords.

It is remarkable how many motifs of Buber's later philosophy are contained in this description of his experience: the contrast between "being" and "seeming"; good is what one does with one's whole being, evil is what one does with only a part of one's being; the "heart-searching" that brings one to one's own unique way; and above all, one's work not as a separate compartment of one's existence but as one's *direction* in response to the claim of the situation.

In February 1906 Buber wrote to Hugo von Hofmannsthal from Florence that he found his play *Oedipus and the Sphinx* the strongest, richest poetry that he had read in ten years. "What you once described as myth has become living in it in a way that in our time has happened only in the work of Rodin." Hofmannsthal responded that "in the chaos of this calling and this epoch" Buber's letter gave him a moment of joy and gladness, and added that his affinity for Buber had been assured since he first saw his handwriting! In his answering letter Buber pointed out one of the sayings of Rabbi Nachman of Bratzlav in the book he planned to send him:

> As the hand held before the eye conceals the greatest mountain, so the little earthly life hides from the glance the enormous lights and mysteries of which the world is full, and he who can draw it away from before his eyes, as one draws away a hand, beholds the great radiance of the inner worlds.

"That is a particularly simple formula for a thought common to Eckhart, the Upanishads, and Hasidism," Buber commented.

"My aim is not to accumulate new facts," Buber wrote Samuel Horodetzky in July 1906, "but simply to give a new interpretation of the interconnections, a new synthetic presentation of Jewish mysticism and its creations and to make these creations known to the European public in as artistically pure a form as possible." How well Buber succeeded in his goal of Europeanizing Rabbi Nachman is suggested by the congratulatory letter sent him by Simon Dubnow, the Russian-Jewish historian of Hasidism and the Jews of Poland: "Your personal characterization of R. Nachman has succeeded very well, only somewhat idealized, for Nachman was not free from many of the errors of his Hasidic 'entourage.'" He followed it by the still more dubious compliment that Buber's masterful reworking and retelling of Nachman's stories had freed them from the *"anima vili,"* the vile, or worthless, spirit, of the originals!

In a letter of December 1906, written immediately after the pogroms at Bialystok, Buber connected the sense of his personal lifework with his concern for Judaism:

I am writing now a story which is my answer to Bialystok. . . . I am now in the first real work period of my life. You are my friend and will understand me: I have a *new answer* to give to everything. Now only have I found the form for my answer. I have grown inward into my heaven — my life begins. I experience nameless suffering and nameless grace.

Buber was, indeed, in "the first real work period" of his life. When he began to translate the allegorical and even fairy-tale-like stories in which Rabbi Nachman of Bratzlav, the great-grandson of the Baal-Shem, clothed his teaching, he discovered that mere translation left them even more paltry and impure than the distortions of form and the insertions of vulgar rationalistic and utilitarian motifs by Nachman's disciples. Rejecting his first attempts, Buber proceeded to the far harder task of real artistic creation: "I had to tell the stories that I had taken into myself from out of myself, as a true painter takes into himself the lines of the models and achieves the genuine images out of the memory formed of them." "The Steer and the Ram," "The Simple Man and the Clever Man," and "The King's Son and the Son of the Maid" became progressively freer and surer until "The Rabbi and His Son" grew unexpectedly into Buber's own work. But his goal was not merely self-expression. It was faithful dialogue with Rabbi Nachman himself, the man with whom Buber so deeply identified himself at this time. In 1917 he still felt that this dialogue was achieved in full measure in the two last tales, "The Master of Prayer" and "The Seven Beggars." "I experienced, even in the entirely new pieces that I inserted, my unity with the spirit of Rabbi Nachman. I had found the true faithfulness: more adequately than the direct disciples, I received and completed the task, a later messenger in a foreign realm."

We have used Buber's own term "dialogue," but perhaps there was an element of genuine dialogue missing that even the above words betray, an adequate sense of otherness. He recognized the distance from which he came to meet Rabbi Nachman, but when he had found his way there through making the material his own, he saw this too much as a *unity* of spirit, too little as a unique, personal response. The same may be said of his report in 1917 of his attempt in *The Legend of the Baal-Shem* to construct the inner process in the life of the master from a selection of traditional legendary motifs. Here too he began with simple translation and met with disappointment. Here too he came to his own narrating in growing independence, and the greater the independence became the more deeply he experienced the faithfulness. The secret of dialogue is certainly contained here, namely, that an authentic word cannot be captured by any mere mechanical rendering but only by daring to make it one's own and to re-create it. Buber could state in 1917 that although by far the largest part of *The Legend of the Baal-Shem* is autonomous fiction composed from traditional motifs, nonetheless, what he wrote in the Introduction in 1907 was an honest report of his experience of the legend: "I bear in me the blood and the spirit of those who created it, and out of my blood and spirit it has become new." Yet here too the language is that of *unity,* a unity which is seen as not only achieved but already present in the "blood": "my inborn binding with Hasidic truth."

Still there was something authentic even here that Buber never ceased to affirm, as far as he grew away from these early attempts. That was the genuine task of the storyteller who carries the story from one generation to another in the only way that it can be carried: by retelling it. The Hasidic legend which Buber strove to tell did not possess the austere power of the Buddha legend nor the intimacy of the Franciscan. It was received and passed on haltingly: "It came to life in narrow streets and small, musty rooms, passing from awkward lips to the ears of anxious listeners. A stammer gave birth to it and a stammer bore it onward — from generation to generation." It was this stammer too that Buber heard and sought to repeat:

> I have received it from folk-books, from note-books and pamphlets, at times also from a living mouth, from the mouths of people still living who even in their lifetime heard this stammer. I have received it and have told it anew . . . as one who was born later. . . . I stand in the chain of narrators, a link between links; I tell once again the old stories, and if they sound new, it is because the new already lay dormant in them when they were told for the first time.

What was missing in Buber's retelling, however, was precisely the stammer. What he received from the *spoken* word stammered by "awkward lips" he transformed into artistic and urbane literature not destined for "the ears of anxious listeners" but for the sophisticated appraisal of readers attuned to the highest in German culture at the time. Buber never simply used Hasidism for the sake of his personal work or as a mere literary project. Rather, he saw himself from the first as an instrument — an honest artisan carrying out a commission to the best of his ability. He saw what commissioned him, moreover, as something hidden in Hasidism which he could and should bring to the world, even against the wishes of Hasidism itself, which "wishes to work exclusively within the boundaries of Jewish tradition." Yet fifty years later, he recognized that he was then, for all that, an immature man, still subject to the power of the *Zeitgeist* — the spirit of the age which led him to mix genuine testimony to a great reality of faith with an inauthentic desire to display the contents of exotic religions to readers motivated mostly by curiosity and a wish to acquire "culture." His *representation* of the Hasidic teaching was essentially faithful, but his *retelling* of the legendary tradition was not, for the form he gave to it was just that of the Western author that he was.

> I did not yet know how to hold in check my inner inclination to transform the narrative material poetically. I did not, to be sure, bring in any alien motifs; still I did not listen attentively enough to the crude and ungainly but living folk-tone which could be heard from this material. . . . The need, in the face of . . . misunderstanding, to point out the purity and loftiness of Hasidism led me to pay all too little attention to its popular vitality.

In at least one case in *The Tales of Rabbi Nachman*, "The Simple Man and the Clever Man," it was not the "vulgar rationalistic" motifs that Buber omitted but precisely what was, from the standpoint of an enlightened Westerner, the *irrational*. "Even when Buber meant the divine," according to Professor David Flusser of the Hebrew University, Jerusalem, "he never meant the irrational." In Buber's version this story ends with the clever man so outsmarting himself that he cannot even believe that his friend the Simple Man, who has become the king's prime minister, sees the king every day. In a passage remarkably anticipatory of Kafka's novel *The Castle*, the clever man jeers at his friend who dares to believe in the madness that there really is a king:

> "What makes you think . . . that he with whom you speak is actually the king? Were you intimate with him from childhood on? Did you know his father and grandfather and can say that they were kings? Men have told you that this is the king. They have fooled you."

To this the minister replies that it is precisely the subtleties of the Clever Man that are preventing him from seeing life, and that simplicity, so far from being easy to come by, is a grace that he will never receive. Thus Buber concluded. But the original continues with a further event in which the Clever Man is trapped by the devil and only the grace of the *zaddik,* the *rebbe,* rescues him and shows him that he who is tormenting him is the devil and not merely an evil man. "Now you see that there is a king in the world," the *zaddik* admonishes him.

Although a neighbor of Buber's, Professor Flusser did not try to have any contact with him for some years because of what he had done to the original of these tales. One day he ran into Buber in the street in Talbiyeh, the quarter of Jerusalem where they were both living, and he reproached Buber because of *Rabbi Nachman.* To his amazement, Buber replied that he himself no longer accepted what he had done there. "I was just a boy of thirty-one," he explained. When he wrote of Rabbi Nachman, he identified himself with him and at the same time used him as a mouthpiece. But long since he had seen that this was not right. Nonetheless, about this particular passage that he left out of the ending of "The Clever Man and the Simple Man" Buber said: "How can one write that?" However distasteful *The Tales of Rabbi Nachman* had become to Buber, he did not entirely reject them; for he allowed them to be reprinted in German and to be translated into English less than ten years before his death.

Buber opened *The Tales of Rabbi Nachman* with an essay, "Jewish Mysticism," in which he set forth many motifs which were later to become central both to his interpretation of Hasidism and to his own philosophy: the essential importance of *kavana,* the strength of inner intention, the possibility of apprehending God in each thing if every action, no matter how lowly, is a dedicated one, the notion that one's urges, far from being evil, are the very things that make greatness possible.

In his picture of the life of Rabbi Nachman, Buber spoke of him — as the year before he had spoken of Herzl — as "a great and tragic man." Nachman's dream for the *zaddik,* the leader of the Hasidic community, was to be "the soul of the people." Nachman did not find the yoke of service easy, "for he had a joyous strong disposition and a fresh sense for the beauty of the world"; yet he finally succeeded in basing his devotion on just this disposition and serving God in joy. He broke out of the centuries of ghetto existence into direct contact with the power of growing things and heard the voice of God in the reeds of the stream, in the horse that bore him into the forest, in the trees and plants, the mountain slopes, and the hidden valleys. Above all, he represented for Buber a new and more meaningful way of turning to the Jewish people — of living with them and bearing their pain and finding in them his consecration. For Nachman, as later for Buber himself, this living with others meant an insistence on the mystery of communication and on the mutuality of dialogue. The true word awakens the hearer so that he himself becomes a speaker and speaks the final word. "The soul of the disciple shall be summoned in its depths so that out of it, and not out of the soul of the master, the word will be born that proclaims the highest meaning of the teaching, and thus the conversation is fulfilled in itself."

Nachman of Bratzlav was a paradoxical and anguished figure. Everyone should cry out to God, said Nachman, "as if he were hanging by a hair and a tempest were raging to the very heart of heaven," for "a man is in great danger in the world" and "there is no counsel and no refuge for him save to remain alone and to lift up his eyes and his heart to God." But solitary and intense turning to God meant no depreciation of the word for Nachman, as it has for some mystics: the words of some men's prayers are like jewels that shine in themselves, while those of others are like windows that are transparent and let the light through. Nor did man's dependence upon God mean, for Nachman, any lessening of the importance of the will and freedom of man, as the emphasis upon grace has often done in Christianity. The world was created only for the sake of the choice and the choosing one; for man is the master of choice. But this freedom is given man so that in every place he should redeem the world and fulfill its needs. From this it follows that there is no obstacle that cannot be overcome; the obstacle is there only for the sake of the willing and exists only in the spirit. By the same token, no limits are set to the ascent of man, and to each the highest stands open. "Here your choice alone decides."

Nachman also anticipated Buber in his emphasis upon the "evil urge," which, if it often deludes one into following that which is hollow, also offers man the possibility of serving God with the very passion that seeks to lead him astray. Equally important was Nachman's emphasis upon uniqueness ("God never does the same thing twice"), upon the dialogue between man and man (a man with joyful countenance may cheer with his joy those who suffer terrible distress and cannot tell anyone of it), and upon guilt, the call of what is not ourselves that restores our dialogue with the world ("If a man does not judge himself, all things judge him, and all things become messengers of God").

The intensity of Nachman's messianic longing corresponded to Buber's own passionate quest for redemption. One must walk in loneliness, said Nachman, so as to be tranquil and composed when the Messiah comes. Perhaps the most moving of the six stories of Rabbi Nachman that Buber retold is that of "The Rabbi and His Son," in which the pathos of just this messianic longing is portrayed. The father will not hear of his son's desire to visit a *zaddik* who, though he has the power to liberate souls, to wipe sorrow and distress from men's foreheads, and to relax the spasm of hatred in men's heart's, is not deemed sufficiently "learned" and "holy." The father finally takes pity on his son, who wastes away when his request is denied, and three times sets out with him to journey to the *zaddik*. Twice he turns back when an accident befalls the carriage, considering this as a sign from on high, and the third time he takes a merchant's statement that the *"zaddik"* is a worldly and sinful man as a confirmation of his own fears of such a muddleheaded and confused heretic. The son dies, visits his father in a dream with a countenance of wrath, and demands that he set out by himself on the journey to the *zaddik*. The father again meets the same diabolical merchant, who now laughs at him openly and informs him that his son had the rung of the lesser light and the *zaddik* the rung of the great light, "and if they had come together on earth, then the word would have been fulfilled and the Messiah would have appeared."

An even more intense story of messianic longing was included in the original editions of *The Legend of the Baal-Shem* but was later renounced by Buber as not being carried through with sufficient effectiveness. It is for this very reason significant for understanding the "immature" Buber. What is more, it is in *this* story that Buber first uses in written form his image of "the narrow ridge."

"Sound the great shofar," the Baal-Shem called to the Lord, "when the circle of the year has come round and the souls of all things plunge into the darkness to attain rebirth. Your pain has racked our hands until they have grown weak before life. Your wandering has hunted our feet until they falter on firm ground.

You have sent the worm into our hearts, and they are gnawed through like sick leaves. Your messenger has laid his hand on our foreheads, and our thoughts freeze into ice. Sound the great shofar, O Lord, for our liberation!

"The angel of the Lord seized me in the night, and I stood in the void. . . . There was a circle between two abysses, a narrow round ridge. And within this circle was a red abyss like a sea of blood, and outside of it stretched a black abyss like a sea of night. And I saw: a man walked on the ridge like a blindman, with staggering feet, and his two weak hands rested on the abysses to the right and to the left, and his breast was of glass, and I saw his heart flutter like sick leaves in the wind, and on his forehead was the sign of ice. . . . And already he was near the end of the circle which is its beginning . . . and the man suddenly looked up and saw to the right and to the left, and he stumbled and out of the abysses arms rose to catch him. . . . Then the man raised his wings, and no weakness and no numbness was in him any longer, and the ridge disappeared underneath his feet, and God's fountains of water swallowed the abyss of blood, and the abyss of the night disappeared into God's light, and the city of the Lord lay there, open in all directions.

"See, our year is a circle. We walk on a narrow, round ridge between two abysses and do not see the abysses. But when we have come to the end of the ridge which is its beginning, then fear and trembling descend upon us like the storm of the Lord, and the lightning of the Lord flashes across the abysses, and we see them, and we falter. . . . And the world shofar sounds and bears on its wings the soul that has been born from our souls and that is the soul of the Messiah, and it swings upward to the kingdom of the mystery and beats with its wings at the gate, and the gate opens wide and behold there is no longer gate nor wall but the city of the Lord lies there, open in all directions."

Even in this early usage the "narrow ridge" is a metaphor for human existence itself: an existence in which one must walk with faltering step, threatened at every moment by the danger of falling into the abysses to the left and to the right. Here we can glimpse Kierkegaard's "knight of faith" who comes slowly creeping forward in "fear and trembling," in a tension that can never be relaxed. Yet in "The New Year's Sermon" the awareness of the abyss comes only at the end of the circle which is its beginning, that is, at the Jewish New Year which is the commencement of the

"Days of Awe." As such it presents a caesura in time which other-wise seems to carry us smoothly along in the regularity of the seasons and the round of the years. When the awareness comes and the man's foot stumbles, he is upheld by arms that arise from the abysses to the right and the left — the abysses are threatening but they are not pure evil. But the man finds deliverance only when both the abysses and the narrow ridge disappear in favor of the fullness of redemption in which everything earthly is transfigured. This exalted tone is very different from the "hallowing of the everyday," the "obedient listening," the moment-by-moment response to the "lived concrete" that marked Buber's later use of the "narrow ridge." Even Hasidism itself Buber later defined as persevering in an *unexalted* life. Messianism became for him later a "messianism of the everyday" rather than an apocalyptic longing for redemption *now*. This is, in fact, the central conflict in his great Hasidic novel, *For the Sake of Heaven*.

In later years, the abysses on either side of the narrow ridge tended to become symbolic for Buber: the evasion of the demand of the concrete situation through one or another type of abstrac-tion — psychologism, historicism, technicism, philosophizing, magic, gnosis, or the false either/or's of individualism versus collectivism, freedom versus discipline, action versus grace. In "The New Year's Sermon" and in many of the other stories in *The Legend of the Baal-Shem* the abysses seem all too real. When in "The Werewolf" the old Rabbi Eliezer speaks to his son Israel on his deathbed, he describes the "Adversary" as "the abyss over which you must fly." In the "Revelation" the abyss confronts Rabbi Naftali each day that he sets out to leave the innkeeper in the Carpathians who has invited him to stay for the Sabbath and whom no one yet knows to be the Baal-Shem. On the first day, he looks up and sees the things of the world dislodged from their places and lost in confusion. "It seemed to him as if an abyss had opened up beneath him, greedy to swallow up heaven and earth." On the second day he encounters a hard, heavy, brazen shell and all of the things imprisoned and sickly in their places or moving in a close and musty cage. Later, he rationalizes the sadness that engulfed him then by saying to himself as he set out on the third day that both the moment when the connections are shattered and the moment when the creatures are transfixed are a play of time. He shuts his eyes for happiness and opens them to see an enormous veil sinking downward.

> Then the world lay before him like an abyss. Out of the abyss emerged the solar disk in silent torment. In agonized birth pangs the earth brought forth trees and plants without number. . . . Each creature suffered because it must do what it did. . . . All things were enveloped by the abyss, and yet the whole abyss was between each thing and the other. None could cross over to the other, indeed none could see the other, for the abyss was between them.

This is the strongest expression Buber had yet made of the abyss *between* each thing and the other, the abyss that must have opened for him personally when his mother left him and that each of his different ways of striving for unity sought to bridge. Redemption here, however, is not pictured as unity or joy but as contact, touching, the restoration of "betweenness" through the very presence of the Baal-Shem.

> The man was here and everywhere, possessed of manifold being and overspanning presence. Now his arm clasped round the body of the trees, the animals clung to his knees and the birds to his shoulders. Then lo, comfort had come into the world. For through the helper, things were joined and saw and knew and grasped one another. They saw one another through his eyes and touched one another through his hand. And since the things came to one another, there was no longer an abyss, but a light space of seeing and touching, and of all that was therein.

In "The Life of the Hasidim" section of *The Legend of the Baal-Shem,* Buber stressed the central place of the word for the Jewish mystic:

> From time immemorial speech was for the Jewish mystic a rare and awe-inspiring thing. A characteristic theory of letters existed which dealt with them as with the elements of the world and with their inter-mixture as with the inwardness of reality. The word is an abyss through which the speaker strides.

The speaker of the word becomes the mouth for creation: "'One should speak words as if the heavens were opened for them. And as if it were not so that you take the word in your mouth, but rather as if you entered into the word.'"

In his Introduction to *The Legend of the Baal-Shem* Buber set up a remarkable opposition between religion and myth in which he asserted that the history of the Jewish religion in particular is in great part the history of its fight against myth. This antagonism, as

Buber spelled it out, is a variation of the ancient tension between the One and the Many, but also of the Nietzschean tension between form and dynamism.

> All positive religion rests on an enormous simplification of the manifold and wildly engulfing forces that invade us: it is the subduing of the fullness of existence. All myth, in contrast, is the expression of the fullness of existence, its image, its sign; it drinks incessantly from the gushing fountains of life.

Tracing the history of this battle within Judaism, Buber declared that religion always wins the apparent victory, myth invariably wins the real one. When Jewish myth had to flee from the official tradition which excluded it, it took refuge in the Kabbala and in the folk saga, and in Hasidism mysticism and saga flowed together in a single stream. Hasidism "is the latest form of the Jewish myth that we know." But Hasidism produced a special type of myth — the legend — and legend, as we have seen, Buber distinguished from "pure myth." In the latter "there is no division of essential being," whereas "the myth of the calling" knows the duality of over-againstness: "The legend is the myth of I and Thou."

Commenting on this passage in the short section devoted to himself in "The History of the Dialogical Principle," Buber wrote:

> Here the dialogical relationship is thus exemplified in its highest peak: because even on this height the essential difference between the partners persists unweakened, while even in such nearness the independence of man continues to be preserved.

But he followed by pointing out how far this insight into legend was from the full reality of the life of dialogue:

> From this event of the exception, of the extraction, however, my thought now led me, ever more earnestly, to the common that can be experienced by all.

It is no accident that this second image of redemption is not the establishment of unity but the establishment of contact — what Buber was later to call the realm of the "between." For it is in the Introduction to *The Legend of the Baal-Shem* that Buber first speaks in a fully developed sense of that mutual relationship of I and Thou which later became the center of his life and thought.

Here Buber distinguished between "pure myth" in which there is no "Thou" over against an "I," and "legend" in which there is "caller and called," "I and Thou."

> The legend is the myth of the calling. In it the original personality of myth is divided. In myth there is no division of essential being. It knows multiplicity but not duality. Even the hero only stands on another rung than that of the god, not over against him: they are not the I and Thou. The hero has a mission but not a call. He ascends but he does not become transformed. The god of pure myth does not call, he begets; he sends forth the one whom he begets, the hero. The god of the legend calls forth the son of man – the prophet, the holy man.
>
> The legend is the myth of I and Thou, of the caller and the called, the finite which enters into the infinite and the infinite which has need of the finite.

This passage contains in seed the dialogue between the "I" and "the eternal Thou" that Buber later set forth in the third part of *I and Thou*. And it is not Feuerbach or Kierkegaard that inspired it but the Baal-Shem, who is seen, like Buber himself in his relation to Hasidism, as the man of summons and sending. "The legend of the Baal-Shem is not the history of a man but the history of a calling. It does not tell of a destiny but of a vocation."

Although it was more than a dozen years before this seed germinated and spread its roots and tendrils throughout Buber's thought, it is not an isolated or nonorganic part of *The Legend of the Baal-Shem*. In two of the stories in particular – "The Return" and "From Strength to Strength" – the ontological reality of the "between" is stated with unmistakable force. In this case, it is the dialogue between man and man and not just that between man and God which is in question. In "The Return" two boys who are the closest of friends are separated by marriage when they are fourteen and go to live in separate towns. At first they write faithfully to each other every month and share their new lives. "But then the world clasped them in its arms and crushed the free breath out of their souls, and they were ashamed to confess to each other in letters that the stillness out of which the living word of love comes had withdrawn from their hearts." Finally, when one became rich and the other poor, the poor man bethought himself of his friend and went to see him. When he broke into weeping and revealed his plight, his friend gave him half of all that he owned. But later when the tables were turned, the man who had been poor and whose poverty had made him a miser was reluctant to share his wealth with his friend who had been rich, and gave orders that he not be admitted. The friend expired from weakness and disappointment, and shortly afterward the miser died too. When they stood together before the judge of the world, the man who had been rich and became poor had won out of suffering and kindness an existence in great glory while the man who had been poor and became rich was condemned to sink to that place where ice burns like fire. Then the poor man cried out amid tears: "Lord, the light itself that proceeds from Thee cannot illuminate the dark sorrow that I must feel through all eternity if this man must enter into the kingdom of torments."*

Aristotle assigns a very high place in his Nichomachean Ethics to true friendship where each cares for the other for his own sake. But the highest virtue and the highest good to Aristotle, as to the Greek world in general and the Neo-Platonic and Christian mystical world that grew out of it, is contemplation and mystical union of the soul with God. In Buber's Hasidism, in contrast, despite its emphasis upon ecstasy, friendship is even a higher intrinsic value than closeness of the soul to God. The mutuality between man and man is possible, however, only if it nourishes and is nourished by the wholeness of the soul. It is this which the Baal-Shem tells the weeping Rabbi Arye in "The Language of the Birds" when the latter has listened with a divided mind to the wisdom that the Baal-Shem has imparted to him because he wishes at the same time to hear the language of the birds: "Could you not devote your soul to me entirely in the moment when I wished to instil the knowledge into it? . . . God's wonders are for those who can collect themselves in one thing and be satisfied in it." A variant of this same demand for wholeness is the story "The Call," in which only when the Baal-Shem shames Rabbi David out of his secret intention of calling down the Messiah is Rabbi David able to weep with the whole of his broken heart. "What are all *kavanot* [special mystical intentions]," said the Baal-Shem once, "compared to one heartfelt grief."

It is *kavana,* the dedication of the whole being, rather than *kavanot,* the conscious intentions of the mind, which Buber stressed throughout his lifetime of work on Hasidism. In this story the complete dedication of Rabbi David awakens the wholeness of each member of the congregation.

---

* See Note C in Sources for Chapter 6, p. 387.

The tears carried away with them in their stream his readiness and
his great will and thereby took with them the kavana of his spirit, the
fruit of days and nights, the tension of the infinite. He no longer felt
and knew anything other than the suffering of his heart, and out of his
heart's suffering he spoke to God and prayed and wept. And from his
suffering the suffering of the community took fire and flamed upward.
He who had spread a covering over the blemishes of his soul now drew
it aside and showed God his wounds as to a doctor. He who had erected a
wall between himself and men tore it down and suffered the pain of
others in his own pain. And he whose breast was heavy because he
could not find the word in it that would press forward to the heart of
destiny now found it and breathed in freedom.

However long it would take Buber to reach the life of dialogue
in its fullness, here is already one of the important milestones on the
way. Even Buber's distinction in Part Two of *I and Thou* between
the free will of the whole man in dialogue and the arbitrariness of
the man who does not stand in living mutuality is as clearly
grounded in Buber's Hasidic contrast between *kavana* and *kavanot*
as in the *wu-wei,* or seeming "nonaction," of the Taoist. Equally
remarkable is the way in which these stories, full of folk material
though they are, do not fall into the usual simple contrast between
good and evil, the divine and the demonic, of which most myths
are full, but recognize from the outset that evil is the footstool of
the good, the "profane" that is waiting to be hallowed. When the
young Israel goes to encounter the werewolf, he goes bravely
forward until he reaches "the dark, glowing heart, from whose
mournful mirror all beings of the world are reflected, discoloured
by a burning hatred," and he senses as he holds it "the infinite
suffering that was within it from the beginning." In the last story,
"The Shepherd," evil is still the Adversary who has confronted
the Baal-Shem "in the beginning, at the turning, and at the fulfillment." But like the Satan of the Hebrew Bible, the Adversary
is no separate power of evil able to stand against God. It is "the
demonic might that opposes the unification of heaven and earth"
and that seduces men just through the false appearance of redemption. Yet the power it holds is from God himself:

There came out of the nameless centre of solitude a voice that was
full and overfull with sadness. The demon fell back in terror. But the
voice said, "The moment is yours and always only the moment until
once knowledge conquers you and you plunge into my light because
you can no longer bear to be the lord of the moment."

The introductory section of *The Legend of the Baal-Shem,* "The Life of the Hasidim," is divided into four parts, each of which deals with a central Hasidic attitude — ecstasy, service, intention, and humility. Each part is illustrated by quotations from the *zaddikim,* but it is given richness and fullness by Buber's own powerful imagery. *Hitlahavut* is the ardor of ecstasy which can appear at all places and at all times. Only the moment lives, and the moment is eternity. Ecstasy is the way without end, the simple unity and limitlessness in which man is beyond all law and above all evil urge. *Avoda* is service. All is God and all serves God: this is the primeval duality. Through creation God is separated from his glory, his Shekinah, but man, through binding all action into one and carrying the everlasting life into each deed, can reunite God with his exiled glory. To perform true service man must say "Enough!" to his inner dissensions and become at one with himself. This wholeness is not attained through God's grace or through man's power alone but through the mysterious meeting between them. "The mystery of grace cannot be interpreted. Between seeking and finding lies the tension of a human life. . . . For God wishes to be sought, and how could he not wish to be found?"

Kavana is intention, the mystery of a soul directed to a goal. It is the ability of man through the singleness and purity of his will to liberate the fallen sparks of divinity that are imprisoned in the people and objects around him and to take part in the redemption of the world. But it is like the Taoist *wu-wei* in that it has no special aim or concrete object but is dependent on quietness of mind and wholeness of being.

> No leap from the everyday into the miraculous is required. "With his every act man can work on the figure of the glory of God that it may step forth out of its concealment." It is not the matter of the action, but only its dedication that is decisive. Just that which you do in the uniformity of recurrence or in the disposition of events, just this answer of the acting person to the manifold demands of the hour . . . just this continuity of the living stream, when accomplished in dedication, leads to redemption.

Shiflut is humility. Humility, for Hasidism, begins not with self-denial but with the affirmation of one's true self, one's created uniqueness that is given one to unfold and to complete. This is the uniqueness which we have already seen in Buber's presentation of

Nicholas of Cusa, but now it has taken on intensity and depth:

> That which exists is unique, and it happens but once. Now and without a past, it emerges from the flood of returnings, takes place, and plunges back into it, unrepeatable. . . . It is because things happen but once that the individual partakes in eternity. For the individual with his inextinguishable uniqueness is engraved in the heart of the all and lies forever in the lap of the timeless as he who has been created thus and not otherwise.*

It is not humility when one lowers oneself too much and forgets that one is "the son of a king." But true uniqueness forbears just that comparison of oneself with others that "individuality" thrives on. "No man can presume too much if he stands on his ground since all the heavens are open to him and all worlds devoted to him."

Here is the link which makes explicit why the understanding of uniqueness is the necessary prerequisite for the understanding of dialogue; for one can be truly open and ready to meet others only if one stands on the ground of one's uniqueness and deepens that ground through each new meeting. But here the corollary of the "between" is present and explicit, as it was not in Buber's discussion of uniqueness in Nicholas of Cusa. Humility is the love of a being who lives in a kingdom greater than the kingdom of the individual and speaks out of a knowing deeper than the knowing of the individual. This greater kingdom and this greater knowing is the realm of "the between," which Buber equated even at this early date with God: "It exists in reality *between* the creatures, that is, it exists in God. Life covered and guaranteed by life. . . . What the one is wanting, the other makes up for. If one loves too little, the other will love more." Nor was this understanding of love as the between something that Buber read into Hasidism; he found it there in all explicitness.

The distinction between true help and mere pity which Buber arrived at through Hasidism deepened his own understanding of the immediacy with which a person may grasp the otherness of the other. Pity is a feeling *within* oneself — a sharp, quick pain that one wishes to expel; whereas true help takes place *between* oneself and the other and arises out of *living with* the other. Real love, then, means to live with the suffering of the other, to "bear it in

---

* See Note D in Sources for Chapter 6, p. 387.

his heart as one bears the life of a tree with all its drinking in and shooting forth and with the dream of its roots and the craving of its trunk and the thousand journeys of its branches, or as one bears the life of an animal with all its gliding, stretching, and grasping and all the joy of its sinews and its joints and the dull tension of its brain." This is the new image of the human in Buber's "The Life of the Hasidim" — the image of the true *zaddik,* the humble, the loving, the helper:

> Mixing with all and untouched by all, devoted to the multitude and collected in his uniqueness, fulfilling on the rocky summits of solitude the bond with the infinite and in the valley of life the bond with the earthly, flowering out of deep devotion and withdrawn from all desire of the desiring. He knows that all is in God and greets His messengers as trusted friends. . . . He is at home and never can be cast out. The earth cannot help but be his cradle, and heaven cannot help but be his mirror and his echo.

The noted Swedish educator Ellen Key wrote Buber that since her reading of *The Legend of the Baal-Shem* he was no longer "doctor" to her but simply "person" and a very dear one. "How beautifully you have retold all this! . . . How deep, how *stirringly genuine*." Buber replied that when praise such as hers came, "so strong, warm and unfettered, it seizes one's heart, opens locks and bolts and touches the mystery. There is too much of me in this book for my soul not to be receptive to your words." He also recalled how he had written an article about her and the Swedish writer Selma Lagerlöf ("Two Nordic Women") in 1901. "I was at that time a very young fellow and had in me more intuitive glimpses than direction."

Martin received untold help in retelling the legends of the Baal-Shem from his "heart's Maugli" Paula, with whom he divided the task of reworking the crude raw material of the originals into artistically fashioned stories. This fact remained a well-guarded secret for over six decades, until after Buber's death, although in retrospect it is clear that it was to this that Martin referred in the poem "Do You Still Know It?" with which he dedicated the collection of his mature *Tales of the Hasidim* that he presented to Paula in 1949!

Elias Lönnrot, the nineteenth-century Finnish doctor who traveled around Finland collecting the runes of the Laulaya, the folk singers, and gave them the definitive form of the great Finnish epic the Kalevala, was at once a model and companion-spirit to Buber in his own lifelong task of uniting ancient and modern, people and individual, through the recounting of Hasidic tales and the translation of the Hebrew Bible. In 1913 Buber wrote "The Epic of the Magician," the long essay introducing the German translation of the Kalevala, which essay he reprinted in 1917, together with "Ecstasy and Confession" and "The Teaching of the Tao," in *Die Rede, die Lehre, und das Lied* (The Speech, the Teaching, and the Song). More than any of his more general statements, this essay shows the depth of Buber's understanding of myth and the central place it played in the development of his thought and of his lifework. Lönnrot, even in revering tradition, became, almost without noticing it, independent of it. In this sense Lönnrot's life foreshadowed Buber's sacrifice of his own "creativity" for the lifelong task of translating the Hebrew Bible, through which he joined himself to the generations of faithful transmitters in whose work "even while the hand makes its alterations, the ear hearkens to the depths of the past" (Martin Buber, *Moses*).

Not to the codification of the Jewish law but to the preservation of Jewish myth did Judaism owe its inmost cohesiveness in times of danger, asserted Buber in his "Speeches on Judaism." The Baal-Shem truly consolidated Judaism by raising a folk religion (Hasidism) to a power in Israel and renewing the people's personality from the roots of its myth. Official Rabbinism, in contrast, emasculated the Jewish ideal. "Myth" Buber defined here as a narrative of a corporeally real event perceived and presented as a divine, an absolute event. Primitive man had a heightened awareness of the uniqueness of each event, and even modern man, in times of high tension and intense experience, feels the shackles of causal awareness fall off him and finds within himself that mythmaking faculty through which the world's processes are perceived as meaningful beyond causality, as the manifestation of a central purpose which can be grasped only by the ardent power of one's whole being. The "man who is truly alive" mythicizes the hero because the mythical approach reveals to him the very being of the beloved. Here, in all but language, is the I-Thou relationship. What is central to *I and Thou* is already central here — that corporeal reality is not an illusion and myth a metaphor, as it was for the Indian sage and for the Platonist, but that myth is a true account of God's manifestation on earth. All the books of the

Bible that tell stories have only one subject matter: YHVH's meetings with His people. To tell such a story is already to speak mythically, for it tells only events that have been grasped in their divine significance. This biblical myth is continued in Hasidism, which teaches that the Shekinah — the indwelling glory, or presence, of God — is dormant in all things, and needs to be liberated by man's intention and his deed. "Thus, every man is called to determine, by his own life, God's destiny; and every living being is deeply rooted in the living myth."*

In "The Spirit and Body of the Hasidic Movement," the 1921 Introduction to his book of Hasidic tales *The Great Maggid and His Followers,* Buber arrived at the specific language of "meeting" and of "I and Thou" as an integral part of his deeper penetration of the myths of the Kabbala and Hasidism. "Our world is in truth the world of man," Buber wrote, and man means the last working out of the otherness, the freedom of creation through which God enters into the fate of the world in order that he may find for himself a partner for mutual knowing and mutual love.

> In other teachings the God-soul, sent or released by heaven to earth, could be called home or freed to return home by heaven; creation and redemption take place in the same direction, from "above" to "below." But this is not so in a teaching which, like the Jewish, is so wholly based upon the double-directional relation of the human I and the divine Thou, on the reality of reciprocity, on the *meeting.* Here man, this miserable man, is, by the very meaning of his creation, the helper of God. . . . God waits for him. From him, from "below" the impulse toward redemption must proceed. Grace is God's *answer.*

Hasidism's fullness of genuine life manifested itself above all in the *zaddik.* The *zaddikim* bear the Hasidic teaching not only as its apostles, but as its working reality. *They are the teaching.* The *zaddik,* the true, or justified, man, now stands in the succession of that series of modern mythical figures that Buber presented in the fifteen years preceding — the perfected man of "The Life of the Hasidism," the central man of "The Teaching of the Tao," the "realizing man" of *Daniel,* and the mythical hero of his essays on myth. In the *zaddik,* heaven and earth meet: "the timeless present reveals itself ever again in the moment where, out of the essential act of the true man, the unification of God and His Shekinah takes

---

* See Note E in Sources for Chapter 6, p. 388.

place." In the *zaddik* the mythical hero becomes, for Buber, a modern human image. "He is . . . the man in whom transcendental responsibility has grown from an event of consciousness into organic existence. He is the true human being, the rightful subject of the act in which God wants to be known, loved, wanted."

Basic to this mythical and modern image of man is that personal wholeness which leads to the spontaneous response rather than to conscious imitation. It is the spontaneity of the *zaddik*'s existence that exercises above all the purifying and renewing influence, to which the conscious expression in words is only the accompaniment. Even in the word what is significant is the unintentional. Thus "the less premeditated the prayer of the zaddik is, the more immediately it breaks forth out of the natural depths of man, . . . so much the more real it is." From this image of man a direct way leads to that mature teaching which expresses the modern relevance of the Hasidic myth in universal terms. The last sentence of "Spirit and Body of the Hasidic Movement" begins with a quotation from Rabbi Nachman of Bratzlav and ends with the very language of *I and Thou*: "To each the highest is open, each life has its access to reality, each nature its eternal right, from each thing a way leads to God, and each way that leads to God is *the* way."

In "Spirit and Body of the Hasidic Movement" Buber used freely the Lurian Kabbalistic myth of the *tsimutsum* whereby "God contracted Himself to world because He, nondual and relationless unity, wanted to allow relation to emerge; because He wanted to be known, loved, wanted; because He wanted to allow to arise from His primally one Being, in which thinking and thought are one, the otherness that strives to unity." In our world God's fate is fulfilled, but our world is in truth the world of man. Yet Buber also contrasted the Kabbala with Hasidism, claiming that only in the latter does real community take place, only in the latter is the concern for magic and special mystical intentions (*kavanot*) overcome in favor of the *kavana* that consecrates the everyday. Hasidism strives to deschematize the mystery of the Kabbala. By virtue of its intensity the principle of the Kabbala becomes a religious *meeting*.

The longing for the Messianic redemption found at times an even more personal expression in conjuring words and storming undertakings. But the work for the sake of the end subordinated itself to the hallowing of all action. In the stillness there ripened presentiments of a timeless salvation that the moment disclosed; no longer a set action but the dedication of all action became decisive. And as the mystery of present fulfillment joined the preparation of coming things, strengthening and illuminating it, winged joy lifted itself above asceticism as a butterfly above a cast-off cocoon.

In October 1921 Gerhard Scholem wrote Buber a long letter in response to this essay which prefigured his later critique of Buber's interpretation of Hasidism. In it he expressed his gratification that Buber had followed his urging and published the sources, but he questioned whether Buber's emphasis upon deschematizing the mystery was not a one-sided presentation of Hasidic teaching which did not do justice to its many historical stages or to its close dependence upon Kabbalistic doctrine for its own teaching.

Buber wrote his tales of the Hasidim not only in "obedient listening" to past tradition but also in response to the call and the need of the present hour. The stories of the many *zaddikim* that he recounted were attempts on Buber's part to make the mythical hero living today, to place before modern man an image of true human existence. For countless readers Buber's legends and tales of the Hasidim have just this effect. At the time of Buber's eighty-fifth birthday, his old friend Shmuel Agnon, the Israeli Nobel Prize novelist, told of just such an impact of Buber's modern Hasidic image of man occurring in the very period about which we are writing, the period between the end of World War I and the final writing of *I and Thou*. A high police official in Leipzig abolished the order to expel a Hasidic family from Galicia because he was an ardent reader of Buber's books and had been greatly impressed by his Hasidic tales.

Buber's understanding of the *zaddik* as the true helper was deepened through an experience that he had four or five years after he wrote *The Legend of the Baal-Shem*. He had emerged by that time from his self-imposed retirement to give his famous "Speeches on Judaism" to the Prague Bar Kochbans. At the end of the third of them, he went with some members of the Bar Kochba Association into a coffeehouse. "I like to follow the speech given before an audience, whose form allows no reply," remarked Buber when he related this incident, "with a conversation with a few in which person acts on person. In the latter I express my view in the dialogue with my partners through going into their objections and questions." They were discussing some theme of moral philosophy when a well-built, middle-aged Jew of simple appearance came up to the table and greeted Buber. When Buber failed to recognize him, he introduced himself as M., the brother of a former steward of Buber's father. Buber invited him to sit with them, inquired about his life, then turned back to the conversation with the young people. Although it was obvious that he did not understand a single word of the abstract discussion, M. listened with eager attentiveness, receiving every word with a devotion resembling "that of the believers who do not need to know the content of a litany since the arrangement of sounds and tones alone give them all that they need, and more than any content could."

From time to time Buber turned to him and urged him to say whether he had some wish, but he vigorously declined. As was usual after such a lively interchange, Buber felt fresher than before and decided finally to go for a walk with the young people. At this moment M. approached him most timidly and said he had a question. Punctuated by pauses, he announced that he had a daughter, that he had a young man for his daughter, and that the man was a student of law who had passed the examinations with distinction. During the long pause that followed, Buber looked at him encouragingly, supposing that he would ask him to use his influence in some way on behalf of the presumptive son-in-law. Instead, to Buber's surprise, he asked: "Doctor, is he a steady man?" and then still further: "But, Doctor, does he also have a good head?" Feeling that he could not refuse to answer, Buber said that the young man must certainly be industrious and able and that he must also have something in his head for he could not have succeeded by industry alone. But in reply to M.'s final question — "Doctor, should he now become a judge or a lawyer?" — Buber could give no advice at all. Then M. regarded him with a glance of almost melancholy renunciation and spoke in a tone, composed partly of sorrow and partly of humility: "Doctor, you do not *want* to say — but I thank you for what you have said to me."

This humorous occurrence gave Buber a new and significant insight into the role of the *zaddik* that went beyond his own teaching of the perfected man who realizes God in the world. Now he understood more profoundly the image he had glimpsed in his childhood: the *zaddik*'s function as a leader. Each person has an infinite sphere of responsibility, but there are persons who are hourly accosted by infinite responsibility in a special way.

These are the leaders — not the rulers and statesmen who turn away from the individual, problematic, personal lives to deal with the external destiny of great communities but the true *zaddikim* who withstand the thousandfold-questioning glance of individual lives and give answer to the trembling mouth of the needy creature who time after time demands from them decision. The true *zaddik* is the man who constantly measures the depths of responsibility with the sounding lead of his words. "He is the helper in spirit, the teacher of meaning whom the world awaits evermore."

In relating this story, Buber did not in any way imply that he saw himself in the role of the *zaddik*. On the contrary, he explicitly contrasted himself with the *zaddik* even at the moment he attained a glimpse into his role:

> I, who am truly no zaddik, no one assured in God, rather a man endangered before God, a man wrestling ever anew for God's light, ever anew engulfed in God's abysses, nonetheless, when asked a trivial question and replying with a trivial answer, then experienced from within for the first time the true zaddik, questioned about revelations and replying in revelations. I experienced him in the fundamental relation of his soul to the world: in his responsibility.

"Endangered before God, . . . wrestling ever anew for God's light, ever anew engulfed in God's abysses," this portrait that Buber gave of himself when he was nearly forty probably continued to hold true of him for the almost half century that he had yet to live. It is, indeed, the very heart of the "narrow ridge" that he walked. Although his friend Franz Rosenzweig could refer to him jokingly as Reb. Martin of Heppenheim (his home in Germany for many years), Buber was never a *zaddik*. Yet the *zaddik* was without question for him an image of the human, and in the years that he lived beyond this essay, he took on ever more powerfully the lines of the "true zaddik" he himself had described. He did not become a leader of a genuine community, but he withstood the thousand-fold questioning glance of countless sorely troubled persons and constantly measured the depths of responsibility with the "sounding lead" of his presence and his words.

CHAPTER 7

The Prague Bar Kochbans and the "Speeches on Judaism"

BUBER TOOK HIS FIRST STEP toward full responsibility in his relationship to others precisely at the time of his story about M., for it was then that he emerged from his five years of seclusion devoted to Hasidism to become the acknowledged leader of the young Jewish intellectuals and particularly the young Zionists of central Europe. The occasion was the invitation to Buber to speak to the Zionist student association in Prague, which called itself the Bar Kochba Union after the famous military leader of the Jewish rebellion against the Romans. The name was given to the group during the heroic era of Zionism that Herzl had ushered in, but the overture to Buber already signified the inadequacy of a merely external Zionism and heralded the entrance into a new period.

A truly momentous encounter took place here between this remarkable group of young Zionists, many of whom later became influential figures in Zionist, Jewish, intellectual, or literary circles, and Martin Buber, who emerged from his self-imposed retirement with a stature and dignity that made men only ten years his junior look up to him as a leader and a sage. This return to activity on Buber's part in no way meant a turning away from

Hasidism. On the contrary, it was precisely through his deep immersion in Hasidism that he was able to make true the words that he wrote in his letter of 1905 — that if he *should* return to activity in the Zionist movement it would be with something more significant and profound to say than the catchwords which he had been uttering during his early years in the movement. The Prague Bar Kochbans, on their part, invited Buber not merely as the man who had been active in the movement five years before, but as the well-known author of *The Tales of Rabbi Nachman* and *The Legend of the Baal-Shem* — the man who asserted that no renaissance of Judaism could take place that did not bear in it some elements of Hasidism.

The heroic epoch of the Prague Bar Kochbans was characterized by the will to make the impossible possible, a new spirit that scorned all difficulties and that willed from the first to bring Jewishness to realization and to make one's personal and one's political life a single unity. Buber and Berthold Feiwel had already spoken before the Prague Bar Kochbans in 1903 on the "Jewish Renaissance," and it is then that Buber first came into contact with his lifelong friend Hugo Bergmann, later one of Israel's most eminent philosophers and moral leaders. The very striving for cultural Zionism that Buber had fought for characterized the position of the Bar Kochbans within the total Zionist organization and led them to a bitter fight with the bourgeois Zionists and the liberals who were closer to assimilation. Bar Kochba represented the democratic and progressive direction, and it was no accident that its delegate to the 1903 Zionist Congress was Martin Buber, one of the leaders of the Democratic Fraction.

After Herzl's death, the heroic Zionist activity subsided but also the "practical" as opposed to the "political" Zionists were few, and the Prague Bar Kochbans suffered the stagnation that followed from espousing a Zionism without content. It was this situation that led to the invitation to Buber. Buber's thought and personality ushered in a new era for the Prague Bar Kochbans and, radiating out from there, for central European Zionist youth in general. The Prague Bar Kochbans became Buber's community, and from it emerged some of Buber's most influential disciples and lasting friends, men such as Hugo Bergmann, Max Brod, Robert and Felix Weltsch, and Hans Kohn. The result was that the Bar Kochba in this era proved itself a much deeper and more revolutionary element in Zionism than in its heroic epoch.

In place of the meaningless annual party that the Bar Kochba Union had held until then, Leo Hermann, after his election as chairman in the fall of 1908, proposed that they sponsor a festive evening for the general public in the ballroom of the Hotel Central, where the foremost gatherings of the city took place. An actor and a young artist were invited to give recitations, as well as the celebrated author of *Bambi,* Felix Salten, to give the proper tone to the occasion. The circle of Jewish intellectuals and of the "better" society that used the word "Jew" only among themselves, if at all, found that because of Salten's presence it was legitimate to come too, and the hall was filled to the last seat. But it was the profound effect of Buber's talk that led from that day on to the Prague intellectuals' recognition of Judaism as an essential cultural problem.

The theme of the evening was the question of how the young Zionists of the West were to find their way back to Jewishness. In a letter of November 14, 1908, Hermann had written to Buber telling him of their isolation in Prague, between German and Czech, between German Jew and Czech Jew, and asking him how the Western Jew was to make his own that part of the Jewish being that he did not possess. Buber had replied warmly, and out of their exchange of letters both the title and the content of his talk developed. Buber arrived unexpectedly ahead of time the night before the festive evening. As a result, his first meeting with the young Zionists took place in walks around the city and in informal talks. Writing more than half a century later, Robert Weltsch declared that of all the many times that they showed distinguished visitors through the streets of historic Prague, it was the walking tour with Martin and Paula Buber that remained foremost in his mind. No other visitors had showed so much genuine understanding and informed knowledge of the architectonic and artistic splendors of the city or felt so deeply its magic and mystery. Buber discovered similarities between Florence and Prague, and from this time on remained closely tied to Prague until the old Jewish Prague disappeared.

The members of the Bar Kochba sat together with Buber in a small circle, and he spoke to them for the first time of his position regarding Jewishness and Zionism. "Then we knew," said Leo Hermann, "that he would help us further on our way." From that time on, they looked on Buber as a man of incontestable authority. Buber too found this meeting of great importance; here there existed *young* people, he realized, who could show once again that there is a new beginning and new hope.

The festive evening began with Felix Salten's speech, which was brilliant and subtle. While he spoke, Buber and Leo Hermann waited in a cold cellar underneath the theater. Buber was concerned because he believed that, following Salten, he would not find any contact with the public. Hermann begged him not to think of the public but to speak only for the members of Bar Kochba. He promised to do this, and they arranged for Hermann to give him a sign when he was to end his address. When Buber, sitting before a small table, began to speak, Hermann went back into the loges. After ten minutes Buber gave him a questioning look, but he made no sign. As a result, Buber delivered his speech to the end, "with his whole being, wholly turned to us," Hermann reported. When Buber joined the members of the Bar Kochba in the loges, Hermann was too moved to do anything other than press Buber's hand. The speech and his talks with them had helped them to recognize in their own Zionism a meaning that the political formulas and goals had not been able to give them.

In the last part of March 1910, Buber was in Vienna and then visited Prague with Paula. Again the Bar Kochbans walked with them in the old city of Prague, along the old city circle and the bridge over the famous Prague castle the Hradshin until, as they stood above, the lights sprang up on the dark city and along the Moldau. When they returned, the others were already waiting in a local union of the Bar Kochba. Buber opened the discussion with a continuation of the conversation that had been begun above the Hradshin. He spoke about the meaning of the concept "blood," about the specific Jewish characteristics, the resolution of one's personal "Jewish question," the relationship of the Western Jews to Palestine, the hope of a great religious upheaval which alone could bring renewal for the Western Jews too. To the question of one woman as to whether he could instruct them in a method of self-liberation, he refused to reply, but to the question whether in the last analysis one really had to accept Palestine as the only way, he answered with a clear Yes.

The next day in the Jewish council house, Buber delivered a public lecture on "Judaism and Mankind." He formulated clearly and strongly the answer to the questions on which the discussion of the evening before had centered: the demand for unity born out of one's own inner division and the redemption from it. Buber spoke this time much more confidently; his voice was better and fresher than in the preceding year. The general public too felt itself drawn to him; it was fully receptive and unwearied. He spoke an hour and a quarter with extraordinary effect and all were completely absorbed until the last word. There was no coughing, no shifting of seats. Buber's distinguished head above the lectern with its impressive composure, his brown eyes often prophetically flashing, and the clear words that he drew forth from a rich treasury of images, as if used for the first time — all these worked together to make of his speech an address to be listened and responded to, not only on an intellectual level but with one's whole being. The applause that broke out lasted until the last guests had left the hall. After the Bubers left, the Bar Kochbans spent the whole afternoon discussing Buber and his speech. "It was remarkable," says Hermann, "that almost every one of us remembered a large part of the speech almost word for word and that we felt as if it had penetrated our blood."

In June 1910 began the first of three relationships in which, according to Grete Schaeder, young men who studied philosophy placed their lives to a certain extent under Buber's direction — that with Ernst Elijahu Rappeport in the period before the First World War to the early twenties, that with Hermann Gerson from the late 1920s through the 1930s, and that with the author from 1950 until Buber's death in 1965. Rappeport wrote Buber then saying that he probably did not remember their conversation after his Vienna lecture for the Bar Kochba Union on "The Land of the Jews." Buber replied that he always forgot only the impersonal and that he remembered well that conversation. Asked for a criticism of Rappeport's thought process, Buber replied that he could not say anything about his views on religion because his own were so nonpolemical. What was pure in Rappeport's thought was that Rappeport accepted the world as it is, unsoiled by any dialectic, that he had reverence even for his own feelings, and that he honored the hours of self-recollection as the decisive ones.

> The impure in it is that you do not allow yourself time, . . . that you do not serve for the sake of the immediate, that your reverence is not strong enough to make you shudder and tremble, that you forget soul-recollection and pursue quick, surface abstraction, our hereditary sin.

Buber urged him to go to the things, to seeing, hearing, and grasping, to battle and service! "Then only will you come to the thought as one comes to himself, dedicated: out of the embrace of the things, through it." Schaeder rightly sees in this a foreshadowing of the first dialogue of Buber's philosophy of "realization," *Daniel.* In November Buber wrote Rappeport that he feared that his frank criticism had wounded him, but that he had his sympathetic cooperation and that he was sending him "The Teaching of the Tao," which he thought would speak to his condition. Rappeport assured Buber in his reply that he had postponed writing only because he could not fully understand his words, that his criticism had in no way wounded him but was a great joy as a serious and stern companion on his way.

In May 1911 Buber congratulated Elijahu Rappeport on the birth of his son:

> When I received your letter, I had just read in the *Zohar:* "When a man is with his wife, he should think of the *Shekinah* [the indwelling Glory of God], for the wife is the image of the *Shekinah.* The husband in his house is surrounded by the longing of the eternal hills." And it is this which I basically wish for you: that you have bequeathed to your son the longing for the eternal hills, that experiences the infinite in the finite. He shall become a friend of the elements and an intimate of the spheres, and all things shall love him and present him the strong world of images that only things have to give.

In September Buber wrote Rappeport that he could not confirm his "Buch Jeshua" (Jesus Book) as a book but only as fragments of a book, not fully matured, compiled prematurely, even though there was much in it that he found worthwhile. Buber told him that his friend Moritz Heimann, one of the most significant human beings alive, had for more than ten years devoted his best inner strength to just such a book. In Rappeport's there were few happenings; it dealt with its subject archaically instead of giving it its own appropriate living speech. Also the writing lacked unity because of the insertion of quotations from the Gospels (the fundamental problem of a Jesus book). The one thing Buber found finished and unconditionally praiseworthy was Rappeport's image of Paul. Despite all this, Buber added that if Rappeport should decide to publish the book, he could count on his advice and help for all individual details. The following month Buber told Rappeport that he could not accept his statement that "Elijahu" was other than himself.

He is not real in spirit like a Kierkegaardian pseudonym. He has exactly so much blood as he has drunk from your wounds. . . . Make your Elijahu wholly real — and you will see what he will write. I speak from knowledge, for I have been in the land of Sheol and know the life of shades.

Inhumanly cruel: You are right — inhumanly cruel and inhumanly merciful was he of whom it is told that he led the Patriarchs from the Land of Sheol.

In the middle of December 1910, Hermann traveled to Vienna, partly to meet with Buber, and there heard him deliver the speech on "The Renewal of Judaism" that he had prepared for Prague. He felt how Buber had grown beyond his first two speeches and was surprised to discover how since his last speech in Prague the Bar Kochbans had come in many points to similar conclusions. In Vienna such great Jewish writers as Arthur Schnitzler, Jakob Wassermann, and Richard Beer-Hofmann formed a part of the enthusiastic audience. Yet Hermann experienced the speech in Vienna as something finished that was placed before a public that was not ready for it, while Buber's speeches to them in Prague had seemed to grow out of questions and conversations. When Buber later gave the speech in Prague, Hermann felt how the conversations with the Bar Kochbans the day before had altered it. This speech had a still stronger effect than his first two great speeches in Prague, and on Hermann a still stronger effect than the same speech heard in Vienna. That was the third of the "Three Speeches on Judaism."

The revolutionary element in Buber's "Three Speeches" is one that today we might call "existentialist," for it turned the "Jewish Question" from an abstract question about whether Jews are to be considered members of a race, nation, or common creed to that of the deepest personal meaning of Judaism to the Jew himself. Buber had already anticipated this approach in his emphasis upon cultural as opposed to merely political Zionism. But now he went a step further to understand Jewishness as an existential choice that is made to create the future out of the inheritance of the past rather than through Nietzschean creativity and will which transcended the past in the name of the future. "Judaism has for the Jews as much meaning as it has inner reality," Buber proclaimed, anticipating his later emphasis upon "realization." Regarded from the standpoint of this inner reality, he added, Jewish religiousness is a memory, perhaps also a hope, but not a present reality. The ages of Jacob and Moses, of early Christianity and of Hasidism, have been followed by no genuine life of fervor that *bears witness* to God and makes out of divine truth a divine reality because it is lived "in his name." There is profession of faith — of a monotheistic humanism — but no fulfillment.

The parallel that Buber then drew between the life of a child and the life of the Jew brings to mind his own childhood and the concern about homelessness, the threat of infinity, and the need for roots that permeate all his thought. The child builds up his feeling of belonging to a community out of three constant elements of his experience — habitat, language, and custom. With the discovery of his "I," the child experiences his limitedness in space and his unlimitedness in time. The longing for continuance leads his glance beyond his own life span. This young man whom the shudder of eternity has touched (Buber himself at fourteen) experiences in himself that there is continuance, and he experiences it with all the simplicity and wonder of the self-evident — in the hour when he discovers the succession of generations, in the series of fathers and mothers the mingling of whose blood has produced him. The people is now to him a community of the dead, living, and unborn who together form the unity that he experiences as the ground of his "I," as his innermost uniqueness, his innermost destiny. The past of his people is his personal memory, its future his personal task.

The Western Jew is a divided person because his community of land, speech, and custom is different from his community of blood. Yet the blood is the deepest level of force of the soul, for it has given us something that determines in every hour each tone and color of our lives. The great heritage of the ages that we bring with us into the world is the destiny, action, and suffering, pain, misery, and disgrace of the fathers and mothers — from the fight of the prophets to the detached intellectuality of the modern Jew. The inner division of the Jew will remain until he recognizes that the blood is the formative element in his life. This recognition does not mean a choice that would free him from the influence of his environment. We are, said Buber, in a more pregnant sense than any other civilized people, a mixture. But we do not want to be the slaves but the masters of this mixture. The choice means a decision about which shall be the ruling element and which the ruled in us. When out of deep self-knowledge we shall have said Yes to our whole Jewish existence, then we shall no longer feel ourselves as individuals but as a people, for each will feel the people in himself. My soul is not with my people, rather my people *is* my soul.

"When I was a child," Buber concluded, "I read an old Jewish saying that I could not understand . . .: 'Before the gates of Rome sits a leprous beggar and waits. He is the Messiah.' Then I went to an old man and asked him: 'For what does he wait?' And the old man answered me something that . . . only much later I learned to understand. He said: 'For you!' "

Of all the doctrines that Buber ever enunciated, this one of the "blood" is perhaps the most problematic and the most difficult to comprehend. We can see it as a reaction to the loss of his mother as a boy of four, to the uncanniness of the infinite that he experienced at fourteen, to the aimless whirl of Vienna in which he lost himself in his student days, to the anti-Semitism that he, like all Jews of that age, encountered. We can also see it as an outgrowth of his early focus on the Jewish Renaissance movement and on cultural Zionism. Also manifest here are his scientific studies, which led him, like many at that time, to adopt biological analogies, and the interest in ethnopsychology stimulated by his studies with the great psychologist Wundt. On the other hand, this grounding of the individual so totally in the community of blood seems strangely at variance with Buber's concern for the problem of individuation in his doctoral dissertation and still more with his concern for uniqueness in *The Legend of the Baal-Shem* three years before, though one might say that here Buber repeats in new guise the Renaissance mystical teaching that each individual contains the whole world in himself. Buber would have seen no contradiction here, however, for his call to inner decision was a call to the realization of one's uniqueness through the uniqueness of one's people. Buber had a remarkable prototype for his dual emphasis in his friend Gustav Landauer, to whom he sent the first edition of *Three Speeches on Judaism* in 1911 with the inscription, "In ever new feeling of unity." In an essay of 1901, most of which he included in his book *Skepticism and Mysticism* (1903), the anarchist Landauer defined the individual, far more one-sidedly than Buber, as the product of the "community of blood."

But what the individual is, that is something that stands firm by virtue of God's grace and birth, that is the hereditary might that we ourselves are, character, which can only superficially be modulated and corrected from without. The firmer an individual stands on himself, the deeper he withdraws into himself, the more he cuts himself off from the influences of the environment, so much the more does he find himself coinciding with the world of the past, with what he is by birth. What man is by birth, what is his innermost and most secret, his inviolable uniqueness, that is the great community of the living in him, that is his blood and his community of blood. Blood is thicker than water; the community which the individual discovers himself to be is mightier and nobler and more ancient than the thin influences of state and society. What is most individual in us is what is most common in us. The deeper I return into myself, so much the more do I become part of the world.

The feeling for the "forebears," as Buber himself has shown in his essay on the Austrian-Jewish poet Richard Beer-Hofmann, was common to some of the poets of this period who stood closest to Buber himself — Beer-Hofmann, Arthur Schnitzler, Hugo von Hofmannsthal. Commenting on Beer-Hofmann's famous "Lullaby to Miriam," which was once printed in Buber and Feiwel's *Jewish Almanac*, Buber wrote in 1962:

> Our being itself is an inheritance from our forebears that we bequeath to our children. The feeling that we are endangered has deceived us. If "all" are really "in us," then the terror of loneliness is forever banished: death has become a servant to life.

Despite his clear statement that the Jewish people, more than any other, is a mixture, Buber's concept of "the community of the blood" has often been identified retrospectively with the type of racial mysticism prevalent in Germany at the time and later in cruder form incorporated into the myths of Nazism. To some, this judgment may seem to be confirmed by the fact that Alfred Rosenberg and his lawyer cited Buber at the Nuremburg trials as evidence that the Nazi philosphy was part of a *Zeitgeist* that had no necessary connection with anti-Semitism. There is, indeed, an element of biological vitalism and irrationalism in this concept of the "blood" that is bound to disquiet those who have lived through the Nazi era. But the differences, for all this, are more important than the similarities. Buber was not emphasizing the *superiority* of one people over another but the precious uniqueness of each. Buber wanted to know the unique potentialities and task of the Jewish people from within. The Nazis, and the racial theorists who preceded them, compared and contrasted from without. "Ignorance and distortion are . . . the pillars of the modern race psychology treatment of the Jewish people," Buber wrote in 1916.

In 1958 Jacob Agus asked Buber whether in the light of "the development of demonic Nazism out of the seeds of romantic nationalism in Germany" and the evident untrustworthiness of the "voice of the blood," he had not reconsidered his earlier views on romantic nationalism as expressed in the "Speeches on Judaism." In his reply, Buber did not disguise his amazement that such a question could be formulated as if he "had not long since answered it in print." Buber characterized his treatment of the national problem in the "Speeches on Judaism" as "all too simple," since he had failed there to stress what was central to his Zionism from the time of his 1921 address on "Nationalism," that "the spirit of nationalism is fruitful just so long as it does not make the nation an end in itself." Yet at the same time he denied Agus's label of "romanticism" even when applied to the "Speeches on Judaism" alone:

> But already in those early "Talks on Judaism" the *core* was not romantic. Essentially, it only modernized the fundamental biblical concepts of "seed" and "land" (Gen. 12:7). It was important at that time to state that in order to be able to develop fully what was intended in it, a community needs biological and territorial continuity. This development is by no means produced by this continuity; and it is just not possible without it.

What Buber really meant by "blood" was illustrated by a comment he made to his former teacher, the German-Jewish philosopher Georg Simmel, around 1909. Simmel affirmed the perseverance of the Jewish *spirit* as highly worth striving for. Whereupon Buber remarked: "But how can you conceive of perseverance of a particular spirit without a biological foundation?" Simmel was thinking as a *Luftmensch*, the intellectual Jew of the Diaspora who meant perhaps a certain quality of spirit but not a total existence. Buber was thinking, in contrast, of a full Jewish existence lived by Jews together in organic community. In a comment on this conversation a half century later Buber added: "If this biological foundation is given and the spirit is now one that wants to be realized in the fullness of public life, then one must give it . . . the possibility of determining its own social and political life-forms." Thus, as even Alfred Rosenberg recognized in however grotesque and distorted a form, there was an integral connection between Buber's concept of "blood" and his Zionism. By "blood" he meant nothing more nor less than the link of the generations, and by Zionism he meant not political action and diplomatic negotiations, but the task of building organic community on the land.

In the second of his "Three Speeches on Judaism" — "Judaism and Mankind" — Buber universalized the inner duality of the Jew to a psychological dualism characteristic of all men, perhaps indeed the most essential and decisive factor of human life. Whether it is experienced as personal choice, external necessity, or pure chance, man experiences his inner way as a movement from crossroad to crossroad. What has made the Jewish people a phenomenon of mankind is that in it this polarity is more dominant than elsewhere and the striving for unity stronger. Persian dualism was objective, but the myth of the Fall of Adam is a subjective duality in which man must choose between good and evil and his future is dependent upon this choice.

It was in this same year — 1910 — in his essay on Herzl that Buber recognized that he and his friends were problematic. It was precisely in this period, as we suggested in our discussion of mysticism, that Buber seemed to be four persons at once. Nothing makes this clearer than his oscillating relationship to the Hindu Vedanta. In "Ecstasy and Confession" he exalted Indian mysticism as the one form in which men have proclaimed the "I" that is one with the All and with the One and have not fallen into the illusion that makes their experience into a multiform mystery. In "Judaism and Mankind," in contrast, he valued the Jewish view of redemption above the Indian, and the multiform above the nondual. The Indian idea of redemption is clearer and more unconditional than the Jewish, Buber stated. Yet it means becoming free not from the duality of the soul but from the soul's entanglement in the world. The Indian redemption means an awakening, the Jewish a transformation; the Indian a laying aside of illusion, the Jewish a laying hold of the truth; the Indian a negation, the Jewish an affirmation; the Indian takes place in the timeless, the Jewish means the way of mankind. The Jewish idea is, like all historical views, the less essential but the more moving. It alone can say like Job, "I know that my Redeemer liveth." From it the messianic idea of Judaism derives its humanity. And when in Jewish mysticism duality was carried even into the conception of God, the Jewish idea of redemption rose to the height of the Indian: it became the idea of the redemption of God — of the reunification of the essence of God, which is removed from things, with the glory of God, which wandering, straying, and scattered lives among the things of the world.

The Jewish mystic carried forward in glowing inwardness the ancient striving for unity. Yet this striving is carried forward today, Buber claimed, by each person who wins unity out of his soul, who decides in himself for the pure, the free, the fruitful, by each who drives the money changers out of his own temple. The people too must also decide and reject the negative, the play-actors, the covetous, the gamblers, the cowardly slaves of the community. For the expulsion of the negative, in a people as in individuals, is the way to becoming one. The distinction here is between those who choose and those who let happen, between those who have a goal and those who have petty ends, between those who create and those who destroy.

The myths of the Kabbala and Hasidism are retained here yet converted into a psychology that flows together with the attack on uncreative intellectuality cut off from life impulses that marked Buber's early essays on the Jewish Renaissance. On the other hand, the teaching of bringing all the passion of the "evil" urge into one's decision that was central to Buber's earlier *and* his later thought is obscured here by a view of decision as the expulsion of the negative in the individual and the community. Buber's whole-hearted rejection of those forms of the Galut, or exile, which he could not bear, preceded his wholehearted realization that it was not enough simply to cut off the impulses — that one must trans-form and use them.

The process of concentrating himself which Buber went through in his period of retirement clearly had as its corollary a facing of his own inner duality in a way that he had not before. His call to his fellow Jews was a call that he himself had answered. "It does not become us," he wrote, "to evade the deep reality of our existence, and there will be no salvation for us before we have confronted it and stood our ground before it." What is in question here, Buber stated, is not basically an *ethnic* but a *human* question. The Jew may experience a specially heightened inner duality because of the disparity between the community of the generations and the community of his immediate environment, but all persons know the inner duality that Buber knew in his own soul and strove to overcome.

If in 1903 Buber proclaimed evolution as *the* modern idea, at the end of 1910 — in the third of his three "Speeches on Judaism" — Buber attacked it unconditionally in a way that clearly anticipated his complaint in *I and Thou* against the domination of modern man by the dogma of unfree process. The difference here is the difference in Buber himself between his earlier hope for a Jewish Renaissance and his later demand for a decisive turning of the whole being. This turning Buber called "The Renewal of Judaism." The concept of evolution that dominates the typical man of this time, he said, is the concept of gradual change coming from the working together of many little causes. "When I speak of renewal," Buber said, "I am aware that I am leaving the ground of this age and am entering that of a new, coming one. For I mean by renewal nothing at all gradual . . . but something sudden and enormous, . . . no continuation and betterment, but radical turning and transformation. Indeed, just as I believe that in the life of an individual man there can be a moment of elemental revolution, a crisis and shattering and a new becoming from the roots to all the branches of existence, just so I believe in it for the life of Judaism." Thus the teaching of renewal that Buber realized in his own life when he turned from active Zionism to the re-creation of Hasidism, he now applied to the Jewish people as a whole.

This new emphasis meant for Buber a turning away from Nietzsche, whose seductiveness had dominated his thought even longer than he himself was aware of. Instead of an unconditioned, heroic life, modern evolutionism leaves only the hope of being the exponent of a little "progress." He who can no longer perform the impossible now performs the all-too-possible. Even the longing for the heroic life is ruined by this tendency of the age. The most tragic example is perhaps that of the man in whom this longing was strong as in no other and who nonetheless could not escape from the dogma of evolution: Friedrich Nietzsche. Buber's new demand for renewal also meant for him a dissatisfaction with Ahad Ha'am's teaching of "the spiritual center" and his own advocacy of a Jewish Renaissance. A spiritual center can further scientific work, can disseminate ideas, can even become a social model, but that from which I alone expect the Absolute, said Buber — the turning and transformation, the revolution of all elements — it cannot effect. Indeed, he added — in what might seem to be an anti-Zionist note — the shattering of the foundations that must precede it, the monstrous dismemberment, the boundless despair, the infinite yearning, the pathetic chaos of many present-day Jews is a more favorable soil than the normal and confident existence of settlers in their own land. What is essential is whether a deed is done in human conditionality or divine unconditionality. This cannot be achieved through the flowering of a new Jewish literature or through those other values "that, with a term more of hope than of experience, we used to designate as the 'Jewish Renaissance.'" All this in no way means a renewal of Judaism. The fight for fulfillment must now begin anew.

If Buber was critical of the inadequacy of Nietzsche, Ahad Ha'am, and his own early teachings, he was still more critical of the claim of liberal and Reform Judaism to be a renewal of Judaism. Rationalization of the faith, simplification of the dogma, relaxing of the rituals — all this is negation, nothing but negation! This is not a renewal of Judaism but its continuation in an easier, more elegant, more European, salonlike form. The prophets certainly spoke of the insignificance of all ceremonies, but not in order to make the religious life easier. They sought rather to make it more difficult, to make it genuine and whole, to proclaim the holiness of the *deed*. Prophetic Judaism demanded that man live unconditionally, that he be whole at every hour and in all things, and that he *realize* his feelings of God at all times. This meant the realization of three interrelated tendencies — the striving for unity, for the deed, and for the future. These tendencies find their strongest expression in messianism — the deepest original idea of Judaism. In messianism the relativity of a far time is transformed into the absolute of the fullness of time. Here, for the first time, the Absolute was proclaimed as the goal — the goal in mankind and to be realized through it. This unconditional demand Buber tried to renew in his time for every Jew who was willing to listen and respond as a Jew. "We stand," Buber proclaimed,

> in a moment of the greatest tension and of ultimate decision, in a moment with a double face — one looking toward death, the other toward life. The renewal of Judaism means to put aside the dualism between our absolute and our relative life in order that the fight for fulfillment may grasp the whole people, that the idea of reality may penetrate the everyday, *that the spirit may enter into life!* Only then when Judaism extends itself like a hand and seizes every Jew by the hair of his head and bears him in the storm between heaven and earth toward Jerusalem will the Jewish people become ripe to build itself a new destiny.

What is at stake here is not the destiny of the Jewish people alone, Buber asserted, but a new world-feeling to be brought to mankind. The formation of this new world-feeling and the renewal of Judaism are two sides of *one* event. The basic tendencies of Judaism — the striving for unity, deed, and future — are the elements out of which a new world will be constructed. "And so our soul's deepest humanity and our soul's deepest Judaism mean and will the same thing."

In Oskar Epstein's 1910 semester report on the activities of the Prague Bar Kochbans, he described Buber's third speech, on "Judaism and Mankind," as of "surpassing significance for the spiritual development of the Union."

> Buber illuminated the center of the question like a flash of lightning. He said to us simply what we wanted and longed for from our deepest hearts. . . . Not only new, valuable knowledge, but the holy seriousness and the deep yearning for truth in Buber's words has powerfully influenced the spirit of the Union and helped to mold it. We can also say rightly that the fact that the Union has become dear to a man like Martin Buber can fill us with satisfaction and justified pride.

In September 1911 Hans Kohn wrote Buber raising critical questions about whether he had not broadened the boundaries of the Jewish beyond recognition but affirming that for no one more than himself had Buber's "Speeches on Judaism" been a turning point in all his views. In October 1912 Kohn wrote Buber that a cleavage had opened between the three or four older Bar Kochbans who had made Buber's ideas their own and the fifteen new members who had not; he urged Buber to come to Prague in January for the sake of reestablishing a personal continuity with the Union. Buber replied that, despite personal difficulties, he could not refuse such a request and proposed speaking on "Myth in Judaism." He also urged Kohn to get in touch as soon as possible with the Berlin actress Gertrud Eysoldt, who, although neither a Jewess nor of Jewish origin, "can read my legends as no Jewess can." In November 1912 in reply to another letter from Hans Kohn, Buber wrote that the "fullness of time" needs first to be realized through our fulfillment: it is not the time but we that are unfulfilled. The inclination to and demand for a Jewish existence in Palestine is the more worthwhile the more it is part of a unified life-connection of the personality and the less it hinders this desire for fulfillment. The most immediately important thing, he wrote

Kohn a week later, is that they help establish those values that characterize the folk religion over those of official Judaism. "We need new life-forms, and they can only arise out of the dominance of those values," a hint of which Buber felt he had given in the two sections on *Kavana* ("Intention") and *Shiflut* ("Humility") in "The Life of the Hasidim" section of *The Legend of the Baal-Shem.*

In 1912 the German-Jewish novelist and playwright Arnold Zweig told Buber that it was thanks to his "Speeches on Judaism" that he could again return to the Jewish problem, and in 1913 he wrote him that "the coming Judaism will be so much the more vital and essential the more it incorporates the ideas that your books . . . pour forth toward it." In June 1913 Max Brod, Franz Kafka's closest friend and himself a distinguished writer and novelist, raised an important critical question with Buber about the mystical element in his "Speeches on Judaism":

> In your presentation ecstasy always has a somewhat strictly ego-centric character. But to me it does not seem sufficient for life in fulfillment that the world be redeemed *in me;* rather it must also be redeemed in itself: I miss the Messiah-idea, the turning to the general redemption.

The German-Jewish poet Ludwig Strauss, later to become Buber's son-in-law, wrote Buber in 1913 that his "Speeches on Judaism" had become for him *the* expression of his Judaism:

> The hours in which I doubt myself and my Judaism turn into an embittered doubt of your strength and your work. And the hours in which I am firm before my goal are full of an overflowing thankfulness to you.

In 1916 Ludwig Strauss wrote Buber in response to *Vom Geist des Judentums,* the second set of three "Speeches on Judaism," that the message of this book had influenced the atmosphere of their lives so much that even a young Jew who did not know it would receive something of its glance of freedom just as the intellectual youth of Germany were influenced by the spirit of Nietzsche often without knowing his works well.

Franz Kafka, who was on the fringes of the Bar Kochba group through his close friendship with Brod, Bergmann, and Felix Weltsch, wrote his fiancée Felice Bauer in January 1913 that he was reluctantly leaving his home to attend an evening in which Buber spoke on Jewish myth for the Bar Kochba festive evening. "I have already heard him, he makes a desolate impression on me, everything that he says lacks something," he wrote Felice, adding that Buber certainly knew a good deal and had "edited Chinese ghost and love stories which, so far as I know them, are splendid." Three days later Kafka wrote Felice: "Yesterday I also spoke with Buber [whom in fact he had gone to see in Berlin twice in 1911, as Buber later revealed] who is personally fresh and simple and significant and seems to have nothing to do with the lukewarm things that he has written." Meanwhile Felice wrote Kafka that she had bought and read Buber's expensive book of Chinese ghost and love stories and praised Buber's style. Visibly annoyed, Kafka replied that he knew the book only through numerous citations in a review, and he questioned her speaking of Buber's "style." "Aren't they then translations? Or are they meddling adaptations, which makes his books of legends unbearable to me." For anything false in Buber's early writings there could be no finer touchstone than Franz Kafka, whose diamond-hard style and artistic honesty are without comparison. Yet we must take Kafka's depreciation of Buber's "books of legends" in his correspondence with Felice with a grain of salt, not only in view of their relationship but also because of the influence of these very books of legends, particularly *The Tales of Rabbi Nachman,* on Kafka's own writings.

One of the ways in which Buber himself tried to "prepare a highway for the Lord" in the desert of the Diaspora was the attempt to establish a College of Judaism in Germany. At the end of March 1913 he sent out invitations for a meeting for this purpose. Among those invited were Moritz Heimann and Gustav Landauer as well as Leo Hermann and many of his friends from the Prague circle. On May 18 a smaller circle met in Dresden, but the plans went no further. Not until Franz Rosenzweig brought Buber into the leadership of the Freie Jüdische Lehrhaus in Frankfurt ten years later was this dream of Buber's partially realized. But the interchange on this subject between Buber and his friend the Viennese poet and playwright Richard Beer-Hofmann was a significant event in itself.

Early in April 1913 Beer-Hofmann wrote a letter to Buber expressing in all frankness his fear that the proposed college would expose Jews still more cruelly than they already were to the anti-Semitism of the time:

...A Jewish college cannot be a college like any other. It must be exemplary or not exist at all. And do you know — and do all of us — how much of tradition we may regard as living, how much as dead? ...

And then: We stand under other laws of judgment than other peoples. Whether we like it or not — what we Jews do takes place on a stage — our fate has hewn it. The conduct and misconduct of other peoples are taken as a matter of course. All the world may slouch on the seats of the audience and stare at the Jews. Glance, voice, carriage, the color of the hair, the proportions of the body — everything will come under the pronouncement of malicious judges — and woe unto us if we do not stride on the scene as demigods.

And now the students of this college! Here — they will say — Jews have now been educated according to their own ideas, undisturbed by alien influences. Every student will be appraised as a representative Jew. Do you really believe that a stroke of luck such as has never yet been will bring us to this institution every year fifty to sixty Jews who will be equal to the burden of this responsibility? Once again: I fear this college.

Beer-Hofmann's letter to Buber was a fully realistic appraisal of the Germany and Austria of that time. Precisely because this was so, Buber's reply gives us a glimpse in rare depth not merely into the philosopher and Jewish thinker but into the man. It anticipates the Buber who twenty years later was to walk on the stage as leader of the spiritual battle of the German Jews against Nazism.

...You ask whether I know how much of tradition we may regard as living. I do not know, but I begin to sense how much of tradition we will to preserve as living. And I believe that this "will" ... is just as decisive as that "may," yes that it is so decisive that we may err in its service....

And you are again right: all that we Jews do takes place on a stage. But what is fundamentally wrong is that for so long we have let this fact determine our doing and our not doing. The great man too is looked at by the world; if he pays any attention to it, his greatness is threatened in its heart. It is not possible for him to live at one and the same time from his power and from his image — no matter whether it is his image in the eyes of his friends or of his enemies. If God looks at me, I cannot show myself more gently to his glance than when I do not concern myself about it, and if Satan looks at me, I cannot put his glance more fully to shame than when I do not concern myself about it.

In 1913 the Bar Kochba group in Prague set about the task of publishing in common a book that would express the view of their circle. Leo Hermann, who had moved to Berlin, was often together with Buber in the city or at Buber's home in Zehlendorf, a suburb of Berlin (which, after Buber's death, named a street after him) in order to discuss with him alone or with others things concerned with the preparation of the collected book *Vom Judentum*. It was astonishing, Hermann later reported, with what careful, downright jealous love Buber took pains over every detail and how at the same time he was careful not to encroach upon the responsibility of the Bar Kochba and to remain himself only the adviser.

At that time (1913) Buber complained again and again that in Jewish life, and especially in the Zionist movement in Berlin, no places for free and creative expression existed such as he had found with the Bar Kochba group in Prague. Consequently, he and Hermann created the "Free Jewish Club," intended from the outset not to be a purely Zionist organization but to include broader circles, such as Nathan Birnbaum and his friends. It was in the Free Jewish Club on November 5, 1913, that Buber delivered the lecture "Jewish Religiousness" — the second of his second series of speeches on Judaism. But the development of the Club did not satisfy Buber and Hermann, for behind it stood no community.

Buber's second series of "Speeches on Judaism" lacks the dialogical quality of the first. If the first three speeches grew out of the real questions that the Bar Kochbans brought to Buber, the second three seem more like attempts on Buber's part to bring together his own wide-ranging thought into some meaningful synthesis. In "The Spirit of the Orient and Judaism," the first speech of this second series, Hasidism, the Bible, Hinduism, the Tao, Zoroastrianism, the Greeks, Plato, and many other elements are thrown together. The result is speculations, some of which strike us today as prophetic, such as the unique role that the Jew might play as mediator between East and West, and others as fantastic, such as his extension to all of the Orient of what he formerly held to be Jewish characteristics — motor rather than sensory orientation, movement as opposed to image, the sense of hearing as opposed to sight, time as opposed to space, inwardness as opposed to outwardness.

In the midst of these speculations Buber attained new and important insights into the relation between decision, personal wholeness, and man's task of bringing unity to the world. Inner division can be overcome by decision, Buber stated, and decision brings unity not only to the divided individual but to the divided world. He who stands in decision knows nothing else than that he must choose, and even this he knows not with his thinking but with his being. He who decides with his whole soul decides himself to God; for all wholeness is God's image and in each whole being God Himself shines forth. In each genuine, united decision the primal meaning of the world fulfills itself in eternal originality. In the province entrusted to him, the united man completes the work of creation; for each thing's completion, the greatest and the smallest, touches upon the divine. In appearance, the deed is inescapably fixed in the structure of causality, but in truth it works deep and secretly on the fate of the world. When it recollects its divine goal of oneness and cuts itself loose from conditionality, it is free and powerful as the deed of God. This recollection is *teshuva,* turning to God with one's whole existence. When God first planned the world, it is told in the Talmud, he saw that it could not persevere because it had no basis; then he created the turning. From this point onward, *teshuva,* or the turning, becomes the term Buber uses for the renewing revolution in the course of existence for which he called in "The Renewal of Judaism."

There are three stages of realization which can be distinguished in Jewish religiousness. In the first, the biblical stage, it was conceived as an *imitatio Dei.* In the second, the Talmudic stage, the realization of God was conceived as an enhancing of his reality. In the third, Kabbalistic, stage realization was raised to the working of man's action on the fate of God. All three stages, asserted Buber, are united in the conception of the absolute value of the human deed. He who does the deed cannot measure its effect, yet he must say, with the Talmud, "For my sake the world was created" and "Upon me rests the world." What is essential to one's deed is not the What but the How. It is not the content of a deed that makes it truth, but whether it takes place in human conditionality or divine unconditionality. Even "profane" actions are holy if they are performed in holiness, in unconditionality. Unconditionality is the specific religious content of Judaism. Where religiousness is effective in building community, founding religion, where from the life of the individual it enters into the life between persons, then the basic feeling that one thing is needful becomes a demand. In the common life of men, as nowhere else, a formless mass is given us in which we can imprint the face of God. The human community is an important work that awaits us; a chaos that we must order, a disapora that we must gather, a conflict that we must resolve. But we can do this only if each one of us in his place, in the natural realm of his life together with men, does the right, the uniting, the shaping: because God does not want to be believed in, discussed, or defended by man; he wants to be *realized*.

When Franz Rosenzweig reread Buber's "Speeches on Judaism" after they had all been collected in one volume, he wrote to Buber:

> I am amazed to see to what degree you have become the representative speaker and the advocate of our generations, mine as well as the one after me. We may have forgotten this at times in the heat of the battle into which your thoughts dragged us when reading your Lectures for the first time; now that we re-read them with calm, and yet not too objectively but with, so to say, autobiographical excitement, we see clearly that it was our own words to which you were the first to give expression.

An equally moving witness to the influence of Buber's "Speeches on Judaism" over that generation of Jews came thirty years later from Gershom Scholem, the distinguished founder of the science of Jewish mysticism and, at the end of Buber's life, the harshest critic of his interpretations of Hasidism. Around 1913 Buber had immense influence on Jewish youth circles in Germany and Austria, as Scholem testified in an appraisal written on Buber's seventy-fifth birthday.

> We secondary school and university students looked for a way. There was much fervor among us, a great awakening of spirit and readiness to listen to voices of the past and present that reached us. Our sources were few: we knew no Hebrew; the first-hand sources were thus closed to us and the way to them seemed very long. We looked for an interpreter of the phenomenon of Judaism and its heritage. . . . Buber's first books on Hasidism and the "Three Speeches" raised a tremendous echo in our ears. The voice speaking from his books was promising, demanding, fascinating, uncovering hidden life beneath the frozen official forms, uncovering hidden treasures, if only we knew how to get in. His power of expression has always been tremendous, fascinating in its beauty and in its resonance. He demanded attachment to and identification with the core of the people as he understood it, demanded of the youth that they be an additional link in the chain of hidden life, that they be heirs to a sublime and hidden tradition of revolt and uprising.

Particularly attractive to the young Jews of that time, said Scholem, was the strong individualistic, personal, and even anarchic note that characterizes the "Three Speeches." More than any other spokesman of Zionism, Buber went to the heart of the problems of the Jew as an individual. The basic conviction of Buber's Zionism was that the decision of every single individual Jew, made in the depths of his heart, decides the fate of the Jewish nation prior to all political and social facts and slogans. When the destiny of the Zionist movement depended upon its *moral* stance, Buber's words had widespread influence. Already in 1913 Gustav Landauer called Buber "the ambassador of Judaism to the nations."

"I know of no other book about Judaism during those years that even approaches the influence" of Buber's *Speeches on Judaism,* Scholem wrote after Buber's death in a comprehensive essay on Buber's conception of Judaism. No one performed greater service than Buber in making visible again precisely those traits in Judaism which were most lacking, indeed, were actively rejected in nineteenth-century Judaism — mysticism and myth. Buber's work on the Hasidic tradition moved between these poles of mysticism and myth. "Buber was a great listener. Many voices pressed toward him, among them ones which had become entirely incomprehensible to the generations before him, voices whose call moved him deeply." Buber sought the mysticism in Judaism and therefore was in the position to perceive it when it arose before him. "What moved him in the Hasidic world for many long years was its mysticism." The first scholarly publication of Buber's and Feiwel's Jüdischer Verlag in 1904 was a little book, *Hasidism: A Study of Jewish Mysticism,* by Professor Solomon Schechter of the Jewish Theological Seminary of America, himself a descendant of the Hasidim. "Buber was the first Jewish thinker," wrote Scholem, "who saw in mysticism a basic trait and continuing strain of Judaism."

The tremendous appeal of the "Speeches on Judaism" was not so much a mystical as an existential one — their personal appeal to the Jew as an individual to decide to join his people — and it was precisely this existential appeal which spread from Bohemia to Galicia to Hungary. "Buber's real influence started with the Speeches," writes Ernst Simon. Buber was a middleman addressing others who also stood between Eastern and Western Jewry, between the masses of traditional Jews and deteriorating Judaism, between a continuous heritage and the loss of all traditional values. What made the Bar Kochba Union in Prague and the youth movement of Hashomer Hatzair in Galicia Buber's ardent followers was that he offered them direction at a time when they found themselves in the midst of three crises — the European crisis of the approaching world war, the crisis of the Jewish nation in the face of the pogroms of Eastern Europe and the intermarriage and assimilation of the West, and the crisis of the modern personality which even then lacked guidance and a definite way of life.

Hugo Bergmann, looking back from the distance of a quarter of a century, found, along with all of its enormous educational impact, a serious flaw in the center of Buber's "Three Speeches on Judaism" with their distinction between "official" and "underground" Judaism. This distinction enabled many young men of the time to shirk the difficult task of going back to the original Hebrew sources, Bergmann claimed, and made Buber's call to renewal of the deed an essentially literary experience. "In the spiritual air of unreality in which we breathed at that time, it had to be thus," Bergmann confessed for his generation. "This was the great spiritual danger of the period before the war. Only through the war was the generation to which the Three Speeches were addressed confronted by reality."

PART IV

The Prophet of "Realization"

(1911-1913)

CHAPTER 8

Realization:
The Kingdom of Holy Insecurity

IN THE COURSE OF HIS EVALUATION of Buber's impact on the young men of that period, Gershom Scholem pointed out that it was Buber's book *Daniel* (1913) that supplied the philosophical background for the emphasis on "realization" in the "Speeches on Judaism." *Daniel* is in no sense a Jewish work, much less a Zionist one. Yet the connection between this first work of general philosophy on Buber's part and his philosophy of Judaism is unmistakable. In 1911 Buber read parts of the unpublished manuscript of *Daniel* to the students of the Bar Kochba Union in Prague. The contrast between "orienting" and "realizing" that stands at the heart of *Daniel* had almost a more lasting effect on the world view of the Bar Kochbans of that time than did Buber's Jewish writings. There is little in *Daniel* to make the reader feel that the author is a Jew. Yet Buber's devoted study of Hasidism and his writings on Judaism influenced *Daniel* just as *Daniel* influenced the later "Speeches on Judaism." Both the "Speeches on Judaism" and *Daniel* deal with the problems of decision and of the unity which is man's task, as well as with the idea of the deed and the future.

Daniel was written in Buber's second period of fame, Ernst Simon points out, his first being the period of *The Tales of Rabbi Nachman* and *The Legend of the Baal-Shem*. From this point onward, Buber's influence developed in two separate streams which had a common origin but were distinct along most of the way — that of his Jewish writings and that of his general philosophy. *Daniel* is the real fountainhead of the second stream, not only anticipating the later developments of Buber's philosophy of dialogue but also many developments in existentialism in general. *Daniel* was a hard-won and crucial step toward that philosophy of dialogue through which, in its many ramifications, Buber was to exercise his most profound, widespread, and lasting influence.

The significance of *Daniel* is best comprehended in the formula that Buber himself used so often in the book — "holy insecurity." Along with the "narrow ridge," "holy insecurity" remained the most important single motif in Buber's writings throughout his more than sixty years of productivity. Like Kierkegaard's *Angst*, what is significant about Buber's "holy insecurity" is not the insecurity itself but the response to it: the willingness to meet it in openness and trust and to answer it with one's life, as opposed to all attempts to guard oneself from it or to reduce it to manageable proportions. Nonetheless, we cannot adequately appreciate the significance of this term for Buber's life and thought if we do not first look at the "insecurity" itself. This we have already done in part in our discussion of the impact on Buber as a child of the sudden disappearance of his mother and the impact on the fourteen-year-old of the threat of infinity. Between these two there occurred another event that illuminates Buber's concern with insecurity — his experience with two of his fellow pupils in the Polish gymnasium.

One autumn, when Buber was twelve years old, was spoiled for the pupils by incessant rain. Instead of rushing to the square outside to play during the recesses, they had to sit at their benches. At this time two of the boys undertook to entertain the other boys as mimics, with clownlike agility, trying their best to remain straight-faced to avoid being seen by the master. After a while, however, this game took on an unmistakably sexual character, and now the faces of the two boys looked like the faces of the damned souls being tormented in hell, which his Catholic schoolmates had described to Buber as if they were experts on the subject. The other boys looked on but said nothing to one another about these occurrences. About two weeks after the game had taken on this character, the master called the young Buber to his office.

"Tell me what you know of what those boys have been doing," he said with the gentle friendliness that the pupils knew to be an essential part of his nature.

"I know nothing!" Martin screamed.

The master spoke again as gently as before. "We know you well," he said, "you are a good child — you will help us."

"Help? Help whom?" the young Buber wanted to reply. But instead he stared silently at the director. Finally a great weeping overcame him such as he had never experienced before, and he was led away almost unconscious. Yet a few hours later when he re-called at home the last look of the director, it was not a gentle, but a frightened one.

He was kept at home for a few days, and then he returned to school. When he came into the classroom, he found that the bench where the two boys had always sat was empty. It remained empty until the end of the school year.

It was many years before Buber understood the full ethical implications of this event and could formulate the lesson that it taught him: that the true norm commands not our obedience but ourselves. But even at that time he began to realize "the prob-lematic relation between maxim and situation" — the shattering of the security which the simple childhood norms of obedience to authority had given him until then. When he wanted to shout "Help? Help whom?" he was aware, as the master was not, of the suffering of the two boys and of the impossibility of his accepting the bribe of being "a good child" who "will help us" in return for betraying them. He also must have known the confusion and pain that he and the other boys experienced who looked on without speaking of it, vicariously taking part in something that they would not have dared to do themselves. Most important of all, he began to realize at that moment the choice that had to be made between finding security in the once-for-all of general moral norms — to be a good child, obeying authority — and living with the insecurity of being open and responding to the unique and ir-reducible situation to which no general categories could ever do justice. It was with this convulsion of his childhood that Buber began the long series of lessons that led him to understand what it meant to stand one's ground before the situation in openness and strength and to respond to it with trust. An important mile-stone on this road was *Daniel.* *

Each of *Daniel's* five "Dialogues on Realization" has its jumping-off point in a particular setting in which Daniel and one of his friends (a different one in each dialogue) happen to be together. What develops from this conversation in every case is discussion revolving around one particular existential problem. Thus the dia-logue in the mountains deals with personal direction, the dialogue above the city with reality, the dialogue in the garden with meaning, the dialogue after the theater with polarity, and the dialogue by the sea with unity. If we are to retain our focus on the events and meetings which were the matrix of Buber's thought, however, we shall have to approach *Daniel* with a very different ordering: the progression from ecstasy and the isolated "I" through the ex-perience of the abyss to holy insecurity and "inclusion." These are the headings under which we may group the personal experiences that Buber incorporated in *Daniel.*

The sea, the night, and the abyss are various symbols of the threat of the infinite which was so basic in Buber's experience and in his thought. Most often it is the sea that enters these dialogues as a symbol of an incomprehensible infinity that threat-ens man's existence or a motherly infinite with which man de-sires to become one. In the first dialogue, "On Direction," Buber does not stop with the experience of the sea as a hostile infinity, as does Melville in *Moby Dick.* He goes on to make of it an oppo-nent who is no longer terrifying as soon as one has chosen one's own direction from the countless possibilities that lie open to one. In the third dialogue, "On Meaning," Reinold tells Daniel of how the childhood security which he had retained even into manhood was lost one day when he went out on the sea in a small boat and the pleasant lapping of the water was suddenly transformed into horror. In the fifth dialogue, "On Unity," the conversation actual-ly takes place by the sea. Lukas shows Daniel the place where their mutual friend Elias sailed out to sea the year before and fell or stepped from his boat and was drowned. Lukas feels as if he sets sail every morning in the boat of his dead friend in which the demon of life sits at the rudder and the goddess of death in the prow. From day to day the question mounts in him: What sort of

---

* See Note to Chapter 8, p. 390.

a sea is it on which we voyage, what sort of a sea is it that has given birth to us, what is the holy sea that bears life and death in its hands?

Reinold's experience of the abyss in the third dialogue is clearly a continuation of many motifs in Buber's earlier writings — the individual's hopeless solitude and eternal distance from the world, the schism between thought and action, life and spirit, the abysses of being which the creative man must face, and the universal inner duality of man. Yet in sharp contrast to Buber himself, Reinold does not encounter the abyss until he is already well into manhood. Although he applies to his own childhood Daniel's quotation from a Celtic song:

> You do not tarry long wandering
> In the land with the living heart,

he tarried far longer than most:

> Meaning, meaning — the falling stars of the August nights had it not more and not less than the cut-off hair that I saw fall down on me; the narrow, immeasurable horizon of my space and my time was golden-rimmed with meaning. . . . When I awakened out of the music of my dreams into the dark, the night had my mother's arms and even mother-ly words like hers. . . .

For Reinold, until his twenty-third year, the world itself was his sister: as long as she was near him and he was turned to her, nothing could harm him. But at twenty-four he is robbed of all meaning and security by a single encounter with the sea. Like Rabbi Naftali in "The Revelation" in *The Legend of the Baal-Shem,* he is moving forward in complete serenity — "a chorus of southern stars sang down on me; my oar cut dark flood and concealed splendor; boundlessness was the bed of my soul, heaven, night, and sea its cushion" — until he looks up casually — and is terrified. The terror here is not just the threat of the infinite experienced by Pascal, Melville's Ishmael, and the young Buber. It is the encounter with a hostile and malicious Other such as Captain Ahab found in Moby Dick:

> Out of a dumb infinity an army of jack-o'lanterns stared into empty infinity; threateningly, thousands of moist lips, sneering cruelly, opened and closed about me, and in the nape of my neck, dark and tangible as

a betrayal, the presence of the night beings grew. Where the bed of my
soul had been, was the void; seduced, betrayed, rejected, my soul hung
in the grey of the night between sea and heaven.

Like the "Modern Promethean," the first type of rebellion against
the Modern Exile that I describe in my book *Problematic Rebel*,
Reinold affirms his own existence *in spite of* his absurd encounter
with an inhuman infinite: "I steeled myself for battle: 'I am there,
I am there,' I cried, 'and you cannot annihilate me.' " But even
when, with renewed strength, he pulls to the shore he encounters
the same abyss on the land. He sensed the abyss between one seg-
ment of the world and another, between image and thing, between
the world and himself. But he also discovered the abyss within
himself and knew himself forever divided into the thousandfold,
Protean doubleness of the bright One and the dark Other, with the
eternal abyss in between. It was this discovery that shattered his
last security, left the world discordant and disjointed for him,
and deprived him of meaning once and for all.

Reinold's experience clearly was not Buber's. If Reinold at
twenty-four "left the last, fearful hiding place of calm and entered
into the harsh storm that would never end," Buber encountered
the abyss at four and again at twelve and fourteen. Yet there can
be no doubt that in Reinold's experience Buber created a vehicle
for the communication of his own experience. What is more, in
the very contrast between Reinold and himself, Buber underlined
the fact that the collapse of the secure and harmonious world of
childhood would come sooner or later to every person and the
abyss at his feet would suddenly become visible. "All religious
reality," Buber was to state many years later, ". . . comes when
our existence between birth and death becomes incomprehensible
and uncanny, when all security is shattered through the mystery."

In the fifth dialogue of *Daniel* the death of Elias leads Lukas to
a realization that life and death do not alternate with each other
but lie in an endless embrace. In a figure strikingly similar to one
that Meursault uses in Camus's much later novel *The Stranger*,
Lukas speaks of the strange wind that, in contrast to the force of
life that bears him onward, is blowing backward toward him from
his future death. Meursault concludes from this figure that the
present is unreal and life absurd, whereas Lukas realizes that it is
foolish to limit death to any particular moments of ceasing to be
or of transformation. It is an ever-present force and the mother of

being. Out of this realization is born for him the holy insecurity: "This certitude was not unholy; it was, indeed, no feeling of being secure in any certainty but the unarmed trust in the infinite." Now that he no longer sees life as handing him to death like a torch that the hand touches only to fling it onward, he is driven to penetrate behind life and death into the infinite that bears them both.

Daniel tells Lukas in turn of an event out of his own youth. What he describes is the response that Buber himself had at the age of seventeen to the death of an uncle who was killed by a fall from a horse while the horrified boy looked on. "Death laid itself about my neck like a lasso," wrote Buber-Daniel. He felt the presence of death in the world to be his own sin for which he had to do penance. His overwhelming sense of isolation prevented him from sleeping, and his disgust with living prevented him from eating. His family did not understand him, and, supported by friends and physicians, they dismissed what he was going through as a problem of adolescence. Only his father met him with a calm, collected glance so strong that it reached his heart, sealed off from all other perceptions. His father then took matters into his hands and sent the boy off alone into a secluded mountain place. This action saved the young Buber and resulted in an experience so profound that he wrote at thirty-four that he believed that images of the time he lived through then would return to him in his dying hour. Stripped clean of his foolishness, he no longer lost himself in penance but won himself through despair. "For despair . . . is the highest of God's messengers; it trains us to be spirits that can create and decide." Here, in contrast to "The Revelation," it was the divided person himself who overcame the abyss between himself and the world, by overcoming the abyss within himself. When his body became united, the world became one for him. Yet the deep union that he now experienced from life to death, from the living to the dead, was a product of his inner unity rather than of any meeting with the world.

At that moment, Buber claimed, the teaching, the one thing needful, came to him and remained with him so that he sensed its presence in all his wanderings. Yet he was not really aware of it until a later time when, as a result of one moment joining itself to another, he reached the final level of the teaching. Walking along the highway on a gloomy morning, he saw a piece of mica lying on the ground, lifted it up, and looked at it for a long time until the light caught in the stone dispelled the gloom of the day. When he raised his eyes from the mica, he realized that in looking at it the stone and his "I" had been one, beyond all consciousness of "subject" and "object." Closing his eyes, he gathered in his strength, bound himself with his object, and raised the mica into the kingdom of the existing. "There," Buber wrote, "I first felt: *I; there I first was I."* He regarded his earlier unity as the marble statue might perceive the block of stone out of which it was chiseled; it had been the undifferentiated, the amorphous, but his "I" was now unification. This unity cannot be found but only created — by him who realizes the unity of the world in the unity of his soul.

In "Ecstasy and Confession" Buber spoke of the grace of unity which may be kindled through looking at a heap of stones. One is no longer aware of looking at a rock, he wrote; one experiences only unity, the world: oneself. All forces are united and felt as unity, and in the middle of them lives and shines the stone which is contemplated. The soul experiences the unity of the "I" and in it the unity of "I" and the world, no longer a content but that which is infinitely more than all content. This is the unity realized apart from the world, the unity of the nondualist mystic which Daniel later was to describe as one of the wrong ways from which the faithful man turned. Commenting on a similar experience of looking at stone, that of the fragment of mica, Buber said three years later that the only real "I" is the "I" that is produced by the awakening of tension. "Only polarity, only stream, only unification can become 'I.'" Accordingly, in the Introduction to *Die Rede, die Lehre, und das Lied* (1917), Buber explicitly rejected his treatment of unity in "Ecstasy and Confession" for that of the fifth dialogue of *Daniel.*

Buber's reinterpretation of his earlier mystical experience in the light of later experience and thought shows the limitations of any one experience, even a mystical one, in providing a permanently valid knowledge. But it also shows how all previous experience may enter into and remain the material for a growth in wisdom that rejects no earlier stage yet does not remain fixed in any one formulation. It is not, as Buber puts it in this dialogue, that one experience simply joins itself to another and thereby reveals the truth of the first. On the contrary, our interpretation of each successive experience is itself a dialogue with that experience. The truth we receive is the product of this active dialogue

rather than the passive imprint of the experience itself. Thus in
I and Thou (1923) Buber took up the experience of looking at
the mica again only to recognize that the knowledge gained from
the experience was limited:

> O fragment of mica, looking on which I once learned, for the first
> time, that *I* is not something "in me" — with you I was nevertheless
> only bound up in myself; at that time the event took place only in me,
> not between me and you.

Thus the event itself stayed with Buber as a hidden store of potential knowledge, not simply reinterpreted but ever more deeply
understood in the light of new events.

"Holy insecurity" was, for Buber, the decisive transition
between his earlier responses to the threat of infinity — his attempts to find unity either apart from or with the world — and the
existential trust of his philosophy of dialogue which does not demand either continuity or unity but accepts the "graciousness"
of the coming of our meeting with the Thou (for it cannot be
willed) and the "solemn sadness" of its going (for it cannot be
held on to). Buber began, as we have seen, with a whirl of possibilities that threatened to overwhelm him. He did not succumb to
the temptation to dissipate his energies by realizing them all,
but neither did he simply reject them; for "in the world of mankind there is no other beginning than reality." Buber's greatness
lay in his insistence on starting with the chaos as the reality
given to him *and* on transforming this chaos through the discovery
of direction. There are men, says Daniel in the fourth dialogue,
"in whom the existence which has not been worked out longs so
strongly for fulfillment that no illusion lasts for them. They shatter on their contradiction, *or* it becomes creative in them." Not
once, but again and again in his life, Buber was such a man. His
whole life, indeed, may be seen as a replacing of his absent mother
with personal direction. Daniel says precisely this in the first
dialogue:

> The directed soul goes forth to meet the whirlpool, enters into the
> whirlpool. And such is its power that it charms it, magically charms it,
> so that it stands naked in the naked and is not destroyed. Rather it
> rests around the soul, as the sheath around the sword, as the earth
> around the grain of corn, as the mother around the child. And then the
> soul knows its mother's lap.

Although the "between" is not reached in *Daniel* as a whole, any more than in the specific experience with the fragment of mica, it is so far anticipated that in the fourth dialogue, "On Polarity," Buber first uses the term "inclusion" (*Umfassung*) in the sense that later became central to his philosophy. Nor is "inclusion" present only as an idea but as a series of events and meetings — Buber's relation to nature, to people, to drama, and to love.

Buber's experience of inclusion in relation to nature is perhaps the most consistent thread in his entire philosophy. The complete intertwining of sensory and spiritual spontaneity out of the undivided depth of the soul was characteristic of Buber's personality. Already as a child left to himself, his intensive life-experience and an elemental openness to the world supplemented and contended with each other. In his 1901 essay on Boehme, Buber illustrated the "wonderful world-feeling" that we have woven into our innermost experience by the desire that sometimes comes to us (certainly to Buber) to put our arms around a young tree and feel the same surge of life as in ourselves or to read our own most special mystery in the eyes of a dumb animal. In *The Legend of the Baal-Shem*, Buber used the relation to the tree and the animal to illustrate that quality of *living with* the other that takes place *between* oneself and them and not just *within* one. In *Daniel* it is the relation to the tree and not the animal that persists. In the first dialogue, Buber has Daniel distinguish between trying to know a stone pine through comparison and contrast, categories and classifications, and knowing the truth of its being "with all your directed power" so that you "receive the tree, surrender yourself to it."

> Until you feel its bark as your skin and the springing forth of a branch from the trunk like the striving in your muscles; until your feet cleave and grope like roots and your skull arches itself like a light-heavy crown; until you recognize your children in the soft blue cones. . .

Yet Daniel remains enraptured by the *inner* and does not really reach the between: the tree "is transplanted out of the earth of space into the earth of the soul." From being just a tree among trees, it had become for him "the tree of life."

A fuller understanding of inclusion is found in the original Preface to *Daniel* which Buber omitted from later editions yet included in his "Autobiographical Fragments." It is in this preface that Buber first used the word "dialogue" not in the literary and dramatic sense of *Daniel,* most of the "dialogues" of which are really monologues, but in his later sense of a meeting with the other in which one retains one's uniqueness, yet experiences the relationship from the side of the other as well as one's own.

He writes there of a descent during which he had to utilize, without stopping, the late light of a dying day; he stood on the edge of a meadow, now sure of the safe path, and let the twilight settle upon him. Not needing a support yet wishing to find a fixed point for his lingering, he pressed his stick against the trunk of an oak tree. Then he felt his contact with the tree both from his own side where he held the stick and from the other where the stick touched the bark. "At that time dialogue appeared to me; for the speech of man is like that stick," Buber concluded his original Preface to *Daniel.* His elaboration on this experience in his "Autobiographical Fragments" made explicit what was already implicit in the original: that it took him beyond the realm of his contact with nature and made of it an "inclusion" of human beings as well:

> That means: truly directed address. Here, where I am, where ganglia and organs of speech help me to form and to send forth the word, here I "mean" him to whom I send it, I intend him, this one unexchangeable man. But also there where he is, something of me is delegated, something that is not at all substantial in nature like that being-here, rather pure vibration and incomprehensible; that remains there, with him, the man meant by me, and takes part in the receiving of my word. I encompass him to whom I turn.

In the fourth dialogue of *Daniel* Buber uses the word "inclusion" in connection with the polarity of the theater in which actor stands over against actor and the audience stands over against both. With the great play both actors and audience have a single heart in common: they are united in the act of inclusion.

> When on the stage the murdering knife is raised, the heart of this dark being, the audience, palpitates in the knife's point; but it quivers at the same time in the flesh that receives the blow. It joins with the fate that guides the hand of Oedipus, and it lives in the blinded eyes. It swings along with that wave that drives Lear to his madness; it circles in the pain of the king, mad like him.

A being stands over against a counterbeing, expresses its own being, yet at the same time swings across to the opposite pole of the other and suffers his life with him.

Daniel represents a clear continuation of Buber's early interpretation of Hasidism in its emphasis on the immanence of God not as an accomplished fact but as a task. The presence of God must be actualized through our every action. The image of the realizing man in *Daniel,* who "wants only to live this here . . . so completely that it becomes for him reality and message," can be identified with Buber's 1908 image of the Hasid, for whom the character of the action is determined by its dedication, the man who is at home in the world without any special protection and greets God's messengers as trusted friends. The realizing man too knows "summons and sending," receiving what befalls him as a message and doing what is necessary for him as a commission and a demonstration. But he can also be identified with the perfected man of "The Teaching of the Tao," who purifies the world through purifying himself, who is helpful to others through unifying himself, and who renews creation through true action, or "nonaction," the working of the whole being. In "The Teaching of the Tao," as in *Daniel,* the teaching means the realization of unity in genuine fulfilled life, lifting the conditioned into the unconditioned by allowing all that is scattered, fleeting, and fragmentary to grow together to a unity. *Daniel* attempts to move away from the unity of ecstasy above the world toward the unity of existence which is brought about through the inclusion of one's day-by-day life. Yet far from completely rejecting mysticism, Buber explicitly fused it with his existentialism. The motto that Buber set above *Daniel* in the first edition, and later left off, was a sentence from the medieval theologian Scotus Eriugena: "Deus in creature mirabili et ineffabili modo creatur" – In a wonderful and inexpressible way God is created in his creatures.

In *Daniel,* as in the early "Speeches on Judaism," mysticism is fused with myth. Myth becomes the "word" of the realizing man as causality is the "word" of the orienting man. Daniel's view of myth as focusing on the unique value of the present event anticipates in all clarity the directness, mutuality, and presentness of the I-Thou relationship. If orientation installs all happenings in useful formulas and rules, realization relates each event to nothing other than its own content and thereby shapes it into a sign of the eternal. But in Buber's language of this period that means it makes of it a myth. Both in his action and in his knowledge, the man who loves the world is related to the primitive, the myth-creating man:

> As in myth, a significant event of nature or mankind, say the life of a hero, is not registered in a knowable connection but is preserved as something precious and consecrated in itself, adorned with the pride of all the spheres and elevated as a meaningful constellation in the heaven of inward existence; . . . so he who stands in the love of the world does not know a part of a continuity but an event which is fully complete and formed in itself, as a symbol and seal which bears all meaning. This is meaning: the mythical truth of the unconstrained knower.

The myth-creator is the forerunner of the poet. In contrast to the general tendency to regard the lyric as the supreme monologue of the poet, or at most his dialogue with his own soul, Buber saw the lyric poet as standing in the meeting of "I and Thou." "Every lyric work is a dialogue the partner of which speaks in a super-human language: what he says is the poet's secret." Even the epic work, to Buber-Daniel, was a dialogue in which the Fates speak along with the poet and the poet interprets for us their replies.

The fourth dialogue of *Daniel* ends with a praise of the poet that gives to him as central a place in the finding and conveying of life-meaning as one would find in George, Rilke, or Hofmannsthal. If the poet is the messenger of the superpolar God, as Plato saw him, he is no less the messenger of the polar earth. He is Enoch, the legendary biblical figure who walked with God. Every man has to live in a mixture of creation and destruction, rejecting the many things that might arise for him, for the sake of the one thing that he chooses. But this holds true of no one in so full a measure as the poet. His writing is a fire that extinguishes as it moves: "Each word of the poet is single; and yet there lies around each a ring of ungraspable material which represents the sphere of infinite vanishing . . . the track of the dissolving force of fire." The poet bears the antitheses of the spirit, and in him they are fruitful, for he represents the marriage of two great loves: the love of the world and the love of the word: *"To speak the world:* that builds the rainbow bridge from pole to pole." Word and world meet and create in the work of the poet and ground all duality in unity. "But out of each work polarity arises for him anew: renewed. Rejuvenated, sharpened, deepened, it summons him to new deed.

> All poetry is dialogue: because all poetry is the shaping of a polarity.

The unmediated polarity of the soul, that is the lyric situation: out of one of his pairs of opposites the poet has lifted the one pole to the absolute and addresses it, treating himself as the other pole. Or the mediated polarity of the world; that is the epic situation: the poet subordinates his love for the world, and the world ascends while the loving spirit stands over against it as that reconciliation in which even the Fates do not terrify. Or the dramatic: then the poet flings his burning contradiction into the world, and it stands in flames.

"All poetry tends toward drama," Daniel says to Leonhard, because all poetry, even the lyrical and the epic, is a dialogue. But "the drama is pure dialogue; all feeling and all happening have become dialogue in it. It stands on the border of its art and points to that fulfillment and suspension in every other art in which the dialogue is spoken." If Buber attributed a central human significance to the poet in the fourth dialogue of *Daniel,* therefore, it is in the dramatist above all others that this significance reaches its highest intensity and its greatest fulfillment.

Daniel describes to Leonhard how he looked at one of the two protagonists on the stage and saw him as *two* beings: the character and the actor who represented him. The heroic character had a mouth firm as a stone bridge and a knee arched like the knee of kings, whereas the mouth of the actor was stretched like a tightrope and his knee like that of a swimmer. The two stood over against each other as opposite poles, as being and counterbeing, and the actor accomplished his task of "inclusion" precisely through the fact that he did not weaken this polar tension. The great, the genuine actor always stands over against the hero as the simulacrum the deed, the possible the actual. This situation would be poisoned if he sought to weaken the opposition, if he crept after and aped the hero. He does not put on masks but penetrates — surrendering his soul and winning it back again — into the center of his hero and obtains from him the secret of the personal kinesis, the union of meaning and deed peculiar to him. He has the particular voice and gestures of the hero: because he has the element that commands and engenders them. If he becomes angry and screams, the substance belongs to the man he plays, and only to him. He sounds the meaning of anger in himself, and the deed of anger resounds. The false actor, in contrast, fingers the hero with his senses, collects the hero's voice, his mien, his gestures. He explores the world of the doer in order to acquire his material and then constructs out of it a mask.

The spectacle of duality that Daniel saw was like the soil of tragedy that the twenty-four-year-old Buber became aware of when he went into Herzl's chamber and experienced the "grave of right and wrong" in the face of the conflict between two men both of whose positions had to be respected. Out of the dialogue of the protagonists resounded the antiphony of *ananke,* or irrational necessity: "There they stood, the tragic pair, like Creon and Antigone, and had neither right nor wrong, neither guilt nor innocence, had nothing except their being, their polarity, their destiny." Each, as Buber later was to say, "was as he was"; the resources of both were too limited to resolve the tension of their opposition into genuine meeting.

Without any weakening of the inner division between the protagonists, indeed at the very time when that division stood in sharpest relief, the polar world of the agon being enacted on the stage had won for Daniel the shape of a single being, standing over against his We–I as the storm the stillness, the mountain of waves the sandy plain, the contradiction the agreement. Daniel saw the severe light of the footlights as a demarcation which produced space and frame, time and scene, audience and tragedy. *There* stood the two protagonists in the fury of their nature and the fate worked itself out between them, and *here* sat the audience, confirming and strengthening the fate that it perceived and willed. The actors and the audience became one in the act of inclusion, in the dramatic tension of real dialogue.

Behind this unity Daniel discovered one more basic polar tension — that of drama and the theater. Even speech for the actor is only a kind of gesture, and among early peoples there are no words at all for representation but only the dance. The poet is the master of the word who moves the theater and yet himself never really enters it. Behind each word of each actor, even the most masterful, Daniel could hear the gestureless, unaccented word of the poem whose decisive simplicity the theater can only draw out, can only interpret.

"On Polarity, Dialogue after the Theater" leaves us with the question of how the word becomes speech and speech becomes event, of how drama relates to the theater. This question is not really answered in *Daniel* any more than it was in "Three Roles of Novelli." Indeed the earlier essay states the question much more sharply: Is the theater "faithful interpretation" of the drama or the drama mere sketch notes for the theater? Buber did not attain full clarity on this subject until after he had broken through to his "I-Thou" philosophy and had acquired a mature expression of this philosophy in the final version of *I and Thou.* But an important element in Buber's developing understanding of the relation between drama and theater was the work that he did in advising and directing experimental theater productions, first in Hellerau and later in Düsseldorf. This work extended from 1912 or earlier through 1920 or later.

In 1913 Emil Strauss and Martin Buber of the "Thursday Society," Jakob Hegner (later famous as the publisher of Jakob Hegner Verlag), and the great French dramatist Paul Claudel founded a Hellerau Dramatic Union for the production of epical dramatic works. Buber took an active part in the preparation of the festival of plays that celebrated the opening of the Hellerau Playhouse. This festival began in 1913 with a production of Claudel's mystery play *Verkündigung* (The Annunciation), translated by Jakob Hegner from the original *L'Annonce faite à Marie.* Buber worked together with Wolf Dohrn, Alexander von Salzmann, and Emil Strauss on the production. Decisive for Buber was the "movement". that the words create. The father of Violaine is a peasant, and the speech of a peasant is simple, not elevated. It cost Buber infinite pains to inculcate into the actors the new style. Then Claudel himself came and overturned everything, insisting, for example, that the father of Violaine should be portrayed as her godfather. He wanted to impose on the play the style of the Comédie Française. Dohrn, Buber, and Emil Strauss absented themselves from the premier in protest.

"The Space Problem of the Stage," the essay that Buber wrote in 1913 for the "Claudel Program Book," is even today a radical approach to the theater and one that anticipates Buber's philosophy of dialogue and still more his later philosophical anthropology with its emphasis on the two primal movements of "distancing" and "relating." Just as the great actor does not weaken the opposition of the polar tension between himself and the hero he represents, the great play does not weaken the over-againstness of spectacle and audience nor attempt to gain "audience participation" through the abolition of its role as spectator. Buber demanded that the scenic event, like all genuine art, be a synthesis of opposites so that the audience be at once fully involved and observing at a distance, vulnerable and safe. This is not the popular distinction between "appearance" and "reality": the scenic event that is genuine art is reality if anything is. "We are encompassed by it; yet it is an image: we cannot enter into it." This is the paradox of all genuine art that transposes us into the midst of a world which we are incapable of entering. Although we abandon ourselves to it and breathe in its sphere, its essence is withdrawn and inaccessible to us.

The modern stage has succeeded in thoroughly destroying the space sense of the spectator, his sense of distance, "the strongest motive of artistic theatrical effect." It does this when with its "advanced" technique it seeks to create the illusion that the space of the stage is of the same kind as ours. The "illusion-stage" aspires to overcome not only the genuine sense of distance, but also the genuine relation that is possible only through activity. All the details of the modern stage destroy the activity of the audience essential to its part in the polar tension. Instead the spectator gazes "in passive and unimaginative astonishment at the perfected technique of its 'scenic design.' " The ancient stage, with the same optic illumination as the space of the spectator, was thoroughly separated from the spectator through its cultic character. Ancient tragedy was born out of sacrifice perceived as vision, and the ancient stage out of the festive procession celebrating the sacramental destiny of god, demon, or hero. Even when this festive procession celebrated a mythical or historical event, it was never mere memory but also present reality. "The spectator, blown upon by the breath of the chorus, is irresistibly carried away by it through awe before the drama that sacramentally and genuinely *takes place* in this space before him wherein he cannot enter."

The basic demand that drama makes of the stage is for a space that is at once unified and changeable. The enduring of space in the midst of transmutations depends upon distance: a space which is self-enclosed and inaccessibly over against us. For space to be changeable in the midst of unity, on the other hand, its metamorphoses must be supplemented by the activity of our perception. The partial experiments to be attempted by the theater performances at Hellerau grow, Buber asserted, out of the recognition that a diffuse and variable lighting is the only element that can bring flexibility to a basically unified stage.

Under the direction of Louise Dumont, the Düsseldorf Playhouse worked in the 1910s and 1920s toward becoming a German "theater of culture." It edited the periodical *Masken* and worked closely with Gustav Landauer and other creative figures in Germany.

Buber took part in the development of the Düsseldorf Playhouse, as he had in the Hellerau experimental theater, and it was in *Masken* that Buber published in 1925 his mature statement on "Drama and the Theater." The road to *I and Thou* is in part identical with Buber's deepening understanding of the relation between drama and theater.

Buber's preoccupation with drama, "inclusion," and distance and relation at this period was not the only thing that led into his philosophy of dialogue. His concern with direction in the first dialogue of *Daniel* both continued and presaged his lifelong emphasis upon combining passion and direction, turning to God with all the strength of the "evil" urge. It also presaged Buber's important later doctrine of personal direction as one's unique path to God through which one fulfills the task to which one is called in one's creation. Direction is neither destiny nor predestination. It is discovered through openness to the seemingly chance, ever-new, present situation. Here is its relation to holy insecurity and to inclusion. For direction is not some fixed goal which excludes the other but a pointing: "It does not know where north is; rather its north is there where it points." Direction is also "the flowering cross of community" — the direction to the other "which pulls me up in the morning and drives me into the wilderness, which visits me at midday and sends me to the living, which takes my hand at evening and leads me to God — the high Lord of my all-solitude."

Only the combination of direction with polarity led Buber to Daniel's full teaching of realized unity. This is not the polarity of good and evil or of any external valuation, but of being and counterbeing — "the free polarity of the human spirit." In human life, as in drama, all high excitement has its origin in a polarity which is to be lived, realized. Polarity as task and realization is the positive content of the holy insecurity which is attained after the discovery of the abyss. Therefore, one must love danger; for one has no security in the world but one has direction and meaning and with them God, the risking God, who is near at all times.

This "risking God" is still the becoming God who is made real in man rather than the "eternal Thou" whom man can meet in lived partnership of existence. As a result, the specific form that "holy insecurity" took in *Daniel* — the doctrine of God's becoming through man's realization of him in all things — is closer to the later works of Rilke and even of Martin Heidegger ("Man is the shepherd of Being") than to Buber's own mature thought. The statement at the end of the third dialogue — "You must descend ever anew into the transforming abyss, risk your soul ever anew, ever anew dedicated to the holy insecurity" — would hold good for all of Buber's thought from this time on. But the earlier statement in this same dialogue — that "God cannot realize himself in man otherwise than as the innermost presence of a life-experience, and . . . therefore it is not the same, but ever the new, the uttermost, the god of this life-experience" — would not. "This is the kingdom of God," Daniel says to Reinold: "the kingdom of danger and of risk, of eternal beginning and of eternal becoming, of opened spirit and of deep realization, the kingdom of holy insecurity."*

Buber later rejected this teaching as still belonging to the "easy word." Yet much in *Daniel* was seminal for Buber's later thought. Daniel recognizes that the individual cannot, any more than the community, always live in direct contact with reality: hours of orientation must follow hours of realization. In this respect *Daniel* forms a clear transition to the alternation between the I–Thou relationship and the I–It relation that lies at the heart of *I and Thou*. As in *I and Thou* authentic existence and redemption mean bringing ever greater provinces of It into the Thou, so in *Daniel* mature orientation is included as a dependent and serving function in the creativity of the creative person. As Buber recognized in *I and Thou* that the accumulation of the world of It makes it ever more difficult to permeate it with the immediacy of Thou, so in *Daniel* he recognized that the task of realization is more difficult than ever before, for in our age orientation predominates as at no earlier time. Although the domination of orientation is linked with the progress of science and of "objective" information about the world, this progress is not repudiated as evil in itself. What is evil is that when confronted by the irrational, people simply become anxious: instead of receiving it into life-experience with the whole strength of the moment, they try to attain a once-for-all security, a solid general truth that will enable them to orient themselves without making their existence real. So they build their ark and name it *Weltanschauung* and seal up with pitch not only its cracks but also its windows in order to shut out the waters of the living world. The thousand petty means of life have each of

---

* See Note A in Sources for Chapter 8, p. 392.

them taken on the features of ends in themselves so that man no longer has a true goal but is ruled by his instruments. Human life, as a result, becomes impersonal and indirect, and realization is replaced by appearance and imitation.

In many of its motifs, dialogue is clearly incipient in *Daniel*. In talking of realization as fulfilled unification, Daniel says that nothing individual is real in itself, that the mystery of reality is communion, that what is actual is actual because it shares in the real. "A something is not real *for* him, but *with* him." Even the I-Thou relationship is explicitly anticipated when Daniel urges the troubled Reinold to speak freely, for, "So long as one is in the calm of his becoming, the Thou that he bears in himself may be enough for him. But when the flood comes to him, then his need and summons is to find the Thou to whom he can speak in the world." The need for the decision of the whole being that is central to the second part of *I and Thou* is also stressed in *Daniel:* "Every doer must, knowingly or unknowingly, reject the many that might arise through him for the sake of the one thing that he chooses."

The essay which more than any other stands as the transitional stage between *Daniel* and *I and Thou* is "With a Monist" (1914). In "With a Monist" we find again the realizing of *Daniel,* the person who sees reality not as a fixed condition but as a greatness which can be enhanced, the person who does not want to remove the world of the senses but wants to intensify it, the person who establishes unity in the world of experienced unity, for "unity is not a property of the world but its task." Now, however, the orienting and realizing aspects of life no longer apply merely to the person himself but to that person's relation to what meets him. The "I" that exists through the "shoreless becoming of the deed" is no isolated self. On the contrary, it is the self that comes into being in its mutual contact with the unique reality that it meets. The world is no longer displaced into the soul, as Daniel did with the stone pine and the piece of mica. It is *met* in its incomprehensible but nonetheless encounterable otherness. I give reality to my world "by bending over the experienced thing with fervor and with power and by melting the shell of passivity with the fire of my being until the confronting, the shaping, the bestowing side of things springs up to meet me and embraces me."

If Daniel's task of creating unity out of duality was one stepping-stone for Buber to the life of dialogue, the immediacy between person and person was another. Only the two together could reveal the full meaning of the insight that Buber attained at the end of *Daniel:* "Human life cannot escape the conditioned. But the unconditioned stands ineffaceably inscribed in the heart of the world." Love, as much as drama, was the origin of Buber's understanding of "inclusion." "The love in which a genuinely present man embraces the creatures, so that he may live, remaining with himself in perfect power, the whistle of the tramp on his lips and the look of the fool in his eyes and, before he takes the poisoned drink, lament like Socrates the beautiful hair that the young Phaedo will sacrifice in mourning for him." But it is the love between a man and a woman that Buber had in mind when he justified his use of the word "inclusion" by referring to "the loving man . . . who has a living experience not only of his struggling desire but also of the blossoming beloved and includes what is opposite him as primally his own."

In an article on Buber written just after the publication of *Daniel,* Buber's friend Gustav Landauer referred to him as a thinker who married abstraction not with reason but with feeling. "As Buber is the apostle of Judaism before mankind," declared Landauer, "so he will be the awakener and spokesman of the specifically feminine thinking without which no renewal and revivification will come to our finished and sunken culture." Only when all abstract thinking has been immersed in the deep ground of feeling will deed grow from our thought, genuine life out of our logical desert. Women will come, are already coming, who will sing in accord with Buber's thought-music. Buber took exception to this statement, perhaps because he saw it as attributing to him an unduly feminine cast of mind or style of writing, rather than as a recognition of the essential feminine side of every human being. "I did not ascribe feminine thinking to you but the gift to awaken feminine thinking," Landauer protested. Buber replied: "The duality of the masculine and the feminine belong, I feel, to the tensions which are spoken of in the last dialogue of *Daniel.* In spirit this tension is formed together. The genuinely thinking man must live through the feminine, the genuinely thinking woman the masculine; each must find therein the counterpole to his own in order to allow the unity of the spiritual life to develop from both. That I mean by that no blurring of opposites and no neutralization, you know. But most forms of manifestation of sexual thought are only forestages and presuppositions of the spirit."

"You could not have corroborated my opinion more strongly," retorted Landauer. "Therefore, we do not yet have any true masculine thought because feminine thought does not yet have its strong share."

Landauer anticipated by a half century the women's liberation movement. He refused to take part with Buber in the founding of a college unless women were included in the student body, and Buber went along with this radical stance, yet Landauer's views on feminine thought boomeranged ironically in his relationship with the Bubers. Landauer had urged Buber to encourage Paula to do writing of her own, and shortly after this last interchange, Paula did, in fact, publish her first book of stories, *The Illegitimate Children of Adam* — under a masculine pseudonym, Georg Munk. Buber confided to Landauer who the author of the stories really was, and Landauer made the mistake of mentioning this at a party at the Bubers', an indiscretion for which Paula Buber never forgave him. No doubt his pleasure in Paula's creativity and his desire to communicate it were entirely in accord with his theories about feminine thought but not with Paula's personal preferences. "My wife has the uncommon, intensive, and steady wish," Buber wrote him, "not to see her relationships to persons and to human society in general influenced by literary activities." This breach Landauer tried to heal through a letter to Buber. "I believe that I have discretion in my blood," wrote Landauer, "but I also have something else: . . . wrestling for wholeness in friendship." He pointed out that Buber had revealed to him Georg Munk's identity freely and with the consent of his wife. "The question is," he continued, using Buber's own concept of inclusion, "whether I also must be discreet in relation to your wife, or whether she will give me permission to include this part of her being when I speak with her." It is not that Landauer wanted to speak with her about her authorship but that he wanted in talking with her to feel that he could really speak to her as whole person to whole person. "Dear, honored Mrs. Buber," Landauer concluded in a touching plea, "please receive in a friendly way these words which particularly and again seek to attain your friendship. The world is very lonely, and breaking through the crusts is a calling that was once given to me and to which I will not become untrue." Martin replied that naturally Landauer did not have to be "discreet" with Paula, but he suggested to Landauer that he erred when he represented to himself the genuine being of women as existing, incomparably more than that of men, in the way of living and not in *what* they did; for this was true of men and women alike.

When in 1905 Buber began to edit his series *Die Gesellschaft* (Society) he planned to write one himself on sex. In a letter to Hugo von Hofmannsthal he described his intention as "a deduction of the interhuman" at whose center would be the sexual problem. The announcement of this projected volume appears in the earlier volumes of the series and then drops out in favor of *The Erotic* by Lou Andreas-Salomé, whose close friendship with Nietzsche, Rilke, Freud, and many other men made her much better qualified for this task. Buber had come to know Lou Salomé through her essay "Der Mensch als Weib" (The Human Being as Woman), about which he wrote to Lou in a letter of 1906: "Every subject, it seems to me, possesses, if, at any time, then surely in ours, a single human mind that is there to present it and express its essence. In my eyes, such a relation obtains between this subject and you." It was then that Buber requested an essay from Lou on "The Erotic" for his series on "Society." Three years later, after she wrote it, Buber called it "an essential, pure, strong work" in contrast to which Rudolph Binion, the biographer of *Frau Lou,* writes: "The tone, incantatory and carnal churchly, was that of a high priestess of Eros, even as the diction, in its poetic density, was just this side of sibylline sing-song."

In 1910 Lou timed a trip to Berlin so as to meet Buber, with whom she struck up a friendship based on mutual esteem. "How alike we think about 'experience,' about idealization as realization, about polarity as the point of departure for experiencing unity!" she once exclaimed, obviously in response to Buber's sharing with her his thoughts or his unpublished chapters of *Daniel.* Binion suggests that Lou had influence on Buber's psychological thought and that she tried to teach him something about psychoanalysis, probably through sharing her own essays on the subject. It was in this same period (1911) that the psychoanalyst Poul Bjerre, to whom Buber later became close in the 1914 "Forte Circle," introduced Lou to Freud at a psychoanalytical congress, and Lou soon became a good friend of Freud's. When Buber proposed to write a critical book on Freud, Lou dissuaded him on the grounds that the young movement of psychoanalysis was just establishing itself. Buber went on sending Lou his books, and she attended at least one of his lectures in Berlin.

"Every man fell in love with her," Buber once said of Lou

Salomé, "but I didn't." Lou always dropped in on important men entirely without ceremony in order to make their acquaintance, with the visits usually ending in declarations of love. It happened thus, Buber recounted, with Constantin Brunner, a philosopher and writer who had a considerable following in Germany during the first two decades of this century. When Lou drove away after visiting Brunner, she was overtaken at a train station in Berlin by a telegram which read: "I love you in all three faculties," referring to the central concept in his book *Die Geistigen und das Volk.* Twenty years later Buber became angry at Lou for the unjust way in which she wrote of her first husband Andreas in her memoirs.

In July 1912 Buber sent to Landauer the first dialogue of *Daniel,* "On Direction," and Landauer responded with enthusiasm and the highest praise. In a paragraph which he repeated and expanded in his 1913 article on Buber, Landauer said to Buber: "You have attained with this work . . . what Nietzsche did not attain with Zarathustra and Dithyrambics." In Nietzsche's works, he explained, there always appear side by side the subject of the discussion and then a person who reveals strong emotion over this subject. In *Daniel,* in contrast, the subject of the speech and the person speaking are inseparable. This comparison with Buber's beloved *Zarathustra* could not fail to encourage Buber, who wrote Landauer that his words had given him more than he could say at that time. "It is for me as if what I have thought and written only now attained its full life since it received this blessing from the mouth of a friend."

Landauer's reaction to the second dialogue, "On Reality," was more critical. "You must still do something for it," he wrote, "so that we readers can feel more strongly, directly, and more from the beginning what 'orienting' is. You must give us more concreteness, visibility, vitality. We are agreed, are we not, that if one remains in abstractions one will not escape from the world of 'orienting.' I still miss their penetration and force. You must bear in mind how long all these things have lived in you and how much your earlier thought bequeaths feeling and content to your present thought."

A still more significant criticism was evoked by Landauer's reading of the fourth dialogue, "On Polarity." "On the whole and in many particulars, your dialogue spoke to me truly and beautifully," wrote Landauer, "but . . . here and there there is only a murky vague feeling coupled with efforts to make finished terminology living in itself. It is a tendency of your spirit that I have often pointed out to you already: You work up something in yourself until it has a certain roundness and compactness, but you do not share the means that you took to reach this conclusion. Here now in this dialogue there is the peculiar fact that Daniel does nothing else at all than to tell of the way that he has gone (in a wonderfully beautiful, ever more intense structure); yet in the description of the way, there is, for my understanding, too little chaos, too little passion of struggling, questioning, forming, too much terminology, finish, and compactness. You must not content yourself with beholding the results within yourself, artistically yet composedly, and transcribing them from your soul. You must compel us in a stronger and more living fashion."

Without any question the criticism of this older man whom Buber looked up to, and who spoke his opinions with honesty and love, must have had a great salutary influence on Buber in weaning him away from abstraction, vague emotion, and the "easy word," to ever-greater concreteness and solidity. Buber's being, suggested Landauer in his article, is a mixture of a tender, melancholy-pathetic nature, the genuineness of which cannot be doubted, a carefully nourished culture, and a talent for beautiful expression, for happy analogy, and for thoughtful, symmetrical speech. One gives oneself to the music of Buber's language; one is magically captivated and dissolved in it — and just thereby falls into the danger of being left with nothing else than impression and afterimage, rhythm and feeling.

However much Buber saw *Daniel* as the "final teaching," Landauer did not. We honor best this productive force, said Landauer, when we see all that has been attained as a beginning and a promise. We thank Buber best if we say to him: You are one on whom we may place demands. We shall not compare you with others but with yourself. We can approach an uncommon nature like that of Buber with the demand, even, that he might let us taste now and again something wholly ordinary, wholly earthly. For truly, no one can and should always speak out of the depths. There are passages in his dialogues where an incongruity exists between the clear beauty of the language and the depths of the life-experience, which demands to be rough and gnarled rather than beautiful and even. When despair is talked about in the last and most significant dialogue of *Daniel,* we long for more agitation, more volcanic and even common expression. Martin Buber is an uncompromising and not easily satisfied man, Landauer concluded. We ought not to bestow any applause on him of which he would be ashamed.

At this very time Buber complained to his young friend Rappeport that the latter did not write with sufficient directness and imagery.

> And directness, my dear friend, is the language in which we have to speak of these things and above all to those whom we want to instruct and educate. The age swarms with concepts, but what counts is not concepts (Begriff) but grasp (Griff), and we living and witnessing ones are obliged to speak thus. I say that out of innermost self-experience: before I wrote *Daniel* (of which you have read a section), and I will not be more gentle with those persons with whom I am concerned than with myself.

One could wish in reading *Daniel* that Buber had applied his advice to Rappeport more stringently to his own writing!

Buber sent *Daniel* to the distinguished German poet Karl Wolfskehl with a letter indicating that he saw it as his true beginning and that, although he cast it into the vortex of the public, it was intended as personal speech for only a few persons, among whom Wolfskehl belonged. Hugo Bergmann, to whom Buber also sent *Daniel,* in a long, appreciative, but critical letter expressed his difficulty with "realization" without content. Lou Andreas-Salomé wrote that she had spent many restful days in May between trees and in the sun letting *Daniel* speak to her of what was important and alive. But she added that Buber's voice came to her still more directly when it was not artistically divided into two different tones by the form of dialogue. Martin's father Carl wrote him that if the world recognized a part of what Landauer wrote about him in his essay, he could be satisfied and expressed joy and happiness at his success. But he confessed that he had tried but failed to understand *Daniel* and voiced a fear that Martin was overstraining himself with such great spiritual and intellectual work.

Though *Daniel* is still of genuine value both as literature and as philosophy, some of it is definitely dated — in thought, spirit, and style. There is much in *Daniel* that is beclouded with aesthetic language and a very special and subjective mystical emotion. We can see this particularly clearly by comparing *Daniel* with *I and Thou,* in which many similar concepts are expressed in much clearer form and illustrated in terms of much more universal experience, while the language has gained in beauty and force. For many years Buber refused to permit the publication of an English translation of *Daniel* on the grounds that it did not represent his mature thought and thus might mislead his reader. Finally, he consented under the express condition that I should "write an introduction explaining, even at some length, that this is an early book in which there is already expressed the great duality of human life, but only in its cognitive and not yet in its communicative and existential character. *Daniel* is obviously a book of transition to a new kind of thinking and must be characterized as such."

PART V

The First World War

(1914-1918)

CHAPTER 9

The First World War and the
Breakthrough to Dialogue

THE FIRST WORLD WAR made real for people all over the world the abyss that Buber had pointed to in *Daniel*. It shattered every comfortable view of individual life and society, every assumption of progress and enlightenment, every once-for-all meaning and world view. This was especially so for the most sensitive and prescient persons of the age, many of whom, like Buber himself, had anticipated the crisis before it came. But anticipation did not mean that they were prepared to withstand the onslaught of chaos or that they could emerge from the slaughter what they were when they entered it.

Although by no means the most dreadful crisis Buber had to confront (the Nazi Holocaust was still to come), the First World War was the turning point in Buber's life. What happened in those years can only be described as a breakthrough, as Hans Kohn puts it — a breakthrough to dialogue. This breakthrough was so decisive that in his will Buber directed his literary executor not to allow the publication of anything written before 1916 if it had not already been published before his death.

What led up to this breakthrough was a process, beginning shortly before the First World War, in which Buber's experience decisively matured him. This process lasted over eight years and was completed only after the war. All the experiences of being that Buber had during the years 1912-1919 became present to him in growing measure as *one* great experience of faith. By "experience of faith" Buber did not mean a conversion in any ordinary sense nor any specific religious experience or religious ecstasy. On the contrary, he meant something that transcended all experience and seized him as a whole, transporting him in *all* his being, his capacity for thought and reason included. The very validity of this religious totality is witnessed by the fact that nothing separate was given to Buber, that he received no message that he might transmit. "As we reach the meeting with the simple *Thou* on our lips, so with the *Thou* on our lips we leave it and return to the world." As he was to say in *I and Thou*, what he received was not a specific "content" but a Presence, a Presence as power. Of this Presence he could only say that it included the whole fullness of real mutual action, the inexpressible confirmation of meaning, and meaning not in any world "yonder" but here and now, demanding confirmation in this life and in relation with this world. The only description that Buber could give of these experiences of being that converged into a single great experience of faith was just a pointing to this ineffable wholeness that transported him in such a way that, all the doors springing open, the storm blew through all the chambers of his being.

As in *Daniel,* this meaning was clearly linked up with the holy insecurity, the trusting response in confrontation with the abyss. The approach of the first stage of the catastrophe in the exact sense of the term became evident to Buber in the year before the First World War, though again it was only after the end of the war that this gradual realization suddenly exploded into certainty within him. The certainty that he attained was no philosophical conviction or existentialist thesis. It was a question, rather, of the claim of existence itself, a claim which had grown irresistible. The philosophy of dialogue that developed at that time was only the intellectual expression of this claim. Buber realized, of course, that the crisis of Western man did not begin with the First World War. It had already been recognized by Kierkegaard over a century earlier as an unprecedented shaking of the foundations of man as man. "But it is only in our generation that we have seriously begun to occupy ourselves with the fact that in this crisis something begins to be decided that is bound up in the closest manner with a decision about ourselves." Partial explanations, such as Marx's concept of the radical alienation of man through economic and technical revolutions, and Freud's concept of individual neuroses, do not yield an adequate understanding, any more than existentialist analyses. "We must take the injured wholeness of man upon us as a life burden in order to press beyond all that is merely symptomatic, and grasp the true sickness." The true sickness Buber described as "massive decisionlessness," dualism, the radical separation between ideas, ideals, and values and personal existence on which the spirit no longer has any binding claim.

The specific form in which the approaching catastrophe made itself known, of course, was the threat of war. That Buber had some premonition of the crisis is suggested by his statement to Arnold Zweig, in connection with the publication of "With a Monist": "I have now a strong need to contend with the things of the time." At that time, under the initiative of the amazing Dutchman Frederik Van Eeden, a remarkable group came into being that had as its purpose some common front across the nations that might serve in some way to avert the catastrophe. Although the ultimate goal of this group, drawn together by some undefined presentiment of catastrophe, was to make preparations for the establishment of a supranational authority, the original number was only eight — five Germans, two Dutchmen, and one Swede. The great writer and peacemaker Romain Rolland had originally planned to attend but was unable to do so. But he stood in close relation to the spirit of the group and to Van Eeden in particular. Van Eeden himself, a doctor whose writings were respected and cited by Freud, was a rebel against urban life who built himself a cottage in the country and called it "Walden" after Thoreau, and a social reformer and utopian who kept up a vigorous interchange with Upton Sinclair, Gandhi, and Tagore, and at the same time a man of such great personal warmth and understanding that he was able to knit together into one spirit eight remarkable persons, each one of whom was a prominent intellectual and author in his own right. Buber had had contact with Van Eeden as early as 1910 when he had corresponded with him about contributing to *Die Gesellschaft,* and there was a remarkable convergence of their ideas, as Van Eeden pointed out after receiving a copy of *Daniel.* Direction, holy insecurity, and polarity were all anticipated by Van Eeden in his own poetry and thought.

What Buber anticipated from this meeting and how it related to his own developing philosophy is made clear by a circular letter that he sent to the members of the group before it met in Potsdam. The main theme of this letter, as in the second dialogue of *Daniel*, was "direction" — the only power that is able to confront a directionless mankind.

In this age the fictitious rules, said Buber, that which is nourished by opinion and calculation. What is needed is to establish in opposition to it the authority of the real as that which is nourished by world meaning.

The signature of the fictitious is that each wills something different; there is no singleness of purpose. If ten men were to be of one purpose, they could tear the planet out of its path and alter its direction. Direction is truth not in formulas, but in willing. In it alone is there decision and turning.

Commingle the men of the age richest in "spirit," let them discuss the essential questions for weeks, months, and nothing will come of it but "spirit," "spirit," and more "spirit," but no decision. But let some men come together who are of whole will, and let them recognize actively, rising above all formulas, that their wills are one, *the one,* and they will reach decision. This will is the true spirit, the pneuma, that *drives.*

But the work of erecting the real in its authority is not to be regarded merely as another experiment; one cannot try it out at one's pleasure, let it fall, take it up again. Rather, what was begun in this sign and expires in nothingness endangers the ground roots, the deep fruitfulness of the crisis. What does not succeed here destroys. The Antichrist is the Paraclete that has failed.

The men who met at Potsdam were Van Eeden, Buber, Gustav Landauer, Eric Gutkind, Florens Christian Rang, Poul Bjerre, Henri Borel, and Theodor Gustav Norlind. Although "I and Thou" suggests at first glance a relationship of only two people, it was not the one-to-one meetings described in *Daniel* that led Buber to a mature understanding of the life of dialogue but *this group of eight.* The conversations of the group, Buber testified, were marked by an unreserve whose substance and fruitfulness he had scarcely ever experienced so strongly. This reality of group presence and presentness had such an effect on all who took part that the fictitious fell away and every word was an actuality.

It was not like-mindedness but mutual presence that Buber re-

THE FIRST WORLD WAR

membered when he looked back on those days sixteen years later. The circle failed to accomplish its goal of bringing the unity of mankind to authoritative expression at that decisive hour. Yet this did nothing to dim the memory of those three days of strenuous and inward being with one another, without reservation, on the part of eight such different men. The more powerfully divided they were in their opinions, the more truly close they became! From the often impassioned difference of opinions there emerged time and again a new shape of truth, which was not that of one or the other of the disputants but was common to them both. A truth not to be expressed in words but in a pressing of the hand, not conceptual truth but existential truth, a truth of human binding, unity, and communion. It was this reciprocal giving that illuminated the persons in their special beings, unprejudiced, unarbitrary, true to creation. Forty years later in his important anthropological essay "Elements of the Interhuman" Buber again alluded to this meeting as an example of the experience of the interhuman in a dialogue in which several have taken part:

> Without our having agreed beforehand on any sort of modalities for our talk, all the presuppositions of genuine dialogue were fulfilled. From the first hour immediacy reigned between all of us, some of whom had just got to know one another; everyone spoke with an unheard-of unreserve, and clearly not a single one of the participants was in bondage to semblance. In respect of its purpose the meeting must be described as a failure (though even now in my heart it is still not a certainty that it had to be a failure). . . . Nevertheless, in the time that followed, not one of the participants doubted that he shared in a triumph of the interhuman.

In this interhuman reality Van Eeden played a special role. "You did not take an active part in any of the questions at issue," Buber wrote to him, "and yet you were present in each of them by virtue of the trusting kindness of the look with which you regarded each of us. You beheld us with your whole soul. You looked at the one and the other of the disputants not neutrally, no, but joyfully and full of love. You saw with loving clarity the to-each-other in the against-each-other, saw the mysterious growth of the union, saw the new shape of the true rise naked and splendid out of the fervor. Most of all of us you were there with your eyes, not as one who consciously observes but as one who looks on naturally. You entered with your glance into the happenings between us. Your glance lived in the space of the events, and when we met in battle and in the mutual redemption of each other, we met at the same time in the life of your glance. And that helped us."

"How long a time has passed since then, what a time!" Buber wrote in 1930. "How long, friend Van Eeden, we have not seen each other! Yet I have not ceased to see you — to see your seeing. It is thus still something wonderful, therefore, to be really contemporary with another person in the world and in the hiddenness of one's own spirit to be within his."*

After the Potsdam meeting, Van Eeden recorded his impression of Buber in his diary, giving us an invaluable glimpse of Buber as a person when he was in his late thirties: "The slender, fragile, subtle but strong Buber, with his straight look and soft eyes, weak and velvety, yet deep and sharp. The Rabbi, but without the narrow mind, the philosopher, but without the aridity, the scholar but without the self-conceit." It is significant to compare this portrait of softness combined with strength with Landauer's article of a little over a year before with its hint of a determined and uncompromising will making its way through the layers of poetic richness and subjective emotion until it became manifest in the person and in his writings. Still more significant is the comparison of this emerging openness and strength with the picture that Landauer's and Buber's mutual friend Margarete Susman has left us of her first meeting with Buber ten or more years before the Potsdam conference. "I came to know Buber in a private seminar of his teacher Georg Simmel [the great German sociologist and philosopher]," she related, "at a time when he was not yet famous. He was," she recalled, "a young man of the utmost sensitivity. My first impression on looking at this delicately built man was: that is no man, that is pure spirit."

"Pure spirit" Buber certainly was not in the dialogues at Potsdam. He was very much present as the body-and-soul person that he was, and he stood his ground in the give and take with as much force as any of the other disputants of which he spoke. But here, more than in any dialogue recorded in *Daniel,* more even than in the dialogue with the monist, Buber discovered the spirit that is in the "between," in the stern "over-againstness" of two or more truly distinct persons who really meet each other without les-

---

* See Note A in Sources for Chapter 9, p. 394.

sening anything of the distance from which they start out. Not the harmony of Plato's chord but of Heraclitus' bow is what these days taught Buber and with it the possibility of confirming the other even in opposing him. Like-mindedness and difference of opinion became minor, though never blurred or overlooked, in the immediacy between the one participant and the other.

It was at Potsdam that Buber met for the first time the lawyer and former minister Florens Christian Rang, a man whose impact upon Buber was perhaps next in importance only to that of Paula, Gustav Landauer, and Franz Rosenzweig. Yet this friendship began in purest opposition. When the members of the circle came to discuss the composition of the larger group from which public initiative should proceed when they met again, as they planned, in August, Florens Christian Rang, "a man of passionate concentration and powerful love," suggested that too many Jews had been nominated, so that several countries would be represented in an unbalanced fashion by their Jews. Buber's position, of course, was that of a Zionist who wanted the Jews to gather into a community of their own, and he saw this as the most effective way in which his people could share in the building of a stable world peace. From this standpoint, he did not actually disagree with Rang. Yet he felt that the way in which Rang had expressed his objection was unjust. "Obstinate Jew that I am," Buber later wrote, "I protested against the protest." At this point, from being a political discussion, it became a Jewish-Christian dialogue — one of the most remarkable ones, surely, that has ever taken place. Buber came somehow to speak of Jesus and to say that the Jews knew him from within, in the impulses and stirrings of his Jewish being, in a way that remains inaccessible to the peoples submissive to him. "In a way that remains inaccessible to you" — thus he directly addressed the former clergyman. Rang stood up; Buber stood up; each looked into the heart of the other's eyes. "It is gone," Rang said, and before everyone Buber and Rang gave each other the kiss of brotherhood. "The discussion of the situation between Jews and Christians had been transformed into a bond between the Christian and the Jew," Buber later commented. This was a bond that was to last and to grow ever deeper until Rang's death in 1926.*

If the "content" of this dialogue was the interchange between

---

* See Note B in Sources for Chapter 9, p. 395.

Christian and Jew, the heart of it was the dialogue itself — the immediacy between one person and another. Within a month after the Potsdam meeting, Buber took part in another dialogue with a Christian, though in this case one that was as much mismeeting as it was meeting. This dialogue was as decisive for Buber as the one with Rang in leading him to the life of dialogue. The content of the interchange was the relationship between man and God, but the context was the imminent catastrophe — the disintegration of the relationship between person and person.

In May of 1914 Herzl's friend and supporter the Reverend William Hechler came to visit Buber in Zehlendorf, the suburb of Berlin where he lived. He apparently had not seen Buber at close range since the time they rode together on the train in 1898; for he brought with him the manuscript and proofs of Buber's youthful Zionist poem that he had taken with him to the Grand Duke of Baden and then published, without Buber's knowledge, in *Die Welt*. When Buber opened the door to Hechler, he was struck by how aged he was, but also how straight he stood. After the warm mutual greeting, Hechler drew forth from one of the gigantic pockets of his havelock a bundle of papers wrapped in a blue-white cloth. Out of it, first of all, he took Buber's youthful poem, but then a large sheet that he slowly unfolded. It was a graphic representation of the prophecy of Daniel on which he indicated to Buber, as if on a "histomap," the exact point in which they now found themselves. Then he said to Buber: "Dear friend! I come from Athens. I have stood on the spot where Paul spoke to the Athenians of the unknown God. And now I come to say to you that in this year the world war will break out."

What struck Buber most forcibly in Hechler's statement was not so much his prediction itself as the term "world war," which he had never heard before. What kind of a war was it, he asked himself, which embraced the world? He imagined it to himself as something terrible, utterly unlike any previous war that mankind had known. From that hour the presentiment grew in Buber that something ever more monstrous was getting ready to consume history and with it men, a premonition that has proved as true of the generations that followed as Hechler's prophecy of the immediate future.

Hechler stayed a few hours with Martin and Paula Buber. Then Buber accompanied him to the railway station. In order to get there, they first had to go to the end of the small street of the "colony" in which Buber lived and then on a narrow path covered with coal dust, the so-called black path along the railroad tracks. When they had reached the corner where the colony street met this path, Hechler stood still, placed his hand on Buber's shoulder, and said: "Dear friend! We live in a great time. Tell me: Do you believe in God?" It was a while before Buber answered. Then he reassured the old man as best he could that there was no reason to worry about him on that score, and they walked on to the railway station.

When Buber, returning home, again came to that corner where the black path issued into his street, he stood still, forced to ponder deeply the event that had just taken place there. He asked himself now whether he had told the truth, whether he really did "believe" in the God whom Hechler meant. He stood a long time on the corner determined not to go farther before he had found the right answer.

Suddenly in his spirit, there where speech again and again forms itself, there arose, word for word, distinct, without having been formulated by him, this answer:

"If to believe in God means to be able to talk *about* him in the third person, then I do *not* believe in God. But if to believe in him means to be able to talk *to* him, then I do believe in God." After a while new words came: "The God who gives Daniel such foreknowledge of this hour of human history, this hour before the 'world war,' that its fixed place in the march of the ages can be predetermined, is not my God and not God. But the God to whom Daniel prays in his suffering is my God and the God of all."

Buber remained standing for a long while on the corner of the black path and gave himself up to the clarity — now beyond speech — that had begun.

Hechler, of course, was proved right, probably sooner and certainly more terribly than he himself could have imagined. But Buber's rejection of Hechler's God had nothing whatever to do with whether his prediction was right or wrong and would not have even if Buber had not realized later that Hechler's certainty stemmed from a peculiar fusion of the Book of Daniel with the indications of imminent crisis that he had unconsciously picked up in the courts of Europe where he was tutor to many royal families. What Buber rejected was the very form of the apocalyptic itself which forfeited the "holy insecurity" of Buber's *Daniel* for the certain future of the biblical book of the same name. Here we can see in a single event one of the most important origins of three of Buber's central and related contrasts — that between prophetic openness and choice and apocalyptic closedness and certainty, that between unconditional trust in relationship (*emunah*) and faith which begins with a proposition in which one believes (*pistis*), and that between the attempt to comprehend the whole of reality and schematize the mystery (*gnosis*) and the willingness to meet what comes and to go forth from that meeting as one summoned and sent (*devotio*).

We can also see here, as in Buber's childhood experience with the two boys in his gymnasium, the first dawning of a realization that only later became conscious and articulated. For just as Buber did not know when he was twelve of "the problematic relation between maxim and situation" but only of an overwhelming stalemate, so here too, in fact, he was unable to find any really meaningful response that would satisfy him. As Rivka Horwitz has shown, only in an event which took place six months before his Lehrhaus lectures in early 1922 and that he recounted in those lectures did he arrive at the radical assertion of the "eternal Thou," the God who is always met as Thou and cannot be known as an object, the God whom we can speak *to* but not *about*. The above story is related as Buber himself told it because his memory had the faithfulness of the Hasidic "legendary anecdote": it telescoped into one event what actually took place in two events seven years apart, both curiously enough connected with a train (for he found the "answer" in 1921 when riding on a train). Though he did not yet have the language in which to put what he was groping for, his discovery, nonetheless, *began* in that *event* of 1914.

As decisive as was the content of this revelation, equally decisive was its context. The sense of impending catastrophe gave a new depth of meaning to Hechler's question: In the face of the abyss one can say only what one really knows, only that truth with which one is ready to descend into the abyss itself. Buber did not understand the demand that this question placed upon him when he first answered it. Only later, after Hechler left, did he know it as a question addressed to his life itself, a question that could be answered only with his life. This wholehearted turning and decision came two months later in July of 1914 in the event that Buber called a "conversion."

About this time, as we have seen, Buber was given to hours of mystic ecstasy. The illegitimacy of this division of his life into the everyday and a "beyond" where illumination and rapture held without time or sequence was brought home to Buber by "an event of judgment" in which closed lips and an unmoved glance pronounced the sentence. One forenoon after a morning of mystic rapture, Buber had a visit from an unknown young man named Mehé. Buber was friendly toward the young man but, inwardly absorbed by the mystical experience that he had just emerged from, he was not present in spirit. It is not that Buber was indifferent or abstracted in the usual sense. "I did not treat him any more remissly than all his contemporaries who were in the habit of seeking me out about this time of day as an oracle that is ready to listen to reason," Buber noted, pointing out incidentally the humorous role in which he saw himself as the middleman between ancient revelation and modern reason, offering hope to young men who desperately needed it yet could not accept it unless it was couched in intellectual terms not too disquieting to their world views. Wherein then was Buber remiss? He conversed attentively and openly with Mehé and answered the questions which he was asked. But he failed to guess the question that the young man did not put. Two months later one of Mehé's friends came to see Buber and told him of Mehé's death *and* of what his talk with Buber had meant to him. He had come to Buber not casually, but as if borne by destiny, not for a chat but for a decision.

The decision was one of life or death. But not in the sense that many assumed. Mehé did not commit suicide, as some commentators have asserted.* Rather he died at the front in the First World War, as Buber himself wrote me, "out of that kind of despair that may be defined partially as 'no longer opposing one's own death.' " Even in a psychologizing age such as ours, the difference between actual suicide and such despair should be evident. The "something monstrous that was getting ready to consume history and mankind" is the qualitatively different era that began with the First World War, continued with the Second, and outstripped imagination in the Nazi extermination camps, Hiroshima and Nagasaki, and the "Gulag Archipelago." In such situations those who do not fight wholeheartedly against their death will certainly be killed, whereas those who do *might* remain alive. The despair which prevents such wholehearted contending may indeed contribute to

* See Note C in Sources for Chapter 9, p. 396.

one's death, but to equate it with suicide is to reduce the dialogue between person and situation in our time to an intrapsychic monologue and just thereby obscure its terrifying reality.

Buber experienced this event as a judgment and responded to it with a "conversion" which changed his whole life. Buber's feeling of guilt was not based on any illusion of omnipotence, as if he *should* have been able to remove Mehé's despair no matter what. Buber told me that Franz Kafka came to see him several times in Berlin in 1910 and 1911. "He was a really unhappy man," Buber added, but with no slightest look or intonation that might suggest that he felt himself guilty for not being able to lighten Kafka's load of despair. In Mehé's case what made Buber personally guilty in the exact sense in which he himself later defined existential guilt was that he withheld himself, that he did not respond as a whole person to the claim of the situation, that through this withholding he injured the common order of existence which he knew to be the foundation of his own and all existence. This withholding of himself did not arise through any conscious decision or willful detachment but through a habitual way of life which removed him from the everyday to a "spiritual" sphere which had no connection with it. With the best intention in the world and with all the resources that he could muster at that moment, he still was not "there" for Mehé, who had come to him in that hour. It is not that he did not *say* the right thing but that he failed to make real, insofar as it was up to him, the possibility of genuine dialogue that that hour offered. The question that Mehé did not ask was not a philosophical or theological question but one much more basic, the question of trust in existence. And Buber did not hear and answer this question in the only way in which it could be answered — through his full presence. "What do we expect when we are in despair and yet go to a man?" Buber asked of himself later when the lips of the questioner were forever sealed. "Surely," Buber answered himself, "a presence by means of which we are told that nevertheless there is meaning." More than forty years later Buber could speak of himself as one who dealt with problematic persons who had lost the ground under their feet, who had lost their trust — not in this or that person but in existence itself. If that became so, it was only because at this crucial point, Mehé's death came home to Buber as a demand that he change his life, that he practice that asceticism that means the giving up of mystical rapture rather than the things of this world.

He answered this demand with the turning of his whole existence to the meeting with reality met *in* the world and not apart from it.

> Since then I have given up the "religious" which is nothing but the exception, extraction, exaltation, ecstasy; or it has given me up. I possess nothing but the everyday out of which I am never taken. The mystery is no longer disclosed, it has escaped or it has made its dwelling here where everything happens as it happens. I know no fulness but each mortal hour's fulness of claim and responsibility. Though far from being equal to it, yet I know that in the claim I am claimed and may respond in responsibility, and know who speaks and demands a response.

Thus Buber gave up the much more perfect and satisfying fullness of mystic rapture, in which the self experiences no division within or limit without, for the always imperfect fullness of the common world of speech-with-meaning built up through ever-demanding, ever-painful meetings with others. Not expansion of consciousness to the All but awareness of otherness, not universality but uniqueness, not perfection but the unreduced immediacy of the "lived concrete" became Buber's way from this time on.

"Let us believe in man!" These words, with which Buber concluded "With a Monist" just a few months before, were destined to undergo trial by fire during the months and years to come. In contrast to the years before 1914, war and crisis were the "normal" situation for the rest of Buber's long life, and the challenge of this crisis, more than any other, was whether in the midst of it these words could be authenticated and confirmed. If the fruitless attempts at finding a meeting of minds in the face of the crisis did not shatter Buber's trust in men, at the very least they sobered it. On the other hand, the monstrous inhumanity of the war itself turned him more and more to direct meeting with persons and completed that breakthrough from inner realization to the meeting with otherness that began in the "conversion." What this extension of "inclusion" meant for Buber during wartime is shown most clearly in the hymn "To the Contemporary" which he put at the end of his book *Events and Meetings*. "To the Contemporary" is the one essay in the book written after the beginning of the war, and, like Buber's "conversion," it represents a turning *away* from the spiritual life that had formerly absorbed him as well as *toward* the irreducible and far less agreeable concreteness of the reality of the present. Written in autumn of 1914, this "hymn" even today needs no footnote as to what was the "invading power of the contemporary!" to which Buber referred. Beautiful as the language remains, there is something about this hymn that breaks out of any "wonderful world feeling" and ushers in a new soberness and concreteness that finally led Buber to recognize that his early meetings with nature took place *within* himself and not *between* himself and the tree or the fragment of mica.

The "event" behind this essay is sublimely simple as Buber described it. He sat once in the steel-blue solitude of the evening, opened his window, and felt suddenly the full reality of the *moment* as if it were a moon-colored bird that had flown into his window laden with the fearful and the sweet. Mixing his metaphor, Buber pictured the bird as laying "the earth-space of this moment" upon his breast like "a skein of wool." With the moment came the inrush of otherness — he breathed the dreams of far-distant beings, impulses of unknown creatures gathered in his throat, and the elements of many souls mixed in his blood. The present entered into him like a music composed of tension, impulse, and rapture of the living. He withstood the infinity of the moment, but he did not know whether it ruled him or he it; he knew only that it was bound into bodily music. He did not yet know that the call of the contemporary meant the renunciation of a life absorbed in the philosophy and wisdom of the ages. He was still able to close his window and feel himself at one with all time. Now they were again with him, Lao-tzu the Old and the golden Plato, and with them, kindred to them, the whole present. Here is still the all-colored mysticism of "The Altar" in which the ages unite and the timeless is near.

But now the invading power of the contemporary broke in upon Buber with a force that could not be denied. Like a robber-eagle or a cruel fate, it roared through his window and fell upon him: the centuries fled before it, and with them the timeless unity of all the ages. Instead it hurled the earth-space of this moment like a firebrand upon Buber's breast. Out of this firebrand, happenings poured into his blood — the dreadful and inhuman happenings of a war such as mankind had never known before: shrapnel wounds and tetanus, screams and death rattle, and the smile of the mouth above the crushed body. Now Buber could no longer see this present as bound into music or imagine in what heritage of aeons it might find its song. Yet, along with the claim of each hour which he took upon himself in his "conversion," he accepted once and for all the terrible, absurd concreteness of the historical hour in which he lived, and renounced forever the refuge which companionship with the great spirits of the ages had afforded him. As Boehme's ternary of fire is transmuted into the ternary of light, as the rabbi in "The Revelation" sees the fire rising over the body of the praying Baal-Shem and being turned into light, so here Buber sees himself as the sacrificial offering in which fire suffers transformation into light:

> But never again, O moment, O instorming power of the contemporary, never will I bid you go. . . . Rather shall I be prey and fuel to your fire all the moments of my life. Out of your fire light is born, and nowhere does it flash except out of your fire. I am consumed in you, but I am consumed into light.
>   . . . Let the timeless be near where the ages unite; I have found what is greater in the inexorable truth of the moment, which commands to work for tomorrow.
>   These wounds and these cries which you have brought to me, power of the contemporary, these wounds give forth light, these cries preach, and the confused destiny helps the struggling eternity.

Far from setting fire and light in an irreconcilable dualism, Buber came to the realization that only out of fire — the fire of horror and despair, of absurdity and death — could come the "hidden light" of meaning, the meaning of the "lived concrete" which derives not from the exclusion of otherness but from the meeting with it. The war added the real world tension to the inner, freely chosen one, Schaeder rightly observes. It taught Buber the weakness of the creature and the fear of God's judgment. It deepened "cosmic unification" into suffering with one's fellow creatures, the "courage to create" into the power to withstand. Out of all this it transformed the "realization" of *Daniel* into the "over-againstness" of *I and Thou*.

This was not a process that took place all at once, however, but, as Buber himself indicated, over a period of a dozen years. Buber was never a German superpatriot, like Hermann Cohen, the great Neo-Kantian philosopher and leader of German Liberal Jewry, nor is there any evidence that he ever signed any document supporting the Kaiser as some German intellectuals of that time did.*

---

* See Note D in Sources for Chapter 9, p. 396.

On the other hand, he was neither a pacifist nor an anarchist like Gustav Landauer, and during the first year of the war he was not able to maintain Landauer's almost fanatic clarity of opposition. Instead he succumbed at times to seeing the war, despite and even because of its frightfulness, as a chaos from which a new cosmos would emerge. In the first instance, he saw this as a "movement" which would transform Germany and Europe into real community, and in the second, as we shall see, he saw it as an upheaval which might decisively improve the situation of the German and still more the Eastern European Jews.

"I am shaken by what has happened as never before in my life," Buber told Rappeport in August 1914, and in September he wrote him: "The time is exceedingly beautiful with the might of its reality and with its demand on each of us." To Ludwig Strauss, Buber declared in the same month: "For the first time the nations have become wholly real for me." Buber's friend Margarete Susman was far more realistic. Although she granted that some illumination might come out of the darkest and heaviest fate, all that she could experience, she wrote Buber, was "the monstrous compulsion over the human of objective powers that are themselves only human." The letters that Buber received from his Bar Kochba friends who were now scattered over various fronts of the war were still less enthusiastic, and Buber was disappointed by their mood. "Here it is entirely otherwise," he informed Hans Kohn. "Never has the concept 'Volk' become so real for me as during these weeks." The Jews in general shared this feeling, Buber claimed, which led many, including the German-Jewish poets Karl Wolfskehl and Friedrich Gundolf of the Stefan Georg school, to volunteer. Buber expressed his own disappointment in not being found suitable to enter the army. He also told Kohn of joining the Jewish Socialists of Germany to organize a committee for the Eastern Jews in Poland and Russia, whom they hoped to "liberate." The last sentences of Buber's letter unfolded for full view what Landauer later called the *"Kriegsbuber"* (War-Buber):

> For each who wants to spare himself in this time the statement of the Gospel of John is valid: "He who loves his life will lose it."
> ... When we Jews then feel, wholly feel to its core what this means: then we shall no longer need our old motto, *Not by might but by spirit*, since force and spirit shall now become one for us. Incipit vita nova!

Thirty-five years later Buber was to say that those Jews who wanted to effect by might rather than spirit were aping Hitler!

"Tonight cannon shots from the sea awoke me," Buber wrote in a collection of war diaries of artists. "I stood at the window above the primevally silent strand and heard the rolling out of the uncertain distance. I did not know 'what' it was — a battle between German and English ships? — only that it was destruction, far-reaching destruction from all sides, and — purification of the spirit. It tore me out of my limits, bore me into the midst of the conflict, I lived for a moment shattered and *liberated*. And now I feel one thing: that the spirit does not submit to all this patiently, that it means and wills all this as the way to it." "When I go through the streets [of Berlin]," Buber wrote in a second war diary, "I recognize, probably more strongly than I should be able to on the battlefield itself, the threefold present reality: the plowshare, the turned-up earth, and the coming seeds. I see, deep beneath all intentions and actions and infinitely more real than they, the preparation."

Kinesis, movement: thus the Greeks named the transition from the quiescent to the acting force, from being able to be to being. The age of kinesis into which we have entered did not begin with this war; it only became manifest in it. This is the age in which the soul of man no longer stands and stares but rises upward to the highest deed; the age in which the deed of man is no longer confined by many petty aims but wins its freedom and its completion in sacrifice. It is not the name of the value for which the sacrifice is made that is the inner truth of the event but the fact that men are willing to die for it. The divine is made manifest not in their creed but in their devotion.

In these words we find an echo of Buber's formulation of *kavana* in *The Legend of the Baal-Shem:* "It is not the nature of the action that is decisive but its dedication." But now, somehow, a new dualism has entered in where the action itself becomes almost indifferent, the inner attitude all. And in this context such a dualism has sinister implications that Buber himself later became aware of. The same holds for the sentences that immediately follow: "They cast aside the familiar, the safe, the conditioned in order to hurl themselves into the abyss of the unconditioned, and just this, that they do it, is the revelation of the unconditioned Absolute in a time that appears to be abandoned by it. For this reason we have to rejoice in the terror and bitter suffering of these days. It is a fearful grace; it is the grace of a new birth. Even he who condemns the war cannot close his ear to the roar of kinesis. Our cause is that it should swell beyond itself and become the power of new aeons — realization." Here the language of *Daniel* and the "Speeches on Judaism" is used to celebrate movement and change as almost a good in itself, something which must inevitably do the work of the spirit! This was the trial by fire of Buber's early philosophy, and in this trial it was found wanting. The emphasis on realization and unconditionality without the check of the faithful meeting with otherness can lead straight into the hell of the most terrible demonism and celebrate it as if it were a path to the divine. "Tomorrow," Buber added, "we shall have to point to the direction, for direction without kinesis is lame, but kinesis without direction is blind. *After* the war the great task begins. Now the plowshare does its work, but then the upturned earth will receive the seeds that fall into it." Buber's acceptance of movement now and direction later made it impossible that the *kinesis* that he celebrated would ever take on the meaning and decision that he desired. Buber was neither a chauvinist nor a militant German nationalist, but his own philosophy helped to seduce him into an enthusiasm in which even his faithfulness to that philosophy became questionable. The bitter disappointments that followed contributed to Buber's breakthrough to the philosophy of dialogue.

Twenty years later another German existentialist philosopher — Martin Heidegger — tied his philosophy to a German nationalist movement in a remarkably similar way. But in marked contrast to Heidegger, Buber learned one of the deepest lessons of his life from this wedding of his thought with the demonic — a lesson which resulted in a decisive change in Buber's philosophy such as is nowhere evident in Heidegger.

During this period Buber remained in close personal contact with Landauer, who did not share his enthusiasm, as well as in correspondence with the members of the Forte Kreis, the circle of those who met in Potsdam and who had planned, before the war broke out, to reassemble at Forte in Italy. It was not the war alone that prevented the group from meeting again, but also the effect of the war on the members of the group. The national feelings that arose were too strong to enable even as deep a unity as was experienced in Potsdam to prevail. Some members of the group, like Landauer, Frederik Van Eeden, Poul Bjorre, and Romain Rolland (who was unable to come to the first meeting but was planning to come to the subsequent ones), remained quite clear in their opposition to the war. Others, like Eric Gutkind and Florens Christian Rang, became strong German nationalists, a position which Rang wholeheartedly and actively turned away from after the war. Buber remained in between the pacifists and the militants, but with enough faith in the war as "movement" bitterly to resent the characterization of that movement as "mass suggestion" not only by the pacifists but also by the neutrals, such as the Dutch still were at that time. In particular Buber resented an "Open Letter to Our German Friends" that Van Eeden published in September 1914 castigating German intellectuals for abetting the current war psychosis and two circular letters to members of the Forte Kreis.

In a letter of September 1914 to Frederik Van Eeden, Buber combined an attack on the "mass suggestion" label with a repetition, in some part word for word, of what he had said about "movement" and "kinesis" in the war diary. "I propose," he wrote to Van Eeden, "to disregard this thin and empty slogan of 'mass suggestion' in speaking of what has happened and is happening in our time. I can speak of Germany from my own view, as you cannot," he said to the Dutchman. "There is nothing here (unless it be in certain circles that pretend to be representative) of that exaltation that you presuppose; everywhere there is evidence of a composed decisiveness ready for sacrifice. At the core there rules, clear to every unprejudiced glance, not 'suggestion' but a thoroughly autonomous feeling: the unreserved faith in an absolute value to die for, which means the fulfillment of life — in a value which cannot be compared with or measured by any other but exists illimitably and in its own right.

"The fact that an age has kinesis does not mean that this age or even this moment means and intends the *right*. Without kinesis nothing essential can happen, but without its being given a right direction (there is only one), the right cannot happen. To discover the one direction ever anew in the vortex of the whirling world is the magnetic life-experience of the spirit; to manifest it is the spirit's inborn summons." Here Buber spoke in the language of *Daniel,* and in particular of the "Dialogue on Direction." But to Van Eeden, too, as in the war diary, he confessed that the age had not yet found its direction, that it had been caught up by a nameless reality that bears all names — the war. One can die for what one feels but does not yet know, Buber recognized, but one cannot yet live for it. Here too he repeated his hope that the spirit, after or even during the war, would begin to find direction. "God waits in all things as a seed and a possibility of becoming, he will be realized through the fervor with which he is experienced, and he will be involved in the world through the might of movement. The decisive people of an epoch, no matter whether it will be victorious or defeated in battle, is the people with the greatest fervor, the strongest movement: because it brings about the completion of God in the event." (Again Buber was using the language of realizing God in man.) But it cannot begin this before it has found God in itself: before it has found in itself the meaning, the justice, the genuine community. "I see in the heart of this war the kindling of a great turning of which today I cannot yet speak," concluded Buber. "But the World-All directs the lightning."

An explicit indication of what Buber hoped from the war is afforded by a note of September 14, 1914, that he later cited: "The frightful thing that is taking place has for me a three-fold promise: the liberation of the Central European man for public life, the awakening of the Russian man to constructive life, the rescue of the Near East for a semitic regeneration." Only later did he come to the painful recognition of what he did not suspect at the time: that in conformity with the nature of our time and the situation in which it took place, each of these events had of necessity to bring forth a new, difficult problematic. It was, indeed, the *problematic* aspect of the war that, despite Buber's deep concern about preventing it, seemed to have dropped out of sight for Buber during the first months of conflict when the stirring and rising of the nation was more evident than the abyss into which it marched. In this respect Buber differed from Landauer, whose pacifist-anarchist opposition to the war remained unchanged throughout. But the friendship between Landauer and Buber continued in undiminished intensity during this same period, and this meant that Buber's enthusiasm necessarily had to accept the polar tension of Landauer's rejection of the war and the perspective which it afforded. Two days after he wrote his long letter to Van Eeden, Buber wrote to Landauer that he believed their relationship to be anchored so deeply that it could not be shattered and hoped he felt the same. He did not want to write to Landauer concerning their differences, as he had to Van Eeden, but preferred meeting with him either in his house or in Buber's own. "There are many things that I could not write to him that I can say to you. . . . Gutkind reports that you reproach me — like him — with aestheticism. Shall you really thus misunderstand and confuse me with others? I cannot believe it."

When Van Eeden proposed that the members of the circle again write war letters to one another, Landauer objected that this letter writing caused more confusion and agitation than clarity and mollification. What is necessary now, he affirmed in November 1914, is a personal meeting of the original eight. In this spirit Landauer and Buber wrote a joint letter to all the members of the Forte Kreis proposing that there be a two- to three-day meeting between Christmas and New Year, and that it take place only if all eight came. "During the war, in the severest test, we shall in direct togetherness establish whether we are doing justice to the rights of one another and to our *most important task: despite and even because of the differences in our personalities and our thinking, meeting one another in the full openness and hope of genuine mutuality.*" The proposed meeting did not take place, however, and Landauer and Buber resigned from the Forte Kreis in protest.

Before writing the second letter in which he definitively took leave of the Forte Kreis, Landauer went to visit Buber to discuss with him his correspondence with Bjerre, as well as to discuss a plan for communal-educational activity. An illuminating picture of Buber's relation to the war at this time and of Landauer's relation to Buber emerges from Landauer's report of this conversation to his second wife, the poetess Hedwig Lachmann. "My answer to Bjerre cannot be entirely agreeable to him [Buber]," Landauer wrote, "because he feels many of the passages to be aimed at himself too. As well he should. Despite this, I feel toward no one as forbearing and as trustfully expectant as toward him. To me it is really touching how, before, I had to defend Germanness, which he regarded as something not at all essential to Jews, and how, today, Germanness stirs so sensitively in him against his will that he would rule out every distinction between the deeds and sins of individual regimes. He loves everything and acknowledges everything that is rooted in the unconditional; he acknowledges fully and without reservation my complete rejection of the war; but he also finds such an unconditional in the unanimity of the German people, the readiness for death of the young generation, and he brings to it no analysis of any sort and is especially embittered if one speaks of mass suggestion. Thus he must, to be sure, admit the facts elucidated by the author of *J'accuse,* Emile Zola; but that is all 'secondary.' He is especially angry in speaking of Van Eeden, whom he reproaches with coming out onesidedly against Germany but not against the war of the states as such. There is some truth in this. I gather from a Dutch paper that Van Eeden is, in fact, making propaganda in Holland for a military intervention of Holland [against Germany]. But I must confess that I understand Van Eeden's perversity no less than Buber's. Both lack the power of their own aim, otherwise they would not seek in the tradition something to which they can in some way adhere. Both are poetically sensitive spectators, onlookers, oriented to the olden times, whose fantasy has to nourish itself upon great utterance — 'the people arise, the storm breaks forth.' And neither is able to sift the ingenious entanglements of peoples and states so that his insight into the madness of a war without a real object goes beyond his understanding and fills his whole feeling. But that is the essential: all this horror is taking place for nothing."

Two days later Landauer wrote his wife that in contrast to Kurt Hiller, with whom he had politely conversed for some time but who was at the antipodes from him in essential things, it was wholly otherwise with Buber. "I understand and love his ardent passion for the heroic and what still separates us in our judgments of things and men (it is no longer much) is wholly inessential." This depth of understanding and sympathy grew during the war years. Buber joined Landauer in withdrawing from the Forte Kreis, expressing his renunciation "in a manner very dear to me," Landauer wrote to Walter Rathenau, and Landauer joined Buber in the attempt to establish an independent circle in Germany and Austria.

In his correspondence concerning plans for forming educational and communal groups, Landauer often indicated how closely he and Buber worked together. "Buber and I are one concerning the essence that we wish to call into life," Landauer said, "and therefore when we are together although we discuss many things we have not once needed to discuss fundamentals."

In September 1915 Buber announced to Landauer that Paula and he had decided to buy a house in Heppenheim that they were going to move into in April. The strongest ground for their change of place was "the need for a life with nature in landscape adequate to our feelings." A few days later Martin wrote Paula that she had misunderstood the letters of Poul Bjerre and Norlind, who were not against Germany or German people, as she supposed, but simply against Rang's war ideology — which they saw, with greater or less justification, as "Lutheran." "Of course," Buber added in an illuminating comment on Paula and his relationship to her, "I already know that one cannot call to the fire-spewing mountain: 'Wait until I have informed you so that you can spew in a more accurate direction!' " Bjerre did Rang an injustice. "But what Bjerre said about Luther was not altogether unjust; for with his teaching that the action of man means nothing in the face of grace this awesome man has also founded an awesome confusion." Martin added that he saw no hope in international conferences, but he did hope to do something together with the people in Germany who sought a way out of entanglement into an atmosphere of freedom and truth and who wanted to build a new Germany.

In May 1916, two months after the Bubers moved to Heppenheim, Landauer came for a visit of several days. "I had not been in the company of the 'War-Buber' and had almost forgotten him," Landauer wrote later. In Buber's opening editorial for *Der Jude* — "The Watchword" — and in "The Spirit of Judaism" in the second three of Buber's "Speeches on Judaism," Landauer found passages that offended him so deeply that he denied Buber the right to speak publicly of the events of the war and "to incorporate these confusions into your beautiful and wise generalities." "I confess that it makes my blood boil when you single out Germany without qualification as the only redeemer nation without reference to how Germany in the last decades had pursued colonization through conquest." "That is War Politics!" Landauer exclaimed. "Virility, manliness, sacrificial courage, devotion" are not implicit in the content and meaning of this atrocity. "The community that we need is far from all that war means today." "Dear Buber, you must at the very least recognize that among the hundred thousand Jews there were, say, 23 or 37 who . . . did not enter this war with a passionate longing." "And if you cannot, then in my opinion you ought not speak."*

When Buber wrote Rappeport in January 1918 telling him of the mustering of his seventeen-year-old son Raffi (Rafael), he commented that for some years they had not been in the age of war but of something else, something nameless. He asked Rappe-

---

* See Note E in Sources for Chapter 9, p. 397.

port to keep an eye on Raffi and suggested that he could have an important influence on his life that Buber as his father could not exercise. "I have a deep concern about this still unfinished, still wholly unformed youth whom I must allow to wander forth into the world of confusion."

The First World War was Buber's breakthrough to dialogue, and this breakthrough was not a single event, "conversion," or experience of faith but an ever-repeated alternation of darkness and illumination, of finding a way forward and of knocking his head against a wall, of repeated efforts to recapture the open immediacy of the Potsdam meeting and of repeated recognition of the limitation of actual community. "During the First World War," declared Buber in 1952, "it became clear to me that a process was going on which before then I had only surmised. This was the growing difficulty of genuine dialogue, and most especially of genuine dialogue between persons of different kinds and convictions. Direct, frank dialogue is becoming ever more difficult and more rare; the abysses between man and man threaten ever more pitilessly to become unbridgeable. I began to understand at that time, more than thirty years ago, that this is the central question for the fate of mankind." It is no accident that out of this experience of the growing difficulty of genuine dialogue Buber came to his first formulation of his classic statement of the philosophy of dialogue. It was at the very height of the war, in 1916, that Buber wrote his first draft of *I and Thou.* What he said of this draft in his 1957 Postscript does not suggest a catastrophic breakthrough that rejected all that had gone before in his thinking and his life. Nonetheless, only the encounter with the terrible realities of the war had enabled Buber to achieve a clearer vision:

> When I drafted the first sketch of this book (more than forty years ago), I was impelled by an inward necessity. A vision which had come to me again, had now reached a firm clarity. This clarity was so manifestly suprapersonal in its nature that I at once knew I had to bear witness to it.

It was only after the war, in 1919, that Buber was able to write a new draft of *I and Thou* and only in the years between 1919 and 1923 that he was able to find the right words as well and rewrite the book in its final form. Before this was to take place Buber had to live through some of the most active and terrible years of his life — the years of his editorship of *Der Jude,* of his renewed

Zionist activity, of his call for religious socialism and true community, of postwar disintegration and the murder of his friends Landauer and Walther Rathenau. But his "conversion" was irreversible. The real turning point in Buber's life that led to ever-greater soberness and concreteness in walking the "narrow ridge" was the First World War.

CHAPTER 10

Der Jude

A VISIBLE SYMBOL OF THE CHANGE that the First World War wrought in Buber was the inner necessity to move from Zehlendorf, the suburb of Berlin in which he had lived since his return from Florence, to Heppenheim an der Bergstrasse, which remained his home until he left Nazi Germany for Palestine more than twenty years later. The first enthusiasm of the war that had led Buber to celebrate Berlin, even in all its ugliness, now gave way to a raw sensitivity that made this center of bustling war activity impossible for him. Almost a half century later, when he was awarded an honorary doctorate at Heidelberg University, Buber testified: "Shortly after the beginning of the First World War — which I already at that time experienced as the beginning of the crisis of mankind — I found living in Berlin all too painful." The income from his father's estate enabled Buber to live independently, and it was not for another eight years that he was to enter academic life as instructor of Jewish religion and ethics at Frankfurt University. Yet even now university life must have attracted Buber, for when he looked around for a quieter dwelling place, his choice fell on the neighborhood of Heidelberg. Buber had not studied at Heidelberg and had no official connection with the university until 1964 when he received the honorary degree. Yet in the world of imagination of young men of that time Heidelberg was "the exemplary abode of great teaching."

Buber's breakthrough to dialogue in these years also meant a breakthrough to a new relationship with Zionism, Judaism, and Jewish education. None of these were new concerns for him; yet all of them had to pass through the refining fire, out of which they came transformed and tempered. The final results of that tempering are not evident until Buber's Foreword to the collected edition of his *Speeches on Judaism* (1923). But there are many tokens in Buber's life and thought during this period of the ever-renewed process of plunging into the fire.

It is of great symbolic significance that the sharpest and most perceptive critique of Buber's early "Speeches on Judaism" was written in 1914 by Franz Rosenzweig, ten years younger than Buber, soon to spend years in the trenches at the Balkan front, and later to become Buber's closest friend and co-worker. The title of Rosenzweig's essay, unpublished until years later, was "Atheistic Theology," and its subject was the life of Jesus school of Christian theology and unmistakably, though not mentioned by name, the thought of Buber's "Three Speeches on Judaism." In this essay Rosenzweig attacked the pseudonaturalistic concept of "race," the replacing of the supranational goal of the people by the "essence" of the people that lives in its "blood," and the use of the oneness of God and the kingdom of God as mere historical examples of the longing for unity that dwells in the Jewish folk character. The consequence of these emphases, said Rosenzweig, is that there is no real place for revelation in this sort of modern Judaism, and the totality of the religious world — the partnership of God and man — is replaced by a one-sided concern for man which largely dispenses with God. "In this theory of the birth of the divine out of the human the new theology is consciously rooted in the old mystics," points out Rosenzweig in anticipation of his later comment on Buber's doctoral dissertation with its identical teaching. But mysticism and rationalism are alike here in that they leave no real room for revelation, for the otherness of God. Thus Rosenzweig criticized Buber's work from the very standpoint that Buber himself was painfully achieving in those years, that of genuine dialogue with otherness, the apex of which is the dialogue between God and man.

This symbolic significance cannot be translated into actual influence, despite what not only Will Herberg but Buber's closest friends and disciples — Hugo Bergmann and Ernst Simon — have suggested.* The very significance of the convergence of such independent thinkers as Rosenzweig, Buber, Ferdinand Ebner, Hermann Cohen, Gabriel Marcel, and many others in those years lay in the impact of the war upon them and not in any form of "intellectual influence." "That is not the way men change," Buber himself said. "It was the First World War that changed my thought." Not the linking of idea with idea but the impact of events and meetings was here, as always, the matrix of Buber's central thought.

If Buber's general expectations of the "movement" set in motion by the war were soon disappointed, his specific expectations of its effect on the situation of the Jewish people were still more bitterly so. Yet it was precisely this situation that prompted Buber to renewed Jewish activity in ways destined to have a lasting effect on the German Jews and the Zionist movement. When the war broke out, Hermann recorded, Buber felt like all of them that the destiny of the Jewish people was bound to be set in "movement" by it. "One must do something — I heard this from him often at that time," wrote Hermann, "almost every day." On the one hand, the fate and danger of each individual who was in the field moved him. On the other, he was open to every initiation that sprang from the concern for the future of the Jewish people and above all for that part of it which was Jewishly alive. Buber belonged to the founders of the Jewish National Committee that was already established in October 1914. "The Jewish National Committee wants to help prepare for a national freedom movement," concluded the sketch of a short program that Buber himself wrote.

It was freedom that was the central motif of the Hanukkah (Feast of Lights) address that Buber gave in the same year. Although it was the destiny of the nations that was at issue in the First World War, Buber maintained that the destiny of Jewry was also, in subterranean ways, being decided at that time. In a remarkable anticipation of the teaching of the Yehudi in *For the Sake of Heaven,* Buber insisted that the obstacle on the way to genuine life was not outside but inside them, not that there was evil in the world but that they did not devote themselves without reser-

---

* See Note A in Sources for Chapter 10, p. 398.

vation to the good. "What inwardly degrades and profanes us is that we are not whole but broken." The task, therefore, is the same as that to which Buber pointed in his "Speeches on Judaism": to overcome inner division and become unified and thereby to become capable of serving the unity of the world. Not just for the individuals, but for the people, purification and consecration were necessary.

The time offered not only questions and tests, however, but answers. In the storm of happenings the Jew had come to experience with elemental force what community is. The essential weakness of the Western Jew was not that he was "assimilated" but that he was atomized: that he lived without connection; that his heart no longer beat in accord with the heartbeat of a living community but followed the arbitrary urging of his isolated wishes; that he was excluded from true human life, from living with others and in others in a holy commune of people. But now in the catastrophic event that he was living through, the First World War, the Jew had discovered the great life of community, and it had seized him. He joined himself fervently to the community that thus revealed its life to him — the community *which at this moment so strongly needed him.* To the question of whether the community of the moment might still further alienate the Jew from the community which needed him eternally, Buber replied that, on the contrary, this experience of community would deepen among Jews the feeling and the recognition of their unity. They had experienced in blood and tears the inner dissension of Jewry, and the longing would come over them to heal it.*

The Jewish National Committee interested important forces in the Socialist Party of Germany in the Jewish national cause, secured valuable support in the fight against the persecution of the Jews in the East by the occupational authorities, and prepared an atmosphere out of which grew, even during the war, a pro-Palestine Committee. It was out of the considerations of this Jewish National Committee too that a decision was born to take seriously the founding of a monthly.

Buber would become the editor only when he was convinced that a strong group of leading intellectuals would really go along. In naming the journal, Buber consciously reached back to the earlier journal which Weizmann, Feiwel, and he attempted unsuc-

---

* See Note B in Sources for Chapter 10, p. 400.

cessfully to launch in 1903 — *Der Jude,* "The Jew." The new attempt succeeded beyond all expectation and lasted through 1924 as the leading organ of German-speaking Jewry, for the most part under Buber's direct, personal supervision. Ernst Simon, who at first assisted Buber and at the end took over the editorship from him, characterized *Der Jude* as having from the the start a double aim: to acquire national equality of rights for the Jewish people, since it is a nation like all the others, and to shape its special being, since it is not like all other nations. Buber here repeated on a higher level, Simon pointed out, the Zionist criticism of the Emancipation during the period of the French Revolution and afterward: "To the Jews as individuals everything, to the Jews as a nation nothing."

Buber's introduction to *Der Jude* — "The Watchword" — not only quoted from his Hanukkah speech but in large measure continued its spirit. This time of the most difficult testing means for Jewry a deep taking stock of itself and thereby the beginning of a true gathering and unification, he wrote. "From all letters from the field, from all conversations with Jewish soldiers who have returned home from the front, I have received the same impression, that of the strengthening of the relationship to Jewry through clarification of vision and determination of will." "This or that one may have fallen away from their Jewishness," added Buber in one of his rare notes of dogmatism. "He for whom this is possible today has never belonged to it." He who is serious about his existence on earth must be serious about his relation to the community: by *feeling* himself *responsible.* "We do not mean the individuals," concluded Buber, "but the Jews as bearers of the people and its task."

> We do not demand freedom of conscience for the adherents of a faith but freedom of life and work for a suppressed national community and that they, who are today for the most part treated as the helpless object of experience, become the free subject of their destiny and its work in order that they may be able to fulfill their obligation toward mankind. To struggle for this freedom is the one watchword of *our* war; but the other is to overcome the hindering forces of greed and destruction which in Jewry itself oppose the task. . . . We want to realize the Jew whose exalted image we bear in memory and in hope.

Although the first issue of *Der Jude* did not appear until March 1916, Buber spent months beforehand preparing for it. An important part of this preparation was inviting contributions to the journal and enlisting wide interest and support for it. One of the first persons whom Buber naturally thought of in this connection was Hugo Bergmann, the elder statesman of the Prague Bar Kochbans. Bergmann at this time was serving in the army in the Southern Tyrol, and his reaction to this proposal from Buber was a skeptical one. Taken up wholly by the experience of the war and the men with whom he had become acquainted in the army, he doubted the efficacy of periodicals and ideas. In a letter of November 25, 1915, Buber replied that he could easily understand his mood without sharing it. What followed was a rare note the like of which can hardly be found in Buber's writings: the praise of genuine idealism as the reality of the coming generations precisely because it does not succumb to reality but sees it as a whole. Buber contrasted this genuine idealism with the spurious "realism" which celebrates reality without mastering it *and* the spurious idealism which floats above reality in a cloud of highflown phrases. The latter evades the task; the former betrays it. To whom shall I turn if men like you refuse? Buber pressed Bergmann. What is necessary in our time which imagines it sees only individual Jews and no united Jewry is to make Jewry visible again as a living totality, but, still more, to summon the German-speaking Jews to living participation in this totality.

In November 1915 Buber also wrote Franz Rosenzweig inviting his participation in *Der Jude,* which he described as not directed to any party but to a deeper treatment of the Jewish problem, an adequate presentation of Jewish reality, and a direct and emphatic representation of the Jewish language. Robert Weltsch, with whom Buber also communicated, responded from the trenches at the front: 'How shall I, lying here in the cold in a sandpit by a stove I have built for myself, wrapped in a heavy mantel without any real opportunity to sit . . . — how shall I write something here?" Franz Kafka informed Buber that he was much too oppressed and insecure to be able to speak in this community with the least voice. But he thanked Buber for the afternoon they had spent together two years before, a meeting which would always remain with him and which was for him his purest memory of Berlin. Kurt Singer told Buber that the German cause lay more on his heart than the Jewish one, whereas for Buber, Singer said, it was the other way round. Singer was too much a part of the poet Stefan George's circle to be able to respond to Buber's call.* Gustav Landauer, on the other hand, although no Zionist, appreciated what Palestine might become and saw it not as reform but a renewal, which Buber too saw as the deepest and most decisive in Zionism.

The first number of *Der Jude* came into the world amid difficulties. The war censor forbade the distribution of the journal because of an essay on "Eastern Jews and the German Reich" by Gustav Landauer and an article "Poles and Jews." As a result a new printing was necessary. The difficulties which Buber faced as an editor were great, as he reported at length to Bergmann: the slowness of mail delivery, especially from America, the hesitations and refusals of many whom he invited to write articles, the preoccupation with the war. "To edit at this moment is a work of art," exclaimed Buber. "If I did not have a few young people who were faithful and were willing to write on a variety of subjects," he added, "I could not make out at all. I have to carry out by myself all of the editorial work down to the technical details and cannot leave it to work further on my book of Hasidic stories and other important matters. If the issue pleases you, I am glad. I see it as nothing more nor less than what can be done under the given conditions but hope that after the war it may be possible to make a good journal out of *Der Jude.*"

The best of Jewish writers and thinkers and a number of non-Jews, testifies Simon, saw it as a great honor to participate in Buber's monthly. This applied to both Zionists and non-Zionists, writers in German, Yiddish, and Hebrew.** The journal combined a wide spiritual scope with high quality, and it overcame the artificial frontiers which cut the Jewish world in half at that time. In its translations, notes, and summaries — political, economic, and literary — *Der Jude* reminded the Jewish world of the unity which it had once possessed and prepared it for that which it might possess again. It thus fulfilled on the highest level, states Simon, a national Jewish task encompassing many countries. Its scope was broad yet centered in a clear and special principle — Zionism according to the national concept of its editor.

The influence of *Der Jude* was very great almost from the first moment, Simon reports. Even an anti-Zionist like Franz Rosen-

---

* See Note C in Sources for Chapter 10, p. 400.
** See Note D in Sources for Chapter 10, p. 401.

zweig wrote to his parents that it was becoming the only organ of German Jewry which could be taken seriously and which deserved support. For seven years Buber tried to influence the Zionist movement through *Der Jude,* fighting for its organic tie with the Jewish nation living and creating all over the Diaspora, for its progressive social and political character. Despite all the freedom of speech and discussion accorded to the many and various participants, this was a consistent tendency of the editorial board.

At this time Buber published the first volume of his collected essays and speeches on Zionism from 1900 to 1914 entitled *Die Jüdische Bewegung* (The Jewish Movement). Ludwig Strauss wrote Buber that he thought this book could have a very great significance for the Zionist movement, as the "official document of its spiritual side, the will to make the spirit living in all Zionist activities." Scholem told Buber that the book convinced him that Buber in his youth had stood where the present Zionist youth now stand. "But suddenly, in most recent time, there is a rift there which I do not yet wholly understand." "We speak two different languages," he added. Scholem then described to Buber at length his own situation as one of the leaders of Jewish youth in his school and his great rage at a statement of Buber's disciple Siegfried Bernfeld in an essay in *Der Jude:* "We march to the war not because we are Jews but because we are Zionists." The reply that Scholem wrote to Bernfeld fell into the hands of the school authorities and led to Scholem's expulsion!

What Scholem apparently was objecting to in Buber was his attitude toward the war, but this was already changing. In August 1916 Buber declared to the playwright and dramatic critic Julius Bab that true Zionism was not concerned with "nationalism" but with the gathering of Jewish force for a supernational task. The same month Buber complained to Rappeport that the work on *Der Jude* proceeded all too slowly: "Out of a hundred 'coworkers' only one knows what I mean, and even he does not know it." A vivid illustration of this fact came the following month from Gustav Landauer, who maintained that Buber saw himself as *wholly* the Jew while he felt himself to be *wholly* the German and saw no reason why the two should exclude each other. Buber replied that he intended to devote the January issue of *Der Jude* to the theme of "Germanness and Jewishness," including an essay by himself which would not coincide with Landauer's position but also not with that of the official Jewish nationalists. He recognized the dualism, as did Landauer, but in contrast to Landauer he saw it "as a dynamic and tragic problem, as an agon of the soul, which, to be sure, like every agon can become creative."

Buber's work as an editor is not to be measured by the results alone. As a successful editor he understood and practiced what was to become a central concern in his philosophical anthropology — confirmation. Franz Kafka wrote Felice that Buber had rejected his prose piece "A Dream," taken from his work on *The Trial,* with a letter that was more respectful than any ordinary acceptance could have been. (Later it was printed in *Das Jüdische Prag,* a collection that Buber coedited.) Buber wrote to Rappeport that the poems he had sent him were "a beautiful proclamation of the soul and had much to say to me — but true poems (this rarest of all things) they are not." But he added, in a foreshadowing of his later distinction between unconditional acceptance and true confirmation that contends with the other, "Affirming a person is infinitely more important than the obligatory objective evaluation of the artistic merit of his expressions."

If true confirmation means confirming the person precisely through being honest about that person's work, it also means confirming persons essentially other than oneself even in opposing them. The most remarkable case in which Buber did this as an editor of *Der Jude* was that of the Prague Jewish lyricist poet Franz Werfel (later author of the famous novel *The Song of Bernadette*). Grete Schaeder has pointed out how often Werfel testified to the quieting effect of Buber's work and presence on his unrest, which oscillated between anxiety and creative exultation and brought peace to his passionate broodings. Already in 1914 Werfel had written Buber about the latter's great power for easing and brightening one's spirit, which had a lasting effect. At the same time Werfel confessed that recently he had been pervaded by a remarkable feeling of anxiety — of an absolute emptiness, desolation, paralysis. Playing on the legend of the Golem, he said that he dreaded that God would take the piece of paper with the holy name inscribed on it out of his mouth. Buber replied that if he knew but one thing it was that there was community in the world, and that is why he had spent time with him the day before. He rightly guessed that Werfel feared that he could no longer write poetry, and in words reminiscent of *Daniel* said that doubt is essential to genuine creativity and that there is no other way.

> You should for the time being set aside the work and live without it. It is nothing more than waiting and accepting God's tempo. Consider only that the things are there for you and the more you have trust, the more you originate and give of yourself. . . . the only thing you have to fear is just this anxiety . . . I know this anxiety from a period of my own life, and I feel more than fond of you: joined with you.

This is reminiscent of Rilke's *Letters to a Young Poet*.

In January 1917 Werfel wrote Buber from the front, offering his hand and his confession of his own feeling of Jewishness but adding that his knowledge was too chaotic for him to express it in writing. "Let me only say to you, dear Martin Buber, that of all the present Jewish-theoretical literature your writings alone delight my soul and evoke my assent whereas most of what the Zionists write almost offends me." He excepted the scholarly articles of *Der Jude* from his attack on "the shmalzy chauvinism of the Ghetto which they take as revelation," but despite his close friendship with Max Brod, his "aversion extended chiefly to the Prague Zionists."

After receiving Werfel's letter Buber told Max Brod that he was convinced that Werfel's feeling for Judaism had to grow of itself and slowly, in peace and undisturbed, and urged Brod most explicitly not to press him or try to influence him in any way. Werfel had a soul constituted "thus and not otherwise"; his relation to community was a very different one from that of both Buber and Brod. This respect for otherness foreshadowed "The Question to the Single One" which Buber wrote twenty years later, but his quotations from Chuang-tzu about holding back, not interfering, not preaching at people but being in harmony with them, anticipated the way in which he was to import the Taoist *wu-wei* into the heart of the second part of *I and Thou*. Brod responded that he was not trying to convert Werfel and even avoided arguing with him except when Werfel came and expressly demanded that they continue their discussion. But he also contrasted Werfel with his friend Kafka, "with whom I do not discuss and into whom, to my joy, Judaism passes slowly, unnoticed." Werfel, in contrast, "is basically very robust and rational. His whole life is discussion indeed. He argues incessantly and with everyone he meets. He longs for clarity, and I would hold it to be a mistake suddenly to stop my working on him."

Buber showed understanding for Werfel's expressionist lyric poetry, with its motifs of alienation and rejection, and published some of them in *Der Jude* with a prefatory remark of his own to try to help the reader understand this poet who not only fought with Judaism but showed strong leanings toward Christianity. "I am happy that what is uppermost in me can stand before you without deception," Werfel confessed to Buber, "and that you without having to force yourself, can know it and still have a good word for it."

The publication of Werfel evoked a violent letter from the twenty-one-year-old Jewish poet Werner Kraft, who complained that Werfel had been published and that Karl Kraus, the Austrian writer and editor of the satirical journal *Die Fackel,* had not been, nor had Rudolf Borchardt of the Georg school. Buber replied coolly that he had asked a contributor some months ago to write an essay on Kraus, "only because I valued him, not because I held him to embody 'the miracle of being a Jew and a person of great will.' " "Having a great will is not a miracle for a Jew," Buber added, "but his nature; the opposite, which you seem to know only, is but his degeneration." Borchardt did not belong in *Der Jude* not only because he had told Buber he was not a Jew but also because he had said, "We want to crush Russia." Buber felt nothing in common with someone who could make such a statement. Buber defended Werfel's Jewishness and declined to "have the courage" to publish Kraft's letter in *Der Jude.* Kraft penned another even longer, more embittered, and impassioned letter but one which showed him as having been hurt by Buber's response. Buber replied with a much warmer and more personal letter because the tone of Kraft's second letter was really different. He understood very well what Kraft had in his heart against Werfel, but everything he adduced Buber saw as derived from the fact that Werfel sometimes wrote poems in despair as Kraft wrote letters in despair. He chided Kraft for taking verses out of context from a young poet the same age as he, denied that Werfel was ill, but also denied that health was the true goal of mankind, people, and the artist. Health is only presupposition, the necessary basic. Werfel, like every Jew, had to face his inner duality and confront the task of bringing it to unity. "I am always ready to listen to you," Buber concluded, "but you should ask yourself first of all whether what you suffer from does not lie in yourself." Thus began what became a lifelong friendship!

A rough breakdown of the contents of the first two years of *Der Jude* shows the overwhelming number of articles to be about

Zionism and the Jewish settlement in Palestine and next to that questions concerning the Eastern Jew, particularly the Jew of Poland, though also of Galicia and Lithuania. In the second year of existence there was, as a result of the urging of writers like Max Brod and Stefan Zweig, a notable increase in the number of literary contributions, in the form either of stories or of discussions of literature and the theater. Aside from this there were a number of political articles, a number on Jewish education, on the Jewish youth movement, and on various aspects of Judaism, and a number of Hasidic stories and articles about Hasidism. The war itself remained in the background, coming into prominence only in the third year in articles on postwar possibilities and on the peace conference. In the third year, too, several of the articles on Zionism focused for the first time on the question of the Arabs in and around Palestine, a foreshadowing of what later became Buber's central Zionist concern.

Buber shared with the other German Jews the expectation that the cessation of party strife proclaimed by the Kaiser would give the Jews for the first time full protection and genuinely equal rights. But this proved to be anything but the case. The anti-Semites soon complained that few if any Jews were to be found in the front line, and the German army itself conducted a fake census to "prove" this contention true. The Jews pointed to the number of Jewish war heroes, many of whom had fallen, including the first member of the Reichstag to be killed, who was both a Jew and a leader of the Socialist youth movement. "The only comment made by the anti-Semites," reports Walter Laqueur, "was that Jews always had to jump the queue." These experiences within Germany, plus the disillusionment with the war itself, led to a gradual change of emphasis which, without weakening his deep ties to the German language and folk spirit, nonetheless led Buber to insist ever more unambiguously that the German Jews' primary identification had to be with the Jewish people, where their roots lay, rather than with the German, even though their language and culture were formed by the latter.

The rising tide of German anti-Semitism made *Der Jude,* precisely in its character of an independent cultural organ of great breadth and high quality, a first-class, great political force, as one of Buber's advisers put it. "Just now when we hear from all sides how the flood of attacks and of defamations and derogations of the Jewish name rises ever higher it is an absolute necessity to say our piece, too, forcefully and courageously. In this sense *Der Jude* is, indeed, the only proper form of a correct defense against anti-Semitism." Only a month earlier, however, Dr. Viktor Jacobson, the writer of these lines, had written to Salman Schocken, Jr., the German industrialist, joining Schocken in his criticism of *Der Jude* for its lack of concrete political material and adding that he had expressed this to Buber but that Buber, as Schocken had no doubt observed, was not so easily handled.

The frequent correspondence between Buber, Hermann, Viktor Jacobson, Julius Berger, and other prominent Zionists over the content of the articles for *Der Jude* suggests that unofficially *Der Jude* was regarded as the spokesman for Zionism, even though independent as far as party was concerned. Without censorship by any organization, there was a remarkable amount of consultative control in the production of *Der Jude.* Jacobson took exception to a central theme in one of Buber's own essays, the one which contained the first reply to Hermann Cohen in the famous debate between them over Zionism. Hermann Cohen was the great Neo-Kantian philosopher of Marburg and the recognized spiritual leader of German Jewry. Cohen identified himself with the Liberal Jews and the anti-Zionists, although, unlike many of them, he had vivid sympathy for and understanding of the Polish Jews and contributed an article to *Der Jude* on this subject. Buber was an atypical Zionist and Cohen an atypical anti-Zionist, as Ernst Simon has pointed out in a historical reevaluation of their debate. The point at issue, nonetheless, was that between a man who, for all his universalism, gave the primacy to the German state, and a man who, for all his allegiance to the community in which he lived, pointed to the Jewish people as a more basic reality for the German Jew than was the German state. Buber looked up to the older man as a great thinker and even a great Jew, but he found himself compelled to reply to Cohen's fiery and unjustified attacks against the whole of Zionism. There was, in fact, as Ernst Simon has said, no one except Buber who could answer Cohen on behalf of the Zionists. This was because only Buber had the intellectual and spiritual stature in the German-Jewish community to make him a worthy opponent of Cohen's. But it was also because Buber was at this point the most representative spokesman, even if not the real political leader, of the German Zionists.

The occasion and implicit central topic of the interchange between Cohen and Buber was the war itself. Buber pointed out at the beginning of his open letter to Cohen that Cohen justified his position by the fear that the danger that he saw in Zionism would become ever greater and more actual as the result of the heightened international tension. The thrust of Buber's further reply was a distinction between people and state that Cohen was not ready or able to make, a distinction that guarded Buber against *both* German nationalism and Jewish nationalism being made ends in themselves. This position contains in germ Buber's much later, central distinction between "the social principle" and "the political principle." But its first application and its first occasion here was a radical and permanent change in his relationship both to the First World War and to the Zionist movement.

Buber sharply attacked Cohen's definition of nationality as a purely natural fact in favor of the understanding of nationality as a reality of the spirit and of the ethos which demands to be realized in our own lives. But at the same time and for the same reason Buber attacked Cohen's definition of "nation" as being identical with a community established and founded by the state. There were levels of German Jewry that Buber confessed he could not regard as a nationality. "But I need only read a verse from Bialik [the great Hebrew poet of the twentieth century] or a letter from Eretz Israel [the land of Israel] and I feel: here is nation, no, here is more than nation — here is a people." "Nation" could be understood after the pattern of modern nationalism; "people" established the link not only with the history of the Jewish people in the Diaspora but with the very covenant that made them a people in the first place and preserved them as a people down through the ages. This simple distinction represents the decisive transition from Buber's Zionism of the Jewish Renaissance, with its celebration of the dynamism and creativity of the awakening people, to his later biblical Zionism, with its understanding of the inseparable connection between the land, the people, and the task of making real the kingship of God. A presentiment of this later Zionism can already be felt here and with increasing clarity in each new statement in the years to come.

> The Jewish people — not a natural fact but a historical reality that can be compared to no other; not a concept but an awesome living and dying before your and my eyes; not the means for the transmission of the religion but the bearer of this religion and with it all Jewish ideology, all Jewish ethos, all Jewish sociality debased as it has been to the dust.

Jews in this or that place, in this or that fatherland may "possess their political consciousness and feeling for a home state"; the Jewish people is the great homeless people.

Cohen subsumed Jewish universalism under German nationalism. Buber transcended German nationalism in the name of a Jewish nationalism, national in its means but supranational in its goal. "We do not want Palestine for the Jews," proclaimed Buber, "we want it for mankind, for we want it for the *realization* of Jewish peoplehood." Here "realization," from being a category of individual life as in *Daniel,* or of the realization of the divine in the immanence of man, as in the earlier "Speeches on Judaism," has become a messianic category. In the name of this messianism Buber not only rejected the anti-Zionist devaluation of the concept of Jewish exile but declared that not only Zionism but every true Zionist in his personal life is *on the way.* *

This was too much even for some German Zionists who felt quite comfortably settled as Germans whatever they might feel about the call of Zion to the Jews in general. One of these was Viktor Jacobson, who wrote Buber that Cohen seemed to him weak on every other point, but on this point of "being on the way" Buber seemed to him not only weak but easily subject to refutation. "Expressed in this general form as a categorical imperative which *practically* would regulate the whole life of every good Zionist, this principle cannot be reconciled with the proper attitude of the citizen. Setting up such a principle must bring the Zionist into opposition to every state, must produce a conflict between Zionists and all others who belong to the state in which he dwells. The principle of 'being on the way' is really the principle of 'being alien' in a sharper and more unreconcilable form."

Buber's reply to Jacobson is a highly significant statement not only of his Zionism but of his personal relation to Germany and the German language. Denying that being on the way intensifies alienation, Buber confessed that personally so far from finding Germanness alien, he loved the language, the landscape, the deeper levels of the people's soul — but nonetheless his roots were elsewhere. How could he otherwise be a true Zionist as opposed to a philo-Zionist? Only in Palestine would a full Jewish life be possible, but even in Germany one could be on the way from an in-

---

* See Note E in Sources for Chapter 10, p. 402.

authentic to a new and whole Jewishness. In this connection Buber pointed to the soon-to-be-published second part of his answer to Hermann Cohen. It is here that he most significantly prefigured the distinction between the political and the social principles. The national groups within the state in no way wish to lead a statelike but rather a national existence, he asserted. The state represents the ordering, the national the creating, principle, and in every age the ordering principle tries to make its order ever firmer and more exclusive while the creating principle withstands it and preserves its claim as the primal law of life. "And so it will remain," Buber concluded, anticipating his mature biblical teaching of the kingship of God, "until the kingdom of God arises on earth; until, in the messianic form of the human world, creation and order, people and state are fused in a new unity, in the community of redemption."

It is not nationalism in the narrow sense, indeed, but the prophetic demand that Buber had in mind here. When Cohen stated that the Jew's whole being is concentrated in the consciousness of the state, Buber asked if one could put those words in the mouth of a Samuel, an Elijah, an Amos, or a Jeremiah. Their being was concentrated in the consciousness of God, and when the state fell away from God, they espoused the cause of God against the state. The wise and venerable Cohen had the wisdom but not the soul of a Prince of the Exile, Buber suggested, for he did not experience this whole exile with all its misery and its shame as the exile of the Shekinah, the "in-dwelling" of God. With all the seriousness with which one must take the duties to the state to which one belongs, Buber did not know of any higher command than that of God to Israel for the sake of mankind. To Buber, humanity was greater than the state, and the duty of the citizen was to hold up to the state the image of genuine humanity as often as it departed from it. This was not the seeming humanity of yesterday's Europe, which was unable to deliver the states from their entanglement in the invisible war of all against all, but the new, awakening humanity gathering and preparing itself for the sake of the living God; not the caricature of humanity that does not know or wish to know what states are, but a new, clear-sighted humanity which has experienced too often what states are capable of and does not want to repeat the experience.

The war clearly was no longer, for Buber, a movement of the German community but an activity of the German state. His unconditional denial of Cohen's religion, controlled by an ethics which is in turn controlled and consummated by the state, was equally an expression of his growing alienation from the war with which formerly, at least in its aspect of a new awakening, he was able to identify himself. This same experience also protected Buber from then on against any narrow Jewish nationalism in which the "Jewish state" should become an end in itself. "I have seen and heard too much of the practical effects of the empty need for power." What mattered for Buber seems sadly unrealistic in the light of the actual and to some extent inevitable development of the Jewish state in the years that followed: "It is not a question of a Jewish state which, in fact, if it arose today would also be constructed on the same principle as every modern state; it is not a question of one more tiny power in the confusion of powers; it is a question of a settlement which, independent of the drives of the nations and withdrawn from 'external politics,' can gather all its forces for the sake of inner development and, consequently, for the sake of the realization of Jewishness." The need for self-realization is not the need for one's own power but, rather, to increase God's power on earth. Such a restored Zion could be a house of prayer for all peoples, the central abode of the spiritual fire in which "the blood-soaked warclothes will be burnt" (Isaiah 9:5) and "the swords beaten into plowshares" (2:4). This new mankind Buber envisaged under a new motif — a whole-hearted human community in the image of God — and an old one — showing how God lives the *genuine human life* in us through our realizing ourselves and God in us.

In 1918 Landauer's friend Fritz Mauthner, the distinguished philosopher of speech, stated, on the basis of his belief that the German Jews should be assimilated into the German population, that the border of Germany should be barred to the Jews from Eastern Europe. Buber was pained by this statement, and, precisely because he cherished his own relationship with Mauthner, felt he could not remain silent concerning it. "In my experience the atmosphere between real persons is only troubled when it remains unspoken." To this he added that even the most German of Jews should — despite all aesthetic considerations — know and recognize that the *Ostjuden* represent "an enormous reservoir of spiritual, moral, and social energy."

Another concern that rose into prominence toward the end of 1916 and continued through 1917 and even later was the plight of the Polish and other Eastern Jews in the territory captured by the German army and now under its administration. Pointing out the importance of finding a firm in Germany which would hire these unemployed Polish Jews, Victor Berger asked Buber for an introduction to the great German-Jewish financier and statesman Walther Rathenau, who would be in a position to further this "great social experiment of exceeding Jewish and political significance." The large number of articles devoted to every aspect of the problem of the Polish, Galician, and Hungarian Jews in *Der Jude* in the first two years of its publication shows how great Buber's own concern was for the Eastern Jews. In an article of October 1917 Buber singled out for special attack those German-Jews who rejected the Jews of the East. The East is the great basin from which the Western Jews, including these self-styled German patriots, have always renewed themselves, Buber declared. When Buber learned that his friend the Jewish novelist Jakob Wassermann had made a disparaging statement about the Eastern Jews, Buber called him to account at their next meeting, and the two men never spoke again.*

Buber's growing alienation from the war is strongly hinted at in one of his most moving utterances of this period, a letter that he wrote to his Prague friends, his disciples among the Bar Kochbans, in September 1916. "Friends," Buber cried, "you in danger and you in prison, you in the trenches (*Gräben*) and you in the graves (*Gräbern*): at this moment at the darkening evening window before a chestnut tree and a plane-tree and children playing at the fountain, I think of you with all my memory's force of love.

"O force, remembering force of love!

"Now I am no longer at home and you are no longer outside, I am no longer secure and you are no longer exposed or lost, but we are together, all together in the streets and rooms of Prague, the immortal city, in those holy hours of great togetherness."

Looking back, Buber now saw with different eyes the charismatic figure that he had been for them at that time: "I spoke, and you heard too much pride; you spoke, and I heard too much humility — but then, time and again, we were silent, silent together, together in a secluded cottage, on an ascending woodpath, in the gate of a hidden garden, on the water. And that of which we did not speak was full of our silence. . . ." The word most full of

---

* See Note F in Sources for Chapter 10, p. 402.

silence in their memories was *Shabbat* — the Sabbath — but the mention of this word recalled the terrible present which no loving memories could efface. Buber related a legend from the lore associated with the Golem, the Frankenstein monster that the great Rabbi Lowe of Prague was said to have created to protect the Jews of seventeenth-century Prague from their persecutors. Every Friday evening before it was Sabbath, Rabbi Lowe drew forth the name of God from under the tongue of the Golem and he became again a lump of clay. But once Rabbi Lowe forgot to do this and went into the Old-New Synagogue to pray with the community. They had already begun to recite the Sabbath song when Rabbi Lowe recollected that he had left the Golem living. Immediately he called out: "It is not yet Sabbath! It is not yet Sabbath! It is not yet Sabbath!" And because, went the legend, the Old-New Synagogue was built out of the stones of the original Temple in Palestine, his wish was granted and it was not yet Sabbath in heaven or on earth. "Friends," Buber concluded, "it is not yet Sabbath! First we must draw forth the name from under the tongue of the Golem!" The redemption of the Jewish people and of mankind, to which Buber and the Bar Kochbans had looked in the days of Buber's "Speeches on Judaism," was obstructed by the Golem, the Frankenstein monster of war that the nations had created but could not control. To draw the name of God forth from under the tongue of this Golem meant to put an end to it by putting an end to the pretense of divine sanction and divine meaning with which it had been endowed.

In November 1916 Leonhard Ragaz, Protestant professor of theology in Switzerland and later Buber's close friend and co-worker in religious socialism, expressed his surprise and delight in Buber's essays, "Imperialism and Judaism" and "Zion, the State, and Mankind," both published in *Der Jude*. "I can now do not other than extend to you my hand," wrote Ragaz in appreciation of Buber's changed attitude toward Germany and the war. "The agreement between what you say and certain cherished thoughts of mine that have evolved in me entirely in silence out of my observation of history and on deeper grounds, is very striking and is for me a promise. We stand in the dawn of a new development, a new aeon or, even, a 'new birth.' "

In December 1916 Buber wrote "A Hero Book" in which he celebrated those who had rejected the false values of Europe and America for the building of values which no success or power guaranteed. The true heroes are those who fell voluntarily guarding the collective settlements in Palestine rather than the soldiers in the war in Europe who did not fight or die of their own free choice. Thus Buber had reached the very standpoint from which Landauer earlier criticized him. This same contrast between the German and the Jewish hero entered into a talk on Jewish education that Buber gave at a Zionist conference in January 1917. Decisive for this task, he declared, is the image of man that one puts before the young, and here it is not indifferent, as some at the conference suggested, whether it be the image of Siegfried or of David. Jewish education must point to the very different heroism of Jeremiah, who proclaimed the truth to the possessors of power because he stood under the law of the spirit.

But here too Buber spoke out against Jewish nationalism as an end in itself. National education without human education is parochial and unfruitful, he insisted, and that means that a leader of the Blau-Weiss (the Jewish youth movement on which Buber had an ever stronger influence in the years to come) should be ready to address all the human needs of a young person, even the most intimate. Only through this could the human and the Jewish ideals merge into one for him: for the completion of his own being.

Here too Buber returned to the ever-present background of the war. He recognized that the twenty-nine months of war had worked deeply on the Jewish people and increased greatly the number of those who belonged to the periphery, the circle close to Zionism. On the day when the soldiers return from the field, they will ask us for bread of the spirit, for life, for a living ideal, Buber asserted. To illustrate this statement Buber told of how in the past year he had repeatedly received letters from unknown men in the field, letters "that have moved me more deeply than anything in these moving years." Out of all these letters came the same question: What shall become of us? It was the feeling of being sacrificed and the longing for firmness, for direction, for footing. If ever there was a time to gather the vital forces to meet the challenge of the moment, it is now, Buber concluded.

For the second year of *Der Jude* Buber wrote an essay on "Our Nationalism" in which he declared that growing everywhere was a not yet manifest bond of "nationalists" of all people who, like the Jewish nationalists, were primarily concerned not with the success but with the shaping of their nations. In any case, he rejected Jewish nationalism's finding its end in itself and he demanded a real and not merely apparent connection with the cause of humanity, one which would reflect the means as well as the ends. The Russian Revolution, too, which had occurred a few weeks before, was greeted by Buber as meaning the freedom of the person, the freedom of peoples, and the freedom of the millions of Russian Jews. If history has proved Buber a false prophet about the character of developing nationalism, about the fate of the Jews in revolutionary Russia, or even about the course of Jewish nationalism itself, nonetheless it is here that Buber first enunciated explicitly what became from then on his most important single emphasis in Zionism: that Zion can be attained only by means that resemble the end. The ripening of the soul of humanity, the beginning of which Buber espied in those apocalyptic times, has certainly not made itself manifest since; yet Buber clung to this faith as the soul of "our nationalism."

A part of this faith still remained bound up with the possibilities contained in the upheaval of war, but with what a difference! The peoples have begun to recognize, wrote Buber in August 1917, that the war has arisen out of the guilt of all of them. They feel with increasing and ever grimmer certainty that it is up to them whether this war is the hopeless hell or the purgatory, the place of purification, of this century. But in order that the latter may come about it is essential that a just cause like that of Zionism, which injures no other national right (the situation of the Arabs had not yet come into prominence for Buber, or, for that matter, for the Arabs), not be exploited by the war. Zionism is not a party in the war and does not want to be a party in it, because the road to Zion is not by way of madness. Thus it was no longer the "movement" of the war itself, still less the political machinations involved in it, that gave Buber hope but rather the community of peoples with a new consciousness of responsibility to the changing wills of the peoples. The day of the final coming to their senses of the peoples will also be the day of Zionism. "What we confessed twenty years ago in the face of the human world and to which we have remained faithful is a politics other than that which obtains in this war. It is a politics of frankness and not of mistrust, of openness and not of ambush, of directness and not of intrigue."

The motif of community had entered permanently into Buber's Zionism at this time. In its name he even shoved aside what until now had occupied the central place in his teaching of the Jewish Renaissance and his renewed Zionist activity — cultural work. Cultural work is a misleading term, laden with misunderstanding, that no longer expresses what we want, Buber declared to the delegates at a meeting of German and Dutch Zionists in February 1917. We do not want "culture" but life. *We want to give a new shape to Jewish life.* I know and praise the eternal Jewish spirit; I desire and hope for a new Jewish creation, said Buber. But neither of these can properly be striven for or willed in themselves; for they are the by-products of community. The *life of Jews* is the *life of individuals.* A *Jewish* life can only be the life of a *community.* Those who try to secure a homeland in Palestine will not have it unless in all their actions they guard the responsibility to found a pure and just human life together. Social education without national education would mean working in a dream, but national education without social education would mean waking in madness. What matters is not proclaiming rebirth, but living with, helping, and serving one another, out of which the great Jewish community shall be built.

Buber saw Jewish politics at this time as an insoluble contradiction, as it had not been in the epoch before 1914, and he felt that it could be legitimately pursued only in full consciousness of this paradox. The external sign of the situation was the contemporary "success" of Zionism. "There are only a very few Zionists who share or even understand the pain that it causes me." At the same time, he wrote Hans Kohn, after spending "a few beautiful days" with Robert Weltsch in Berlin: "Everything has now become more serious, responsible, and thereby basically more essential and the Jewish cause appears tied up as never before with the human." He had done no writing in the last two years, he reported, because of his work on *Der Jude.* Of his new home in Heppenheim he said, "We live in a silent little place in an old doctor's house with a beautiful garden and things are as good as one can effect at this time." He also spoke of a newly formed Committee for Jewish Culture in which he was active together with Moses Calvary, Hugo Bergmann, Max Brod, Kurt Blumenfeld, and Salman Schocken.

By October 1917 Buber's critical attitude toward warring Germany as the antithesis of everything he stood for had become so sharp that he published a bitter attack on the growing German anti-Semitism and the German nationalism that had bred it. Equal rights cannot be made dependent upon belonging to the nation dominating in the state, Buber declared. The fiction was abroad in the country that the German nation not only ruled in the German Reich but was the only nation that existed in it, as if there were no Poles or any other minority in Germany. This fiction had to be got rid of if Germany was to tread other paths than it had in this war. Like Landauer, Buber now stood in unequivocal opposition to the war, but his ground was not only humanity but also Judaism. In explicit opposition to his friend Walther Rathenau and all the other apologists who tried to make Judaism respectable by presenting it as a minimal religion, Buber declared that Judaism was founded on the memory of a great and meaningful destiny and the hope of the fulfillment of its meaning in a messianic future. One can no more tear out of Judaism this connection of the generations, without shattering its structure, than one could tear the person of Christ out of Christianity. "He who does not *remember* that God has led him out of Egypt, he who does not *await* the Messiah is no longer a true Jew." Buber did not call here for *belief* but memory and hope, not for acceptance of revelation in a fixed form but for that openness to past and future revelation which can bring the historical dimension of existence to life by receiving and responding to it in the present.

Not "blood" but history now gave Buber a solid ground from which he could publish a clear and unprecedented denunciation of the perverted attitude that had become common in wartime Germany. Only a country that nourishes mistrust would lay the ground for new mistrust, he wrote. Only a country that refused to share civilian rights and freedom until they can no longer be withheld lives in fear of their consequences. At the beginning of this war the German people declared unmistakably through its spiritual leaders that from now on the foreign elements and the men of other religions in its midst would be regarded and treated as having equal rights with itself. Woe to Germany if that was only an intoxication!

In 1918 Viktor Jacobson wrote Buber criticizing the independent attitude of Nahum Goldmann, later to become the head of the World Jewish Agency. In defending young Goldmann against Jacobson's criticism, Buber wrote: "*Der Jude* is no party organ and will have a greater impact on the young — its most important circle of readers — the more thoroughly its innermost independence becomes manifest." Jacobson's criticisms of Buber

undoubtedly stemmed in no small part from the innate mistrust of the practical political actionist for the man of ideas
and ideals when the latter impinges on his realm. It is inevitable
that it should also include the mistrust of the plainspoken man for
the artist and the philosopher. We find here indeed a clear echo of
the criticism that Weizmann made of the affected language of the
young Buber. But Buber was now a far more mature man and
much less subject to such criticism. As a part of his overall task
of criticizing the contents of each issue of *Der Jude,* Jacobson
suggested to Buber that he should simplify his style and sacrifice
artistic words for plain speaking. In the midst of a warm letter,
Buber explicitly rejected Jacobson's complaint that his diction
lacked simplicity. "You have apparently the mistaken conception
that I could say what I say in another, simpler manner," Buber
replied. "I cannot simplify and complicate my diction as I
choose. Rather it comes about necessarily from my mental consti-
tution and my relationship to the subject, and I cannot change it.
The only thing that I could do would be to leave what is not
simple unpublished. I have no 'art of words,' as you imagine, . . .
when I write, it is the subject itself that inspires my words. . . . In
short, my dear Dr. Jacobson, allow me this friendly if brutal remark: You can be rid of my style only by getting rid of me —
it is inseparable from me and independent of my will."

Far from being a "politics of eternity," as Jacobson held,
Buber's "Jewish politics out of idea and reality" was from this
time on far more concrete and close to the actual situation than
that of the "practical" politicians who concentrated on diplomacy
and political maneuvers at the expense of the task of building
the Jewish settlement in Palestine. In January 1918, after Lord
Allenby conquered Palestine from the Turks, Buber wrote an
article insisting that only that people could "conquer" Palestine
who could make it its own. England with all its freedom and force
could no more awaken Palestine than could the Turks. No other
people could accomplish this except that one which once constructed in this land the dwelling of the spirit. But even it, the
Jewish people, could not do this through hugging it to its breast
and saying: You are mine! "Conquest of the land through armies:
a bold madness. But conquest of the land through money: a miserable deception. And have they not fallen to this deception, those
Jews who went and bought the earth of Canaan and had it cultivated by strangers, imagining themselves to be great doers and

possessors when they were only exploiters?" Thus Buber categorized the *bilui*, the first Aliyah, or wave of Jewish immigration to Palestine, who copied Western colonial methods and let the land be worked by the Arabs. But in opposition to them, Buber pointed out, stand the second Aliyah, "the genuine, the honest, the decided, who know, and show by practice, that one cannot truly pay for this earth in any other coin than with life-long work and the involvement of one's whole person; the young, the pioneers, who have in truth begun the conquest of Palestine." "The claim of being able to create out of the land its fullest potential, is that which belongs alone to the Jewish people."

That Buber did *not* think this capacity native to every Jew is shown by his criticism of the *bilui*. That such a capacity did inhere in the majority of the Jews who ascended to the land has been proved by subsequent history. In this case, at any rate, history has borne Buber out. That no other people could have such a capacity does not follow of itself and certainly does not accord with Buber's own later call for a Near Eastern Federation of Jews and Arabs who should cultivate the Middle East together. Yet something in the very conviction of those Zionists who, often under Buber's influence, went forth to settle and cultivate the soil of Palestine made this a self-fulfilling prophecy. Within this conviction there was at least in part what became for Buber more and more important: the unfinished task of realizing the kingship of God in true community built on *this* land. What was needed was the return of the farmer's soul and the farmer's life to Israel. "Not out of contact with the earth, only out of the marriage with it through work will the rebirth be fulfilled."

In February 1918, in reply to a long anti-Zionist letter from Stefan Zweig, Buber declared that he knew nothing of a "Jewish state with cannon, flags, and medals" even in the form of a dream. His concern was to build community. He saw a Jewish Palestine only as the beginning of a movement in which the spirit would be realized. To Trotsky, at that time one of the leaders of the Russian Revolution, realization would be denied because the ideal lived only in the doctrine but not in the method. Buber came close to despair when Viktor Jacobson said to him, "We must as soon as possible, hence using all means, create a majority in the Land." This approach to Palestine made Buber's heart stand still, particularly since it was one that most of the leading Zionists at that time shared. They were unrestrained nationalists after the European model, indeed imperialists, unconscious mercantilists and worshipers of success. "If we do not succeed in erecting an authoritative counterforce the soul of the movement will be ruined, perhaps forever," Buber proclaimed; he invited a number of persons to contribute to a collection of essays against the penetration of imperialism and mercantilism into Palestine, essays which would not be polemical in character but would point to the threatening danger and would offer an image of community. Gustav Landauer rejected this invitation out of hand, reflecting not only his non-Zionism but also his reaction to the events of the time, including the Russian Revolution:

> The more Germany and Turkey on the one side, England, America, and the political Zionists on the other interest themselves in Palestine, the cooler I become toward this subject, to which my heart has never drawn me and which is for me not the necessary geographical precondition for a Jewish community. The real event that is significant and perhaps decisive for us Jews is only the liberation of Russia.

Landauer's response foreshadowed his own tragic participation in the Munich Revolution.

One of the most effective forms in which Buber himself carried on Jewish politics during those years was in his relation to the Jewish youth and in particular the Jewish youth movement. During the war and during the 1920s Buber also had a considerable influence on the German youth movement in general, earlier through his presentation of the parables of Chuang-tzu and the teaching of the Tao, later through his emphasis on community. But he also had a quite specific and much greater impact on the Jewish youth movements of Germany and Austria, including the famous Blau-Weiss group which had established itself when Aryan clauses excluded Jews from the Wandervögel and other general youth groups during and after the First World War.

In March 1917 Buber wrote Franz Werfel that in his view youth is indeed the true bearer of *every* great movement, but it cannot be the *object* of a true movement; it is the immortal shaper of the program of humanity, but it may not itself become that program.

> Today's youth movement seems to me a partial and early form of a great religious movement — like every form misunderstanding itself; like every form, ready for sacrifice and destined to sacrifice. Every

movement that is concerned about itself as subject is of this nature and destiny. Zionism is nothing other than just such an early form: I have always stressed precisely that this is its transitional and preparatory character. But a people that must escape ruin may at such a time (and only then) will itself — the youth may not.

This criticism of the youth movement in no way meant a withdrawal from it on Buber's part. Siegfried Bernfeld, a psychoanalyst in Freud's second circle, leader of the Jewish youth movement in Austria, and later Buber's own secretary, wrote Buber in September 1917 telling him how central his participation in a youth day for the Vienna Jewish youth groups would be. "In our feeling the conference is senseless if it is not you who form its center."

In March 1918 Buber attended a conference of Jewish youth organizations of Germany the program of which he had helped to prepare many months before. The *primacy of Jewishness* above every other community — "not only in our feeling and our insight but in our active love, in our work, in our life" — must be the presupposition of *any* Jewish youth movement, Zionist or otherwise, Buber declared there. In May of 1918 Buber published in *Der Jude* a classic address on "Zion and Youth" that was destined to have a far-reaching effect upon the development of the Jewish youth movement in the years to come. "Youth," said Buber, "is the eternal chance for happiness of mankind, the chance for happiness that is offered it ever anew and injured by it ever anew." But it was not youth in general that Buber was speaking about but the youth of that apocalyptic time, the youth finishing their fourth year of war. Now for the first time Buber saw the call to youth as made up of three inextricable elements — the national, the social, the religious — and its task as the fight for freedom, revolution, and apostleship.

The German youth movement errs, Buber stated, because it imagines that youth is its own goal and does not recognize that it shall 'be the instrument of a fulfillment. Yet it also has truth in that it preserves the pure strength of the youth, and the direction slowly begins to reveal itself. The delusion of the past age with its talk of personality, will to power, and culture has vanished away. Youth has recognized that personality is a glorious reality but not a goal and that genuine personalities are enclosed within the heaven of their *cause*. It has further recognized that power is an unavoidable means but no goal, and that those only have great sacred power on earth who seek it in humility and for the sake of the realization of their *cause*. It has recognized finally that culture is certainly the flower of community life but that it cannot be *made*, and that to be without culture is infinitely preferable to the artificial culture in which we live — that a new culture, a new totality of the intellectual and spiritual world, can arise only when there exists again real community, a real living with and in each other, a living immediacy between human beings. The age in which they lived was an age of decision — decision for humanity, decision for the nations, and the return of the people to Palestine. A true Jewish community cannot be any other than that in which the commands of Moses for the equalization of property and the call of the prophets for social justice become a reality in a form including and mastering the economic relations of our time. To build Zion means to found a living immediacy between men.

Hence the very goal that Buber saw or hoped he saw as the dawning direction for the youth movement in general, he saw as the special task of the Jewish youth movement — a task that could be realized only on the free earth of the Land. But the national liberation of the Jews he saw not as a war but as a redemption, and the social transformation he saw not as a revolution but as a creating. Even Jewish religiousness, Buber now believed, would renew itself in Zion and create a new word of God for Israel and mankind. In the Diaspora the holy sparks gleam here and there only intermittently. Where else than in Zion can they be fanned into flame? As the last great religious movement in Eretz Israel was that of the tillers of the soil — the Essenes — so also Buber's hope and faith now rested on the new tillers of the soil in Israel, the pioneers (Halutzim).

The distinction that Buber made between the surface success of Herzl and the underground "dark charisma" of his defeated opponents within Zionism, Buber now applied to the contrast between "this world's madness for success, which today presumes to be the real world and is in reality only a power-swollen puppet," and the very different world history of Amos, Jeremiah, Jesus, and Spinoza, the earthshakers who died without "success." He called to the Jewish youth to reject the former for the latter, rejecting thereby the world of lies and God-forsaken dualism, in which men substitute the rhetoric of ideals for personal commitment. In a note reminiscent of his "Bereitsein heisst bereiten" (To be prepared means to prepare) of his early "Speeches on Judaism," Buber concluded: Zion will not arise in the world if it is not prepared in the soul.

PART VI

Crisis and Revolution

(1918-1921)

CHAPTER 11

<hr>

Communal Socialism and Revolution: The Murder of Landauer

<hr>

MARTIN BUBER was not the first Jewish thinker to unite Zionism and socialism. Moses Hess, to whom Buber devotes a chapter in *Israel and Palestine* (1945), had already done so in the midnineteenth century in his famous book *Rome and Jerusalem*. But Buber's philosophy of community, which came to its flowering in the last year of the First World War, was quite independent of Hess, going back rather to Gustav Tönnies's distinction between *Gemeinschaft* (communtiy) and *Gesellschaft* (association) and to that stream of "utopian socialism" that flowed from Proudhon and Lassalle through Kropotkin and Landauer. One should also mention in this connection Buber's friendship and association with the great German sociologist Max Weber, which began as early as 1910 and was especially close during the years 1916-1918.

One of the important foreshadowings of Buber's philosophy of community in his own early thought is the emphasis on community that Buber found in Hasidism and set forth in his interpretation of it, though never centrally until his 1917 essay "My Way to

Martin's paternal
grandmother, Adele Buber.

Martin's paternal
grandfather, Solomon Buber.

Martin's mother, Elise
Buber, née Wurgast.

Martin's father, Carl Buber.

Martin at about seven.

Martin at about four.

The student in Leipzig
(1897).

(ABOVE) Martin (*lower right*), Berthold Feiwel (*lower left*), Davis Trietsch (*rear right*), Chaim Weizmann (*rear center*), E. M. Lilien (*rear left*)—Martin's special friends, leaders of the Democratic Fraction of the Zionist Party.

(OPPOSITE) In circle of fellow students at the University of Vienna, with Martin in center holding sword.

Paula Buber (Martin's wife) as a young woman.

(OPPOSITE TOP) Paula (*right*) with children Eva and Rafael.

(OPPOSITE BOTTOM) The Buber house in Heppenheim an der Bergstrasse, Germany (1916-1938).

Gustav Landauer.

Hasidism." Of equal importance was the collection of forty social-psychological monographs that Buber edited from 1906 to 1912. In this collection Buber succeeded in bringing together the thought of the leading representatives of sociological research of the day in a brilliant series of significant and often groundbreaking presentations. This series included such titles as "Manners and Customs" by Tönnies, "The Revolution" by Landauer, "Education" by Rudolf Pannwitz, "The Party" by Carl Jentsch, "The Church" by Arthur Bonus, "Spiritual Epidemics" by Willy Kellpach, "Politics" by Alexander Wan, "The Erotic" by Lou Andreas-Salomé, "Religion" by Georg Simmel, "The Strike" by Eduard Bernstein, "The Newspapers" by J. J. David, "World Commerce" by Albrecht Wirth, "The Doctor" by E. Schweninger, "The State" by Franz Oppenheimer, "The Parliament" by H. von Gerlach, "The Woman Question" by Ellen Key, "The Workers Movement" by Eduard Bernstein, "Trade," "Architecture," "The Warehouse," "The School," "The Theater," "The Colony," "The Engineer," "The Stock Exchange," "Sports," "Inventors and Discoverers," "The Judge," and even "Dilettantism" by Rudolph Kassner.

In 1905 Buber wrote an introduction to the collection which appeared in the first edition of the first volume, Werner Sombart's *Das Proletariat*. The collection was devoted to the "Problem des Zwischenmenschlichen" (The Problem of What Is between Man and Man), an expression used for the first time in Buber's Introduction. The range of subjects covered by this problem, according to Buber, is the life of men together in all its forms and interactions, and its way of looking at things is social-psychological. The problem goes behind individual existence, asserted Buber, to what can be understood only in the action or suffering of two or more men together. What happens between individuals happens between complexes of psychological elements and can only thus be understood. Social action is essentially the transformation of the life of the soul in its rhythm, tempo, and intensity of expression. Thus the problem of what is between man and man is at bottom a social-psychological one. Its subject is the social seen as a psychological process. It is precisely this approach to "the between" that Buber rejected with all his force in his essay on "Elemente des Zwischenmenschlichen" (Elements of the Interhuman) written a half century later! Whereas in this later essay Buber protested against the analytical, derivative, and reductive way of looking at things which threatens to destroy the mystery of personal life, in the earlier he called for an analysis of what the person experienced as his own action and suffering in terms of "an impersonal process in which men participate, that which happens between men." Economics, sociology, ethics, law, history, and history of culture — none of these disciplines can escape from psychology if it does not want to be fully detached from the roots of real life. Buber did not, of course, mean that there existed anything like a group soul transcending individual souls. But the mutually complementing and interacting events the community of which forms "das Zwischenmenschliche" is not located whole in each separate soul but only in the relations between souls. "The individual does not experience in himself an *example* but only a *part* of the process. This process is fully revealed in polar relations, such as that between man and woman."

Nonetheless, the whole idea of the *Gesellschaft* contained the seed that would later blossom into Buber's ontology of the "between." In a 1905 letter to the Silesian poet and mystic Hermann Stehr, Buber described *Die Gesellschaft* as a presentation of the psychic realities that arise out of the cooperation of persons. "Through reciprocal relationships between individuals, new values, new psychic facts are created that are not possible in isolated individuals. Every situation in which this takes place is the subject for social-psychological observation." In asking Gustav Landauer to write the monograph on the Revolution, Buber stressed the psychological problem of the revolutionary and of the experience of revolution as a social-psychological one. Landauer later replied that he was indeed writing his essay based on the psychological states of mind of persons and of their relationships. Buber wrote to Landauer that he had read his essay "with that tender strong joy that one experiences in the early morning in the Tyrolean Alps when the far away things appear wholly clear yet also wholly in the mist of the distance." Landauer replied that it was interesting that Buber used the metaphor of the landscape; whereas he during all his work of the last period had had the feeling of a musical composition with its repetitions, variations, heightenings, and complications.

Without question the single most important influence on Buber's teaching of community was his friend Gustav Landauer's socialism. The chapter that Buber devoted to Landauer in *Paths in Utopia* (1949) clearly coincides with Buber's own views and is, indeed, a memorial to his friend whose own writing was tragically cut off along with his life. Landauer's opposition to the war was not only pacifism but also an inherent antagonism to the state which made him as clearly an anarchist as a socialist, or, putting it differently, a socialist of community and of communities of communities as opposed to a socialist of the state. "In our souls we take no part in the compulsory unity of the state," Landauer proclaimed, "since we wish to create a genuine human bond, a society proceeding from the spirit and therefore from freedom."

In his funeral speech for Landauer's daughter Charlotte in 1927, Buber summarized Landauer's socialism in a single sentence: "Gustav Landauer had recognized that the new community of mankind for which we hope cannot coalesce out of individuals, that it cannot arise out of the chaos in which we live, out of this atomizing of individuals, so that individuals would come to individuals and join with them, but that there must exist cells, small community cells out of which alone the great human community can be built." Elsewhere Buber characterized the building of socialism, as Landauer in his mature spirit understood it, not as political action but as immediate beginning, as an elemental commitment to living and realizing. "No one has preached socialism in this epoch so fervently and powerfully as he, and no one has so led the great attacks on the party programs and party tactics which are almost universally identified with socialism." Buber said of Landauer that he fought not as one who belonged to a group but as a solitary man and not with slogans but discovering and pointing to hidden reality. "He understood socialism as something that one could and should begin only there where one was really situated, and his own existence was for him a place of realization."

Landauer, like Buber, had no Marxian theory of historical development, dialectical or otherwise, that made revolution inevitable. On the contrary, for both Landauer and Buber, human will and decision, the path that man himself takes, have a decisive influence upon the unfolding of the future. Like Buber in his early dialectic of religion and culture, Landauer contrasted that past which is living in us as movement and way and plunges at every moment into the future, with that other past that has become rigid and must be destroyed and built anew.

Because of the closeness of their friendship, the impact of Landauer on Buber was not merely one of ideas and doctrines but also of personality. Indeed the former were inseparable from the latter. The glimpses that we have had of that personality in its relationship to Buber are supplemented by the testimony of another close friend of Landauer's, Julius Bab:

> ... In the midst of this ever-new interest in works, men, and groups, Landauer was still solitary, had very few friends in the full sense of this difficult word and also not many lasting comrades. ... The demon in Landauer that sacrificed all the forces of his inner life to a passionate goal, also sacrificed friendships and comradeships in great number. In the midst of his tireless strivings he could have no patience with men; he was not patient, he was not tolerant — as the wholly unavoidable reverse side of his truly great courage a frightfully rigid pride at times became visible. ... Landauer recognized himself to be a "man-eater," a restless consumer of men. ... Thus this prophet of the commune was in his personal life almost a solitary man, and he was, remained and had to remain a *poor* man.

From his earliest beginnings in the anarchist movement Landauer was pursued by the Prussian authorities, and for years he was continually trailed by police spies. He was one of the most-watched men in Germany. He passed eleven months of his youth in prison because of his statements on freedom and later another six months because he wanted to save an innocent man who was imprisoned as a murderer and to this end advanced weighty, solidly grounded, but not fully provable complaints against the police prosecutors.

Even within the sphere of the anarchist and revolutionary movements Landauer's enormously creative writings remained almost unnoticed. His whole life he was without means, without security, without regular occupation, not only in terms of his practical needs but, above all, with regard to the possibility of expressing and furthering his cause to the full extent that he longed to. Gustav Landauer's downfall came, according to his friend the noted language scholar Fritz Mauthner, because he was no politician and yet was driven by intense sympathy with the people to declare himself politically. Too proud to join a party, not narrow enough to form a party in his own name, he was thrown back on himself, a leader without an army. Once, before the turn of the century at an international party meeting in Switzerland, he was publicly abused by August Bebel, the German Social Democratic leader, as an *agent provocateur* of the German government and in consequence was beaten by some of the comrades. He did not get angry, but instead said to Mauthner: "And this Bebel is one of the best, an exemplary man; he is only so stupid because he is a politician."

Landauer possessed an extraordinary spiritual power over the people to whom he spoke, according to Mauthner. "He could have been a demagogue of the first rank, like Ferdinand Lassalle." Perhaps it is because Landauer did not fall into the temptation of becoming a demagogue that his image remained intact for Buber as that of Lassalle, the hero of Buber's early youth, did not. Whatever the fragmentation of his gifts and alternation of his goals, Landauer involved himself to the full in every task that he took up and remained a whole person even when his actions were fragmented. Undoubtedly important, too, was the trait to which another friend of Landauer's attested, the mildness of his nature which prevented him from dealing abusively with the view of others or making propaganda for his own, and kept him from demanding even of his friends that they go along with him in what was most important to him.

"There was in Germany in the time of its greatest distance from God," wrote Buber after Landauer's death, "a man who, as no other, summoned this country and this hour to the turning. For the sake of a coming humanity that his soul beheld and longed for, he strove against the inhumanity in which he had to live." Landauer rejected the centralistic, mechanistic pseudosocialism because he bore in his heart a federalistic, organic, community socialism. Thus in a society in which all public life was narrowed to politics and creativity frozen to party activity, he had to remain without allies and to propagate his truth with great difficulty. As powerful and impassioned as his speech was, it always moved only individuals: the few who were inwardly open and ready. For he demanded something unheard of: that one not be content with acknowledging an idea and espousing it but that one must take it seriously and begin to act upon it; that socialism is not an affair of then and there but of here and now. Proletariat and intellectuals alike were impervious to such a demand: the proletariat because they had grown up in the doctrine that socialism is an inevitable end product of an unalterable, scientifically accountable development, and because this teaching had stifled in them the courage to dare that is the primal principle of all real beginning; the intellectuals either because they were fully estranged from social events or because they imagined they could master them with political slogans.

In the beginning of the war, before his voice was silenced, Landauer was the first to speak the words that others only later were to repeat but at that time no one listened to or answered: "None is guilty, all are guilty. All — we too are guilty." Buber was one of those who spoke later. During the war years, as we have seen, Buber and Landauer grew closer and closer. On receiving Buber's little book *My Way to Hasidism,* Landauer wrote Buber that this progress from report to confession to teaching had done his heart much good and begged him not to take it amiss if he could not join him in this or that undertaking. "Each needs his own forms and springboards," he said, "but that does not touch on our oneness and community which in these years have grown much deeper and which have much to do with my wish and will to preserve life and strength for the future." It is striking that it is precisely in *My Way to Hasidism* that Buber expressed most explicitly, up to that time, his teaching of community. "At that time there arose in me a presentiment that common reverence and common joy are the foundations of genuine human community." Similarly in *The Holy Way,* which Buber wrote in 1918 and dedicated, when it was published in 1919, to Landauer's memory, Buber pointed in particular to Hasidism "as a bold endeavor to establish," in the midst of the confusion of the Diaspora, "a true community, and to create a brotherly union out of all the people bent under the yoke of an alien environment and threatened by degeneration."

If Buber's socialism had got no further than Tönnies's simple contrast between organic community and atomized society, it could not have withstood the great perversion that Nazism later introduced when it combined the very two elements to which Buber pointed as central: nationalism and socialism. But, as Hans Kohn has pointed out, Buber modified Tönnies's basic concepts in such a way as to bring them nearer to socialism. Buber's "community" was not the natural community of the family or the village commune in which powerful instinctive traditions ruled, perhaps, but also coercion, violence, exploitation of one's fellowmen, disregard of their freedom and worth. Buber's community, rather, was a community of choice around a common center, the voluntary coming together of men in direct relationship. Thus in contrast to the romantic nationalists, Buber never held that the formation of community could be the mere return to the medieval communal forms.

It was not to the medieval community, indeed, but to the biblical that Buber turned more and more in this last year of the First World War. In May 1917 Buber wrote Siegmund Kaznelson that the spirit can directly *create* institutions only where a new communal being, a social, religious, economic whole, a colony, a church, or a fellowship *enters into life.* Only power, authority, or revolution can *change* institutions directly — the spirit can do so only indirectly: through example and education. In February 1918 Buber wrote Rappeport that in the period that lay ahead, as in every period, those who sought a pure living together among men would find God. The following month he declared to Kaznelson, "I believe in a transformation out of the spirit itself, not merely through direct working on the inwardness of men but also through the establishing of spirit-born, remolding forms of community."

The Holy Way, which Buber wrote as "A Word to the Jews and to the Nations," is a way in which God is not seen merely as seminal in all things but is realized *between* them, and with man this means in community. Not Jewish culture or Jewish renaissance was the keyword now but the overcoming of that most fateful assimilation of all: "the assimilation to the Occidental dualism that sanctions the splitting off of man's being into two realms, each existing in its own right and independent of the other — the truth of the spirit and the reality of life." It was only contemporary events, however, and in particular the war in which the nations were embroiled, that led Buber to the mature understanding that "realization" does not take place *within* "the realizing man," but in "the seemingly empty space . . . between man and man," in the preparation of a place for the divine in true community. From this time forth, "realization" to Buber means the realization of the biblical covenant to become a kingdom of priests and holy people — "We will do and we will hear" (Exodus 24:7) — in which what is heard is revealed out of the deed of community, and what is revealed is "that realization of the Divine on earth is fulfilled not within man but between man and man, and that . . . it is consummated only in the life of true community."

All of Buber's later understanding of revelation is contained just here. We do not find revelation by going back to the past — not even the past of the Bible — and applying it to the present, but by hearing the word of the present situation so deeply that within it even the word of the past may become renewed in full concreteness and full presentness. It is, in fact, no longer a word of "the past," but a word that speaks again and anew and fully uniquely in the present. Thus in "Herut: On Youth and Religion," the last of Buber's early "Speeches on Judaism" (1919), Buber went from the loneliness and confused and inauthentic gropings of contemporary youth to the teaching of community, and not the other way round:

> Intellectualization, in the making for centuries and accomplished within recent generations, has brought a depressing loneliness to the youth of present-day Europe.... Because the bridge of immediate community, whether its name be love, friendship, companionship, or fellowship, connects only man with man, and hence spirit with spirit, but not thinking apparatus with thinking apparatus, this intellectualization begets loneliness. Not the exultant loneliness of the summit experienced by the first climbers who are waiting, with silent hearts, for their companions who have fallen behind, but the negative loneliness of the abyss experienced by the lost and the forlorn. Out of the anxiety and depression of such a state of mind, modern Europe's youth longs for community, longs for it so powerfully that it is ready to surrender to any phantom of community, as we have so abundantly experienced.

What were the "phantoms of community" to which the youth of that time surrendered and to which Buber referred? To understand this we must turn, however briefly, to the history of this period of crisis, the period of W. B. Yeats's "Second Coming" (1920), in which

> Things fall apart; the centre cannot hold;
> Mere anarchy is loosed upon the world. . . .
> The best lack all conviction, while the worst
> Are full of passionate intensity.

It was, to begin with, a time that was still feeling the first wave of impact from the Russian Revolution, a wave which had rolled to the very soil of Germany and now broke, with less force indeed than in Russia itself, but nonetheless with devastating effect. When the revolution first broke out in 1917, Buber welcomed it, as we have seen, as a promise of freedom — freedom for the peoples of Europe and freedom and political and social equality for the millions of Russian Jews. How drastically Buber had altered his opinion within a year is shown by his comment in *The Holy Way* on that unawareness of the soul, life, and history of the people "that has in our day engendered the tragic conflict between political doctrine and national character that is the initial product of the Russian Revolution." Not only was the religious socialism that Buber developed in 1918 and 1919 a *national* socialism; it was also a *social* and *decentralistic* socialism in the strongest possible contrast to the *political* and highly centralized socialism that was developing in Russia in the aftermath of the Bolsheviks' taking power. Even in 1919, Buber saw the true nature of the socialist power-state which, in the name of compulsory justice and equality, makes impossible spontaneous community and genuine relationship between man and man. True to the "narrow ridge," he refused the clamoring either/or of the modern world — the demand that one accept a centralized socialist state because of the defects of capitalism or a capitalist society because of the defects of socialism.

The most immediate historical events of this period for Buber were, of course, the defeat of Germany by the Allies and the establishment in Germany of the democratic but fatally vulnerable Weimar Republic. At the very time when the German nationalists were beginning to join forces to throw off any vestige of German war guilt in favor of the myth that Germany was knifed in the back, Buber not only accepted the German war guilt *and* that of all the other nations but saw it as rooted in that very "Occidental dualism" between spirit and life in response to which he put forward his teaching of community. The form of this teaching, like the guilt to which it was a creative response, Buber set forth in terms of Judaism. But the real substance of both was the contemporary situation. "To me, the most repulsive of men is the oily war-profiteer, who does not cheat any God, for he knows none. . . . From there, a step-by-step progression leads to the most subtle rationalizations. *And who among us dares* to deny his own part in this guilt?"

Arnold Zweig wrote Buber that he had read *The Holy Way* with the happy feeling that it was "a radical description of our present situation and just as radical a pointing to the way out." He sympathized strongly with the freedom of spirit that he sensed in Buber's words. Aware of Buber's continual wrestling with the problem of expressing what is inexpressible and of tying in the infinitely important subject with the most propitious word, Zweig attested that never before had Buber's speech come to them so good, free, and simple. "There is a strong simplicity in your tone and an energy that compels." Five months earlier Zweig had written Buber in response to another essay:

> The style of your latest essay has something that your earlier prose lacked: ease and fluency, along with passion and meaning. In the "literary Buber" what was for you a necessity and an unsubdued remainder was taken as intention: the decorative style. The new essay contains nothing of this; it is spoken with great strength.

This appreciation of Buber's social and political writing is particularly striking in the light of Arnold Zweig's later Marxism that led him to leave Israel to spend the last years of his life in East Germany.

If Buber rejected Marx's economic determinism and the Soviet state centralism, he did not fail to recognize the part that the profit motive at the heart of the capitalist system played in causing and prolonging the war. If Marx saw revolution as the bursting of the integument of the capitalist system because of the latter's inherent contradictions, and as the midwife which liberates the new society ingested in the womb of the old, Buber, like Landauer, saw it as the breaking up of the old order — chaos with the possibility of rebirth but with equal possibility of still further disintegration. If Marx's theory that revolution would arrive in the most advanced of the capitalist societies proved to be palpably false in the case of Russia, forcing Lenin to enunciate the theory of the weakest link in the chain, it would have served no better for Germany immediately after the First World War. The true historical atmosphere of those chaotic years and the promise which lay within them was grasped with incomparable clarity by Buber in his little essay, "What Is to Be Done?" written in 1919. It is to this essay that Buber himself pointed forty years later in response to the sociologist Kurt Wolff's question as to whether the I-Thou philosophy does not contain the danger that it will be used as "an instrument of political reaction." The only safeguard against this danger, replied Buber, is that all its true friends must fight against this misuse with the weapons that they find within themselves, and this includes the injunction in "What Is to Be Done?" against "withdrawal into one's private garden."

Not objective appraisals of the situation but listening to its call to *you* is what is essential, Buber declared. The person who asks not the theoretical question "What is *one* to do?" but the real, existential question, "What have *I* to do?" is taken by the hand by as yet unknown comrades who answer: "You shall not withhold yourself." Only this personal involvement in the common situation can lead to "the bond of togetherness" and breaking through the shells into which society, state, church, school, economy, and public opinion have placed you, to lead to a direct contact with others.

> Ancient rot and mould is between man and man. Forms born of meaning degenerate into convention, respect into mistrust, modesty in communicating into stingy taciturnity. Now and then men grope toward one another in anxious delirium — and miss one another, for the heap of rot is between them. Clear it away, you and you! Establish directness, formed out of meaning, respectful, modest directness between men!
>
> You shall not withold yourself.

Not withholding means directness; it means betweenness; it means awakening in the other the need of help and in yourself the capacity to help; it means coming forth from behind the fortress of your spirit in which you have enclosed yourself and from which you exchange signs with fellow conspirators in the secret alliance; it means finding the new word and sign that will unite the coming torrent — the torrent that you facilely call "the crowd." It means forgoing that withdrawing into oneself and standing apart which makes up the solitude of individuals incapable of community. But, by the same token, it means establishing and consolidating the necessary experience of ever again becoming solitary. As Buber was later to write in his critique of Kierkegaard *and* of Nazi totalitarianism, it does not mean fleeing from the crowd but making it no longer a crowd. This may mean sometimes retreating into solitude in order to go forth with new strength to the community, at other times throwing oneself into the crowd to plant the seeds of community. No longer through *exclusion* and *subduing,* but only through *inclusion* and *redeeming* can the kingdom be established. "Out of forlorn and impotent men, out of men who have attacked one another through forlornness and impotence, the shapeless thing has come into being — deliver man from it, shape the shapeless to community!" To those who look to a new chaining to succeed the unchaining, Buber cried that history no longer held, that soon their well-informed security would be pulverized in their souls. "Recognize this before it is too late!"

In the face of this situation it was no longer possible for Buber to address himself principally to the Jewish youth. "The experience of the boundary that has visited me again and again for a year now," Buber wrote Ludwig Strauss, "has recently become so powerful that I began to tear down the firm enclosure, the work of my hands, and to speak to men" in general rather than "to the Hebrews." In a series of *Words to the Age* planned in 1919 for the Three Country Publishers of Munich, Vienna, and Zurich, Buber published two pamphlets on "Basic Principles" and "Community" and announced eight further pamphlets in preparation which in fact were never published: "Beyond Politics," "The Problematic of Culture," "The Religious Force," "On the Peoples," "Of the Madness of Institutions," "Domination and Leading," "The Principle of Revolution," "To the Youth."

The "basic principles" of which Buber spoke in the first pamphlet were Man, Earth, Work, Help, Spirit, Community, Communal Existence, Mankind, and the Name of God — a list almost identical with that in *The Holy Way*. Immediacy will exist between men only when the veil between them is torn away — the veil born of the profit motive which leads people to see one another not as persons but as members of a category, as citizens of the state, as belonging to classes. Only places filled with the immediacy of living with one another can be regarded as examples of communal existence, as opposed to states — those surrogates of community which maintain themselves only through coercion.

It is in "Community," the second of Buber's *Words to the Age,* that he set forth most clearly his criticism of Marxism as the completion of that very process of development from community to association that capitalism has begun. The state of universal paradox in which we have lived until now is that of a fever-ridden tyrant whose spasms mean the suffering and ruin of millions, yet in whose kingdom the holy child of community lies concealed in the trappings of unions and comradeships. The state of the socialist order, if it ever attains undisputed sovereignty, will be a blank-eyed, indifferent ruler who will prevent all exploitation of men by men yet in whose realm there will be no room for community.

Two movements in our time have risen up against the dizzy power intoxication and feverish greed for power. One is aboveground, visible and effective, its goal clearly formulated, based on the primacy of economy as the ordered satisfaction of human needs. The other is an underground movement which is apparent only to the person who looks deeply, borne by the striving of all true humanity for genuine community. New laws are but empty shells, or mere window dressing, when justice does not manifest itself in the life between man and man. In order that "the inescapable evolution" away from community may be halted and the "turning," the true revolution, take place, the unheard-of is needed: a powerful will toward community. Here, despite all, history proves to be an event of truth and meaning. The divine has sunk into the possibility of genuine life between persons and wills to reveal itself only through its realization in true community.

The signal importance of the events and meetings of this period and of the response which Buber made to them through his developing religious socialism can be seen from the fact that "Community" (*Gemeinschaft*), of all Buber's early works, most clearly looks forward to *I and Thou* both in language and in thought. It was during this very year 1919, indeed, that Buber completed his first draft of *Ich und Du*. Yet we cannot understand the road to *I and Thou* adequately without examining the other terrible events of this period. The most important of these, not just for *I and Thou* but, one suspects, for the whole of Buber's life to come, was the murder of Gustav Landauer.

Landauer's second wife was the noted German poetess Hedwig Lachmann, who composed the libretto for Richard Strauss's opera *Salomé*. When she succumbed to a fatal illness in February 1918, dying at the age of thirty-five, it was for Landauer a fearful blow. "One could since then observe something unsteady in him," testified a friend, "an unrest that drove him to expend his life. I believe that since then an impatience came over him for some definitive self-involvement and action from which a contemplative aspect of his personality had formerly held him back. The calm warming light of his being was caught upward into a self-destroying flame. This was his state of mind when he was taken hold of by the revolution that demanded and needed him."

The so-called German Revolution was really a series of revolts in a number of major cities occasioned far more by the defeat in the war than by the example of the Russian Revolution, itself a product of war and the virtual breakdown of the Russian army. On November 11, 1918, the Allies signed an armistice with Germany and the Austro-Hungarian Empire, and it was in that same month that the "Revolution" began in Munich, Berlin, and other parts of Germany, lasting sporadically until the following May. Fritz Mauthner reported that Landauer came to him in the fall of 1918 in feverish expectation of the "world revolution" that he had helped prepare and for which he had for thirty years suffered privation. When the revolution broke out soon after, Gustav Landauer was ready, ready for death.

The German Revolution meant for Landauer no lessening of the isolation in which he had always lived and no real illusion that this revolution would differ from the others about which he had written. In April 1918 he wrote: "Ah, how I am needed! And how I have no more desire to give advice that will not be taken and to criticize what is not done." In fact, his advice was not taken, and the great hope that he had cherished for so many years was lost.

When the German Revolution broke out, Landauer was fully aware of the tragic failure of all previous revolutions and of the fact that socialism had never once existed as a reality. The feeling with which he entered the revolution was not hope but grim decision to do in this crisis what he was obliged to do, not as a spiritual leader and pathbreaker but as one of the small band of constructive German revolutionaries: to effect what he could of the blessings of revolution and avert what he could of its curse.

On November 15, 1918, Landauer announced to Buber that he was bitterly opposed to the coming summons to a so-called national assembly. "Behind it is hidden only the long-dead party." Nonetheless, he did want to take part in the preparation for the new democracy. "I should like to go to Berlin as representative of Bavaria," he wrote Buber, "and that you should work in Vienna in the same capacity." This dream of his was not to be realized. In its place came the revolution in Munich, and on November 22, exactly one week after the earlier letter, Landauer told Buber that he wanted to return to Munich where he found himself in the closest agreement with Kurt Eisner, German journalist and Socialist leader in Bavaria. "The situation is very serious: if the Revolution emerges intact from *this* liquidation of *this* war, it will be almost a miracle. . . . Despite all, this I can promise you, Bavaria will not give up its autonomy." Landauer then asked Buber to sketch for him his thoughts on the education of the people, the nature of publication, etc., or better still, come soon to Munich. There Buber would find Landauer working splendidly together with Kurt Eisner, whose democracy was as anarchistic as Landauer's own. It is clear that Landauer saw Buber as someone essentially on his side, but not as comrade and co-worker in the same sense as Eisner, who was a revolutionary as Buber was not. On December 13 he wrote Buber urgently asking for information on the fight of the Bolsheviks against the Left Social Revolutionaries. Yet Buber did not take part in the preparation for the Munich Räterepublik in which Landauer briefly held power. As Buber himself explicitly said: "Landauer and I were friends, but I in no way cooperated with him in his revolutionary action and in particular in his preparation for the Räterepublik." Landauer appreciated Buber's article in *Der Jude* on "The Revolution and Us," but wanted from him something more definite. At the same time, Landauer promised Buber to take part in a conference of German-speaking socialist Zionists that was planned for Munich, if he were still there at that time.

Buber could not go along with Landauer's revolutionary activities and remain faithful to his own insights. Landauer entered the revolution ready for sacrifice not only of his person, but of his cause, so Buber wrote after his death. While bitterly resenting the calumnies against Landauer in the press, Buber confessed in his memorial speech that in his opinion Landauer made the wrong choice.

> According to my insight, there existed on November 7th, 1918, a higher duty and a greater responsibility for Gustav Landauer: namely toward his cause and thereby toward the cause of a true transformation. For what the revolutionary mass lacked, a lack which tore it to pieces and made it directionless, was an *image*, a whole, genuine, accessible image that should and could be realized: an image of institutions, of relationships, of conditions, the image of a new society; not an arbitrary image constructed out of the intellect, but a legitimate image formed from the view of historical connections and growing out of the seed of community preserved in the depths of the natural life of the people. . . . Landauer had created fragments of an image; now it was up to him to bring that image to a unity. He knew it, he thought about it, he worked toward it, he proclaimed it during the Revolution. But he did not decide on the 7th of November to detach himself and concentrate on his work, or even, if that were possible at the same time, to speak his word and to await the reverberations from it, or even to unite the true socialists and out of them then build the kernel of the new community. Rather he decided to throw himself into the breach, which needed a human body to fill it up. Stronger than his responsibility to the future, the dreadful need and problematic of the moment pressed down upon him, and he succumbed. I believe that he erred; but I also believe that no man has ever erred out of purer motives.

In the terminology of Buber's later philosophy, Landauer not only sacrificed himself and the "social principle" of fellowship to the "political," which he had always attacked, but he also sacrificed to "the social," in the sense of the collective movement of the revolution, that very element of "the interhuman" — the direct relationship between man and man — which was essential to building true socialism.

It was those days of postwar chaos and revolution that paved the way for the coming to Germany of the blackest reaction. The milestones on this path were a series of fateful murders and assassinations of revolutionaries and later even of liberal statesmen who, despite all the differences between them, had in common their dedication to the task of building a new social order in Germany *and* the fact that they were Jews — a fact which probably played no small part in the assassinations and certainly in the justifications of them after the fact. The first of these were the brutal murders in Berlin of the famous socialist leaders Rosa Luxemburg and Karl Liebknecht, killed in their cells after long imprisonment. These murders, still remembered among socialists and communists everywhere, troubled all German liberals exceedingly, testified Margarete Susman, "and gave us a foreglimpse of a frightful German future that was near at hand." In June 1919 Arnold Zweig told Buber that he encountered in Tübingen "an unimaginable mood of counterrevolution, which is identical with anti-Semitism." In August the actress Louise Dumont asked Buber if he knew of the anti-Semitic agitation in German countries. "It assumes forms that seem to mean a final battle — if it is decided that this is what it means to be German, then one can no longer remain in the country; then the die will finally be cast against Germany." Buber, with less prescience of the future than Louise Dumont, responded that the persecution of Jews, like all the troubled waves of the moment, did not concern him very much. "I am used to excesses, they belong to the present turmoil, but I do not see a final battle."

Although Landauer represented a very different type of socialism from Liebknecht and Luxemburg, he delivered a memorial address for them in Munich on February 6, 1919. Landauer used this occasion to point to the Janus-faced nature of social democracy which, as the representative of socialism and justice, attracts every daring man of spirit, yet repels him by its bureaucracy and militarism. From this he moved to the ambiguous death of the revolutionary himself, contrasting the heroic death of the Hungarian revolutionary poet Sándor Petöfi (fallen 1849), foretold by the poet himself in a poem translated by Hedwig Lachmann into German, and the death of Rosa Luxemburg and Liebknecht, who also died in the fight for freedom but not on the field of battle: "In the street fight of the licentious, antirevolutionary soldicry, led by professional non-commissioned officers and officers of the General Staff, Karl Liebknecht and Rosa Luxemburg were taken prisoner, in prison they were cowardly murdered." Three months later Landauer himself was murdered by the same "licentious anti-revolutionary soldiery," Buber pointed out.

About two weeks after Landauer's memorial address on Karl Liebknecht and Rosa Luxemburg, Buber was with him and several other revolutionary leaders in a hall of the Diet building in Munich. Landauer had proposed the subject of discussion — the terror. But he himself hardly joined in. To Buber he appeared dispirited and nearly exhausted. His wife had succumbed to illness the year before, and now he was clearly reliving her death. The discussion was conducted for the most part between Buber and a leader of Spartacus (Liebknecht and Luxemburg's subversive organization which disseminated illegal propaganda against the War), who later became well known in the second communist revolutionary government in Munich that replaced the first, socialist government of Landauer and his comrades. The Spartacus leader, who had been a German officer in the war, walked with clanking spurs through the room. Buber declined to do what many apparently had expected of him — to talk of the moral problems. But he set forth what he thought about the relation between ends and means. He documented his view from historical and contemporary experience. The Spartacus leader, too, sought to document his apology for the terror by examples. "Dzertshinsky," he said, "the head of the Checka, could sign a hundred death sentences a day, but with an entirely clean soul."

"That is, in fact, just the worst of all," Buber answered. "This 'clean' soul you do not allow any splashes of blood to fall on! It is not a question of 'souls' but of responsibility." Buber's opponent regarded him with unperturbed superiority. Landauer, who sat next to Buber, laid his hand on Buber's. Landauer's whole arm trembled. "I shall never forget that night," wrote Buber. When he had returned to Heppenheim from Munich, Buber reported to Ludwig Strauss that he had "spent a deeply moving week in steady interaction with the revolutionary leaders."

> The innermost human problems of the revolution were discussed without holding back. I entered into the happenings, questioning and answering, and we experienced night hours of an apocalyptic heaviness in which silence spoke with eloquence and the future became clearer than the present. . . . At times I was expected to play the role of Cassandra before them. I beheld Eisner in the demonry of his divided Jewish soul. . . . Landauer persevered in his faith in Eisner, with the utmost exertion of his soul and protected him by virtue of a shocking self-deception. The whole a nameless Jewish tragedy.

More terrible and fateful for Landauer than the murders of Luxemburg and Liebknecht was the murder of his close friend and co-worker Kurt Eisner, which took place on February 21, 1919, the anniversary of Hedwig Lachmann's death one year before, and, as it chanced, on a day when both Landauer and Buber were away from Munich. Landauer had been called away on that day to where his children (Lotte and her two younger sisters) were living outside of Munich. When at midday on the anniversary of his wife's death, full of the thoughts of that occasion, he descended from the train, he received the message that Eisner was dead. "In the weeks that followed," Landauer wrote to Buber, who had sent him words that comforted him, "I was so racked that I now know how suffering can become strength. When the heroic epoch was at an end and the scandalous episode of party intrigue took over, I came here [Krumbach in Swabia] for a rest. But my rest takes place, as I should have expected, under an extraordinary tension."

Instead of withdrawing from further activity, as might have been expected after this trauma, Landauer returned to Munich and attempted to accomplish alone what he and Eisner had not been able to do together. He sought to carry on Eisner's task with inadequate means and to make the seething Munich proletariat into that socialist community of which he had so long dreamed. In the beginning of April 1919, the independent socialists overthrew the majority socialist government, and the Räterepublik was proclaimed. In the governing central council sat Landauer. "Landauer is now the most important man in Munich," wrote the German writer Stefan Grossmann to the novelist Auguste Hauschner on April 13, 1919, "because he is the only one in the ministry with a feeling of responsibility, also with insight." Buber's judgment was not so sanguine. Landauer's "entrance into the revolution seemed to me a failure in his task," wrote Buber later. "His entrance into the government was certainly a failure in his reasoning. He joined himself with men of whom in earlier days — in the time of the full integrity of his spirit — he would have recognized at first glance that in cooperation with them no work, and least of all this most difficult, sheerly hopeless work, could succeed. But his anguish over the crumbling away of the revolution had clearly impaired Landauer's superior powers."

Landauer was actually in power only a few days. The communists very soon came to the helm, and the Spartacist, second Räterepublik succeeded the first. From that time on Landauer no longer had an active part in all that happened in Munich. He remained close to the government only in a restraining, advisory capacity. In continual conflict with the Spartacists, Landauer sought to hinder the shedding of blood. The days that now followed were, according to all reports, the hardest in Landauer's extremely hard life. All around him were destruction and dissolution, contradiction and absurdity: in the masses, among the leaders, in his closest surroundings. He bore his head high through it all and did what was his to do. That was, above all — as much while he took part in the government as afterward, until the end — the fight against acts of violence. A young student who experienced all the wild upheavals of those weeks in Munich declared that nothing had moved him nearly as much as the kindness, the humaneness, with which Landauer spoke in all the squares, street corners, and halls — not only to large crowds, but also to small groups and individuals. He was always ready to help, to encourage, to revive, to instruct, to comfort. Concerning these activities of Landauer, so-called reporters issued such a flood of lies that Buber and his friends were overcome with horror.

Despite Buber's criticism of Landauer's entry into the first Räterepublik, Buber insisted that Landauer remained faithful, from the time he first espoused it until his death, to the cause of nonviolence. In 1901 Landauer had written: "A goal can only be reached if the means are in consonance with its essential nature. One will never attain non-violence through violence." In 1914 he said: "Now it can become clear to man that freedom and peace of the nations can only come when as Jesus and his followers, and in our time above all Tolstoi advised, they choose to fully abstain from any violence." "This truth Landauer served until his death," asserted Buber. "When I think of the passionate glance and words of my dead friend, I know with what force of soul he fought to protect the Revolution from itself, from violence."

The precariousness of Landauer's political position and even of his personal safety was fully evident to Buber during the very days when Landauer was in power. Two days after Grossmann wrote to Auguste Hauschner about Landauer's key position in the ministry, Buber wrote to her from Heppenheim, concerning what Buber and Landauer's other friends wanted to undertake in his behalf. "An action is . . . not possible at this time," Buber stated, "because the situation has not yet been clarified, and we cannot therefore formulate clearly what we demand." What is more, so long as the fighting continued in any form, they had to remain altogether inactive, Buber declared.

> On the other hand, we must already now prepare for the moment when a public appeal shall perhaps be necessary. To this end a committee should be immediately formed from his circle of friends who will turn to the personalities we shall consider in Germany and German-Austria with the request that they allow their names to be set down on a possibly necessary appeal. To this committee should perhaps belong: you, me, Dehmel, Einstein, Dumont, Mauthner, Mombert, Susman — Who else? Of these I am not certain only in the case of Professor Einstein whether he stands close enough to Gustav; will you speak with him? . . .

On April 15 Buber wrote to Fritz Mauthner about the formation of a committee that might publicly intercede for Landauer. Mauthner replied that they must indeed attempt to rescue Landauer, without approving his politics. He placed his name at Buber's disposal but left the leadership of the undertaking to him. "We cannot protect him from himself," he added; "he would reject that." "It is very sad," he concluded, "that it is precisely the idealism of his circle [that] . . . will let loose a new wave of anti-Semitism over Germany." On April 19 Mauthner reported to Auguste Hauschner that he had heard that Gustav was apparently not hindered in his movements at all but lived unmolested in Munich. A manifesto had just appeared, in fact, in which Landauer declared himself in agreement with the most radical movement. On April 25 he wrote again that the children of Gustav Landauer (with the children of Kurt Eisner) were in Meersburg living with

Landauer's cousin, that Landauer was quite certainly not arrested, but was still in Munich. On April 30, Landauer's friend, the famous actress Louise Dumont, wrote to Auguste Hauschner from Düsseldorf, conveying the latest report on Landauer, from a nephew of hers studying in Munich. Although he had little good to say of Landauer's health, he spoke of "his astonishing activity in work which occupied him day and night" and of his remarkably inexhaustible patience. On April 28 Buber informed Siegmund Kaznelson that Landauer had been only a few days in the first revolutionary government and not at all in the present one. "That he entered the first was a serious error but not at all the offence that you suppose; he had no part in the bloodbath." Buber also pointed out that Landauer stood firmly on his side when Buber expressed to the Munich leaders the inadmissibility of all forms of terror and the ruinous influence of the use of violence.

While these rumors and alarms were circulating among Landauer's friends, Landauer was, in fact, staying outside Munich in the house of the widow of Kurt Eisner, his murdered friend, not secretly but having notified the police. He came several times to Munich for consultations with those close to his views and planned an exodus of women and children in order to avoid a possible bloodbath. Meanwhile the Munich assembly entered a vote of no-confidence in the communist regime of the Spartacists. On April 30 the dictatorship of the Red Army was proclaimed in Munich. On the morning of May 1 the troops of the German Reich marched into that city. On May 1 and May 2 a fearful battle raged in the streets there, which claimed hundreds of lives. In the course of it the Red Army succumbed to the superior might of the Reichswehr-truppen. All this time and especially when the situation became critical because of the approach of the government troops, and threats and warnings became vociferous, Landauer's friends offered to help him escape and implored him to do so. At first he refused, but then he let himself be talked into it and preparations were made to flee across the Lake of Constance to Switzerland. But on the next day he declared himself unwilling to go, and thereafter no argument of any kind could change his mind.

On the afternoon of May 1, Landauer was arrested in the house of Mrs. Eisner, on the basis of a denunciation, and at first taken in Lastauto to the cemetery, a quarter of an hour distant, to be shot there. A member of the colony intervened, pointing to the fact that Landauer had not belonged to the communist Räterepublik. He persuaded the lieutenant that Landauer not be shot merely because of a denunciation but should be brought first to a hearing. Thus Landauer was taken to Starnberg and put in the prison of the lower court, where he underwent a hearing. There, according to the report of an eyewitness who photographed Landauer escorted by the White Guards on his way to prison, Landauer defended himself splendidly.

On the morning of May 2, Landauer was transported with three other prisoners to Stadelheim. From the moment of his delivery there, Landauer was turned over, defenseless, to the soldiers who, far from being restrained from their bloody act by their officers, were incited to it by them. It was an officer who called to the group of soldiers in whose midst Landauer was walking, "Halt! Landauer is to be shot at once." Another officer, Freiherr von Gagern, beat him over the head with the handle of his horsewhip. This was the signal for the soldiers, who now fell on him like a pack of hounds. Landauer was shot and beaten and literally kicked to death. According to one account, Landauer's last words were: "Now comes death, now one must hold one's head high." According to the report of another witness, Landauer cried to the soldiers: "Kill me then! Since you are men!" (Dass Ihr Menschen seid!).

Meanwhile none of Landauer's friends could find out exactly what had happened. Lotte had telegraphed Buber that her father was not in danger, others did not respond to Buber's telegrams, and from Auguste Hauschner he received a telegram on May 5 saying, "Just the awful certainty." "I have no more hope," Buber wrote Mauthner on May 7; yet he could not dismiss the possibility that Lotte's information meant something. "In these days and nights I have myself wandered through Sheol," Buber concluded. It was only later that his worst fears were confirmed.

"Gustav Landauer died the death that matched his life," wrote his friend Margarete Susman, "—not a gentle, not a gradual, not a passive death, but the bitter, sudden, ugly death of the revolutionary, which is at the same time a radiant sacrificial death." "Beaten to death like a dog," exclaimed Fritz Mauthner, "interred like a dog in a mass grave, treated like a dog by the German nationalist and Catholic papers!" The most atrocious calumnies, in fact, continued to spread after Landauer's death: Landauer had incited men to attack the honor of women; Landauer had directed hordes to break their way into the fenced-in yards of dwelling places to plunder; Landauer had instigated violence and murder.

In April 1922 Buber informed Mauthner that he had learned from Lotte that her father's ashes were preserved in a cellar; he saw this as an indignity. "Transporting them to a more worthy place should be a cause for those in whom his memory is alive, I feel." Buber saw a summons to his closest friends as the best way to achieve removal of the ashes, and he invited Mauthner to join Louise Dumont, Margarete Susman, and himself in signing a letter proposing this, "without any party matter mixing in." In 1923, the year of Hitler's unsuccessful beer-hall Putsch and the year in which Buber published *I and Thou,* a simple but imposing obelisk was erected in the woods of Munich bearing the inscription "1870 Gustav Landauer 1919" and over it the words from his "Summons to Socialism": "What is needed now is to bring a sacrifice of another kind, not a heroic one, but a silent, unpretentious sacrifice in order to give an example of a true life." Ten years later, when Hitler came to power, the obelisk was torn down.

Buber concluded his own essay "Landauer and the Revolution" with a comparison of Landauer and Jesus: "In a church in Brescia I saw a mural whose whole surface was covered with crucified men. The field of crosses stretched to the horizon, and on all of them hung men of all different shapes and faces. There it seemed to me was the true form of Jesus Christ. On one of those crosses I see Gustav Landauer hanging." Robert Weltsch also used the image of crucifixion in a letter he wrote Buber after he learned of Landauer's murder:

> How is it possible that something so frightful could have happened! These days I have been as though lost and can still not always take it in. Is there really so little feeling for true greatness, can such a splendid life be annihilated by human hand? I have here found almost no persons who have felt this event in its full seriousness. One is Czuczka [later Sidney Lens, the future husband of Miriam Beer-Hofmann]; yesterday we walked the whole night and spoke and were silent, and something stirred in us dully, like a sudden understanding of Golgotha, and burning despair.

The social psychiatrist Ernst Joël wrote that his first impulse on his return to Germany from the war was to visit Gustav Landauer; for he hoped to find in him at long last a person he could follow. Now that he learned the news of Landauer's murder he suffered because he had not fought with greater zeal for the cause of freedom.

To the personal responsibility of the revolutionary, which, despite all, Buber saw as embodied in Landauer, Buber ascribed the central point in his own developing social thought: the teaching of the "line of demarcation" that is drawn anew at all times and in every situation. The watchword of the revolutionary's spirit is "Up to here," and for that "Up to here," for that drawing of the line, there is no fast rule. The revolutionary lives on the knife's edge, not of "selling his soul to the devil" in order to bring the revolution to victory, but of the practical tension between ends and means. "I cannot conceive anything real corresponding to the saying that the end 'sanctifies' the means," wrote Buber. "But I mean something which is real in the highest sense of the term when I say that the means may profane, actually make meaningless, the end, that is, its realization!" The farther the means are from the goal, the farther is what is achieved too. It is in this connection that Buber developed his all-important teaching of the "crossfront," the true front that runs through each party or group and through each adherent of a party or group. On the true front each fights against his fellows and himself for the sake of the genuine realization of the cause. The "democratic centralists" say of these men that they have weakened the fight, but in fact it is they who keep alive the truth of the battle. Such a man was Gustav Landauer.

> Landauer fought in the revolution against the revolution for the sake of the revolution. The revolution will not thank him for it. But those will thank him for it who have fought as he fought and perhaps some day those will thank him for whose sake he fought.

When Buber spoke at the funeral of Charlotte Landauer in 1927, he spoke of the life of this faithful daughter in the context of the uncanny, "to us barely graspable meaning of Gustav Landauer's death. . . . a death in which the monstrous, sheerly apocalyptic horror, the inhumanity of our time has been delineated and portrayed."

Landauer became for Buber the image of the authentic social and political person, the image of the person who has to stand and withstand in the "lived concrete," the situation in which he finds himself, "whether in the field of work or the field of battle." It was Landauer whom Buber had in mind when in a public discussion in 1929 he spoke of the religious tragedy of the revolution, namely, that its means are untrue to its end. That is the real unfaithfulness of the revolutionary that perhaps even the religious person may not escape. But when the latter does enter into the revolution, then he has the special responsibility of fighting step by step for the purity of the image. His function in the revolution is to be *defeated* in an exemplary fashion, as one who bears the organic substance *through* the abyss into a new world. Thus in a remarkable fashion the religious revolutionary fused for Buber with the man of the "dark charisma," who knows no historical success, the "suffering servant" who works in the depths of history. As the suffering servant is an arrow that remains hidden in the quiver, so the true religious revolutionary is a person the effect of whose work is ultimately shrouded in mystery.

Buber's response to the news of Landauer's death was probably, next to his "conversion" and the early separation from his mother, the most important single event in his life. Yet this is one "autobiographical fragment" that Buber could not write. When I urged him to do so in Jerusalem in 1960, he confessed that he had tried and found himself still too close to this event to be able to write about it beyond his reference to the "death of a friend" in the dialogue with the American psychologist Carl Rogers in 1957. Two years before Buber's own death, when he was eighty-five, he was still so preoccupied by this event forty-five years earlier that he was impelled to describe Landauer's murder again and again to Naemah Beer-Hofmann, younger daughter of his old friend Richard Beer-Hofmann.

In his dialogue with Rogers, Buber spoke of "a certain inclination to meet people," to change something in the *other,* but also to let *himself* be changed by *him.* This inclination was enormously strengthened by the First World War, at the end of which he realized for the first time how "terribly influenced" he had been by the necessity of expanding "inclusion" to "imagining the real" in the most concrete sense of what was happening in the world at just that moment. The climax and the most important event of *imagining the real* came when he received the news of Landauer's barbaric murder. "Now once more − for the last time − I was compelled to imagine this killing, not only visually, but with my *body.*" By this Buber meant that he had to feel in his own body every blow that Landauer suffered in that courtyard where he was beaten to death. Not, as in the example Buber gives in "Education" (1926), suddenly experiencing from the other side the blows that one is inflicting oneself, but experiencing at a distance the blows that others, strangers, had inflicted on his friend. "This," said Buber, "was the decisive moment, after which, after some days and nights in this state, I felt, 'Oh, something has been done to me.'" From then on, his meetings with people, and particularly with young people, took on a different form. Now he had to give them something more than just his inclination to exchange thoughts and feelings. He had to offer the fruit of a profound experience, that of the four years of the war and, capping it all, the trauma of Landauer's murder.

CHAPTER 12

Zionist Socialism and the Arab
Question

THE POLITICAL REALISM that Buber brought to the Russian and German Revolutions he also brought to that political-military gambit which co-workers within the Jewish Renaissance, such as Ahad Ha'am and Chaim Weizmann, saw as "the last chance for the salvation of the Jewish people" — the British Balfour Declaration in 1917 officially committing Britain to the support of the creation of a Jewish Homeland in Palestine. No less a Zionist than they, Buber did not look to any such purely political document, tied as it was to the shifting political interests of the British Empire, as a secure hope for the Jewish settlement in Palestine. What is needed, Buber told Moritz Spitzer in January 1919, is the foundation of groups and unions of groups dedicated to the creation of a genuine community in Palestine and the willingness to work there themselves on this task. In the same month he wrote Hugo Bergmann that he was entirely in agreement with him concerning Palestine but could not think of going there himself before 1922 because of his work on what was to become *Ich und Du.*

In the middle of March 1919, Buber saw the Zionist movement as facing a critical decision caused by the deliberations in Paris by the representatives of the great powers concerning the new order of European and Near Eastern territorial relations. True to the teaching of nonviolence and genuine social constructiveness that Landauer had espoused, Buber rejected the notion that the Jewish people could be liberated by any actions that did violence to the immanent demand of Judaism that there *be justice and truth between the peoples.* What was being prepared in Paris, Buber prophetically asserted, was a league of state structures, not of peoples, even though the peoples, through every type of propaganda, were being persuaded to identify themselves with the states. If we let Palestine be included in the dominant politics, economy, and culture, declared Buber, it will never really be ours. In the place of the assimilation of the individual, we shall have simply brought about the assimilation of the people. A truly Jewish Palestine might play a mediating function between West and East. But if an agent of economic and political imperialism — of "English-American capitalism, swollen with power yet soon ready to collapse" — is erected on Zion, then all our efforts will be in vain. The bridge, which the unholy spirit of Versailles will never bring about, the Jewish people can build — out of its own socialist truth.

In September 1919 Buber wrote to Hugo Bergmann, in response to an article on "The Hebrew Book and the German Zionists" that was later published in *Der Jude,* that Bergmann seemed less universal in his inner Judaism than before and that he, Buber, could not go along with that or with his radical Hebraism. As highly as Buber valued language for our life, he could not make it central but, rather, what it was that the word communicated. Bergmann tended at times to treat the religious as merely a content among other contents. Buber recognized, of course, that Bergmann was trying to establish a direct relation to the actual situation in Palestine, to which he had immigrated. Bergmann replied that he recognized more strongly than ever that the entire hope of Zionism in the world today lay not in official Zionism, but in the generation that Buber had educated. Just because of that he also saw, more clearly perhaps than Buber, the monstrous danger that because of the alienation of the people and its language the whole movement might remain what it had been until then: literary. When someone as close to them as Max Brod could write a basic book on Judaism without reading Hebrew, "how can we take on ourselves the enormous responsibility of Judaism if, without becoming farmers in Palestine, we do not at least take the step toward reality that would place us within Hebrew literature and detach us from the other languages?" Bergmann said this above all to Buber himself, who had until now been their leader. "For me Hebraism is simply an attempt to remain true and to preserve the word," Bergmann concluded. Buber replied that he had to recognize that what Bergmann wrote about Hebraism was correct and said that he was himself working a great deal on his Hebrew and hoped to be able to compose a free essay in it in a year or two. "Whether I shall ever be able to express myself *creatively* in this language, I doubt — rather I do not believe it."

During all these years Buber's interest in the idea of the Hebrew University continued active. In 1913 when Weizmann learned from Berthold Feiwel that Buber was unhappy at having been excluded from the Committee for the University, he wrote him twice, inviting him to take part, apparently without result. In 1920 Buber told Bergmann that he was unreservedly against a university in the European sense. What he preferred was, on the one hand, a scientific institute and, on the other, a genuine folk school. In the previous summer after he had lectured at a conference on the renewal of culture, he had been offered a great castle on the left bank of the Rhine for that purpose. "I declined because here in this land I do not feel myself called to erect an institution so deeply bound not only with the folk culture but also with its crisis. It would be otherwise in Palestine." Actually Buber was to become deeply involved in *Jewish* folk culture in Germany during the Nazi period *and* in Palestine after the establishment of the state of Israel. In both cases the folk schools that he helped establish were, as he wrote to Bergmann in 1920, closer to Nikolai Frederik Grundtvig's nineteenth-century Danish folk schools than to any traditional university.

In 1921 Buber wrote to his friend Louise Dumont about his meeting with the Hindu poet and philosopher Rabindranath Tagore, whom he found to be a lovable, childlike, worthy person with a touchingly beautiful faith, though one not suited to them. In their conversation about Zionism Tagore wanted to relieve the burden of the Jews in Palestine by getting them to lay aside modern Western techniques. But we must bear the full weight of our burden and either carry it to the heights or plunge into the abyss with it, Buber confided to Dumont. In the same year Buber informed Ernst Elijahu Rappeport that he was beginning hours of conversation in Hebrew. An incomparable picture of Buber's family life at this time is given us by Paula's portion of the letter to Rappeport. Their daughter Eva was at home for the winter and was receiving lessons in Hebrew and English. Raffi was in Berlin at the school for agricultural economy. He was still an "unbaked piece of bread," Paula wrote, and she regretted not having Rappeport nearby to help prepare Raffi's parents for his various transformations! In the fall Paula had planted her garden almost anew, "also with beautiful and rare shrubs which I have never yet seen bloom, and I await it in my full garden-joy." Paula did not fail to tell Rappeport about the cats:

> Do you still remember the little cat whose matted hair you cut off? He is still with us and I hope to have him for a long time. He has become my favorite. At every meal he sits on my knees and lays his forepaws on the table. He lives among us like an imp. He loves Martin most respectfully, me most tenderly, Eva he trusts boundlessly, but with Raffi he has, with reason, some anxiety.

In the midst of all this Paula was actively writing and in 1921 published her second book of stories, *Sankt Getrauden Minne.* Martin's father Carl wrote her of the specially strong overall impression made on him by the poetic structure of the whole, the particularly successful transition from the living into dead souls clothed and acting with the forms of life, and finally the conclusion with its return to Hades.

The decade between 1919 and 1930 in Buber's life, writes Ernst Simon, can be compared to the days of his youth between 1898 and 1904. Both were periods in which a devoted and desperate attempt was made by Buber to influence Zionist policy directly through its institutions and central figures, as well as indirectly through articles, speeches, and intermittent activities with small sectarian circles that intentionally deviated from the *via regia* of the movement. The preparation for this decade of activity was Buber's indefatigable work as editor of *Der Jude,* the teaching of Zionist communal socialism in *The Holy Way,* and his implacable hostility to all forms of narrow, self-serving nationalism. The lesson of the First World War had not been lost on Buber, and once learned it was never forgotten, nor was there ever, from this time until his death, any relaxation in his warnings against the *Yishuv's* (the Jewish settlement in Palestine) becoming "a nation like all the nations." Modern nationalism, to Buber, meant idolatry, and it was not any less so if the idol bore a Jewish name. The "dominant dogma of the century" is "the unholy dogma of the sovereignty of nations," which makes every nation its own master and judge, "obligated only to itself and answerable only to itself." A genuine renaissance has never emerged from exclusively national tendencies, but from a passionate reaching out for renewed human content. "Not Hebraism but Hebrew humanism . . . will have to be at the core of a Jewish movement for regeneration." To accomplish this liberation and redemption, a land of one's own and true community are necessary. Such liberation and redemption can be blocked by those who cling to the old forms of the Jewish law. To Buber this meant receiving the law from the hands of the people rather than from the hands of God. "For we know as yet only the eternal aspect of God's will," but we ourselves must prescribe the temporal aspect by setting the stamp of the eternal's command upon the stuff of reality. "We can tolerate nothing that comes between us and the realization of God," and this realization means a new beginning, a reconstruction, a new world that will reveal itself to us in the *true life between man and man*. "True community is the Sinai of the future."

It is at this point that Buber's teaching coincided with the new form of collective settlement that was already being built in Palestine, the kibbutz. Buber called for a "revolutionary colonization" which would reject already existing structures in favor of a transformation and reshaping within and through the Jewish settlement conducive to its growing into a truly communal structure. This "revolutionary colonization," for Buber, was also a turning back to the past in exactly the same sense as he had spoken of Landauer's revolutionary labors: "A buried ancient treasure is being uncovered, a forgotten direction found again, and a neglected human potential reactivated." As in the Hebrew Bible, the establishment of true community depends upon the agrarian life being elevated to so devoted a service of God that it would spread to other social classes and bind them too to God and the soil. Now Buber's "Jewish Renaissance" took on a whole new meaning: choosing within the Jewish tradition only those elements that lead to closeness to the soil, the hallowing of the everyday, and absorption of the Divine in nature. Thus here again, as in "Community," Buber's religious socialism is based upon community, soil, work, mutual aid, leadership, the commonwealth, mankind, and the spirit. And here too it is recognized that no socialist structure that leaves unchanged the life between man and man can bring about a true transformation of society. "Our hope is rooted in the belief that in the generation of Jews who are returning to their homeland at this moment of our history, after so great a shock and motivated by so great a decision, the preconditions for a transformation of relationships are raised to a power never known before." Many of the Jews who went to Palestine at this time were motivated by the desire to build a new community, a large number of them, including Buber's friend Hugo Bergmann, because of Buber's influence.

Buber's idea of the realization of community contributed to the rise of the Halutz, or pioneer, movement during and after the First World War, and to the beginnings of so-called Labor Zionism. In his conception of Zionist socialism and "revolutionary colonization" Buber's thought converged at many points with the community of workers of the land that had arisen in Palestine as the Young Workers, Hapoël Hazaïr. Until 1920 Hapoël Hazaïr was not a party but a living community of closely bound men. Its emphasis, like Buber's own and that of Landauer, was not on politics or the state, but on personal realization, the involvement of one's whole humanity as the bearer of the Jewish rebirth. At the center of Hapoël Hazaïr stood the labor philosopher and pioneer A. D. Gordon, who came to Palestine from Russia at the age of fifty and lived on a kibbutz until his death sixteen years later. Like Buber and Landauer, Gordon was concerned about immediacy, about making the crowd no longer a crowd, about the fight against the secret lust for power in man which makes the oppressed potential oppressors.

The last figure that Buber dealt with in his book *Israel and Palestine: The History of an Idea,* the man who took on more significance for Buber than any other modern exponent of Zion, from Moses Hess, Pinsker, and Herzl to Ahad Ha'am and Rav Kook, was A. D. Gordon. Buber had chosen Ahad Ha'am the teacher over Herzl the leader, but he found in A. D. Gordon, even more than in Ahad Ha'am, "the true teacher" whose teaching was that of the human image, the teaching of Gordon's life itself, self-evident, casual, where silence is more important than words, and the way in which the spade strikes the earth shows the way in which the eye rests on the stars. "The whole of his life speaks of the teaching," Buber wrote. Ahad Ha'am proceeded from Spirit to People to Land; A. D. Gordon from Land to People to Spirit. Both movements are necessary, but it is in A. D. Gordon that Buber found the realized man of Zion. Indeed, according to Ernst Simon, there was no one whom Buber admired more than A. D. Gordon, with the possible exception of Franz Rosenzweig. Buber saw in Gordon the man who in fact *realized* the idea of Zion, the idea of *realization* that Buber himself *taught* but was not able to embody. In *Israel and Palestine* Buber wrote:

> Of all those who came to the land in the period of new settlement the man Ahron David Gordon appears to me to be the most remarkable. Compared with the others he seems like a natural phenomenon where they seem like merely social phenomena. Just as Gordon is independent *vis-à-vis* society, he is independent *vis-à-vis* history. . . . He is without peer in the Jewry of our day. . . . The wound in Gordon's heart is caused by the Jews having fallen not from political self-determination but from the Cosmos. . . . Whitman sings the praises of pioneering, . . . but Gordon *is* the pioneer . . . only Gordon can say: "Our way — to Nature through work." . . . he was better able than anyone else in the modern Jewish national movement to renew the insight into the unique relationship between the people and the land of Israel.

This last statement must seem strange indeed if we think of the religious fullness of Buber's teaching of Zionism and of the biblical foundation that he increasingly gave it, as opposed to the "land-nature-cosmos-people" axis of Gordon's philosophy. Gordon, Buber pointed out, was not concerned about abstract Being; only about the concrete experience of Being. In that sense, Buber saw Gordon as anticipating his own later teaching of "the eclipse of God," nor would any pragmatic "as if" compensate Gordon for the fact that "we lack religious faith in everything we do." "All 'as ifs' are alien to his soul," Buber declared. "The 'main thing,' Gordon says, is to establish for ourselves a new relationship 'to the mystery of existence and life.' " Just as Israel can participate in the Cosmos only in the land of Palestine, "so too it is only there that it can regain a religious relationship to the mystery of existence." Probably no one has ever suffered and struggled so much as Gordon, Buber asserted, for the sake of his own relationship to the land and for his deep insight into the relationship between the people and the land. "Only when you begin to look for something . . . that no Jew can find anywhere else," said

Gordon, "will you be competent to do something . . . of vital importance for Palestine."

Though Buber met Gordon only once, at the Zionist labor conference in Prague in 1921, this encounter must be seen as one of the significant "events and meetings" of his life, to be placed alongside that with men whom he saw and met hundreds of times, like Landauer and Franz Rosenzweig. The encounter could not have been so meaningful if Buber's whole thought and being had not been moving him toward it in the years immediately preceding, including all he endured with Landauer during the German Revolution. When it did take place, Buber and Gordon met as equals, the man from Europe and the man from Palestine joining forces in creating a new surge of Zionist socialism within the larger Zionist movement. Yet its significance for Buber also lay in the fact that Gordon's existence testified to this fusion of Jewish nationalism and socialism in a way that Buber's existence did not. Gordon returned to Kibbutz Degania, where he died two years later, while Buber returned to his life as an intellectual, a writer, an educator, an activitist and thinker of every type, but not as a man working on the soil of the Land, a pioneer in a true communal settlement. When Buber visited Gordon's grave in Kibbutz Degania in 1928, he wrote for the kibbutznikim a tribute that shows in its very language how Gordon had become for him through that one meeting one of the important Thou's of his life:

> But I see you, you old man with your face that has remained open, you old peasant and thinker, I see you in the evening walking from your village to the river, there where it flows forth from the lyre-shaped sea. You sit down by the water, lean your back for a while on a cypress and let the fresh breeze blow in your face. Then you lay yourself flat so that your body also touches the earth, and even the two palms of your hands you press against the ground. Only now do you look up at the stars. O stars over the Land of Israel, O Land under the stars of God!

Both the plow and the stars belonged together in Gordon. "No real There without a real Here, no real Here without a real There! Only he who produces with the earth, can include the world-space in human life; only for him who loves the stars does the sense of the boundless vibrate through everything near." Thus Gordon became for Buber the image of the true pioneer who called to his comrades on the kibbutz not to lose themselves in the moment and to his fellow Jews in the Diaspora not to lose themselves in history, but to bind the present work to the eternal, the truth of the millennia to authentication in the everyday.

Out of the similarities of their thinking concerning "revolutionary colonization," Buber and his followers and Gordon's Hapoël Hazaïr merged forces during the years 1919 to 1921, producing a fresh spurt in the Halutzim movement. These were the years, according to Hans Kohn, in which the best of the Jewish youth prepared themselves in many ways to leave Europe and go to Palestine, in order to take up there a life of work and community for the building of a new Jewish and human society.

> Sons and daughters of the middle class, educated for middle-class and academic callings, forsook their middle-class existence: not as in war for a short time only to return later to their secure existence, but in earnest and forever because they felt that this bourgeois existence could not be the clothes of their souls. . . . They wanted to reverse the development of the bourgeois age . . .: from the great city back to the land, from industry to agriculture, from abstract learning to concrete, close-to-earth forms of life in accord with nature's rhythm.

At the end of March 1920 there took place in Prague, the city from which Buber's new Zionist activity had emanated, a conference in which the representatives of Hapoël Hazaïr from Palestine under the leadership of A. D. Gordon, and the representatives of the Zionist youth of Central and East Europe under the leadership of Buber, came together. The first action of the conference was the formal unification of Hapoël Hazaïr and Zeïre Zion, Buber's Zionist youth group, to establish a world union of socialist, but not Marxist, Labor Zionists. Comrade Buber set forth the suggested program for this world union, the first principle of which was that the national and the social problems of the Jewish people form an indivisible unity, and that this indissoluble unity would be the principal tenet of Zionist socialism. Through Buber's intervention the two opposing views of the nationalists and the socialists were brought closer together, and the goal of socialism itself accepted as being not a mechanical regulation of social relations but first, and above all, the creation of direct relationships between men, the creation of organic communities bound together through shared living experiences. But Buber went even further than this. He brought together the two seemingly distant and unrelated worlds of the German Revolution and the Palestinian revolutionary colonization. Buber acknowledged Gordon as the man who *lived* this national communal socialism, Landauer as the man who prepared for it by his writings and his life and who might have been, who should have been, its real leader.

Gustav Landauer was a predestined leader of the new Judaism, and it is a sign of the tragedy of our fate . . . that he was murdered in a strange, hostile land in despairing work for a hopeless building of a new life. It is a tragedy of our fate that this man and the cause for which he was created did not come together.

"Landauer's idea was our idea," Buber asserted. It was the knowledge that what counts is not changing institutions but transforming human life, the relations of men to one another. The "dizzy infinity of the new world image," which was Buber's own vision of chaos as a young man, led the individual to take refuge in the emerging structure of nationalism and change a healthy creative power to a sick will-to-power, a destructive will that wants to be "more powerful than" the other nation. "Not power but power hysteria is evil," and the chief mark of this hysteria is surrendering the responsibility of the "demarcation line," the task of constantly demarcating anew one's own rights, as an individual and as a nation, from the rights of others. A people need not be united biologically: it only need be shaped into a new entity by a great molding fate experienced in common in some great creative hour. When such a people acquires a new awareness, a new self-consciousness, it becomes a *nation.* But nationalism is a hyper-awareness, a programmatic hubris which makes of the nation an end in itself. The values of a true nation are *unique;* they need not be compared with the values of any other. But the nationalist declares his people *the best* while at the same time considering his nation responsible only to itself. Such a nation becomes "a Moloch which consumes the best of the people's youth."

This distinction between legitimate and arbitrary nationalism is, for Israel more than for any other people, the distinction between life and death. At the Zionist Congress in Karlsbad Buber asserted, "Israel cannot be healed, and its welfare cannot be achieved by severing the concepts of people and community of faith," but to include both as organic parts of a new order is to recognize the supernational responsibility and obligation at the base of Israel's unique history and situation. Addressing the Congress at what he himself recognized was a very troubled moment in its proceedings, Buber asserted that the group of Zionists to whom he had belonged since his youth had hoped to save nationalism from the error of making an idol of the people, but that they had not succeeded. "Jewish nationalism is largely concerned with being 'like unto all the nations,' with affirming itself in the face of the world without affirming the world's reciprocal power." Repeating this in biblical terms, Buber accused the majority of Zionists of forgetting that Israel's Sovercign is also the Sovereign of its rivals and of its enemies, that the Lord who led the children of Israel out of the land of Egypt also led the Philistines out of Caphtor and the Syrians out of Kir (Amos 9:7). In the spirit of this internationalism, Buber and some friends on the occasion of the Congress made an attempt to found a "Jewish Society for International Understanding," a union of genuine human communes which would replace the present all-powerful method of politics — as the open or secret attempt at *exploitation* of the human soul — by the method of *education* — as the great attempt at an *unfolding* of the human soul.

The most remarkable outcome of the Prague Conference at the Karlsbad Zionist Congress was not the Zionist Socialism that Buber put forward or even the internationalism that was so far ahead of its day, but the practical corollary of these two which only he and a few of his friends saw at that time: namely, the necessity for cooperation with the Arab peoples living in and around Palestine, to go hand in hand with the task of building up communal settlements and making Palestine a center and example of social regeneration in the Mideast.

Ernst Simon, who was present at the Political Committee of the Zionist Congress, testifies to the many things that Buber said about the Arab problem there; most importantly, the universal historical law that he enunciated: The advance and progress of one people will lead to the advance and progress of neighboring peoples; the Zionist movement will hasten the acceleration of the unity of the Arab nations. The Jews in Palestine are to help their Arab neighbors progress rather than to turn them into sworn enemies with whom reconciliation would be very difficult. This argument, which turned out to be a prophecy, found no listeners, says Simon, and instead of increasing Buber's influence detracted from it.

Simon tells of one exception to those who paid no attention to Buber's prediction, namely, "one young usher who was removed from his voluntary service because he manifested his agreement with this attitude, which in view of his job he should have treated with utter indifference." His "unseemly" demonstration was clapping, as Simon has reported, and the twenty-two-year-old usher was Simon himself! The impression that Buber's two great speeches made on Simon has remained with him to this day, as he testified in 1966, but it was in the Political Committee that he was able to recognize and observe Buber as the far-seeing realistic politician (*Realpolitiker*) that he was, even if not as an unusually clever tactician. "Since that time Buber's words did not leave my heart and were one of the factors determining my way of Zionism at the side of Buber these forty years," adds Simon. Anyone who knows the part that Simon has played in Israel's politics, and above all in the attempts of B'rith Shalom and Ihud to bring about rapprochement with the Arabs, will not think this an inconsequential effect of Buber's words.

On September 2, 1921, three days before he gave his address on "Nationalism," Buber gave another address to the Twelfth Zionist Congress, this one specifically addressed to the Arab problem. Beginning with a reference to Herzl, at whose feet he sat even when he opposed him, Buber rejected his own earlier ideas of the Jewish Renaissance as too narrow and too simply historical. The real rebirth of the nation means the turning — turning with one's whole existence to respond to the claim of the situation, in biblical terms the *teshuva*. The first essential task was to be the education of the people to be ready for the true turning; the second, the preparation of the land through pioneering; the third, putting to one side external hindrances independent of people and land, such as diplomacy. First, work and social reality must be created; then rights may be demanded and obtained. Diplomacy had made possible a first step — the creation of the presuppositions of the task, the minimum that was necessary in order that they could work undisturbed on their goal. The reason for the fight of Chaim Weizmann and Buber and their friends against Herzl was the recognition that only actions can provide the support for politics and not the other way around. But now, Buber said, diplomacy has become the master, real work the serving maid, and our work has taken on an inorganic, mechanical, improvised character. Then Buber addressed a word directly to his old comrade Chaim Weizmann, who more than any man was responsible for the Balfour Doctrine, and who now stood at the head of those Zionists committed to diplomacy, cooperation with

England, and European state-politics.* "You are indispensable to us," Buber said, "but take care not to let your indispensability become for us a humiliation instead of a pride." Agitation instead of education, the demand for money instead of the demand for the involvement of the whole person, a false military heroism instead of the genuine heroism of work — all these prevail, Buber charged. Yet four years after the Balfour Declaration they still had to fight for the right for free immigration. In other words, placing political affairs ahead of the real work of building community had not even secured the minimum for their real work!

After this wholesale indictment, Buber turned to the Arab problem. Recognizing the enormous difficulties in establishing relationships with a people not yet constituted and without legitimate representatives, he insisted nonetheless that such relationships must be established — and not merely with one or two Arab notables. The grounds for this would be a planned beginning of a great real effort of colonization and a concrete political and economic program, both of which were lacking. In this fearfully difficult hour which demanded awareness and decision, and in the face of the historical insight into the enduring reality of the Near Eastern peoples, Buber put forth the following resolution in the name of the union of Hapoël Hazaïr and the Zeïre Zion that he represented:

> In this hour, in which for the first time after eight years of separation the representatives of those Jewish people aware of their identity have assembled, be it declared anew before the nations of the West and of the East that the strong core of the Jewish people is resolved to return to its old homeland and in it to erect a new life founded on independent work, a life that shall grow and endure as an organic element of a new humanity. . . .
>
> But this national will is not directed against any other nationality. . . . Not to oppress or dominate any other people do we strive to return into that land with which we are tied by imperishable historical and spiritual bonds and to whose now so-thinly-populated soil we offer, by intensive and consistent cultivation, room enough for us and for the tribes that presently populate it.
>
> Our return to Eretz Israel, which must take place in the form of a steadily increasing immigration, will not injure any alien right. In a just union with the Arab people we want to make the common dwelling place into an economically and culturally flourishing commonwealth whose extension will guarantee each of its member nations an undisturb-

---

* See Note A in Sources for Chapter 12, p. 405.

ed autonomous development. Our colonization ... does not have the capitalistic exploitation of a sphere as its goal and serves no imperial aims whatsoever; its meaning is the creative work of free men on the communal earth. In this social character of our national ideal lies the powerful warranty for our confidence that between us and the workers among the Arab people a deep and lasting solidarity of real interests will manifest itself which must overcome all the antagonisms produced by the confusions of the moment.

From this resolution it is clear why the Zionist socialism that Buber represented for Hapoël Hazaïr was inextricably connected with the concern for the Arab workers and the Arab peoples and with the refusal to transplant European methods of imperialistic colonization to Palestine. In this lay the great advance of the second Aliyah over the *bilui* who hired Arabs to do their work for them. But the Zionist movement at large had not yet caught up to the communal socialist realities that were being built in Palestine *or* to the absolute top priority of working toward a co-operation with the Arab inhabitants of the land. Here and there a brave voice, such as that of Ahad Ha'am, spoke up clear and true at this time, but otherwise the problem was largely ignored. Yet at that time there still *was* the possibility of which Buber spoke; for the situation had not yet polarized, in political slogans or in tragic reality, into Zionism versus anti-Zionism, the Jews in Palestine at the expense of the Arabs or the Arabs running the Jews into the sea. In 1921 and every year of his life thereafter, Buber pointed to the "narrow ridge" between the disastrous extremes, with all the realism, earnestness, fervor, and responsibility at his disposal. What was at issue was not merely an "Arab problem," important as this was, but the whole question of Jewish nationalism. Buber and his friends recognized the central significance of the Arab question for Jewish nationalism precisely because they recognized that the uniqueness of the Jewish people could not be preserved if they became a "modern" nation putting its own interests above all others.* "Buber's Zionism," writes Ernst Simon, "can be concisely formulated in the paradoxical demand: to remain a chosen people in normal conditions."

On the face of it, Buber was successful; for they were able to get through the Congress a resolution in this sense. With the exception of the 1901 Congress, it was, indeed, Buber's only success

---

* See Note B in Sources for Chapter 12, p. 407.

in practical Zionist party politics. But it was a success in appearance only. By the time Buber got it through the Editorial Committee it had lost most of its effectiveness. Nor was any serious attempt ever made to carry it out in practice. The Congress would not have dared reject such a proposal, Robert Weltsch points out, because that would give substance to the Arab and the English anti-Zionist claim that the Zionists wanted to oppress or suppress the Arabs. But the Editorial Committee sought to water down Buber's original text as far as possible, as Buber himself revealed twenty-six years later on the occasion of Judah Magnes's seventieth birthday. Buber experienced this as a deep personal shock that led him to withdraw once again from active Zionist politics:

> Many years ago when I fought in the Zionist Congress for the concept of a Jewish-Arab unity, I had an experience that was like a nightmare to me and that determined my future life. I had put forward a draft resolution emphasizing the community of interests of both peoples and pointing the way to a cooperation between them — the only way that can lead to the salvation of Palestine and its two peoples. ... Then something happened which is entirely usual and self-evident to a professional politician, but which so horrified me that to the present day I have not been able to free myself from it. In the Editorial Committee, which was composed for the most part of old friends of mine, one little amendment was proposed and still another little amendment and so on. Each of these little amendments had apparently no decisive significance, and all were explicitly justified on the grounds that one must formulate the resolution in such a way that it would be agreeable to the Congress. Again and again I heard the words: "Are you only concerned about a gesture or do you want the Congress to accept the thesis of Jewish-Arab cooperation and make it its own cause? If you want the latter, you must agree to this little amendment."
>
> Of course, I was not concerned about a gesture; I wanted to bring about a fundamental change in the attitude of the Zionist movement toward the Arab question. Therefore I fought each time in defense of the text that I had proposed but gave in time and again when the fate of my resolution depended upon this giving in. When the Editorial Committee had finished its labors and the agreed upon version was brought to my hotel in a clean copy, I saw, to be sure, a series of beautiful and convincing statements, but the marrow and the blood of my original demand were no longer in them.
>
> I accepted it and agreed to bring the resolution before the Congress. I contented myself with emphasizing in my introduction and explanation which preceded my reading of the text the fundamental transformation that I had intended with this resolution. But I felt: my role as a "politician," i.e., a man who takes part in the political activity of a group, was finished. I had started something and had to finish it but

henceforth I would not start anything where I would have to choose between the truth as I saw it and what was actually being achieved. From now on I would have to do without formal resolutions and content myself with speech-making.

If we compare the resolution that was passed with the original one that Buber proposed, we can see that what was left out was not just the organic wholeness and fullness of the original but the very thing which gave Buber and the Zionist youth for whom he spoke the assurance that these were not just empty phrases: namely, the necessity of a communal socialist building of the land that would *not* entail the evils of exploitation and suppression that every capitalist expansion of Europe had always brought with it. Buber's misgivings in relation to the resolution as finally passed proved to be only too well grounded. The Zionist leadership of the Congress paid no attention to Buber's demand for the initiation, as soon as the state of war was at an end, of a great, systematic, well-prepared, well-organized work of colonization or to his demand for direct economic and political cooperation with the Arab population already existing in Palestine. "It has so mixed up *our* claim with furthering the cause of *England's* Mandate over Palestine," wrote Buber, "that we pass in Europe and Asia as the handy man of British imperialism — a false slogan, but one that it is very difficult to correct."

What particularly amazed Buber was the failure of the Zionist leaders at the Congress to grasp the changing nature of British imperialism: assuring the continuance of the Empire through a relaxation of the connection of its members, that is through a *centrally instigated decentralization.* Even the most bitter disappointments never weakened Buber's unswerving political realism and his refusal to bend to the wind of political slogans. This course was already set, Buber pointed out at the end of these Congress notes, in the policy of *Der Jude* since he began editing it in 1916:

A healthy, decisive pessimism, . . . the world-view of clenched teeth, the belief in the decision through work and through nothing else — that is the attitude that has found expression in these pages since they existed, that has found stronger expression since we have become "a political factor," and that they will remain true to.

PART VII

Education

(1917-1922)

CHAPTER 13

Education and Politics

BUBER'S POLITICAL AND SOCIAL CONCERNS during these years of crisis contained the seed of one of his most important later contributions to the philosophy of education: the distinction between the propagandist who imposes his "truth" on those he manipulates and the true educator who is concerned with the unfolding of others and trusts that each will find his own unique relationship to the truth for which the educator witnesses. "All true education is help toward self-discovery and toward self-unfolding." From about 1910 on there was a radical swing in Germany from education as the assimilation of knowledge to education as the capacity for making one's own judgments out of one's own experience. In these years Buber took an active part in the development of the Hohenrodter Bund. The folk education of this group was concerned with the formation of character to meet the needs of the present rather than the mere dissemination of culture.

A second, important educational activity of Buber's during these years was his leading role in the foundation and continuation of the Jüdische Volksheim in Berlin under the direction of the great Jewish educator Dr. Siegfried Lehmann. This Jewish People's Home grew in part out of the activity of the Jewish Culture Committee which Buber and Salman Schocken, Jr., headed in Berlin from 1916 on, the date when the Volksheim was established. The immediate occasion for it was the influx of Eastern European Jews into Berlin and the desire on the part of those German Jews who, like Buber, were passionately concerned about the situation of the Polish and other Eastern Jews, to help them in some positive way. The home was a combination of a settlement house and school, since the pupils lived and worked with Dr. Lehmann and with the many dedicated young German Jews who came to help there. Of the five men to whom the report of the first year of the operation of the Home was dedicated as "supporters of our work," three of them are already well known to us: Martin Buber, Gustav Landauer, and Max Brod. An insight into the importance of the Jüdische Volksheim for dedicated Jewish youth during the war years is afforded us by Franz Kafka's letters to his fiancée, Felice Bauer, whom he persuaded to work at the Home and who for a while gave a great deal of her time to it, working in the office, editing the reports, and taking part in the life of the Home.

"From his dwelling place in Heppenheim an der Bergstrasse," writes Hans Kohn, "Buber worked with silent determination in ever widening circles of public life." In the years from 1919 to 1928 a number of conferences took place in Heppenheim precisely because this was Buber's home and he was, for some of the most seminal movements of the time, the personal and spiritual center. One of these conferences at Heppenheim was the Conference for the Renewal of the Essence of Education, which took place in the summer of 1919. Buber addressed the participants on the idea and methods of a general higher school, i.e., a folk high school, or "school for adult education," as it was later called. Out of the 1919 conference on education at Heppenheim grew a circle in southwestern Germany stressing a political attitude stemming from conscience. Thus as Buber's political activity led him toward education, giving him insight into it, so his educational activity led back to his concern with the political. The leading spirits of this "Frankfurt Union," as it was also called, were Florens Christian Rang and Martin Buber, and its members included Otto Erdmann, Hermann Herrigel, Ernst Michel, Paul Natorp, Alfonse Paquet (a noted German literary figure), Heinrich Richter, and Theodor Spira. The distinguished social and religious thinker Eugen Rosenstock-Huessy also was involved with this group.

Alfonse Paquet described Florens Christian Rang as jurist, philosopher, and theologian, *and* as a practical man of eminent experience. Even in 1914 when Rang and Buber were at great odds in their attitude to the war, Rang shared in that spirit that was leading Buber toward *I and Thou*. In 1914 Rang used the language of "I and Thou" and "the between" in a way that anticipated Buber's later use of it. "Love spans a relationship from person to person," Rang wrote, "not as a summation in one individual but between two; only that one of the two is not man but God." Faith and love were essentially one to him: each a movement of an I toward a Thou, except that faith strives toward a transcendent Thou.

The experience of the war years compelled Rang to come full circle: the complete rejection of his earlier militarism and an intensely active commitment to the cause of international understanding and peace. For this to take place he had to make a decisive break with that German Idealism that formerly held him in its spell and that he later characterized as a philosophy of "world-death" rather than "world-life," will-less, cowardly, not meaning what it says, not wanting to know, a not-living which is also a not-wanting-to-die — precisely the sort of cloudy and romantic thinking that Landauer had complained about in Rang in 1915. When Rang and Buber came together again in the Gelnhaar Group after the war, Rang had become as radical as Buber in his opposition to war, and in Rang's case this expressed itself in concern for economic reparations for what Germany committed during the war. Conscience does not want to be a general ideal but to be real here and now, Rang declared. The examination of one's conscience as to whether to reject participation in war will demand, if the answer is affirmative, steps that will form this refusal into something possible and effective.

Two leading German educators with whom Buber worked closely in those years and throughout the 1920s were Elizabeth Rotten and Karl Wilker. At this time Buber was moving in his life and thought to the centrality of meeting, and an explicit and important part of this development was his work in education with this circle. In 1922 when Rotten and Wilker were commissioned to edit for the German-speaking circle of nations —

Germany, Switzerland, Austria, Bohemia — a German-language pedagogical journal with an international orientation, the principles which they formulated under Buber's influence were those of Buber's philosophy of "meeting" and "relationship." In intensive conversation among Martin Buber, Paul Natorp, Karl Wilker, and Elizabeth Rotten, three basic propositions evolved that were printed for several years on the inside page of the cover of the journal which they founded, *Das werdende Zeitalter* (Developing Age):

> Education is interaction, is the working together of giving and receiving, an intensification, heightening and purification of the life-process. Youth is for man openness to all, without biological age limit, so long and so far as his own inner growth incessantly renews him. . . .
>
> Education is for us . . . the confident daring to *open up* human life in renunciation of pressure and force which in the finer and more concealed forms of authoritarian education is more furtive and perhaps more dangerous than in the cruder forms the evils of which lie exposed for all to see. . . .
>
> Education is for us, therefore, no occasion that concerns only the relation of the older to the younger generation. The readiness for *opening up* of the brother-soul in each human being is for us the great attempt, touching *all aspects of human togetherness,* to establish a *decisively changed relationship of man to man.* Thus education becomes the spiritual force which overcomes the prevailing state of open or hidden exercise of power over human souls — the politicization of all human life spheres — through a new reality of genuine, creative human and national community.

The last sentence echoes Landauer's and Buber's complaint against the substitution of party politics for the real task of building community and at the same time adumbrates Buber's call in the 1950s for breaking through the politicization of all human life in order that true social fellowship within the nation and true dialogue between nations might come into being. They saw that power over men, while *specifically political,* nonetheless entered deep into all human relationships and poisoned them. Conversely, politics can be healthy only if it is penetrated by an element of "the educative," namely, that going out from oneself to the other that leads to an appreciation of points of view different from one's own. "Education is the meeting of two spontaneities," said the Italian educator of teachers Lombardo Radice. "What is fruitful in this meeting of spontaneities," said Elizabeth Rotten, "is the

humanly enlivening, the reciprocal opening. For we have all experienced the fact that through what we seek to give the pupils
we ourselves grow, that we thereby receive from them something
essential. There takes place in us, if we devote ourselves wholly
to our task, a rejuvenating process that keeps us flexible, guards
us from rigidity and from . . . routine.''

In 1922, for the second issue of the first volume of *Das werdende Zeitalter,* Buber wrote an essay called "The Task" in which
the language of "I and Thou" is used in explicit connection with
that contrast between the "political" imposition of values and
true educative "opening up" on which *Das werdende Zeitalter*
was founded. Buber characterized "the public life of the present"
as springing from this dominant tendency of persons to relate to
one another in terms of how they can use one another. This basic
relation, moreover, "extends far into personal life, only now and
then interrupted by cursory vistas of love, friendship, comrade-
ship, fleeting revelations of the Thou, after which, as if nothing
had happened, people resume the usual practice." The "primal
evil of modern man" is that "politicization" of all of life "which
is already preparing to annihilate him and his world." The educative attitude that opposes this domination of the political is not
a theory or point of view but a *response* in this hour of pain, of
question, of rebellion "on the part of the genuine bearers of world
conscience, faith and love." Before these educators there arises
"the word of exorcism and of healing: not your It but your Thou
is what is essential.''

"Educating is opening up," or "unfolding," but this means
more than letting the youthful person develop by himself and
merely watching over his development. Whether we like it or not,
we, the adults, the teachers, are partners in his unfolding, not
through our interfering and imposing but through our addressing
and responding. "For in our meeting, even when we no more want
to intervene than the heavens and the forest, there is something
powerfully stirring — our saying of Thou." Even the least willful
person exercises power, for which he must be responsible. Our
taking responsibility for what we are educating toward depends
upon our willing without willfulness, without arbitrariness (the
"nonaction" of the central person of the Tao). To will without willfulness is possible only in that relationship in which
we face and respond to others rather than experience and use
them: "facing the beings in their true presence and truly present

to them, saying Thou to them, awakening the Thou in them."
To face the other in his true present and be present to him was,
for Buber here, to lead others into the eternal *presence*. "Only he
can educate who stands in the eternal presence."

"Religious education as a special sphere," Buber asserted at the
conclusion of "The Task," must become increasingly problematic.
But true education is the education of the whole person and is
thus religious in the deepest sense of the term, i.e., religion not as
one human province among others but as the demand placed upon
the whole of human life, the demand for wholeness, for whole response. Not just politics but man as man must be transformed if
the educative principle is to set its face against the annihilation
threatened by the political and if this world is to become "the
human realm." It is in this spirit that Buber joined with Rang in
his call for moral and political action born out of the response
to the demand of the unconditional in the concrete situation. In
this precise spirit, too, he affirmed that attack on the dualism
between "religion" and making real God's rule that underlay the
political position of Leonhard Ragaz, the great Christian socialist
with whom, in the years immediately following, Buber worked
in ever closer cooperation.

> Either religion is a reality, rather *the* reality, namely the *whole*
> existence of the real man in the real world of God, an existence that
> unites all that is partial; or it is a phantom of the covetous human
> soul, and then it would be right promptly and completely to replace
> its rituals by art, its commands by ethics, its revelations by science.

CHAPTER 14

Franz Rosenzweig and the Frankfurt Lehrhaus

BUBER'S INTEREST IN GENERAL FOLK EDUCATION stood in fruitful interaction over the years with his concern for Jewish adult education. The great impetus to his participation in the latter during the post-World War I years came through the "free Jewish House of Learning" founded at Frankfurt by Franz Rosenzweig. Buber's most significant personal encounter, next to Paula Buber and Gustav Landauer, was his friendship with this profound existentialist philosopher and interpreter of Judaism. In July 1913, a year before Rosenzweig's first visit to Buber, Rosenzweig had decided to convert to Christianity. He wished to enter Christianity as a Jew and not a pagan, and for that reason he waited until Yom Kippur, the Jewish Day of Atonement, and went to the service so completely open that he emerged converted not to Christianity but to Judaism! From that time on, his path and the path which he showed to others was that of the Baal Teshuvah, the "master of the turning" who has turned away from Judaism but is now turning back. As he swung away from Judaism to a degree unthinkable to Buber, so in his swing back he went beyond Buber in both observance and belief. Yet the kinship between the two leading Jewish religious philosophers and existentialists of the twentieth century was recognized by both men in a fruitful personal and intellectual interchange that made their friendship one of the most memorable episodes in recent Jewish history.

Martin Buber was already famous in Germany as a Zionist, the re-creator of Hasidic legends, and the author of the widely influential "Speeches on Judaism," before Rosenzweig, younger by eight years, had met him. Rosenzweig, on his part, stood in the stream of late German Idealism, as Buber never did, and produced a two-volume work, *Hegel and the State*, before turning away from Hegel in his *Star of Redemption*. The distrust which this rationalistic non-Zionist young philosopher felt for Buber's mystical thought and poetic writing was reinforced by Buber's famous controversy with Rosenzweig's teacher and friend Hermann Cohen, the great Neo-Kantian philosopher of Marburg from whom Buber finally wrested the leadership of German Jewry. In this controversy Rosenzweig at first found himself much closer to Cohen. But struck by his admiration for Buber's journal *Der Jude* and by the force of Buber's writing, Rosenzweig became more and more torn between the two thinkers. "Cohen *abstracts himself* in writing," Rosenzweig wrote his parents from the front in 1916, "while Buber *concretizes himself,* so that *although* Cohen is more than Buber, nonetheless Buber's essay is more than Cohen's." "I stand exactly as far from Buber as I stand from Cohen," he wrote his parents in 1917. "I have with good reason anxiety for my future life." Buber's *Der Jude* smuggles Judaism into the German Jews, Rosenzweig wrote a friend in 1918. "The address on the cover reads: To the Intellectuals. But inside speaks Reb. Martin Salmonides." In 1919 Rosenzweig referred to Buber in similar fashion as Reb. Martin of Heppenheim and stated that it was necessary to go beyond Buber and his "ecstasies."

Although Buber and Rosenzweig had met once in 1914, it was not until their second meeting in 1921 that they really came to know each other. The war years, which had had a decisive effect on the thought of both men, had brought them closer together without their realizing it. In 1919 Rosenzweig wrote Buber asking that he read the manuscript of *The Star of Redemption* and put in a good word with the Jüdische Verlag or with Löwit Verlag. Rosenzweig justified his bold request on the ground that the book would eventually find its circle of readers, Buber among them (a true prophecy!). "I have the unshakable feeling that I have attained here the summit of my intellectual existence and that all that follows will be merely appendices." At the same time Rosenzweig wrote that he was not at all sure of receiving a favorable verdict from Buber. "For so far as I can see, the whole manner and direction of my work lies rather far from yours — perhaps not so far as the various schools of 'Idealist' philosophy but for all that still far." Rosenzweig counted, nonetheless, on the breadth and openness which Buber had time and again shown as editor of *Der Jude* and asked him to judge "whether you see an objective necessity for the view that I here put forward being published as a Jewish view, whether or not this view pleases you yourself."

Rosenzweig's *Star of Redemption* was the product of the war in an even more literal sense than Buber's *I and Thou,* since the first part of it, in Rosenzweig's own words, "was written down on army postcards, in the midst of conversation with comrades and superiors — 'What a whale of a correspondence that fellow Rosenzweig has!' " In the years to come, as we have seen, Buber recognized that Rosenzweig's *Star* had explicitly shown the gateway to the Bible as a reality in a way that he himself had done implicitly in *I and Thou* — through the faithful distinction between creation, revelation, and redemption as stages, actions, and events in the course of God's intercourse with the world. "The catastrophes of historical realities are often at the same time *crises in the human relation to reality,*" wrote Buber in 1930, a year after Rosenzweig's death. "Of the special way in which *our* time has experienced this crisis, I know of no greater and clearer example than that of Franz Rosenzweig."

> Such a crisis of the human relation to reality shatters our familiar manner of orienting ourselves, and compels us to withstand, with our knowledge and our lives, a reality stripped of orientation, a reality that threatens us with the horror of meaninglessness . . . such a crisis summons individual spheres of the spirit to attempt to master the new chaos. . . . It enables these spheres to recognize one another . . . as also addressed and claimed by one another. Out of this encounter . . . an existential co-operation in the task of mastery can arise, a self-verifying thinking with one another and serving one another that stands firm in knowledge and life. Rosenzweig's *Star of Redemption* represents such good fortune in the interchange between philosophy and theology in our time.
>
> The architectonic of *The Star* is of a purity and legitimacy of corre-

spondences such as I have not found in any other writing of our time, and it is a dynamic one. . . .

This candour in the face of the spirit which does not wish to philosophize by grace of the spirit, but by grace of Him whose grace the spirit is, this insatiability that refuses to be put off with spiritually-formed "essences" but dares to seek out the reality itself concealed by these "essences," this rebellious courage, awakened in the crisis, for life "in the Face," makes Rosenzwieg's book a work both of the future and for the future. . . . He fights "with both hands" . . . for the liberation of reality, the *whole* reality. . . . Only now is existential thinking present.

Existential thinking, to both Buber and Rosenzweig, meant that truth must be discovered and confirmed by the whole human being. Such an approach set them in unalterable opposition to all philosophy which seeks for the "essence" of things in abstraction from the concrete reality of personal existence. This reality includes time, change, the limitations of each person's perspective, and the necessary acceptance of the fact of death. The sickness of reason, wrote Rosenzweig in *Understanding the Sick and the Healthy* — an attack on Idealist philosophy — is an attempt to elude death by stepping out of life into the paralysis of an artificial life above time and change and reality. The cure of this sickness, conversely, must be the realization that to live means to move forward to death, that death is the ultimate verification of life.

In his supplement to *The Star of Redemption* Rosenzweig proclaimed the "New Thinking" that had sprung up simultaneously and largely independently in such European thinkers as Eugen Rosenstock-Huessy (the friend in dialogue with whom Rosenzweig had come to the conviction that he must convert to Christianity), Hermann Cohen (whose concept of "correlation" in his posthumous work *Religion of Reason out of the Sources of Judaism* brought him surprisingly close to both Rosenzweig and Buber), Ferdinand Ebner, Martin Buber, and himself. The fundamental concept of the new theory of knowledge, wrote Rosenzweig in "The New Thinking," is that truth ceases to be what "is" true and becomes a verity that must be verified in active life. From the unimportant truths, such as "two times two are four," on which people agree with a minimum use of their brains, "the way leads over those truths for which man is willing to pay, on to those that he cannot verify save at the cost of his life, and finally to those that cannot be verified until generations upon generations have given up their lives to that end."

The old thinking is timeless and monological. Just because it is thinking in general and for all the world, it is thinking for no one else but the thinker, a logical process which goes on within the isolated philosopher. The New Thinking is "grammatical." It uses the methods of speech which is bound to and nourished by time. Because it takes the other seriously and happens *between* oneself and him rather than within oneself alone, it cannot anticipate what the other will reply or know where it will end. This *Sprachphilosophie*, or philosophy of speech, always means that one is speaking to someone quite definite, someone who has not only ears but a mouth. Even when several philosophers philosophize together, each is still really isolated, wrote Rosenzweig, and that is "why the great majority of philosophic dialogues – including most of Plato's – are so tedious." But in actual conversation something happens, and that is why real dialogue is the way to existential truth. The New Thinking "needs another person and takes time seriously – actually, these two things are identical." "To require time means that we cannot anticipate, that we must wait for everything, that what is ours depends on what is another's." "Whatever *The Star of Redemption* can do to renew our ways of thinking is concentrated in this method."

For Rosenzweig, the beginning of all thinking is the real seriousness of the separation of independence of God, man, and the world. Idealist philosophy attempts to find the "essence" of God, world, and man – to reduce all three to one substance, what each really "is." "But experience, no matter how deeply it probes, will find only the human in man, the worldly in the world, and the godly in God."

> If in the "deepest core" the other were identical with myself, as Schopenhauer asserts, I could not love him, for I should be merely loving myself. If God were "within me," or if he were "only my loftier self" then . . . this God would hardly have anything to tell me since I know anyhow what my loftier self wishes to tell me. And if there were such a thing as a "godly" man, a theory proclaimed by some German professor fresh from the impact of Rabindranath Tagore's robe, this man would find himself barred from the path to God that is open to every truly human man.

This means too that God is not everything. The world does not need to be shelled and husked, nor need man's self be deprived of its reality for God to exist. But the converse is also true. For God really to exist he cannot be mind or nature, he cannot be of the essence of man or of the essence of the world. The popular modern idea that God is in process or evolution deprives him of reality, even as it deprives man of the privilege of being human — of meeting God in the present moment. Idealism turns God into the subject of knowing. It cannot bear the existence of a God who is something other than a supreme consciousness or a supreme self. Its final secret is the victory of reason, of rational consciousness. The highest object of this reason is its own self. There is nothing which is inaccessible to it. For Rosenzweig, in contrast, God, world, and man transcend one another and each is equally far from the other. Yet they can come near one another in that series of relations between God and world, God and man, and man and the world which makes up existence. God was from the beginning; man became; the world becomes. Each represents to Rosenzweig a moment of real time — the past, the present, and the future. Although the world is still incomplete, it is no shadow, painting, or dream. Its being is real existence (*Dasein*) — created creation.

My self exists, but only along with other selves who have consciousness as well as I, who see from a different perspective from mine, yet whom I can know as "Thou," even as they can know me as "Thou." My self is not everything but neither is it nothing. The world too is something, a limited something which exists only because it enters into the stream of relation with God and man. It is God's incessant creation and man's world — the names which man gives to the things and the seal of language which he affixes on them — which bring the world into real existence. The world as such does not exist: "To speak of the world is to speak of a world which is ours and God's." New things happen at every stage of the process and become events. This course of events never comes to an end, and the world of things must itself suffer the process of history through which it is realized. "The world is real only insofar as it enters into this process, a process which brings all of it within the context of the human word and God's sentence."

Language similarly is the bridge between oneself and the other person. Through being called by my name, I escape from the power of the past and of causation and receive from the future at each moment the gift of being present to myself. Through his surname man belongs to the past, but through his proper name, even when such liberation is not intended, he is summoned to live his particular and unique present. God too we call by His name, but the name is there for our sake, not His. He does not need to be called into existence, as we do, but our names for Him express our encounter with Him that is established and transmitted by the very alteration of the names we use. Indeed it is only through calling upon God that we become a "We." "God cannot be spoken of unless, at the very same moment, a bridge is constructed to man and the world." This bridge gives man trust in existence, but it does not obliterate the line between God and the world.

> Man should remain human; he should not be converted into a thing, a part of the world, prey to its organization. And the world's law and order should neither be rescinded nor sentimentalized. Man ought to be able to abide by the world's constitution . . . and yet remain human. He should feel no necessity to withdraw from the world's order because of his humanity. . . . Yet how could he act, were he not sure that his actions and the world-process . . . interrelate and agree? . . . In the same way as man has achieved certainty concerning the reality of the world and has found the courage to live his life, he must also have faith in Him who brought him into existence. . . . The proper time . . . is the present — today. To avail himself of today, man must, for better or worse, put his trust in God.

The relationship between God, man, and the world in Rosenzweig's thought is seen in terms of three separate yet interrelated moments of time — creation, revelation, and redemption. The great weakness of nineteenth-century theology, wrote Rosenzweig in *The Star,* is that in its concern with the present of revelation, it overlooked the past of creation. It is the thought of creation which first tears the world out of its elementary shut-in-ness and inertia into the stream of the all, which opens its eyes, until then turned inward, to the outside. But God the creator is also God the revealer. Creation is the prophecy which is confirmed only in the wonder of revelation. Man as the creature of God is only the forerunner of man as God's child. When God says "I" in creation, His "I" is still impersonal and the Thou to which He speaks is not yet fully independent and real. But in revelation man has complete freedom and absence of limits over against God even though he is limited in relation to the world.

It is speech which is the real morning gift of the Creator to mankind. It is the common good of man and the seal of his humanity. As man becomes man, he speaks; as he speaks, he becomes man. The word is the visible witness of the soul without which man ceases to be man. Although the way of God and the way of man are different, the word of God and the word of man are the same. This word is revelation. The relationship between God and man in revelation is that of the I to the Thou. It is the relation to the person who cannot be reduced to an object — a He, a She, or an It — to the person who is loved by God just in his unique and particular existence and not as a part of any generality or as a thing that can be compared with any other thing.

In the speech between God and man, the difference between transcendence and immanence is obliterated. God reveals Himself to us as at once near and unutterable.

> The remote God is none other than the near, the unknown God none other than the revealed, the Creator none other than the Redeemer.... This is the thought which was discovered over and over in the sphere of revelation, which inside and outside that sphere was forgotten over and over throughout the centuries from Paul and Marcion to Harnack and Barth.... What matters is that, near or remote, whatever is uttered, is uttered before God with the "Thou" ... that never turns away.

We know God directly only in revelation and not in creation or redemption, and for this reason revelation is the eternal middle point. It is the concrete standpoint of the stubborn and resistant human "I" which is thus our starting point. Revelation is the unmotivated love of the loving God which man who receives the love feels as a constant care. It is a sense of being carried which enables man to turn in love toward the world as God was turned to him. There is no content to this revelation but love, and God's only command to man is love. "Thou shalt love the Lord thy God with all thy heart, with all thy soul, with all thy might." This is the only directly revealed commandment. All the rest are commentaries — the ways in which love implements itself. This love is not an attribute of God, but an activity. God *is* not love. He loves. The imperative of love never leaves the circle of I and Thou, never becomes a third-personal He, She, or It addressing the individual merely as a part of some totality. Rosenzweig compared the aloneness-togetherness of man with God with that of the two partners in a marriage. "Everyone knows that though unutterable the relationship between man and wife is not a self-delusion (which a third person [such as a psychologist] might well think it! It is your own fault if you run within striking distance of the psychologist's knife! Why did you blab?)."

The command to love God has as its corollary the command to

love one's neighbor, and by neighbor is meant just the "next one," the person with whom one has to do at this and at the next moment of one's life. It is only because God loves us that we are able to love our fellowman and the world. This love which God gives to the world is the beginning of redemption, but this process can be hindered and cut short by the person who loses himself in the love of God and fails to turn outward toward the world. This is the guilt which the mystics bear, according to Rosenzweig. Man's deed of love is not a premeditated one. It has no set aim or goal and no guarantee of success. Each person who comes before me becomes simply the "next one," the one whom I am to love as God loves me. Through the love of the next one, the love of the I for a Thou, we become "We." Into man's hands is placed that task of relation to other men and the world which is necessary for redemption.

Yet redemption is ultimately from God. Redemption can be accomplished only in God's time and not man's. If man seeks to hasten the end, he changes the effective deed of love into ineffective action by having a set goal. The love of the I for the Thou is stronger than death, but in the present of revelation this love is always exclusive. It is the love of two, or the love of a "We" which becomes "We" only at the price of seeing a "You" or a "They" outside it. Only in redemption, in the triumphant cry of eternity, does the "We" become fully real and fully inclusive. In this "We," death plunges into nothing and life becomes immortal in redemption's eternal song of praise.

Each successive moment must be capable of being the moment of redemption, yet no moment can be fixed as such. The oneness of redemption, the uniting of God and his exiled Shekinah, really takes place in time, unlike that of Idealism, which posits a timeless redemption that knows nothing of creation and revelation as separate realities. For God, eternity *is,* for God is eternity and in him creation, revelation, and redemption are all equally present. But for man and the world, eternity *becomes.* Yet the unity that is thus attained must be already rooted in the eternity of God for the separateness of yes and no, of the universal and the particular, of nature and culture, to work together toward the final end of redemption. Man gives the world the completeness which it needs. The world presents itself to man as the "next one" whom he must love. Together they work in time for the coming of the eternity which eternally *is* in God. Thus Rosenzweig in *The Star of Redemption* arrived at that same "becoming of the God that is" that Buber matured to in *I and Thou.*

The remarkable parallels between Rosenzweig's and Buber's thought ought not obscure the highly significant differences. Buber's concern with Hasidic tales and Jewish mysticism was as foreign to the more rationalistic Rosenzweig as Rosenzweig's tremendous philosophical-theological system was to the intuitive, largely unsystematic, and only reluctantly theological Buber. Despite his great respect for Buber's position, moreover, Rosenzweig never came to see Zionism as other than a final aspect of redemption rather than as an immediately attainable goal. Rosenzweig's understanding of language as the bridge between God, world, and man can be contrasted with Buber's understanding of language as I–It as well as I–Thou and of genuine dialogue being silent as well as spoken. Rosenzweig saw Judaism as already in eternity and Christianity as in history forever on the way to eternity, whereas Buber saw Judaism as bound to the concrete historic situation — tempted, but less strongly than Christianity, to move away from this situation through apocalyptic emphasis on a fixed future or through faith with a knowledge content that fixes God in a certain image.

The two philosophers of speech came together as persons and as co-workers in Rosenzweig's Freies Jüdisches Lehrhaus. In his essay "It Is Time," written at the front, Rosenzweig had proposed a new type of Jewish academy that should go beyond the old "science of Judaism" (*Wissenschaft des Judentums*) both in its relevance and in finding scholars who were at the same time teachers of the people. The first part of Rosenzweig's suggestion was adopted by Hermann Cohen and others, and an academy was founded which lasted until 1929. But the suggestion about scholar-teachers was ignored. Rosenzweig consequently planned an entirely different sort of institution in his essay "Renaissance of Jewish Learning," and this plan he brought into being himself in the form of the "free Jewish house of learning" in Frankfurt am Main. "Books are not now the prime need of the day," Rosenzweig wrote. "What we need more than ever . . . are human beings — Jewish human beings." To work for the movement for today we "must take the Jewish individual seriously, here and now, as he is in his wholeness." What Rosenzweig was concerned with was not one or another tendency within Judaism but the Jew as a man, the image of man as a Jew.

> All recipes, whether Zionist, orthodox, or liberal, produce carica-
> tures of men, that become more ridiculous the more closely the recipes
> are followed. And a caricature of a man is also a caricature of a Jew;
> for as a Jew one cannot separate the one from the other. There is one
> recipe alone that can make a person Jewish and hence — because he is
> a Jew and destined to a Jewish life — a full human being: that recipe
> is to have no recipe. . . . Those who would help him can give him
> nothing but the empty forms of preparedness, which he himself and
> only he may fill. Who gives him more gives him less.

These "empty forms of preparedness" could be offered by a
school of Jewish adult education. Those who would come to the
discussion room of such a school would prove by this very fact
that the Jewish human being is alive in them, but the teachers too
must prove themselves — by being able within the same discussion
hour to be both master and student. Essential for both teachers
and students would be the power to wish, the urge to question,
the courage to doubt.

> It is as unlikely that "stuffed shirts" will stray in among these stu-
> dents . . . as it is that the lions of the lecture-platform will be heard
> among their teachers. There has been enough of speechmaking. The
> speaker's platform has been perverted into a false pulpit long enough
> among us — just punishment for a rabbinate that, for the most part,
> has been able at best to convert the pulpit into a speaker's platform.
> The voices of those who want these desirous students to desire them as
> teachers must lose the "true ring" of dead-sure conviction.

In his address at the opening of the Lehrhaus in Frankfurt,
Rosenzweig proposed a learning in reverse order — "a learning that
no longer starts from the Torah and leads into life, but the other
way round: from life, from a world that knows nothing of the
Law . . . back to the Torah." The mark of the men of the time is
that there is no one who is not alienated or does not contain
within himself some fraction of alienation. For the new sort of
learning, then, he is most apt who brings with him the maximum
of what is alien. For this reason Rosenzweig often chose laymen
over scholars and rabbis as the teachers of his courses, laymen
who would be learning themselves in order to teach their students.
Ironically enough, Rosenzweig's own lecture course during the
first year of the Lehrhaus (1920–1921) was a failure, according to
his disciple and interpreter Nahum Glatzer. Although he was
able later to inveigle Buber into discussion instead of lectures,

the young genius was not able to make himself over into the type
of teacher he envisaged, reports Glatzer:

> Rosenzweig's own lecture course, attended by about one hundred
> persons, was a failure. He was motivated by a passionate urge to teach,
> to interpret, to clarify. But he was simply unable to realize the intellec-
> tual limitations of even intelligent, university-trained men and women.
> He did not talk their language and they did not understand his. His
> listeners sensed his greatness; yet he did not want to be admired, but
> understood. There was something tragic in the situation of a man who
> so fully believed in the power of the dialogue and the discussion to be
> doomed to a monological, one-sided, activity. Thus his direct and
> immediate influence extended to a small group of men and women;
> only indirectly . . . did his word reach wider circles.

The most striking and successful lectures, in contrast, were
those of Rabbi Nehemiah A. Nobel, the leading Conservative
rabbi in Frankfurt. Two hundred people came to hear him speak
on Halakhah, the Jewish law, and his appeal reached free-thinking
modernists quite as much as dogmatic traditionalists. Rabbi Nobel,
in addition, had a group of distinguished followers, including
Franz Rosenzweig himself, Ernst Simon, Erich Fromm, and
Nahum Glatzer. Ernst Simon, who had turned from assimilation
to Zionism under the impact of Martin Buber's presence at the
Zionist convention in Karlsbad, joined the faculty of the Lehrhaus
its second year, lecturing on the rise of the modern Jewish Renaissance movement. Simon, then in his early twenties, was to
become, in the words of Nahum Glatzer, "one of the most honest
and most passionate advocates" of the prophetic message of
justice in our time. "His Jewish consciousness grew in depth and
urgency as its application to life situations grew more and more
difficult." "He has a refreshing quality of personal uprightness,"
Buber wrote Rosenzweig. It was indirectly through Simon and
Nehemiah Nobel that Buber came to teach at the Lehrhaus.

Rabbi Nobel announced a series of three lectures on Goethe's
religious thought, but fell ill the day following the second lecture
and died two days later, in January 1922. The shock to Rosenzweig
was so great that he described it to Buber as a piece of life's foundation being taken from under his feet. "One can never know his
future," Rosenzweig wrote to Buber, "but one can still see before
him the beginning of the way that leads into the future. At the
least one calls a man who sees this beginning of the way before

him fortunate. Until yesterday I would have called myself that. ... It may be no accident that in the last hours of that good fortune that is lost to me, I had with you that dark and hopeless conversation which nonetheless — even if in the darkness — compelled me to move forward. Remain here for us, remain here for me!''

For his fiftieth birthday celebration in November, Rabbi Nobel had been presented by Franz Rosenzweig with a Festschrift in his honor. Although Buber had had little contact with him, he consented to contribute to the Festschrift at Ernst Simon's urging. When, however, an old essay of Nobel's in praise of Conservative Judaism was included in the volume, Buber wired that he could not allow his name to be placed on the dedication page. "With these words written twenty-five years ago you have formulated the views of all of us about the essence and task of the rabbinical calling," Rosenzweig had first written, but after Buber's wire, he and Simon reread the essay and discovered that most of the contributors, including themselves, could not stand behind the dedication. Shamefaced, they telegraphed to Buber a new wording simply saying that the essay on the values and burdens of the rabbinical calling had been written twenty-five years before. Buber telegraphed back, "Agreed." In a letter to Rudolf Hallo of December 1922, Rosenzweig commented: "That was then an awesome indication of what is great in Buber, whom everyone, of course, regards as a king in the realm of the spirit but who is in truth a genuine king only in his underpants" — a play on Hegel's dictum that no man is a king to his valet.

The way Buber handled this whole matter engendered an urgent longing in Rosenzweig to renew the acquaintance begun in 1914, and as soon as the week celebrating Nobel's fiftieth birthday was over, he went with his wife Edith to visit Buber in Heppenheim. He had no thought in doing so of inviting Buber to teach at the Lehrhaus. But in the middle of the conversation, while they were having coffee, Rosenzweig "suddenly noticed that even intellectually Buber was no longer the mystical subjectivist that people worship, but that even in this realm he was becoming a solid and reasonable man. I was astounded, and I was gripped by the great honesty with which he dealt with all things."

In talking with the Rosenzwiegs about his Hasidic books, Buber said that it astonished him that in all these years only one person had ever inquired about the sources. His new book, *The Great*

Maggid, would include an indication of the sources, at Gershom Scholem's suggestion. Rosenzweig said that, although he had not written Buber, he too had wondered about the sources and had tried in vain to locate them. To this Buber replied that he would gladly lay the sources before a few people. Rosenzweig said he would bring these people to Buber, if not in the winter, at least in the summer. Rosenzweig added that two students were already present and proposed to Buber that they have a tryout on the spot. So they went into the other room, where Buber disappeared into his rows of bookshelves and returned with two or three books. Rosenzweig found Buber at first a rather awkward teacher, especially since he sought to make Rosenzweig aware of the importance and reality of the word in the text — something of which Rosenzweig was already aware, Buber was to discover later when he read *The Star of Redemption.* "Only on the trip home," wrote Rosenzweig with charming and characteristic irreverence, "did it occur to me that it was cheaper to transport the prophet than twenty of his disciples." Accordingly, he invited Buber to teach a course at the Frankfurt Lehrhaus, and Buber, to his own astonishment, accepted, despite years in which refusing such requests had become a matter of course.

It was Buber's first experience with the give and take of real discussion during a presentation. Until then he had always lectured. It was the uniqueness of the Lehrhaus that attracted him, the interruption of a presentation to answer a question, teaching instead of speechmaking. From that time Buber was one of the pillars of the Lehrhaus, and, what was most beautiful to Rosenzweig, not the finished and past Buber but the becoming and future one. He had brought into the Lehrhaus the event of his own rebirth and maturing so that it was a proper marriage. In January and February 1922 Buber spoke before writing down what was to be the first volume of his five-volume systematic presentation of *I and Thou* and the following winter the second, with it being understood that he would accompany the other volumes with lectures at the Lehrhaus. Buber found that these lectures took some pains because it was in the course of them that he first learned with what difficulty an audience hears, and in particular how unwilling they were to hear his new words because of their familiarity with his old ones.

In November 1921, not long after he had written metaphorically of the paralysis of Idealist philosophy, Franz Rosenzweig noticed symptoms of a disturbance of his motor system which his friend Dr. Viktor von Weizsäcker diagnosed as the beginning of a literal paralysis. This diagnosis was confirmed by Rosenzweig's friend Professor Richard Koch the following February. In a few months this paralysis, as Nahum Glatzer has expressed it, "turned the young, vigorous man into an invalid deprived of movement and speech," though he lived on for almost eight more years and not just for a year as Koch expected. At an early stage of his paralysis Rosenzweig forewarned Buber that when he came to see him, he would not find him much different in appearance but that, aside from his being unable to walk, his speech was disturbed. "I can still be understood — more than it will appear to you in the first moment. One can get used to that. But my speech sounds like that of a very old man and comes out in a dreadfully tiresome way, still more tiresome for others than for myself. All nuances are impossible for me. In appearance, if I do not speak right away, I appear pretty much unchanged. I am wearing pyjamas. So — after this tragicomic rendez-vous signal, you will easily overcome your first shock."

Rosenzweig persuaded his friend Dr. Rudolf Hallo, a young art historian and archaeologist (whose son Professor William Hallo of Yale many years later translated *The Star of Redemption* into English), to carry on the work of administering the Lehrhaus as his deputy. Hallo, like Rosenzweig, had gone through a period of estrangement from Judaism. In a letter to Buber, Rosenzweig commended Hallo to him as someone who needed, like every man, two teachers, and in his particular case not only "masters of the return" like Rosenzweig and Eduard Strauss but also the noble "apikorer," or heretic, like Buber. To a friend Rosenzweig wrote a few months earlier that not only was Buber's *Der Jude* one of the best if not *the* best German periodical and the representative organ of German Jewry but that Martin Buber himself, without wishing it, had become recognized by intellectual and spiritual Germany as *the German* Jew.

It is at this period that the real friendship and closeness of Buber and Rosenzweig began. "Buber has meant a great deal to me personally," Rosenzweig wrote to a friend. "My acquaintance with him would have been epochal in my life if there had been opportunity. Even the similarity of thought is very great in his lectures; have you not noticed it? But of greater importance to me is the awesome (indeed almost unhealthy because superhuman) genuineness of his being." A few months later he declared to Buber himself that he could understand it when someone else's thought differed sharply from his own, as with Georg Simmel, for example, or when two who had been on a common course thought the same. But when neither was the case, as with the two of them, when "our thoughts *themselves* met and would have met even if you and I had not," then the question of how to understand this grows enormous. "I have always been reluctant to accept books as realities," Rosenzweig added, "but I feel compelled to here."

> A different beginning, different grounds on which one must think, different contents that enter into one's thought, differences in what one spares, differences (at the very least differences) in what one rejects, in a word: different men, and yet a community, – not an "objective" community based on a "goal" to which different "ways" lead but one in which the way itself belongs to the community; yet we have different ways.

Nahum Glatzer describes Buber's lectures on "Religion as Presence" to the Jewish and Gentile public at the Lehrhaus as "a present-day event of startling immediacy" in which Buber criticized all attempts to reduce religion to a philosophical fiction, a branch of culture, or a means of personal self-assertion. "Religion is not a variant of undirected life," Glatzer paraphrases, "but a knowledge which gives life direction and determines its law." Rosenzweig wrote to Buber before the lecture series saying that it had best be called "Religion as Presence" even when it afterward in truth will deal with "God's Presence." "That that is the case," he added, "I saw with glad astonishment at your home on Sunday." Buber followed his lectures with a Hasidic seminar limited to those who could follow the Hebrew text. "These two courses established Buber's central position in the Lehrhaus," writes Glatzer, and, in turn, "took him, in his middle forties, out of the solitude of his Heppenheim study" to a lifetime of contact with students.

Buber himself made plain the personal connection between this event and his friendship with Rosenzweig. "Already with the second sentence of your letter my answer was assured," he told him. "Of course, I shall undertake the lectures if I can thereby fulfill a personal wish of yours." Rosenzweig raised the question with Buber as to whether he should not have some literary starting-point for the discussion hour following the lecture. He could, for example, expound upon a Psalm the first hour and then really read it, thus transforming evoking into showing. Buber replied that the idea of linking Psalms to the discussion "is beautiful and dear to my heart. . . . Psalms always preserve for me the vivid meaning that they had for my childhood (a motherless childhood, but one spent dreaming of my mother who was living but too far away to be accessible): *You have removed from me my loved ones and comrades* (Psalm 88:19). As a result, after I had not concerned myself with them for the whole of a bad year, once during a wandering in the mountains after scaling what seems in memory a downright impossible grade, *Thou hast delivered my foot from stumbling* (Psalm 116:8) came to me not as a prayer but as a — report (that is still figurative, but you certainly understand). At that time the 116th Psalm opened up to me, out of which now almost all the others have yielded themselves to me. Should not Psalm 116 be understood together with the 22nd and the 23rd Psalms in one mystery?"

In his Afterword on "The History of the Dialogical Principle" Buber recounted that he was able to begin the final writing of *I and Thou* "after he had set forth his train of thought in a course that he gave at the Freie Jüdisches Lehrhaus in Frankfurt founded and directed by Rosenzweig" (a statement which was inadvertently left out of this writer's translation of the Afterword for the Macmillan paperback edition of *Between Man and Man*). Rivka Horwitz has set these lectures on "Religion as. Presence" at the center of her book on *Martin Buber's Way to I and Thou* because the fourth, fifth, sixth, and eighth of them form an early version of segments of the first and third Parts of *I and Thou*. Buber asked that they be taken down by a stenographer, and her manuscript, including his responses to questions, served as the basis from which Buber wrote a good deal of *I and Thou*. This is a remarkable example of an oral and dialogical origin of a classic piece of writing. If the poetic quality and the mastered whole came only later, nonetheless passage after passage was taken over almost word by word. In this early version Buber had an "It world" and a "Thou world" instead of "I-Thou" and "I-It," but in the answer to a question, Buber already had begun to speak of "basic words." The "It world" is the world of the perception and categorizing of objects, of experiences, whereas the "Thou world" is the world of realization, the world of the relationship to a Thou that we really make present or that really makes us present.

"This second world is the true world of the spirit," of closeness to God; for presence exists in life only insofar as there is a relationship to a Thou. "Through the fact that something steps up to us, that it becomes our exclusive partner (*Gegenüber*), through the fact that it becomes present to us, presence arises, and only by the strength of this is there a present."

When presence (*Gegenwart*) is changed, as it must be, into object (*Gegenstand*), then present becomes past. Every finite Thou to which we stand in relationship always becomes again an It, is included in the connection of the experienceable world. Therefore a continuum of a Thou-world is impossible. There is, however, a hidden Thou-world that can be lifted out, based upon the relationship to the "absolute Thou which by its nature cannot become an It." This absolute Thou establishes a living connection between the isolated Thou relationships so that they do not remain detached atoms but form parts of a living whole. Every real relationship into which we enter is suited to further, to help, the decisive relationship, if we let it stream into it. This is the true continuity which cannot be *deduced* from the absolute Thou but can become "a shining, streaming constancy":

> In the pure relationship, the relationship to the absolute Thou, there the way is given to unite these moments to a connection . . . through the authentication that uplifts all It to Thou emerging from the pure relationship, so that this absolute Thou can radiate in all relationship, into all life. . . . The decisive is, if I may use this image, that the lines of the pure Thou-relationship of men meet in God, that every human being enters of himself into the pure relationship and that these relationships stream together into that of an absolute Thou. The true human community is only possible in God, only just through the fact that the true relationships of men to the absolute Thou create a center, all these radii that proceed out of the I's of men to the middle, create a circle. . . . The Shekinah is between the beings.

The relationship to the beloved person, the relationship to nature as a Thou, the relationship to one's own creation as a Thou, the relationship to the deed in decision as a Thou — all this cannot be grasped psychologically as something that takes place *in* man, Buber asserted, but as what happens *between* the human person and an existing Thou. "Every real happening of the spirit is meeting (*Begegnung*)." But meeting can be made real only through the decision, or "nonaction," of the unified man who acts out of his unity (as in "The Teaching of the Tao"):

> What concerns us in the meeting, that is, what we know of it with our life, from our side, is not a waiting, not a being open, but a collected activity — an activity that is not felt to be such because it is essentially different from the sense of activity that we know from everything else, from all that is separate, from all that is divided. . . .
>
> That is the activity of the person who has become whole which in particular religions is called non-action where nothing individual, nothing partial any longer touches the person, thus also nothing of the person interferes in the world, but the whole person enclosed and resting in himself, effects, goes out, where the person has become an effecting whole.

Religion as Presence is a matter of "the narrow ridge between abysses." The multiplicity and exclusivity of the religions, their decline into the world of It, of objects, is not a matter of human willfulness but of human tragedy. The history of religions with its displacement of God into the world of It and the torturing and murdering of one another that follows from that is closely bound to the way of history as a progressive distancing from and returning to God. Just as there is a metacosmic movement away from God and toward God, so the history of religions may be seen as the eternal struggle and settlement of the movement against each other and the binding to each other of God and religion.

In these lectures Buber revealed what thirty years later he forgot: that the answer to Reverend Hechler's question of whether he believed in God in May of 1914 before the outbreak of the First World War did not come to him at that time, but only seven years later on a train. In this account Buber explained that when Hechler said, "Dear friend, we live in a great time," he meant by that a pre-Paraclete, premessianic time. When he asked Buber if he believed in God, "that was so humanly important in all its childlikeness and naïveté that it really became very difficult for me in my heart to answer the man." He could neither affirm nor deny the question the way it was stated and sought the best he could to set him at rest, since he really seemed disquieted. "But at any rate I did not give him a real answer." Only some months before this lecture, riding on a train to a reunion with some friends, did the answer suddenly come to Buber without his thinking about it ("I do not reflect on such things") and in language that he had not before considered, language formed into whole sentences:

> If to believe in God means to be able to speak about him in the third
> person, then I certainly do not believe in God, or at least I do not know
> whether I may say that I believe in God. For I know well that if I speak
> of him in the third person, when that again and again happens, and it
> cannot at all be otherwise than that again and again happens, then my
> tongue is so quickly lamed that one cannot at all call that a speaking.

But, Buber insisted, he did not in any way experience this answer
that he received as a negative one.

After the first, still unwieldy draft of *I and Thou* in the autumn
of 1919, Buber underwent two years of "a spiritual *ascesis*" in
which he could do almost no work except on Hasidic material
and read no *philosophica* with the exception of Descartes's *Dis-
cours de la Methode.* According to Buber's own statement in "The
History of the Dialogical Principle," he read Ferdinand Ebner's
book *The Word and the Spiritual Realities* (1921) plus Hermann
Cohen's *Religion der Vernunft aus den Quellen des Judentums*
(1919) and Rosenzweig's *Der Stern der Erlösung* (1921) "only
later, too late to affect my own thought." "As I wrote the third
and last part, I broke the reading ascesis and began with Ebner's
fragments." Buber happened to see some of them that were published in Carl Dallago's journal *Brenner,* which he often read, and
then sent for the book. "His book showed me, as no other since
then, here and there in an almost uncanny nearness, that in this
our time men of different kinds and traditions had devoted themselves to the search for the buried treasure. Soon I also had similar
experiences from other directions." Along with a sense of nearness, Buber also experienced a sense of farness because of Ebner's
emphasis upon Christ, as Buber wrote to the Swiss theologian
Friedrich Gogarten. The nearness Buber experienced was the
insistence that God is a Thou that cannot become It. The farness
was not only Ebner's Christology but his turning away from the
I-Thou relationship between man and man. In both these senses
Ebner was a true disciple of Kierkegaard, as Buber was a rebellious
one. This sense of farness is reflected clearly in the paragraph
Buber devoted to Ebner in "The History of the Dialogical Principle":

> In February, 1919, the *Star* was completed. But in the same winter
> and in the spring following, Ferdinand Ebner, a Catholic schoolteacher
> in the Austrian province, heavily afflicted by sickness and depression,
> wrote his "pneumatological fragments." . . . Ebner proceeds from the

experience of the "solitude of the I" (*Icheinsamkeit*) in that existential sense that it has won in our time: it is for him "nothing original" but the result of the "closing off from the Thou." Starting from here, following the trail of Hamann, but binding the insights more strongly to one another, he penetrates more deeply into the mystery of speech as the ever-new establishment of the relation between the I and the Thou. He acknowledges himself, in a more direct fashion than Kierkegaard, as one who is not able to find the Thou in man. Already in 1917 he had indicated the danger of going under spiritually in the consciousness of this "impossibility." He finds salvation in the thought: "There is only one single Thou and that is just God." To be sure, he also postulates, as does Kierkegaard: "Man shall love not only God but also men." But where it is a question of the authenticity of the existence, every other Thou disappears for him before that of God. If we ask here, as with Kierkegaard, about what is finally valid, we stand again before the self-relating individuals who look at the world but are in the last instance acosmic, who love men but are in the last instance ananthropic.*

---

* See Note to Chapter 14, p. 408.

PART VIII

The Threshold of Fulfillment

(1916-1923)

CHAPTER 15

From the Easy Word to the Hard Word: The World as Word

WHEN READING THE MANUSCRIPT of my book *Martin Buber: The Life of Dialogue,* Buber came across a quotation from his book *Daniel* in which Daniel speaks to Reinold of the kingdom of God as "the kingdom of danger and of risk, of eternal beginning and of eternal becoming, of opened spirit and of deep realization, the kingdom of holy insecurity." "Today," Buber declared, "I would no longer describe the kingdom so extravagantly! (*Daniel* is still too much a book of the 'easy word')." The corollary of that breakthrough to dialogue that came to Buber through the war years and the murder of Landauer was his painful progression from the "easy word" to the hard one.

Not only Hofmannsthal and the poets around him but the Viennese culture as such had seduced Buber to the easy word. Later he definitely detached himself from it. His spiritual journey led him to an ever more intense struggling for seriousness and concreteness and, in consequence, impelled him to ever sharper renunciation of all that was playfully romantic, of all mere mood and beauty, of every word that was not spoken with the full earnestness of responsibility. This renunciation, as Hans Kohn points out, was also a renunciation of a danger in his own being, of a temptation in his own soul, toward which he was often naturally inclined.

"Buber was bound to the world from the beginning of his life," writes Werner Kraft; "yet the breakthrough into the world was one of the decisive motifs of his spiritual experience." Kraft sets 1916 as the time at which Buber broke through to an active relationship with the world, with his first sketch of *I and Thou*. What preceded it was not negative but, Kraft concludes in the very words that Kafka wrote his fiancée, Felice Bauer, "something was lacking." Buber himself said that he had written much in the first period of his life, but he had become aware of the right way of writing only in the second. In the first epoch of his writing, Hofmannsthal's nonchalant heir who squandered the treasure of antiquity enchanted him and permeated his reading and writing. The second epoch began during and because of the First World War:

> Two decades passed before, in the storm of the World War, which made manifest the innermost threat to man, I struggled through to the strict service of the word and earned the heritage with as much difficulty as if I had never supposed that I possessed it.

Buber saw this earning of the heritage through the strict service of the word as taking place in other kindred writers of his day, one of whom was Hofmannsthal himself.

> When several years later I saw Hofmannsthal again after a long interval, I marked in his traits, gestures, and accent what his later work had already communicated to me: that he had gone the same way of renunciation, of effort, and of new beginning.

"Hofmannsthal was a litterateur who in the course of his life became a true human being," Buber remarked to Kraft. Buber hinted elsewhere at a parallel development between himself and Rainer Maria Rilke. "My way has led me forward from *The Legend of the Baal-Shem,*" he wrote in the 1950s, "in a manner similar to that which had led Rilke away from the *Book of Hours* [which Buber saw as lacking in humility]. On those paths we both reached a region of deeper responsibility."* Without comparisons with himself, Buber noted a corresponding breakthrough in Hermann Hesse when he turned, at this very period — 1917 — and again as the result of the world war, from "delightful narrative books" to "the service of the spirit."

> In the middle of his life the hand of the spirit had torn the poet Hesse out of carefree storytelling and compelled him to report his, the spirit's wrestling, its dangers and risks, epically, that is as events of the life of man with man. Through this his concern became, from work to work, in an ever more exact sense a spiritual one.

The difficult ascent from the "easy word" to the hard one was not just a significant event in Buber's own life and that of a few other writers close to him in spirit. It was a stage in the history of the spirit itself, a stage that shows as no other the existential bond between language and our actual life. "In language as in all realms of human existence," wrote Buber in 1961, "no continuity can any longer be assured." Even to read a book, he asserted in 1924, one "must labor with it hours at a time as with a headstrong horse, until covered with sweat he stands in front of it and reads this book that he has tamed."

> The real reader knows this, but far better still the real writer — for only the writing of a real book is actually danger, battle, and overpowering. Many a one loses his courage midway, and the work that he began in the reading of the signs of the mystery he completes in the vain letters of his arbitrariness. There exists only a little reality of the spirit in this book-rich world.

Buber was widely recognized, even from the time of *The Legend of the Baal-Shem* and *Daniel,* as one of the master German stylists of the age, compared by some to Goethe, Schopenhauer, and Nietzsche; by others to Rilke, Hofmannsthal, Werfel, and Kafka. His style bore the stamp of the German classics and of the romantics and had taken into itself Old German elements preserved in Yiddish. In *I and Thou,* however, the poetic quality and beauty of *Daniel* were now mastered by an all-encompassing purpose. The poetic element, as Grete Schaeder puts it, plays at once a crowning and serving role in Buber's writings because in them the

---

* See Note A in Sources for Chapter 15, p. 412.

whole person comes into play, and the reader's feelings as well as his thought are spoken to. "The speech of poetry remains indispensable to him," writes Schaeder. "But he does not succumb to intoxication or confuse religious dedication with aesthetic enthusiasm. He opens himself to the whole of reality." In a similar manner, Wilhelm Michel, writing in 1926, three years after the publication of *I and Thou,* could see Buber's style as that of an ordered and fully disciplined spirit yet as including the sensuous as well as the aesthetic within its discipline:

> It is rich with presence and corporeality; it has drunk much of the sensual into itself and has become dense with it. But it has remained full of deep feeling and organic; each of its forms gleams with living meaning. . . . It is the pure devotion to the word on the part of a man simplified for the sake of God.

Buber managed to find that right relationship between power and love and word that made all three living for him. Although this relationship was sometimes expressed by him in a poem (such as "Power and Love," which he also retained in his "Gleanings"), it more often expressed itself in a language, such as that of *I and Thou,* in which the poetic power of speech and the faithfulness of thought were inseparable. "Buber remained an occasional poet the whole of his life, in Goethe's sense," remarks Grete Schaeder, and adds, "the poetic speech alongside the scholarly was an indispensable form of expression for him." One might go further and say that Buber's greatest "poetry" came when the two forms became one. Among the mature poems that Buber selected for *A Believing Humanism,* there are a number of exceptionally fine ones — the gleanings or harvest of a lifetime of poetizing, most of which will never be published and may even have been destroyed. Many of Buber's mature poems were the direct products of close personal relationships and were originally composed as inscriptions in books to his wife or close friends or are dedicated to them: to Paula Buber, to Ernst Simon, to Ludwig Strauss, and his last and, perhaps, greatest poem — "The Fiddler" — to Grete Schaeder herself. But Buber attained his greatest sustained poetic power — and this comes through even in translation — in *I and Thou,* in which poetic language and conceptual language are perfectly fused as one. An occasional exclamation in the form of a purely lyrical line does not come as an ornament, but as a culmination, as in

Buber's description of the persons who close themselves off in the world of It and protect themselves from the openness of the Thou:

> But they, having become disinclined and unfitted for the living deal-
> ings that would open the world to them, are fully equipped with infor-
> mation. They have pinned the person down in history, and secured his
> words in the library. They have codified, in exactly the same way, the
> fulfillment or the breaking of the law. Nor are they niggards with ad-
> miration and even idolatry, amply mixed with psychology, as befits
> modern man. O lonely Face like a star in the night, O living Finger laid
> on an unheeding brow, O footstep whose echo is fading away.*

When Buber wrote to Viktor Jacobson, "You can only be rid of my style together with me," he was saying that he could not simplify the complexity of his style by any conscious act of will. By the same token, however, the ten years of experiences of faith which Buber went through at this time had as radical an effect upon his style as it did upon the man. He had to bring to speech and then, insofar as he could, to the written word, the events and meetings through whose dark gate he passed and in which he ex-perienced that uncanniness and shattering of all security that sent him back to the "lived concrete," directed and assigned to his task.

In "Spirit and Body of the Hasidic Movement" Buber spoke of the *zaddik* as one who shunned the "beautiful," the premeditated.

> A learned man who was a Sabbath guest at Rabbi Baruch's table,
> said to him: "Let us now hear words of teaching: you speak so beauti-
> fully!" "Before I speak beautifully," answered the grandson of the
> Baal-Shem, "may I become dumb!" and spoke no further.

The road from the "easy word" to the hard one was for Buber a road from "speaking beautifully" to rejecting any expression not fully mastered by intention and devotion to the word. Thus to the *ascesis* of mystical experience and of reading that Buber experi-enced during this period there was added an asceticism in rela-tionship to the poetic itself. This renunciation of all the literary possibilities and means at his disposal also entered into Buber's retelling of Hasidic legends, which moved from the multicolored fabric of his earlier books to the rough, crude, and fragmentary

---

* See Note B in Sources for Chapter 15, p. 413.

events that he later called "legendary anecdotes." Buber himself, as we have seen, described his first attempts to testify to the great reality of faith which he encountered in Hasidism as the work of "an immature man," who did not yet know how to hold in check his inner inclination to poeticize the narrative material.

The First World War, which brought to Buber's awareness the crisis of dualistic Western man, also led to an ever more basic transformation in his relationship to Hasidism. Although he knew from the beginning that Hasidism was a way of life to which the teaching provided the indispensable commentary, it was only now that it became overwhelmingly clear to Buber that this life was involved in a mysterious manner in the task that had claimed him. This claim was at once a spiritual and a literary one, the two together in such a manner that any attempt to be faithful to the one without the other meant faithlessness to both. Buber could not, like Kafka's friend Jiri Langer, become a Hasid himself; he could not revert to that total affirmation of the Jewish law in which the Hasidic spirit found its starting point and from which it again and again took its form.

> It would have been an unpermissible masquerading had I taken on the Hasidic manner of life — I who had a wholly other relation to Jewish tradition, since I must distinguish in my innermost being between what is commanded me and what is not commanded me.

Buber's task, rather, was to take into his own existence and convey in his writing as much as he could of the realization of dialogue that had been truly exemplified for him in Hasidism. Thus the very material that Buber transmitted and which he saw as having become new in him placed an existential claim on his life itself that the young litterateur who began that task in 1905 and earlier never dreamed of. If Buber's own thought had shown him the possibility of making dialogue real, it was Hasidism that made this possibility concrete for him and fully serious. In the Foreword to *The Great Maggid* (1924), Buber wrote:

> Since I began my work on Hasidic literature, I have done this work for the sake of the teaching and the way. But at that time I believed that one might relate to them merely as an observer. Since then I have realized that the teaching is there that one may learn it and the way that one may walk on it. The deeper I realized this, so much more this work, against which my life measured and ventured itself, became for me question, suffering, and also even consolation.

In addition to his work during these years on Hasidic legends and tales and his creative philosophical writings, such as *Daniel* and *Events and Meetings,* Buber edited and wrote important introductions to the parables of Chuang-tzu, Chinese ghost tales and love stories, the Finnish epic *Kalevala,* the Celtic legends of the Mabinogi, Flemish miracle stories, and the parables of Ferid-eddin-Attar, the Sufi mystic. In this same period he gave sympathetic encouragement and help to his wife Paula, who had begun her own writing, under the pseudonym Georg Munk, with *The Illegitimate Children of Adam,* an adaptation of a Kabbalistic legend, and then continued with the legends and stories of her native Bavaria. "Paula Winkler has become at the side of her husband," wrote Hans Kohn in 1930, "one of the most significant and most independent German story-tellers." There was, in fact, much resemblance between her literary direction and that of Buber's. Only a few years ago a collection of Buber's stories was published in America under the title *Tales of Angels, Spirits, & Demons.* A similar title could be used for many of Georg Munk's stories. As Buber collected and reworked the literature of many peoples, so his wife Paula went to various sources to describe the incursion of the demonic into human life. What is more, as Kohn pointed out, motifs that in Martin's writings became anecdotes or wise sayings became in Paula's writing variegated, fully narrated action.

"To create a story or poem," wrote Buber in introducing a volume of three books of Paula's that he put together after her death, "means to fulfill the bidding of meetings." Within this general understanding of literature as the giving of form to meetings *(Begegnungen),* Buber saw the special calling of his wife as composing "genuine tales of spirits . . . which in a special kind of natural mystery enter into our lives and perhaps abandon themselves to them."

> In her youth Paula Winkler had already beheld the hidden reality that I mean, especially in the landscape of Southern Tyrol: childhood memories from the Bavarian forest also seem to have played their part. But that she could receive the mysterious, the alien to us that encountered her, without timidity, derived from the primal character of her being. She knew about the elemental from its own ground. There she was "the blessed woman" who ventured upon the brokenness of the human house. Her receiving of the elemental, however, was precisely a formative one: not afterward, not in a willed elaboration of the experienced, not even in that unarbitrary activity of the formative memory

did she lend form to the formless: she saw, she experienced it as form. And what then followed, when she wrote down something of it and thus presumed to hold it fast, was made possible by the fact that what she received, as it were, in an unextended moment she transposed into a course of time, gave it a history, told it. She was a narrating person, one of those to whom images become events and then the events become the course of narrated life. From there she imparted to the elemental spirits, who know only cosmic, destinyless time, our human time, that into which the dark threads of our afterknowledge of our birth are interwoven with the still darker threads of our foreknowledge of our death.

It was on this road from the "easy word" to the difficult one that Buber developed his philosophy of the "word," of the word that is spoken, of speech as event and event as speech, of the world as word and human existence as address and response. In 1917 Buber received from the International Institute of Philosophy of Amsterdam an invitation to join in a program, initiated by Henri Borel and Frederik Van Eeden of the Forte Circle, to found an academy the task of which would be "to create words of spiritual value for the speech of Western peoples, new words which had not yet been falsified." The ever-renewed task of the faithful community, Buber replied, is to rediscover and purify the meaning of old words.

> The coming into being of words is a mystery that is consummated in the enkindled, open soul of the world-producing, world-discovering man. Only such a word engendered in the spirit can become creative in man. Therefore, in my view it cannot be the task of a community to *make* it. . . . What is needed is not teaching the use of new words but fighting the misuse of the great old words.

Spoken as opposed to written speech is the great discovery, the great rediscovery, of the life of dialogue. Plato lamented in his Epistles that the written dialogues, which he composed in the name of his teacher Socrates, lacked the authenticity and full reality of the spoken dialogue as Socrates himself practiced it. A passage that Buber returned to again and again as pointing explicitly to the "between" was the image of leaping fire that Plato used in his Seventh Epistle. If Goethe in *I and Thou* served Buber as an example of the "I" of mutual sharing in the relationship with nature, Plato's master, Socrates, was for him the prototype of the man who made his "I" real by virtue of sharing in the dialogue between man and man:

> But how lovely and how fitting the sound of the lively and impressive *I* of Socrates! It is the *I* of endless dialogue, and the air of dialogue is wafted around it in all its journeys, before the judges and in the last hour in prison. This *I* lived continually in the relation with man which is bodied forth in dialogue. It never ceased to believe in the reality of men, and went out to meet them. So it took its stand with them in reality, and reality forsakes it no more. Its very loneliness can never be forsakenness, and if the world of man is silent it hears the voice of the daimonion say *Thou.*

Yet Socrates was not, for all that, an adequate image for Buber of the life of dialogue. The Greek philosopher went forth to people, trusted them, met them, never suspended the dialogue with them. Yet his emphasis upon dialectical thought often put him in the position of the essentially monological thinker whose dialectic, even when it brings in other people, is little more than a moving forward through the opposition and interaction of different "points of view" rather than an interaction *between* persons.

This contrast between dialogue and dialectic has much to do with the importance of the *spokenness* of speech in the becoming real of the "between," of the Each-Other. When the word really becomes speech, when it is really spoken, it is spoken in the context of relationship, of over-againstness, of mutuality, and takes its very meaning from the fact that it is said by one person and heard by another who has an entirely different relationship to it, even as he stands on an entirely different ground from the speaker. Only that drama which includes in embryo that elemental fact of over-againstness is capable of being taken up into the living over-againstness of real theater. This is what Buber learned in the course of an intensive concern with drama and the theater for more than a quarter of a century and what he brought to life in two essentially dramatic works, *For the Sake of Heaven* and his mystery play *Elijah.*

In 1922 Buber complained of "the spirit-forsaken fiction that one can 'give back' the 'content' of a work 'in other words.'" It contributes to killing in young persons the glimpse of the spiritual world in which no word can take the place of another and propagates an unholy swarm of persons who dwell in a spectral realm in which writers do not write because they *must* write

but merely because they *can* write. This "spirit-forsaken" separation between "form" and "content" has as its parallel the errone-
ous notion that "meaning" in general may be separated from the
form and the way in which it is "expressed." But for a thinker
like Buber, the "word" was inseparable from thought; for it is itself the very substance of thought.

Buber's statement in *I and Thou,* "In the beginning is relation,"
is not an alternative to the Johannine "In the beginning was the
Word" but a restoration to it of the biblical dynamic and mutuality of the word as "between." The true beginning of relationship
is the speech of God which creates the world and addresses man.
The world really becomes through God's word, and the world
takes place and becomes real for man in the word. Speech is thus
the face-to-face existence of the creatures, and pure creation coincides with pure speaking. That we can say Thou is to be understood from the fact that Thou is said to us. All speech, therefore,
is answering, responding.

*This is only comprehensible, of course, if the spoken and the
genuinely two-sided and dialogical character of the word as the
embodiment of the "between" is borne in mind.* It is this that
Buber expressed in a small poem in which it is not the tree but we
ourselves that are the words of God, words that need, nonetheless, to join into the *word* before the full reality of the world as
word is attained:

> *We are the sounds that the primal mouth speaks,*
> *And yet we are only words, not word.*
> *When shall we become words that join themselves*
> *Into a sentence to satisfy the primal speech?*

To say that we are "the words of God" in no sense means that we
are God's instrument. Even Moses, who is spoken of as God's
mouth (Exodus 4:16), is not a "mouthpiece" but "an autonomous,
sounding organ; and to sound means to modify sound" (lauten
heisst umlauten). In an unpublished Foreword to *I and Thou*
Buber wrote: "What is here called speech is the primal act of the
spirit whose human execution the spoken languages and all sign
languages serve as helpers and workmen." The meaning of dialogue
lies in the real difference of those who are speaking to each
other, even when they seem to be using identical concepts. For in
this latter case, even the "same" concept involves two different

standpoints and two different worlds of experience and inevitably has different meanings plus a potential of common meaning that may arise through the interchange of the two. But this latter depends upon preserving the tension of the relationship in the concepts themselves.

At many points Buber came close to the *Sprachphilosophie* developed at this time by Franz Rosenzweig and Rosenzweig's friend and partner in dialogue, Eugen Rosenstock-Huessy.* Thus, in an unpublished lecture on Lao-tzu, Buber gave a dialogical interpretation of the name very much like that of these two friends with whom he came into increasing contact. There is, said Buber, an "inwardness of the name" that proceeds from the things themselves that wish to form themselves in men and through them attain to the sphere of the spirit — of the word. The name is not invented; it is discovered. "Name is meeting, like all reality. The reality in which we live is the reality of the relationship between the things of the world and me, the human person." The difference here, however, is that Rosenstock-Huessy and Rosenzweig emphasized the names of *persons,* whereas Buber, true to the I-Thou relationship with nature and art, extended the name to man's relationship to each existing being that confronts him. If the first finds biblical precedent in the statement "I have called thee by name," the second finds even earlier biblical precedent in that version of the creation story in the Book of Genesis in which Adam names all the animals, not conferring existence upon them thereby, but entering into relation with them. This relation often, to be sure, becomes merely that of an "I" to an "It," and the naming of the natural world is followed by the desire to categorize and use it. In this case the pronoun stands for the name and the name for an object. But in the I-Thou relationship, which Buber saw as primary, the Thou is not metaphor, not a pronoun that stands for a name. Rather, the spoken name takes on its ring of authority precisely through the fact that I know that when you call my name, you really mean me in my uniqueness, are really addressing me as Thou. Thus for Buber the meeting with the Thou, rather than the fact of the name, was the ultimate touchstone of reality, as it could not be for Rosenstock-Huessy and Rosenzweig. The difference here is between an emphasis upon the *nature* of what one meets — whether it is a person or a thing

---

* See Note C in Sources for Chapter 15, p. 414.

— and an emphasis on what *kind of relation* one has to what one meets: I-Thou or I-It. Buber's two primary words do indeed yield a twofold world and a twofold I, but these derive from the relation rather than the relation from the nature of what is related to.

The structure of address and response characterizes the I-Thou relationship in man's relationship with nature and art as well as with his fellowman. But it is only in what Buber later called the "interhuman" dimension that language is consummated in speech and counterspeech and the moments of relation bound together by means of the element of the speech in which they are immersed. Speech is the high road on which the Thou attains its full reality in knowing and being known, loving and being loved, and as such it is the real simile of the relation with God. "In it true address receives true response; except that in God's response everything, the universe, is made manifest as language." For this reason too Buber characterized the moments of man's relation to God as the birth of the Word in man's turning to God, the expansion of the Word in which it enters the chrysalis form of religion, the rebirth of the Word with new wings at the moment of fresh turning, and the disintegration of the Word when institutionalization and rigidity of religion suppress the movement of turning so that the forms of religion no longer point the way to a meeting with God. Thus the Word, as Buber used it, includes alternation between I-Thou and I-It and that false autonomy of the It which prevents the return to the Thou. This also entails alternation between the immediate Word of address and response in man's relationship to God and the mediate words that grow out of that relationship, point back to it, or obscure it. Thus Buber wrote to Ronald Gregor Smith, who at the time was translating *Ich und Du* into English:

> It not only means that one cannot fully express it in human speech but that one cannot in general come near to the essential with human words, cannot touch it with words, cannot speak "about it." *Because* I cannot speak "about it," the immediate address with "thou," independent of this or that language, this or that expression that establishes the relationship, remains the primal act of the spirit, the Word, the Logos, and thereby makes unimportant the inadequacy of words, of individual languages.

"Who speaks?" asked Buber in "Dialogue," four or five years after the completion of *I and Thou,* and answered in a way that

united myth, drama, and poetry in the "holy primary word"
of "mutual action."

> Who speaks?
> It would not avail us to give for reply the word "God," if we do not
> give it out of that decisive hour of personal existence when we had to
> forget everything we imagined we knew of God, when we dared to keep
> nothing handed down or learned or self-contrived, no shred of knowl-
> edge, and were plunged into the night.

After we rise out of this "dark night of the soul" and are plunged
into new life, we reach that state in which myth has its origin —
the "moment Gods" [of which the nineteenth-century scholar
of religion Usener spoke]. The "moment God" is not yet a person
or even a continuous divine function, but only that flash of Mana
the traces of which remain in the image of an elemental relational
event. What we know of "God" is only what we experience from
time to time from the address of the situation — the "bestowing"
side of things that comes to meet us when we come to meet it.
"If we name the speaker of this speech God, then it is always the
God of a moment." A myth may carry over the dramatic reality
of this God of the moment without reducing the polar tension of
over-againstness that Buber early recognized as the essence of true
dramatic dialogue.*

But the next stage goes beyond the myth to poetry, without
losing thereby any of its dramatic tension. For Buber could find
no better way of describing that recognition of God from which
there arises for man the One, the Lord of the Voice, than through
the example of the poet, each of whose poems one reads as a unique entity in itself, yet finally hearing in each particular poem not
only the "moment God" of the poem itself but the voice of the
poet as person speaking through his poems.

> When we really understand a poem, all we know of the poet is what
> we learn of him in the poem — no biographical wisdom is of value for
> the pure understanding of what is to be understood: the *I* which
> approaches us is the subject of this single poem. But when we read
> other poems by the poet in the same true way their subjects combine in
> all their multiplicity, completing and confirming one another, to form
> the one polyphony of the person's existence.

---

* See Note D in Sources for Chapter 15, p. 414.

This recognition of the voice of the poet is not attained through any process of abstraction or generalization and still less through any literary-historical study. It is the renewed presentness of the Thou met in its immediacy yet bringing into that immediacy the past moments of the Thou through which a speaking voice becomes discernible.

The best, perhaps the only real, way to understand just how seriously Buber took the world as word and the word as the living "between" of dialogue was to talk with him alone and, still better, in a group. We can get a glimpse into his approach to such a discussion through the guidelines he set down for the three evenings that he conducted with Hugo Bergmann and a small group in November and December of 1923, the year of the publication of *I and Thou*. "We want first of all to be *critical of concepts*," he said. "That means: we do not want to employ any concept without our conceiving thereby something real, something present." When a concept is named, each will have a different meaning in mind, and this difference will set up a tension which in itself is valuable. Real speaking takes place out of tension. Speech is not community, but multiplicity. It is born of a living dynamic. This fruitful essential tension shall be expressed through speech and will act as a stimulus for us to come toward each other.

"Our conversation shall be thus: when one person asks or states, then the other, who has had or is having a similar or contrary experience — not an opinion — shall express it. Thus we will discuss questions which are urgent for us.

"When we have conquered a concept, when it appears capable of bearing its weight of meaning, then we shall each time ask: Is that the reality? This question we can answer only out of our most inward experience. We do not mean thereby out of the experience of individuals in opposition to the experience of the world, out of detached self-experience. We mean, on the contrary, self-experience evolving from contact with others. We mean certainly from the innermost core of individuals — not as detached from the world, however, but as bound with it."

More important than Buber's having developed a philosophy of the word is the fact that he became and remained a person of the word, of the lived word that is spoken. In Buber thought constantly expresses itself purely and cleanly *as* speech, says Hans Fischer-Barnicol, truth takes place as word.

This direct address to the "Thou" fills all Buber's speaking. But it also gives his conceptual prose its incomparable resonance, from the inner rhythm of which the reader cannot escape: No doubt can persist that this thinking is addressed to me, that for my sake it was thought, was said.

One of Buber's tales of the Baal-Shem relates how he went to a marketplace and started to tell a story. First one person came up, then another, and then another. Each hearer as he listened felt that the story was addressed in particular to him, and each when it was over started saying this to the other until suddenly they all fell silent with astonishment. Martin Buber, too, spoke to the person and the condition of his hearers with such compelling directness that persons of the most varied and even incompatible opinions, creeds, and temperaments have felt the immediate, personal address of his voice, oral and written, a voice to which they have listened and responded.

CHAPTER 16

The Overcoming of Erlebnis

So, waiting, I have won from you the end:
God's presence in each element.

Goethe

EACH OF THE ROADS that we have followed has appeared in turn to
be *the* road on which Buber came to *I and Thou*. Actually no one
road is *the* road. Rather all of them converge like the spokes of
a wheel, and from this convergence there appears a phenomenon
that not even the sum of all of them accounts for: *I and Thou.*

In 1958 Buber said to me that were he to write the book again,
he would not deny the I-Thou relationship with nature but neither
would he use the same terminology for the relationship between
man and man and that between man and nature. But, he added,
he would not now change the original text, since the whole was
written in a type of creative ecstasy that even the author himself
had no right to tamper with retrospectively. Commenting on his
sentence in *I and Thou* "In the beginning is relation," Buber
wrote:

> Today the use of the expression "in the beginning" does not seem to me exact enough; it is too rich in associations. At that time I wrote what I wrote in an overpowering inspiration. And what such inspiration delivers to one, one may no longer change, not even for the sake of exactness. For one can only measure what one might acquire, not what is lost.

Hugo Bergmann singles out "Herut: On Youth and Religion" (1919), the last of Buber's eight "Speeches on Judaism," as the first proclamation of the great shift from the manifestation and realization of God in man to God as "the great confronter" who cannot be identified with His manifestation. "Herut" was by no means the first of Buber's writings that revealed this shift. It is already there quite clearly in *The Holy Way.* But it is in "Herut" (Freedom) that Buber made those clear distinctions that he repeated in 1922 in the Foreword to the collected *Speeches on Judaism,* distinctions that warned him as much as his readers against the misinterpretations that his earlier language of realizing God in man might lead to.

Reaffirming that the absolute is experienced by man as over against him, as the Thou as such, Buber now asserted, in contrast to his earlier teaching, that it is not God who changes but only the theophany, the manifestation of the divine in man's symbol-creating mind — until no symbol is adequate any longer and the life between man and man itself becomes a symbol — "until God is truly present when one man clasps the hand of another." The person who lets his whole being be affected by his contact with the unconditional must guard against psychologizing it into an "experience" (*Erlebnis*), Buber added, turning his back on one of his own key terms, which he now associated with mood and superficial emotionalism rather than real response. "I am to some extent accustomed to the hell that the misuse of this word [experience (*erleben*)] means," said Buber in his 1922 lectures on "Religion as Presence." "I know wholly precisely how it happens in this world, in this hellish world in which we live, to whose pain we are exposed every day, every morning."* Correcting Walter Kaufmann, who asserted that his concept of meeting originated in *Erlebnis,* Buber later testified:

> In reality it arose, on the road of my thinking, out of the criticism of the concept of *Erlebnis,* to which I adhered in my youth, hence,

---

* See Note A in Sources for Chapter 16, p. 427.

out of a radical self-correction. *"Erlebnis"* belongs to the exclusive, individualized psychic sphere; "meeting," or rather, as I mostly prefer to say, precisely in order to avoid the temporal limitation, "relationship" transcends this sphere from its origins on. The psychological reduction of being, its psychologizing, had a destructive effect on me in my youth because it removed from me the foundation of human reality, the "to-one-another." Only much later, in the revolution of my thinking that taught me to fight and to gain ground, did I win reality that cannot be lost.*

Erlebnis has its place when in the course of one's life one needs to stress individual points of subjectivity, Buber conceded in 1922. But what is today called *Erlebnis* is just the opposite:

> It means that life is subjectivized, that out of a great continuum, out of a great continuity, space-time continuity in which we stand, in which we are inserted, in which we take part, life is transformed into a fetching forth of things for the use and task of our subjectivity . . . so that the continuity is entirely torn apart and nothing remains but unsteady moments, not even events which are inserted in being but experiences (*Erlebnisse*), precious moments of the soul as they put it. And religion is made into one of these precious moments, so to speak, to a real refinement of this heightened life. . . . Of all the fictions that are made out of the religious, this is the most fictitious.

What is in common to all these attempts is that they see the religious as happening *in* the person, in that encapsulated sphere that this psychology calls soul. They lead to the mixture of religious events with illusory and hallucinatory psychopathological processes. This attack on *Erlebnis* Buber coupled with an attack on the great foolishness of our time — that of a becoming God who needs to be realized and brought forth by the human spirit.

What is understood by the "religious" today, Buber stated in the still sharper "explanations" of his Foreword to *Speeches on Judaism,* is mostly inwardness, religious "feeling." The false objectivism of the philosophical attempt to possess the divine cannot be corrected by the subjectivism of those who wish to reduce God to a feeling or process within them. This is not only a psychological but a cosmic perversion. What matters is not the "experiencing" of life but life itself, not the "religious experience," but the religious life. What "emerges" in the religious life is not God Himself but man's going forth to meet God, and what is "re-

---

* See Note B in Sources for Chapter 16, p. 427.

alized" in this life is not God, who then becomes a mere abstract truth dependent upon man for His existential reality, but rather, preparing the world for God, as a place for His reality, making God and His world one. Here Buber was not merely explaining, as he claimed, but correcting; for his earlier uses of "realization" did indeed fall in whole or in part into what he now called that "hopelessly perverted conception that God is not, but that He becomes." "Only a primal certainty of divine *being* enables us to sense the awesome meaning of divine becoming, that is, the self-imparting of God to His creation and His participation in the destiny of its freedom." What was essential here was not the rejection of "becoming" for "being" but the rejection of the elaboration of subjectivity for the wholehearted meeting with *otherness,* the "conversion" which began with the death of Herr Mehé in 1914 but fully matured in Buber's thought only eight years later.

At the end of this Foreword, Buber reached that tension of the universally human and the specifically Jewish that was to mark all his mature thought, and that led him to write to Bergmann three years before of "the strange melancholy, the feeling between two worlds, the experience of the boundary that grows ever stronger in me." "All men are, at some time, no matter how fleetingly, aware of an encounter with God." There is no man who, in the loneliness of his pain or his thought, does not somewhere come close to God. But the task of making the world a place of God's realization was once heard by a people *as a people.* Israel is enduringly aware of the meeting with God not only in their blessings but even more in downfall and dissolution. "The Jew, bound up with the world, immured in the world, dares to relate himself to God in the immediacy of the I and Thou — as a Jew." The people that was the first to respond as a people to the One who spoke will not "cease to prepare itself anew for His word that is yet to come."

At the time Buber wrote the final version of *I and Thou,* he was fully immersed in Jewish education and Jewish spiritual concerns. It was at Franz Rosenzweig's Free Jewish Lehrhaus, in Frankfurt, as we have seen, that Buber gave the lectures that became the basis for much of the Third and some of the First Parts of *I and Thou.* For all this and for all the fact that *I and Thou* is unthinkable without the wisdom of Hasidism and of the Hebrew Bible, it is in its form and its intent a universal book. It does not address itself to Jews as Jews, and even when it thinks in terms of community and history, it has no concern other than that of modern Western man. What is more, for all the smaller breakthroughs that paved the way for *I and Thou,* it was clearly necessary for Buber to attain the major breakthrough to this classic universal statement before he could go forward (not back) to the more particular work on Hasidism and the translation and interpretation of the Hebrew Bible that occupied so much of the rest of his life. When a biblical scholar asked Buber in the last years of his life whether he regarded his biblical studies and his translation of the Bible from Hebrew into German as the quintessence of his lifework, he replied:

> If I myself should designate something as the "central portion of my life work," then it could not be anything individual, but only the one basic insight that has led me not only to the study of the Bible, as to the study of Hasidism, but also to an independent philosophical presentation: that the I-Thou relation to God and the I-Thou relation to one's fellow man are at bottom related to each other. This being related to each other is — if I may retain the expression — the central portion of the dialogical reality that has ever more disclosed itself to me.

In his Introduction to his 1947 book *Dialogisches Leben* Buber told of the fact that when he began to grasp and to express in writing his philosophy of dialogue, he knew of no related teaching from his own time.

> When within a few years thereafter I encountered one related teaching after the other — as the most important for consideration I name that of Ferdinand Ebner and in a specific part that of Franz Rosenzweig — it came to me that the vision that had had for me the character of a personal discovery, to begin with barely expressible, was to be seen in the context of a number of attempts undertaken independently of one another: attempts to lay a new foundation for human possibilities of life through the clarification of a category of existence that is as old as man. In the stillness a small, dispersed band arose to reveal, out of the fullness of suffering from the great aberration, a new meaningful and saving world-view.

The "great aberration" to which Buber referred was the First World War. This might lead one to think that the other thinkers to whom Buber referred had, like him, discovered the central reality of the dialogue between man and man. Actually, this was not so. Of Ebner in particular Buber had to add that his basic idea was that of the solitary relationship of the human I to God's Thou.

The steady clarity of vision and the inward necessity of writing *I and Thou* came to Buber some years before he received the right word as well and was able to write the book in its final form. When Buber wrote the first sketch in 1916, he envisaged it as the first volume of a five-volume systematic and comprehensive work. Even in 1919 he wrote Bergmann that he was working on "a general foundation of a philosophical ... system to the construction of which the next years will be devoted." The very systematic character of this projected work increasingly alienated Buber from it, and the "right word" came to him only when he condensed what he had to say into a small, unsystematic volume. Everything — God, man, the world, I and Thou — was there, bound together by discursive thought, but Buber broke through this to the I that really speaks and the Thou that can really be addressed.* To insert his experiences into the human heritage of thought he had to relate the unique and particular to the general, to express what is by its nature incomprehensible in concepts that could be used and communicated, to make an It out of what he had experienced in and as I-Thou. But if he could not communicate his experiences as such, in their personal, autobiographical form, neither could he develop the insights that resulted from them into a comprehensive system. He had to make manifest that duality of primal words which "is the basic relationship in the life of each man with all existing being" yet which was, until then, barely paid attention to. "A neglected, obscured primal reality was to be made visible." But this did not entitle him to treat being as such but only the human twofold relationship to it. Therefore, his philosophizing had to be essentially an anthropological one with the question of how man is possible as its central theme. His task was not to expound a doctrine but to point to a reality — to take his partner by the hand, lead him to the window, open it, and point to what is outside. "I have no teaching, but I carry on a conversation," Buber testified. A conversation can never be a system; for a system is always monological.

> No system was suitable for what I had to say. Structure was suitable for it, a compact structure but not one that joined everything together. I was not permitted to reach out beyond my experience, and I never wished to do so. I witnessed for experience and appealed to experience.

---

* See Note to Chapter 16, p. 415.

The experience for which I witnessed is, naturally, a limited one. But it is not to be understood as a "subjective" one. I have tested it through my appeal and test it ever anew. I say to him who listens to me: "It is your experience. Recollect it, and what you cannot recollect, dare to attain it as experience." But he who seriously declines to do it, I take him seriously. His declining is my problem.

I and Thou, as Werner Kraft says, has the compelling quality of all great "breakthrough" writings. What Nietzsche's *Thus Spake Zarathustra* was to the nineteenth century, *I and Thou* has been and is for the twentieth, no less because of the way in which it was written as because of the "ideas" it contains. The "overpowering inspiration" in which it was written is reminiscent, in fact, of Nietzsche's way of writing *Zarathustra.* But the style of the two books, as Buber himself pointed out, is decidedly different. In this respect, Landauer was far more on the track when he compared *Daniel* to *Thus Spake Zarathustra.* Rejecting emphatically a statement that his language remained as close as possible to the biblical, Buber used Nietzsche's *Zarathustra* as the very example of the inauthenticity that such an attempt entails:

> If I had to choose my language, I should least of all have chosen one imitating the biblical; for whoever has dared in our age to take on lease the style of the prophets — as Nietzsche's "Zarathustra" announces most clearly to the present-day reader — has transformed it into an effective but basically inauthentic pathos. Now happily I did not need to choose my language; that which was to be said formed it as the tree its bark.

There are, at the same time, poetic remnants in *I and Thou* of the style of earlier works: "So long as the heaven of *Thou* is spread out over me the winds of causality cower at my heels, and the whirlpool of fate stays its course." And poetical motifs reappear. The celebration of danger in *Daniel* as the "holy insecurity" of the realizing man now reemerges in the spiral descent of cultures through the spiritual underworld which is also an ascent to the turning, the breakthrough, the "trial of the final darkness." This passage ends with an unmarked quotation from Hölderlin, whose spirit also informed *Daniel:* "Where danger is, the delivering power grows too."

PART IX

I and Thou

(1923)

CHAPTER 17

-•——————————————————————————•-

Spirit as Response:
Knowledge and Art

-•——————————————————————————•-

WE NEED ONLY BRIEFLY RECAPITULATE the road to *I and Thou* to become aware of how these seemingly divergent streams converge in *I and Thou*. Meeting and "mismeeting," politics and economics, mysticism, Hasidism, and the philosophy of realization, the World War and the breakthrough to dialogue, crisis and revolution, socialism and peace, education and politics, the world as word and the overcoming of the subjectivization that robs life of its real otherness — all these find their mature and unified expression in *I and Thou*.*

Instead of offering an *explication de texte,* as I did in Chapters 10 to 12 of *The Life of Dialogue,* I wish here to highlight a number of central themes in *I and Thou* that might not be immediately obvious to the reader and to supplement them with other material from around this time. Through this it should become evident that the *road* to *I and Thou* is in no way discontinuous with the fulfillment that is reached in *I and Thou*. Thus I shall set the

---
* See Note to Chapter 17, p. 428.

themes of knowledge and art, love and marriage, politics and community, psychologism and psychotherapy, the "eternal Thou," Jesus and the Pauline Christ, and creation, revelation, and redemption in the context both of *I and Thou* and of the larger framework of Buber's writing and correspondence of the time.

The theory of knowledge and theory of art that Buber labored to develop in "The Teaching of the Tao," *Daniel,* and "With a Monist" finally reached maturity, though not their full unfolding, in *I and Thou.*

In *I and Thou* the sense of relatedness to nature — to trees and animals and stars — that marked Buber's writings from his early essay on Boehme is fully present but now not in any way that implies empathy or identification or minimizes the otherness and the distance of that nonhuman reality that one responds to. The tree, transcending any play of imagining or mood, "is bodied over against me and has to do with me, as I with it — only in a different way." Now it is not merely the horse on his father's farm that is uncanny but the household cat (Martin and Paula were great lovers of cats and always had a number in the house). The domesticated animal does not have a truly "speaking" glance, as we imagine, but it can "turn its glance to us prodigious beings" and acquire thereby a quality of amazement and of inquiry that Buber could experience as indisputably questioning him: "Do you really not just want me to have fun? Do I concern you ? Do I exist in your sight?" — silent questions in which the "I" is a transcription for a word that we do not have, which denotes self without the ego. The glance of the cat, "speech of disquietude," rose in its greatness — and set almost at once. Buber's glance endured longer, "but it was no longer the streaming human glance." This minute event, "this barely perceptible rising and setting of the spirit sun," happened to Buber more than once and left a lasting impression on him:

> No other event has made me so deeply aware of the evanescent actuality in all relationships to other beings, the sublime melancholy of our lot, the fated lapse into It of every single You. For usually a day, albeit brief, separated the morning and evening of the event; but here morning and evening merged cruelly, the bright You appeared and vanished. . . . the animal had sunk again from its stammering glance into speechless anxiety, almost devoid of memory.

What Buber's childhood "mismeeting" taught him — that his

unique experience of losing his mother concerned all persons — he now grasped as basic to every child's becoming a person. Now Bachofen's "Great Mother" (the ancient priority of the Mother Goddess and the matrilineal which the Swiss jurist and historian Johann Jakob Bachofen was the first to maintain) which Buber had thought of bringing into *Daniel,* becomes the cosmic connection which the child loses – not in exchange for the terror of the infinite, but for the ever-renewed distancing and relating of I-Thou. The great mother provides a kindlier separation for the child than the bodily mother at time of birth or, as in Buber's own case, later:

> Every child that is coming into being rests, like all life that is coming into being, in the womb of the great mother, the undivided primal world that precedes form. From her, too, we are separated, and enter into personal life, slipping free only in the dark hours to be close to her again; night by night this happens to the healthy man. But this separation does not occur suddenly and catastrophically like the separation from the bodily mother; time is granted to the child to exchange a spiritual connexion, that is, *relation,* for the natural connexion with the world that he gradually loses. He has stepped out of the glowing darkness of chaos into the cool light of creation.

The "cool light of creation" is not something that is given to a child to possess. Rather he must draw it out and make it into a reality for himself, as in "With a Monist" the man who bends over things with fervor is met by the "bestowing side of things." There are, in fact, no "things" for the child until this groping and reaching out has taken place, as "the correspondence of the child . . . with what is alive and effective over against him."

This implies a theory of knowledge, but underlying this theory of knowledge, in turn, is an anthropology – an understanding of what man is *as man* – and an ontology – a judgment as to what is "really real." At the deepest level of all is the existential trust that was already implicit in the link between Buber's accepting the separation from his mother and his willingness to go out again and again to meet what came to meet him. It is only through the I-Thou relationship, through going out to meet *and* through being met, that the infant, the individual, becomes a person at all. "We live our lives inscrutably included within the streaming mutual life of the universe."

The meeting with the Thou is like Daniel's "kingdom of holy insecurity" – "Strange lyric and dramatic episodes, seductive and magical, but tearing us away to dangerous extremes, loosening the well-tried context, leaving more questions than satisfaction behind them, shattering security" — but it is the insecurity not only of danger and openness but of personal involvement and mutual giving, of the trust that accepts "the exalted melancholy of our fate, that every *Thou* in our world must become an *It*," no matter how exclusively present the Thou was in the direct relation. You cannot make yourself understood with others concerning it.

> But it teaches you to meet others, and to hold your ground when you meet them. Through the graciousness of its comings and the solemn sadness of its goings it leads you away to the *Thou* in which the parallel lines of relations meet. It does not help to sustain you in life, it only helps you to glimpse eternity.

The comings of the Thou are gracious not because we are entirely dependent upon grace but because we cannot will both sides of the dialogue. We will only our own side, which is indispensable to any I-Thou relationship, but not sufficient. Its goings are solemnly sad because we cannot hold on to it, because we must return to the world of It. What is more, no depreciation of the world of It is implied. "Without *It* man cannot live." Yet the man who lives with *It* alone has so fully missed authentic human existence that he is not a man. Buber would not, like the Buddha, say of human existence itself that it is suffering and thus project as a meaningful goal the release from *samsara*, the wheel of life and death with its cycle of rebirths. The individual does not find the meaning of his existence in his suffering or freedom from it, but in the "between," in the reality of the spirit, which in its human manifestation is a response of man to his Thou. The "delusion" in which God and the world are "psychologized" — drawn into man — the colossal illusion of the human spirit that is bent back on itself, is that spirit exists in man. Actually it is man who lives in the spirit, if he is able to enter into relation with his whole being and respond to his Thou. "All real living is meeting."

Those words of Paracelsus with which Buber concluded his early poem "The Disciple" — "If you can be your own, never be another's" — are resumed in *I and Thou*, not in the context of individuation as a goal in itself, but as a preparation for going out to the meeting with the Thou and as a vain possession when cherished for itself: When the soul becomes a unity, "the being is alone in itself and rejoices, as Paracelsus says, in its exaltation."

This is the decisive moment for a man. Without it he is unfit for the work of the spirit; with it, he decides, in his innermost being, if this means a breathing-space, or the sufficient end of his way. Concentrated in unity, he can go out to the meeting, to which he has only now drawn quite close, with the mystery, with salvation. But he can also enjoy to the full this blessed unity of his being and without entering on the supreme duty, fall back into dispersion of his being.

Again and again natural "objects" "blaze up into presentness" and are "lived in the present by men." Before man grasps what is over against him as an object, compares it with other objects, classifies and analyzes it, and registers it in the structure of knowledge, he sees it with the force of presence and thereby grasps it in its incomparable uniqueness. We know this uniqueness as we meet it and as it, in a sense, comes to meet us. Along with all the perception of the senses and the categories of the mind, we feel the impact of real otherness. Buber related that several times in his youth he wanted to fix an object, to compel it, as it were, in order to find through so doing that it was "only" his conception. Every time that he tried to do this, the object refuted him through the dumb force of its being! This irreducible impact of otherness is what sets Buber apart from Edmund Husserl's philosophy of phenomenology. When Buber wrote in *I and Thou,* "In lived actuality no one thinks without something being thought; rather is the thinking no less dependent on the thing thought than the latter on the former," he sounded very much like Husserl. But when he added: "A subject that annuls the object to rise above it annuls its own actuality," he separated himself not only from the mystical doctrine of immersion, the context of this sentence, but also from Husserl's Idealist concept of a "transcendental ego" which somehow includes all that is thought and yet transcends it.

The man who frees the event from the *It* of established ideas "and looks on it again in the present moment, fulfills the nature of the act of knowledge to be real and effective *between* men." This contrast between the knowledge of subject and object and the knowing of *I and Thou* is already implicit in the biblical sentence, "Adam *knew* his wife Eve," in which knowing is, to begin with, mutual contact.* From here the way opens out to an entirely different approach to knowing in love, marriage, friendship, and any type of dialogue in which "inclusion," or experiencing the

---

* See Note A in Sources for Chapter 17, p. 430.

other side of the relationship, is central. From here too an approach to "knowing God" arises that is entirely different from that of ordinary philosophy of religion. Thus if *I and Thou* is not a system, it is, in the profoundest and most original sense, philosophy, having an inner consistency to which few philosophical systems can lay claim.

There is a close and necessary tie between Buber's theory of knowledge and his theory of art. If the mutual contact of the I-Thou relationship is the source of our sense perceptions and of our elaborations of them in articulated knowledge, it is also, as Buber wrote in *I and Thou,* "the eternal source of art." Buber's earliest unmistakably dialogical statement was made in his 1903 essay on the Jewish painter Lesser Ury:

> The thing is activity, not substance. Close it off, and you take from it its life. The most personal rests in the relationship to the other. Tie a being to all beings, and you entice from it its ownmost self.

In "Productivity and Existence" (1914) Buber pointed to the genuine artist as one who brings forth a natural creation, in a gradual selective progression from experience to thoughts, from thoughts to words, from words to writing, and from writing to public communication: "That man is legitimately creative who experiences so strongly and formatively that his experiences unite into an image that demands to be set forth, and who then works at his task with full consciousness of his art."* Through experiencing the "bestowing side of things," wrote Buber in "With a Monist" (1914), there appears to the true artist "the secret shape of that thing which appeared to none before him."

It is precisely this that Buber meant when he wrote in *I and Thou* of our life with "spiritual beings" in which we perceive no Thou yet feel that we are addressed and that we answer. The "forms" that man meets as Thou are not Platonic archetypes but merely the potentialities of form that arise from man's meeting with the world: "what of spirit has not yet entered the world but is ready to do so, and becomes present to us."

> A man is faced by a form which desires to be made through him into a work. This form is no offspring of his soul, but is an appearance which steps up to it and demands of it the effective power.... He

---

* See Note B in Sources for Chapter 17, p. 430.

who gives himself to it may withhold nothing of himself. . . . I can
neither experience nor describe the form.which meets me, but only
body it forth. . . . To produce is to draw forth, to invent is to find,
to shape is to discover.

As the artist gives the form embodiment, he banishes it to be a
"structure," an It. But the nature of this structure is that it can
be freed for a timeless moment by the beholder who brings the
form to life again in the presentness and immediacy of the I-
Thou relationship. Thus in art as in life the alternation between I-
Thou and I-It is necessary and desirable. But the origin and the
renewed presentness of art is again and again a reality of the "between." This was stated by Buber in a clearer and simpler form in
his lectures on "Religion as Presence":

> An artist who has a conception of his work and stands over against
> this work as his Thou . . . does not know this in such a way that he
> could say anything about it, describe it, indicate its place in space and
> time, but only so that he can realize it. And nonetheless one would
> totally deceive oneself under the spell of academic philosophy if one
> wanted to conceive this work as if it were a psychic event, a fiction,
> something that this person devises and which he only then makes
> real. But in truth this work is as much in the world of the real of which
> we speak as the beloved person or as nature addressed as Thou. This
> relationship is not a relationship to something fictitious but to some-
> thing that is there but not as It, only as Thou.

Here too Buber grounds his thought on an event or meeting
from his own life, though one "associated with strong memories"
for many:

> Take the Doric column, wherever it appears to a man who is able
> and ready to turn toward it. It confronted me for the first time out of
> a church wall in Syracuse into which it had been incorporated: secret
> primal measure presenting itself in such a simple form that nothing indi-
> vidual could be seen or enjoyed in it. What had to be achieved was
> what I was able to achieve: to confront and endure this spiritual form
> there that had passed through the mind and hand of man and become
> incarnate.

What music in particular meant to Buber is hinted at in his autobiographical fragment in which he tells of his false confirmation
of his youthful hero Ferdinand Lassalle. Before he mentioned
this incident Buber wrote of the effect of Bach, not only on his
life but on his thinking:

What had the strongest effect on me there was undoubtedly hearing Bach's music, and in truth Bach's music so sung and played — of that I was certain at that time and have remained certain — as Bach himself wished that it be sung and played. But it would be fruitless for me to undertake to say, indeed, I cannot even make clear to myself — in what way Bach had influenced my thinking. The ground-tone of my life was obviously modified in some manner and through that my thinking as well.

After recounting the episode concerning Lassalle, Buber spoke of how "slowly, waveringly" there grew in him "the insight into the problematic reality of human existence and into the fragile possibility of doing justice to it." This momentous statement is followed by the simple but poignant phrase, "Bach helped me." From this we may conclude that the perfection of art was in some way directly related in Buber's mind to the problematic of man and we can anticipate the later development of his philosophical anthropology along just these lines. This relation was clearly for Buber one of fruitful tension — not one of the collapse of art into life or of the escape from life into art. Even though the artist is not fully addressed *as a person* in art, art remained for Buber one of the primary forms of the I-Thou relationship, one that demands the response of the whole being in addressing the invisible but nonetheless real "forms" that accost the artist, as well as of the visible but not yet fully real finished works that require the appreciating person to complete their reality.

CHAPTER 18

Love and Marriage, Politics and Community

TO GRASP THE FULL SIGNIFICANCE of Buber's approach to love and marriage in *I and Thou*, we must speak of his relationship to his wife Paula — an influence probably more decisive for the development of his I-Thou philosophy as a whole than any of the events and meetings with which we have dealt. Buber's dialogical thinking could have grown only out of his marriage to this strong and really "other" woman, this modern Ruth who left her family, home, and religion, and finally even her country and people, for him. The fundamental reality of the life of dialogue — that it is a confirmation and inclusion of otherness — was understood and authenticated in the love and the marriage, the tension and the companionship, of his relationship to Paula. Over Buber's works, Fischer-Barnicol suggests, stands Paula Buber's motto: "Responsibility is the umbilical cord of creation." Buber himself wrote in *I and Thou*:

> Love is responsibility of an *I* for a *You*. In this consists what cannot consist in any feeling — the equality of all lovers, from the smallest to the

greatest and from the blissfully secure whose life is circumscribed by the life of one beloved human being, to him that is nailed his life long to the cross of the world, capable of what is immense and bold enough to risk it: to love *man*.

Feelings are within man, but man stands within love; for love is between I and Thou.

At the end of the first dialogue of *Daniel* it is the woman who adds to Daniel's vertical thrust — the mysticism to which the young Buber was given — the horizontal crossbeam that keeps him bound to community:

THE WOMAN: . . . Give me your hand, Daniel.

DANIEL: Here.

THE WOMAN: . . . What do you see?

DANIEL: My hand in yours.

THE WOMAN: A horizontal, is it not?

DANIEL: A horizontal.

THE WOMAN: Might you — might you remove the crossbeams?

DANIEL: Not for anything.

THE WOMAN: How so?

DANIEL: Because this is not the compulsion by the other which is valid to overcome, but the choice of the other: the direction of the holy spirit, the flowering cross of community.

If the failure of Buber's mother to return when he was four years old was the crucial "mismeeting" of his life, Martin's marriage to Paula was the crucial *meeting* — one that could be so only because of the remarkable personal strength that each of them possessed, their very real otherness, and the greatness of their love. If this meeting did not entirely remove the inner division that his mother's disappearance had brought about, it nonetheless made possible a life of trust in which Buber found again the strength to go forth to meet the unique and unforeseeable person or situation as his Thou. The threatening insecurity of Buber's being, Grete Schaeder perceptively comments, receded when he met and married Paula Winkler. One can go further and say that the existential trust that underlies *I and Thou* and all of Buber's mature works would have been unthinkable without his relationship to Paula. In this sense we have before us in full reality a philosopher whose thinking did not emerge from his individual being but from the "between," which he knew first and foremost in his marriage.

The precise effect of Paula's strength — her integrity, her honesty, and her responsibility — is movingly depicted in a poem that Buber wrote for her on his fiftieth birthday in 1928:

ON THE DAY OF LOOKING BACK

The roaming one spoke to me: I am the spirit.
The iridescent one spoke to me: I am the world.
He had hovered round me with wings.
She had encompassed me with her play of flames.
Already I wanted to pander to them,
Already my heart was duped,
When there stepped before the demons
A presence.

To the roaming one it said: You are madness.
To the iridescent one it said: You are deception.
Then both spirit and world became open to me,
The lies burst, and what was, was enough.
You brought it about that I behold, —
Brought about? you only lived.
You element and woman,
Soul and nature!

A similar acknowledgment came from Martin to Paula a year later in the dedicatory stanza to his little book *Dialogue*:

TO P.

The abyss and the light of the worlds,
Time's need and eternity's desire,
Vision, event and poem:
They were and are dialogue with you.

"On the Day of Looking Back" describes how Paula helped Buber to escape from the danger presented by the very multiplicity of his gifts, to find serious and responsible direction amid his wealth of talent. Commenting on this poem, Hugo Bergmann writes:

Paula Buber warded off the great dangers that threatened the young Buber. The powerful gifts of Buber were set within the literary milieu of the turn of the century, which were fully aestheticizing and unbinding, and his gifts would have become for him a fatality, he would have been the victim of his early fame, had not Paula Buber been at his side at that time, had she not liberated him from deception and lies and pointed him toward the difficult way of work, of responsibility, of truth.

For Buber, as for Kierkegaard, true existential decision meant putting aside the many of the aesthetic man in favor of the one thing that a person is called to do. But to Buber that call did not come through impersonal duty and universal morality, nor could it be responded to except by the channeling of that very passion which formerly was at the mercy of "the roaming" and "the iridescent" spirits that deceived and misled him. Hence the great emphasis upon decision in *I and Thou* is also a call for personal wholeness and direction, for openness and response, for what the Talmud and the Hasidim called "serving God with the evil urge."

> Only he who knows relation and knows about the presence of the *Thou* is capable of decision. . . .
> The fiery stuff of all my ability to will seethes tremendously, all that I might do circles around me, still without actuality in the world, flung together and seemingly inseparable, alluring glimpses of powers flicker from all the uttermost bounds: the universe is my temptation, and I achieve being in an instant, with both hands plunged deep in the fire, where the single deed is hidden, the deed which aims at me – now is the moment! Already the menace of the abyss is removed, the centreless many no longer plays in the iridescent sameness of its pretensions; but only two alternatives are set side by side – the other, the vain idea, and the one, the charge laid on me . . . he alone who directs the whole strength of the alternative into the doing of the charge, who lets the abundant passion of what is rejected invade the growth to reality of what is chosen . . . decides the event.

A later testimony of Buber's reveals how after he found his path in his work on Hasidism, Paula and he built together a common world of mutual discovery, a world which still called and claimed them when Buber wrote the dedicatory poem that he inscribed in the copy of *The Tales of the Hasidim* that he gave to Paula in 1949:

DO YOU STILL KNOW IT . . . ?

Do you still know, how we in our young years
Traveled together on this sea?
Visions came, great and wonderful,
We beheld them together, you and I.
How image joined itself with images in our hearts!

How a mutual animated describing
Arose out of it and lived between you and me!
We were there and were yet wholly here
And wholly together, roaming and grounded.
Thus the voice awoke that since then proclaims
And witnesses to old majesty as new,
True to itself and you and to both together.
Take then this witness in your hands,
It is an end and yet has no end,
For something eternal listens to it and listens to us,
How we resound out of it, I and Thou.

Even the epigraph with which Buber opens *I and Thou* is understood by Grete Schaeder and, following her, Walter Kaufmann, as a concealed dedication to Paula Buber. This epigraph, from Goethe's *West-östlichen Divan,* reads in German:

So hab ich endlich von dir erharrt:
In allen Elementen Gottes Gegenwart.

and in Smith's translation:

So waiting I have won from thee the end
God's presence in each element.*

A much more commonplace indication of the great importance to Martin of his relationship with Paula came in a conversation between Buber and Schalom Ben-Chorin in which Buber affirmed marriage as the life-form most suitable to man. Looking gratefully at his wife, he humorously commented that in marriage each partner has to supplement the other even in external things. He complained of his own lack of manual dexterity, the blame for which he laid at the door of his grandmother, who had kept him from manual activities. Then Buber remarked dryly that without the help of his wife, no packet of books would ever have left his house; for only she could tie up the packages.

Buber's attitude in *I and Thou* toward the relations among politics, economics, and the state, on the one hand, and genuine community, on the other, is identical with his attitude toward the relation between sex and love. Here, too, politics, economics, and the state are not evil in themselves, as they were for Gustav

---

* See Note A in Sources for Chapter 18, p. 431.

Landauer, but only when they became independent of the aim of building genuine community to which they are legitimate means. Is it not unfortunate, asked Buber, that the greatness of the leading statesmen and the leading economists is inextricably joined to their regarding and treating men as He, i.e. It, rather than Thou? Have not modern work and property destroyed in the workers themselves every trace of significant direct relationship to others? But, Buber affirmed, economics (the abode of the will to profit) and the state (the abode of the will to be powerful) share in life only as long as they share in the spirit — as long as the structures of man's communal life draw their living quality from the power to enter into relationship.

In *I and Thou* Buber pointed out that two basically different notions are confused when people use the concept of the social:

> ... the community built of relation and the amassing of human units that have no relation to one another — the palpable manifestation of modern man's lack of relation. The bright edifice of community, however, for which one can be liberated even from the dungeon of "sociability," is the work of the same force that is alive in the relation between man and God.

The presence of the Thou moves over the world of It like the spirit upon the face of the waters. This does not mean any dualism between spiritual ideal and material reality but rather the continuing task of drawing the line of demarcation according to the uniqueness of each concrete situation. The statesman or economist who obeys the spirit "does in communal life precisely what is done in personal life by the man who knows himself incapable of realizing the *Thou* in its purity, yet daily confirms its truth in the *It*, in accordance with what is right and fitting for the day, drawing — disclosing — the boundary line anew each day." What matters is that the spirit which says *Thou*, which responds, is bound to life and reality and not made into an independent realm. The dualism which would keep "spirit" in one compartment and economics and the state in the other would mean yielding up to tyranny once and for all the provinces that are steeped in the world of It *and* thus robbing the spirit completely of reality. "For the spirit is never independently effective in life by itself alone, but in relation to the world: possessing power that permeates the world of *It*, transforming it." Hence no "I-You" relationship is needed in addition to the I-Thou and the I-It, as Harvey Cox asserts in *The*

Secular City. Cox's effort to guard against the sentimental or tyrannical intimacy of the small town not only is based upon a complete misunderstanding of I-Thou but also falls directly into the danger of excluding a priori a large province of life from the possibility of any mutuality, leaving to it only the pseudopersonal element of courtesy without immediacy.*

I and Thou is not a teaching of compromise but of spiritual realism. The question is not what one ought to do in general, but what is possible and desirable for us at this moment and in this situation. Those who instead profess the ideal of total love and renunciation of power rob power of its direction, love of its force, and life of its reality. This is what Buber stated clearly in the poem "Power and Love" (1926):

> *Our hope is too new and too old —*
> *I do not know what would remain to us*
> *Were love not transfigured power*
> *And power not straying love.*
>
> *Do not protest: "Let love alone rule!"*
> *Can you prove it true?*
> *But resolve: Every morning*
> *I shall concern myself anew about the boundary*
> *Between the love-deed-Yes and the power-deed-No*
> *And pressing forward honor reality.*
>
> *We cannot avoid*
> *Using power,*
> *Cannot escape the compulsion*
> *To afflict the world,*
> *So let us, cautious in diction*
> *And mighty in contradiction,*
> *Love powerfully.*

What Buber said here of persons he also said of society in a conversation in this same period with the great Indian poet and philosopher Rabindranath Tagore. Tagore invited Buber to meet with him at the home of the Sanskrit professor Moritz Winternitz in Prague to discuss Zionism, which Tagore feared might weaken the reverence for the spirit and universalism that he saw as the Jewish people's finest, most valuable characteristics. Grown to self-determination, the Jewish people would adopt the narrow-

---

* See Note B in Sources for Chapter 18, p. 431.

hearted nationalism and soulless pantechnicism of the Western nations. Buber agreed about the existence of the danger but not that it could or even should be avoided:

> As in the life of individuals, so in that of peoples, there exists in a certain stage of their way threatening dangers necessary for life, so to speak, which one must attack directly in order eventually to overcome them. If in the pressing historical hour one flees from them, one loses the capacity for advancing further, becomes paralyzed, and expires; what is important is to direct one's best forces to meeting the danger, for then it will either evaporate or we must fight and conquer it with our concentrated forces.

Tagore protested that the civilization of the West, despite the manifestations of decline in it, is still too powerful for a people to be able at the same time both to accept it and to protect oneself from it. He proposed instead that to the machines and cannons of the West be opposed the genuine meditation of the East, demonstrating to the Occident the emptiness and meaninglessness of its freneticism and teaching it, together with the Orient, to immerse itself in the vision of the eternal truth. Buber compared this to telling a man who was carrying a heavy sign up the mountain that his ascent would be much easier if he cast it off. "Not so," the man would answer. "I climb upward precisely to erect this sign up above. I hold it, and it holds me." This, Buber asserted, is the situation of the human spirit today. "It may not cast off the burden of its civilization; for in it a higher value is hidden that will only shine forth when from the sphere of inner conflict it attains the pure summit air of justice and peace."

Buber began an address that he delivered on "China and Us" at the Sessions of the China Institute at Frankfurt am Main in 1928 with a reference to this same conversation with Tagore. On the basis of the development of Japan and even of India, Buber prophesied that Asia could not be spared the road of the West. The West would lose its own way forward if it were to renounce its industrializing, technicizing, and mechanizing, said Buber. Only by bearing and overcoming the problematic as it is, may the West hope to meet an Asia advancing to meet it.

This by no means implies capitulating before the mechanization of Western society but finding an image of man which can give that process meaning. "The ages that possess real culture are ages where a universally-valid image of man stands above the heads of men," living in their imagination, and educating and forming the young through imitation of that image. Buber saw the possibility of receiving from China something of Lao-tzu's teaching of *wu-wei,* or "nonaction." This Taoist teaching of the noninterfering action of the whole being remained central in Buber's mature thought when other aspects of his mysticism fell away and issued into his contrast between "person" and "individual," "free man" and "willful man."

> The free man is he who wills without arbitrary self-will. . . . He must go forth with his whole being: that he knows. . . . He must sacrifice his little will, which is unfree and ruled by things and drives, to his great will that moves away from being determined to find destiny. Now he no longer interferes, nor does he merely allow things to happen. He listens to that which grows, to the way of Being in the world . . . in order to actualize it in the manner in which it, needing him, wants to be actualized by him.

The willful man, in contrast, knows neither meeting nor presentness, but only a feverish, cluttered world of purposes and his feverish desire to use it.*

---

* See Note in Sources to Chapter 19, p. 432.

CHAPTER 19

The Self and the World:
Psychologism and Psychotherapy

IN *I and Thou,* Buber spoke of a "demonic Thou," the man who like Napoleon is Thou for millions yet knows no Thou himself, the man who does not respond genuinely in the personal sphere but only in his Cause.

> This demonic *Thou,* to which no one can become *Thou,* is the elementary barrier of history, where the basic word of connexion loses its reality, its character of mutual action. In addition to (not between) person and individual, free and self-willed man, there is this third, towering in times of destiny, fraught with destiny. Toward him everything flames, but his fire is cold. To him a thousand several relations lead, but from him none. He shares in no reality, but others share in him as though in a reality.

The demonic Thou sees the beings around him as Its, as machines capable of various achievements, which must be taken into account and utilized for the Cause. He sees even himself this way, only he experiences his own power as unlimited. When he says I, he expresses no human reality, only the desperateness of his own self-contradiction. Since he does not make real his inborn possibility of relating to the Thou, in extreme cases the Thou strikes inward and becomes an inner double, a *Doppelgänger.* "Here is the edge of life. What is unfulfilled has here escaped into the mad delusion of some fulfillment; now it gropes around in a labyrinth and gets lost ever more profoundly."

The self-contradiction produced by the Thou striking inward has profound implications for our understanding of schizophrenia, and profounder implications still for the sickness of modern man in general, the sickness of existential mistrust. In the last section of Part II of *I and Thou* Buber described the man shuddering at the alienation between the I and the world, "as when in the grave night-hour you lie, racked by waking dream — bulwarks have fallen away and the abyss is screaming — and note amid your torment: there is still life, if only I could get through to it." Spurning the way of turning through sacrifice, this man calls thought to his aid to paint a reliable picture of the world and patch up the relation between his wretched, empty I and the world — his one-time playfellow who looks at him now with mocking, cruel eyes. Thought produces for him two moving pictures shown on two walls. On the one wall there is the universe.

> The tiny earth plunges from the whirling stars, tiny man from the teeming earth, and now history bears him further through the ages, to rebuild persistently the anthill of the cultures which history crushes underfoot.

On the opposite wall there takes place the soul.

> A spinner is spinning the orbits of all stars and the life of all creation and the history of the universe; everything is woven on one thread, and is no longer called stars and creation and universe, but sensations and imaginings, or even experiences, and conditions of the soul.

Although these two series of pictures are opposite, they both have written under them: "One and all," and they both serve the purpose of reassuring the empty I when the world strikes terror in its heart. Either the I is really embedded in the world and there really is no I at all — so the world can do nothing to the I; or the world is embedded in the I, and there really is no world at all. But he will not long be at ease; for "a moment comes, and it is near, when the shuddering man looks up and sees, in a flash, both pictures together. And a deeper shudder seizes him."

Modern man's wish to be all or nothing is born of his dread of the infinite universe that confronts him and still more of his mistrust in the possibility of living vis-à-vis either nature or his fellowman. In the "Modern Promethean," the rebel of the either/or who intensifies the problematic of modern man, this all or nothing takes the form of a heroic defiance, a romantic posture behind which lurks both terror and despair. In the more ordinary modern man it takes the form that Buber described in Part II of *I and Thou* — a life neatly divided into two tidily circled-off provinces, one of institutions and the other of feelings — the It and the I.

> Institutions are "outside," where all sorts of aims are pursued, where a man works, negotiates, bears influence, undertakes, concurs, organizes, conducts business, officiates, preaches. . . .
> Feelings are "within," where life is lived and man recovers from institutions. Here the spectrum of the emotions dances before the interested glance. . . .
> Institutions are a complicated marketplace, feelings a boudoir rich in ever-changing interests.

People try to escape from the impersonal golem of institutions to the "personal" world of feelings, but feelings per se are no more personal than institutions. They are personal only when they are brought as by-product and accompaniment into the response of the whole person to what meets him, not when they are themselves assumed to be the touchstone of reality. "And if, like the modern man, you have learned to concern yourself wholly with your own feelings, despair at their unreality will not easily instruct you in a better way — for despair is also an interesting feeling."

What is common to the Modern Promethean and the man who divides his life between institutions and feelings is that neither has to risk that openness in which one meets real otherness with full personal involvement. Institutions equal "otherness" without involvement, feelings equal "involvement" without otherness. The philosopher's construction of the world often has the same effect of protecting the I from real contact with the Thou. Positivist and Idealist alike paint the very pictures which the alienated man saw on either wall — in which the I is included in the world or the world is included in the I. In contrast to these traditional philosophical opposites, Buber affirmed in *I and Thou* the distance and relation of self and world as two independent yet interacting realities:

> Certainly the world "dwells" in me as an image, just as I dwell in it as a thing. But it is not for that reason in me, just as I am not in it. The world and I are mutually included, the one in the other. This contradiction in thought, inherent in the situation of *It* is resolved in the situation of *Thou*, which sets me free from the world in order to bind me up in solidarity of connexion with it.

The I-Thou relationship is, in fact, a *coincidentia oppositorum,* to go back to Nicholas of Cusa, who occupied an important place in Buber's early thought. Plato's logical categories of the same and the other and Aristotle's logic of A and not-A can never comprehend the simultaneous reality of distancing and relating, separateness and togetherness, arrows going apart and arrows coming together, concrete situation and free response, which make up the meeting of I and Thou. "Here no further 'reduction' is possible," wrote Buber, possibly in conscious reference to Husserl's "phenomenological *epoché,*" or "bracketing." "Whoever does not honor the ultimate unities thwarts the sense that is only comprehensible but not conceptual."

What is vital here, however, is not philosophical theory but human attitude, not whether I "affirm" or "deny" the world in my soul, but how I let my soul's attitude toward the world come to life, life that acts upon the world. He who merely "experiences" his attitude, merely consummates it in his soul, however thoughtfully, does not concern the world. All his tricks, arts, ecstasies, enthusiasms, and mysteries haven't the slightest effect upon the world. "Let us love the actual world that never wishes to be annulled, but love it in all its terror, but dare to embrace it with our spirit's arms — and our hands encounter the hands that hold it. . . . Whoever goes in truth to meet the world, goes forth to God."

"I knew from the time that I was young," confessed Buber in a striking personal comment in the midst of an essay on Hasidism, "that I was destined to love the world." But to love the world means to be ready to meet the real world with all its uncanniness, horror, and evil. Those who are afraid to do this escape the meeting through *psychologizing* the world, through removing it into the sphere of one's feelings, one's thoughts, or one's analyses.

Buber's opposition to psychologism was in no sense a disparagement of psychology or psychotherapy per se but only of the attempt to subsume all reality under psychological or psychoanalytic categories. Buber stated this clearly in February 1922 in the third of his Lehrhaus lectures on "Religion as Presence." The "soul" with which psychology concerns itself and deals with as an object is often not the soul of which the person is immediately aware in relationship to the world, things, creatures, human beings, and Being, but "something lifted out of the relationship to the world, isolated, abstracted."

> It is, so to speak, the isolated share of the human being which is treated as though it existed for itself, as though it were an apparatus closed in itself . . . and in which one now distinguishes different kinds, different groups of phenomena, which one divides up into different partial spheres, thinking, feeling, willing . . . in which one knows different characteristics of perception.

In 1923, the year of the publication of *I and Thou,* Buber gave an informal lecture on "The Psychologizing of the World" for the Psychological Club of Zurich, the most eminent center of Jungian therapy at that time. Buber's sketch notes of this lecture throw a remarkable light on *I and Thou* by recapitulating some of the central motifs of that book — particularly the one of the self and the world — in an entirely different language and context.

By the psychologizing of the world Buber meant that inclusion of the world in the soul that goes so far that the essential basic relation from which our life receives its meaning is damaged: the facing of I and world in which the real happens. *Psychologism* regards the world as an idea. *Cosmologism* regards the soul as an element, a product of the world. Both pervert the reality of an immediate connection between I and world in which the arch of relationship rises on two clearly individual pillars. In opposition to *psychologism* and *cosmologism,* Buber offered a third perspective which might contain within it the world's inclusion of the soul and the soul's inclusion of the world without abolishing the independence of either partner. This is a greater apprehension of reality than we are accustomed to, a *pneumatic reality* in which the concepts of the psychic and the cosmic can come together. Buber also called this reality of the spirit "ontologism," emphasizing the basic reality of the *between* as that existent in which all that is psychic and all that is cosmic and all that is opposite and all that is inclusive of the two are embedded. If we regard more deeply what we call psychic phenomena, we find that all of them, and their connections, have arisen dynamically only out of the relationship between the I and the other and are comprehensible only through this relationship. The soul stands in a continually developing double movement — in the unfolding or realization of the relationship and the I's withdrawing-into-itself or being-withdrawn from the relationship.

Insofar as the soul is comprehended exclusively as I, however, it is comprehended in amputation, in abstraction, not in its *whole* existence.

"Psychologizing of the world" thus means an attempt of the soul to completely detach itself from its basic character of relationship.

> The spirit in its condition of highest differentiation is inclined to bend back on itself, i.e., the spirit to the extent of its individuation is inclined to forget, to deny that it does not exist *in* man (in I), but between man and what is not man. . . . Then Being is psychologized, installed within the soul of man. The world no longer confronts the soul. That is the soul-madness of the spirit. . . . An all-penetrating substance is created: all is transformed into soul. This fact is the true fall. Here first the fall takes place.

This passage is very close to one in the third part of *I and Thou*:

> All doctrines of immersion are based on the gigantic delusion of a human spirit bent back into itself — the delusion that spirit occurs in man. In truth it occurs from man — between man and what he is not. As the spirit bent back into itself renounces this sense, this sense of relation, he must draw into man that which is not man, he must psychologize world and God. This is the psychical delusion of the spirit.

How important this fall of man into psychologism and the bending back of the spirit on itself was for Buber can be seen from the fact that the major categories of "Dialogue," Buber's first major application of the I-Thou relationship to the interhuman as such, are defined in terms of it. The essence of genuine dialogue lies in the fact that "each of the participants really has in mind the other or others in their present and particular being and turns to them with the intention of establishing a living mutual relation between himself and them." The basic movement of the life of "monologue," in contrast, is not turning away from the other but "reflexion" (*Rückbiegung*) in the physiological origin of the term — bending back on oneself. "Reflexion" is not egotism but the withdrawal from accepting the other person in his particularity in favor of letting him exist *only as one's own experience,* only as a part of oneself. Through this withdrawal "the essence of all reality begins to disintegrate."

Buber was a leading influence at this very time in the German Youth Movement, that powerful stream of political, philosophical, and social ideals that succeeded the Wandervögel. But he saw quite clearly how the relation between man and reality was referred by each member to his own person: "*My* kind. . . . *My* blood. . . . *My* destiny." This clear insight also carried over to the erotic. The erotic is almost throughout only differentiated self-enjoyment, Buber declared, and what is elementally perceived is what takes place in one's own soul. Even the attempts at the spiritual and religious life are soaked through with the same poison — the poison of the human spirit bent back upon itself and deluding itself that spirit occurs in man.

Going beyond legitimate self-experience, the natural growth of consciousness, man falls into *self-observation,* Buber said, an interference which wills to further the growth of the self and in so doing thwarts it. The deeper self-experience that one seeks and seemingly finds is actually a distortion and a belaboring which produces the disintegration of the self. One can only legitimately experience without willfulness. Similarly, that "analyticism" which regards its psychoanalytic method as being universally valid does not know what any healthy psychology must know, that it is merely a method and as such only *provisionally* usable and must always be ready to be given up. "Psychosynthesis," in contrast, knows that though it dissects the life of the soul, the soul is a unity. In Jung's school of analytic psychology Buber often encountered this wise limitation. At the same time, Buber pointed to the problematic of the province of psychotherapy that none of the schools had begun at that time to face: that the therapist deals with the patient as an individual yet his sickness is a sickness of the "between."

> The sicknesses of the soul are sicknesses of relationship. They can only be treated completely if I transcend the realm of the patient and

add to it the world as well. If the doctor possessed superhuman power, he would have to try to heal the relationship itself, to heal in the "between."

Thus in psychotherapy itself Buber was aware of the need to burst the bounds of psychologism, which refers all events and meaning back to the psyche, and to reach the ground of "healing through meeting" — a healing *in* and *of* the "between."

Psychopathology had exercised an active fascination upon Buber since his student days:

> When I was a student long ago I studied three terms of psychiatry and what they call in Germany *Psychiatrische-Klinique.* I was most interested in the latter. . . . I studied it three terms: first with Flechsig in Leipzig, where there were students of Wundt. Afterward in Berlin with Mendel, and a third term with Bleuler in Zurich, which was the most interesting of the three. I was then a very young, inexperienced, and not very understanding young man. But I had the feeling that I wanted to know about man, and man in the so-called pathological state. I doubted even then if it is the right term. I wanted to see, if possible to meet, such people and, as far as I can remember, to establish relations, a real relation between what we call a sane man and what we call a pathological man. And this I learned in some measure — as far as a boy of twenty or so can learn such things.

Buber attended Freud's lectures in Vienna, and seriously intended to write a book on Freud, as we have seen, until Lou Salomé dissuaded him.

In "Body and Spirit of the Hasidic Movement," which was written in September 1919, Buber, in conscious opposition to Freud's "psychoanalysis," stressed the term "psychosynthesis," which already appeared in his notes for *Daniel*, a term which was also used by the Italian psychologist and educator Roberto Assagioli as the focus of a whole movement in Italian psychotherapy. Taking as his problem the understanding of the healing practiced by the *zaddik* on the Hasidim who came to him with their diseases, Buber suggested that one could best do justice to its deeper dimension if one bore in mind "that the relation of the soul to its organic life depends on the degree of its wholeness and unity."

> The more dissociated the soul, the more it is at the mercy of its sicknesses and attacks, the more concentrated it is, the more it is able

to master them. It is not as if it conquered the body; rather through its unity it ever again saves and protects the unity of the body. This power rules suddenly and unmistakably where in a dispersed soul in an elemental moment it accomplishes a crystallization and unification; there takes place rapidly and visibly there what otherwise only grows in vegetative darkness, the "healing." Through nothing else can this process be effected so simply and directly as through the psychosynthetic appearance of a whole, united soul laying hold of the dispersed soul, agitating it on all sides, and demanding the event of crystallization.

The healer fashions in the fellow-soul a ground and center in order that the soul that calls to him for help might look through him, as through a glass, into Being. The more fully and genuinely this ground and center is fashioned, the less does the appealing soul remain dependent upon the helper. But the less, too, does he fall back into psychologism.

At the end of his lecture on the "Psychologizing of the World" Buber brought his concern with psychologism back into the context and language of *I and Thou*. Psychologism develops into self-contradiction when it becomes so intensified that man can no longer bring his inborn Thou into the meeting with others, with the world. Here at the farthest point of emptiness is also the point of the turning, a turning which cannot be accomplished by the individual alone but only by community. But community itself, in a time like ours, can happen only out of breakthrough, out of turning, when the need aroused by the uttermost sundering of self and world provides the motive force for it. Genuine community now begins with the discovery that reality is more than psychological and rests upon the belief in this reality.

If one knows this, then one also knows that community in our time must ever again miscarry. The monstrous, the dreadful phenomenon of psychologism so prevails that one cannot simply bring about healing, rescue with a single blow. But the disappointments belong to the way. There is no other way than that of this miscarrying. That is the way of faithful faith.

CHAPTER 20

The "Eternal Thou"
The "God of the Philosophers"
versus the Living God

AS DESPAIR IN *Daniel* is the gateway to reality, so despair in *I and Thou* is the soil out of which the turning grows. The self-willed man, who is wholly and inextricably tangled in the unreal, directs the best part of his spirituality to averting or veiling his thoughts about his real self. But it is only these thoughts about the I emptied of reality and about the real I that enable one to sink and take root in the soil of despair, so that out of self-destruction and rebirth, the beginning of the turning might arise. Through that turning alone can he meet the "eternal Thou."

Every real relation with a being or life in the world is exclusive in the sense that while it lasts the Thou steps forth free and single and confronts you and all else lives in *its* light. Only the relationship with the eternal Thou is both exclusive and inclusive. The eternal Thou is met in each particular Thou; yet it cannot be fixed in any of them. The eternal Thou does not become "It" when the others do — not because it is some universal essence of Thou, but because it is the present reality, the ever-renewed presentness of meeting, *eternally* Thou. "Although we on earth never behold God without world but only the world in God, by beholding we eternally form God's form." It is the bond of the Absolute with the concrete and particular, not with the universal.

> Men do not find God if they stay in the world. They do not find Him if they leave the world. He who goes out with his whole being to meet his *Thou* and carries to it all being that is in the world, finds Him who cannot be sought.
> If you explore the life of things and of conditioned being you come to the unfathomable, if you deny the life of things and of conditioned being you stand before nothingness, if you hallow this life you meet the living God.

This position is neither transcendent nor pantheist but again the *coincidentia oppositorum*. God is the "wholly Other" of Karl Barth, but he is also the wholly Same, the wholly Present. He is Rudolf Otto's *Mysterium Tremendum* that appears and over-throws, but he is also the mystery of the self-evident, nearer to me than my I.* This is the one, all-embracing relation in which potential is still actual being, the only Thou that by its nature never ceases to be Thou for us.

> He who knows God knows also very well remoteness from God and the anguish of barrenness in the tormented heart; but he does not know the absence of God: it is only we who are not always there.

Thus the man who meets the eternal Thou is the free man of dialogical will of Part II of *I and Thou*: Ready, "not seeking he goes his way; hence he is composed before all things, and makes contact with them which helps them. But when he has *found,* his heart is not turned from them, though everything now meets him in the one event." All revelation is summons and sending, rather than static theological "truths." "Meeting with God does not come to man in order that he may concern himself with God, but in order that he may confirm that there is meaning in the world."

Thus for Buber, in contrast to Kierkegaard, there is no such thing as an I-Thou relationship with God which comes when man turns away from one's fellowmen and the world. Buber described God in deliberate paradox as the "absolute Person, i.e., the Person who cannot be limited." What is more, it is not some personal

---

* See Note in Sources for Chapter 20, p. 433.

manifestation of the Absolute but the Absolute itself that we encounter as Thou, and the "personhood" of this Absolute is not its "nature," about which we know nothing, but the act of meeting itself. "It is as the absolute Person that God enters into direct relation with us." The Absolute speaks personally in Buber's sense of "person" − the sharing of the I-Thou relationship − but it *is* not a person in any finite, person-alongside-other-persons sense of the term. It is because of this paradox that the relationship with the eternal Thou is at once exclusive and inclusive.

> As a Person God gives personal life, he makes us as persons become capable of meeting with him and with one another. But no limitation can come upon him as the absolute Person, either from us or from our relations with one another; in fact we can dedicate to him not merely our persons but also our relations to one another. The man who turns to him therefore need not turn away from any other *I-Thou* relation; but he properly brings them to him, and lets them be fulfilled "in the face of God."

The world of It is set in the context of space and time, but the context of the world of Thou is the Center where the extended lines of relations meet − the eternal Thou. By virtue of the privilege of pure relation there exists the unbroken world of *Thou*: the isolated moments of relations are bound up in a life of world solidarity. As a result, spirit can penetrate and transform the world of It, and we are not given up to alienation from the world and the loss of reality by the I − to "domination by the ghostly." In the turning − the recognition of the Center and the act of turning again to it − the buried relational power of man rises.

The "eternal Thou" did not mean "God" for Buber. "God" meant the "eternal Thou." The "eternal Thou" was not just another up-to-date way of reintroducing the God of the philosophers and the theologians − the God whose existence could be proved and whose nature and attributes could be described as he is in himself apart from our relation to him. It was the reality of the "between," of the meeting itself, and there and nowhere else did Buber find the unconditional which no fathoming of the self or soaring into metaphysical heights could reveal.

For this reason, what matters is not creed or belief but a life-stance. The man who *profits* from the world will also *profit* from God, and it is he, and not the "atheist" who addresses the Nameless out of the night and yearns from his garret window, who is the godless man. Even the man who abhors the name and believes himself to be godless addresses God when he gives his whole being to addressing the Thou of his life as a Thou that cannot be limited by another. "The man who says Thou ultimately means his eternal Thou." In the eternal Thou — not as separate from the interhuman, the communal, and the social, but as the radial center of all of them — Buber found at last that home wherein modern man could live in spite of the threat of infinity which had tormented Buber from his childhood.

> Only when these two arise — the binding up of time in a relational life of salvation and the binding up of space in the community that is made one by its Center — and only so long as they exist, does there arise and exist, round about the invisible altar, a human cosmos with bounds and form, grasped with the spirit out of the universal stuff of the aeon, a world that is house and home, a dwelling for man in the universe.

At the time when Buber was working with the Hohenrodter Bund and the small group of educators that included Elizabeth Rotten, Karl Wilker, and Paul Natorp, he took an active part in adult education. Sometime in 1920 or 1921 Buber spoke on three successive evenings at the adult folk school of a German industrial city on the subject "Religion as Reality." What he meant by this, like his attack on psychologism, was that "faith" is not a feeling in the soul of man but an entrance into the *whole* reality. Concerned because none of the workers in the audience spoke up, Buber readily agreed to meet with them alone the next day, all the more so because real listening, he believed, is found most often among workers, who are not concerned about the reputation of the person speaking but about what he has to say. When an older worker, whose intentness had particularly struck Buber, said, "I do not need this hypothesis 'God' in order to be quite at home in the world," Buber decided that he must shatter the security of the man's *Weltanschauung,* which caused him to regard "world" as that in which one "felt at home." Drawing on a knowledge of twentieth-century physics that the worker had no access to, Buber asked him essentially the same question as he asked in his lecture "On the Psychologizing of the World": Is there some larger reality that can encompass both the I and the world and that meeting between them in which each is included in the other without either losing its own independence and otherness?

The red that we saw was neither there in the "things," nor here in the "soul." It at times flamed up and glowed just so long as a red-perceiving eye and a red-engendering "oscillation" found themselves over against each other. Where then was the world and its security? The unknown "objects" there, the apparently so well-known and yet not graspable "subjects" here, and the actual and still so evanescent meeting of both, the "phenomena" — was that not already three worlds which could no longer be comprehended from one alone?

When Buber was through, the worker, whose eyes had been lowered the whole time, said slowly and impressively, "You are right." Buber then realized with horror that he had led the man to the threshold beyond which there sat enthroned the majestic image which Pascal called the God of the Philosophers, rather than to him whom Pascal called the God of Abraham, Isaac, and Jacob, the living God to whom one can say Thou. He could not enter into the factory where this man worked, become his comrade, live with him, and win his trust through real life-relationship.

Buber had tried to point to the reality of the life of dialogue by making use of philosophical dialectic. But the worker heard only the dialectic and not the dialogical voice speaking through it. As a result, his acceptance of Buber's statement as "right" was nothing more than the substitution of a new *Weltanschauung* for the old one, a new security of It which would make unnecessary the going forth to meet the Thou. But Buber himself had pointed to "the being that gave this 'world,' " which had become so questionable, its foundation," and in so doing had pointed to an It, and not a Thou. He had not pointed to the life of dialogue itself but to an objective, third-personal concept that was supposed to stand for it. That is why Buber described this talk as one which apparently came to a conclusion, as only occasionally a talk can come, and yet in reality remained unconcluded.

There was a sequel, however, of which Buber said just the opposite: though it was apparently broken off, it found a completion such as rarely falls to the lot of discussions. Some time later, in 1922, Buber was the guest of the German philosopher and educator Paul Natorp, whose acquaintance Buber had originally made at a conference where Natorp gave a lecture on elementary folk schools and Buber gave one on adult folk schools. Natorp asked Buber to read aloud the galley proofs of his Foreword to the collected *Speeches on Judaism*. He listened courteously but with growing amazement which ended with an intensely passionate protest: "How can you bring yourself to say 'God' when what you mean is something above all human grasp and comprehension? The word 'God' has been defiled and desecrated by all the innocent blood that has been shed for it and all the injustice that it has been used to cover up!"

"Yes, it is the most heavy-laden of all human words," Buber replied. "None has become so soiled, so mutilated. It is for just this reason that I may not abandon it."

> Generations of men have laid the burden of their anxious lives upon this word. . . . Certainly, they draw caricatures and write "God" underneath; they murder one another and say "in God's name." But when all madness and delusion fall to dust, when they stand over against Him in the loneliest darkness and no longer say "He, He" but rather sigh "Thou," shout "Thou," all of them the one word, and when they then add "God," is it not the real God whom they all implore, the One Living God, the God of the children of man? Is it not the word of appeal, the word which has become a *name* consecrated in all human tongues for all times?

Natorp came over to Buber, laid his hand on his shoulder, and said, "Let us say Thou to each other."

Jesus said, "When two or three are gathered in my name, I shall be there." Buber, at the end of this account, turned the saying around. Instead of the name coming first and then the presence, the presence of God came first and then the name: "For where two or three are truly together they are together in the name of God." The word "God" is indispensable, not because the name itself is sacred, but because in every language it is first of all the word of appeal and only later a name. "All God's names are hallowed," said Buber in *I and Thou,* "for in them He is not merely spoken about, but also spoken to." The repetition of many of the same phrases from this story in the first section of Part III of *I and Thou* shows the lasting impact of this meeting with Natorp on Buber's thought.

THE JEWISH JESUS VERSUS THE PAULINE CHRIST

The name of Christ too was hallowed for Buber *as a word of address* but not as a theological proposition that says that in this form only can one meet God. To Buber, Jesus the man, Jesus the Jew, who stood in unique and unmediated relationship with God, was not identical with the Christ of Christian faith whom men worshiped as the Savior. If Buber used Goethe in the second part of *I and Thou* as the example of the man who spoke the legitimate I of pure intercourse with nature and Socrates as the example of the man who spoke the I of endless dialogue, it is Jesus whom he chose as his illustration for man's relation to the eternal Thou:

> How powerful, even to being overpowering, and how legitimate, even to being self-evident, is the saying of *I* by Jesus! For it is the *I* of unconditional relation in which the man calls his *Thou* Father in such a way that he himself is simply Son, and nothing else but Son.

Buber saw Jesus as man, not God, and as standing on man's side of the dialogue. Jesus's uniqueness does not lie in his being inseparable from God, but in that immediacy which uses even separation for greater solidarity of relation. Buber did not see Jesus's uniqueness as consisting in something *in* him — a power in itself — for this would mean to empty the real, the present relation, of reality. Rather Jesus's uniqueness lay in the strength, the immediacy, the unconditionality of the "between." But even here Buber set up no qualitative difference. He did not hold, as Karl Barth was later to do, that Jesus as the "one man sinless" was the only man who could really relate to God as Thou. "Every man can say *Thou* and is then *I*," Buber wrote at the end of this passage about Jesus; "every man can say Father and is then Son." Jesus is not the exception but the illustration, not the image of God but the image of man. Buber's confidence in his understanding of Jesus's I-Thou relationship with the Father was so great that in the third part of *I and Thou,* he dared to interpret the Gospel According to John, generally taken as the most mystical of the four Gospels — "I and the Father are one" — as "the Gospel of pure relation." What is more, the relation, to Buber, was not just that of the Father and the Son, in the Christian sense of Jesus alone, but of God and man:

> The Father and the Son, like in being — we may even say God and Man, like in being — are the indissolubly real pair, the two bearers of primal relation, which from God to man is termed mission and command, from man to God looking and hearing, and between both is termed knowledge and love. In this relation the Son, though the Father dwells and works in him, bows down before the "greater" and prays to him. All modern attempts to interpret this primal reality of dialogue as a

relation of the *I* to the Self, or the like — as an event that is contained within the self-sufficient interior life of man — are futile: they take their place in the abysmal history of destruction of reality.

Because of the traditional association of Jesus with Christ, of Christ with Christianity, and of Christianity with its claim of exclusive salvation and free or compulsory proselytization of the Jews (not to mention the long history of Christian anti-Semitism), it is difficult for the average Jew to understand Buber's relationship to Jesus. "From my youth onwards," Buber wrote in the Foreword to *Two Types of Faith,* "I have found in Jesus my great brother. That Christianity has regarded and does regard him as God and Saviour has always appeared to me a fact of the highest importance which, for his sake and my own, I must endeavor to understand." There are many Jews who cannot understand how a Jew could confess such a relationship to Jesus and still be a good Jew. A first step toward such understanding would be to recognize that for Buber, as for various Christian scholars in the early years of this century, Jesus was and remained a Jew, as Buber said to Florens Christian Rang in their first encounter at the Van Eeden circle in 1914. To Buber organized Christianity was a distortion of the essentially Jewish teachings of Jesus and of the communal immediacy of the life of the early Christians.

That Buber wrote his doctoral dissertation on the Christian mystics from Nicolas of Cusa to Boehme is not in itself important in this connection, since he interpreted their mysticism in such an immanentist way that he left out precisely those elements that were specifically Christian and transformed the Christian communion into "a wonderful world-feeling." On the other hand, in "Renewal of Judaism" (1910), the second of the first three "Speeches on Judaism" that he delivered at Prague, Buber brought in the motif of early Christianity that was to reappear again and again in these speeches, and he claimed the movement as explicitly Jewish and *not* Christian! In this speech, as we have seen, Buber put forward the three related "ideas" of Judaism: unity, the deed, and the future. The tendency toward the deed began to be thwarted in Judaism by the ritual law, Buber held, leading to the isolated rebellions of the Rehabite and Essene communities and finally, as the ritual law became more rigid and alienated from life, to a revolution of ideas in the very core of the people, that is erroneously and misleadingly called early, original Christianity. It is much more closely related to Judaism, Buber declared, than to what today is called Christianity. Yet it is a peculiar phenomenon of Galut, or Diaspora, psychology that "we not only tolerate the fact that this significant chapter was torn out of our history of ideas, but that we ourselves aided and abetted the tearing."

It is common for many Christians to regard whatever they can see as creative and real in Judaism as being essentially Christianity — in embryo, in likeness, or in cause. What Buber now asserted, speaking as a representative of the minority religion in the midst of the majority, was anything but common: "Whatever was not eclectic, whatever was creative in the beginnings of Christianity, was nothing but Judaism." Not only did it originate in Judaism, was spread by Jewish men, and addressed to the Jewish people and no other, but it proclaimed the renewal, in Judaism, of the Jewish religiousness of the deed, in contrast to the syncretistic Christianity of the West in which faith assumed primary importance. "Early Christianity teaches what the prophets taught: the unconditionality of the deed." For the Buber of 1910, therefore, the answer to those Christians currently recommending to the Jews a "rapprochement" with Christianity should be:

> Whatever in Christianity is creative is not Christianity but Judaism; ... we carry it within us, never to be lost. But whatever in Christianity is not Judaism is uncreative, a mixture of a thousand rites and dogmas; with this — and we say it both as Jews and as human beings — we do not want to establish a rapprochement.

This answer, of course, depended, Buber recognized, upon repossessing this creative element in Judaism *and* upon overcoming "our superstitious horror of the Nazarene movement" and placing it "where it belongs: in the spiritual history of Judaism." Although Buber's position was opposed to the Paulinian attitude which favored faith over deed, it came quite close to the synoptic Gospels in its attitude toward what it held to be the rigidity of the law and its alienation from life. The aim of early Christianity and Hasidism, Buber held, was not to abolish the law but to fulfill it: "to raise it from the conditioned to the unconditioned, and at the same time to transform it from the rigidity of a formula into the fluidity of the immediate."

Buber's response in the same year to the question "Did Jesus live?" was remarkable as an address to a generation obsessed with "the quest for the historical Jesus." Buber confessed himself not particularly interested in the question as to when so powerful a reality in the spirit had come into being. "Only a generation so spiritually unsure as ours can subordinate its own inner experience to the external experiences of a generation long past. . . . To him for whom Jesus is immediately real (and only he is noteworthy or important to me), no investigation of a mediate reality can make this immediacy questionable." The power of myth that lives in Jesus, Buber declared, is a power of the living spirit before which all genetic questions are without force or substance. "That our age is dominated by the genetic method should not blind us to the truth that only the utterances of the spirit have a history, not the spirit itself which is its own deed and is to be understood not from history but from itself."

In 1913, in "Jewish Religiousness," Buber again inserted the movement of early Christianity into the flow of Jewish history. "Just as the prophets had not turned against the sacrificial cult as such, so the early Christian movement did not turn against Scripture but against a perversion of its meaning from the unconditioned; it wanted to restore the ardor of the demand." But early Christianity was lost as a source of renewal for Judaism when it became untrue to itself and narrowed the idea of the "turning" to a communion with Christ by grace. Even though Christianity rose to dominion over the nations, and Judaism sank into rigidity, humiliation, and degradation, the core of Judaism "unshakably maintained its claim to be the true ecclesia, the ever-faithful community of divine immediacy."

In 1914 Buber found the public and private misinterpretations of his views of early Christianity so numerous, not only from ill-wishers but also out of bona-fide misunderstanding, that he found it necessary to publish a statement in the Zionist journal *Die Welt* in order to establish what his position really was. He wrote this statement not to polemicize, which seemed to him vain and unfruitful, but to make his position as clear and simple as possible.

Be it established therefore:
first, that the radical Jewish movement that is called original Christianity and that we once gave another, more accessible name to, is not important to us *because* but rather *despite* the fact that it issued into Christianity in which the Jewish elements did not unfold but were displaced;
second, that the central man of this movement, Jesus of Nazareth, is for us as an object of religiousness forever insurmountably distant and

alien, but worthwhile and essential as the *subject* of religiousness as one who has lived the depths of Jewish religiousness, as Socrates the Greek and Buddha the Hindu;

third, that there can be no peace between us pure, whole Jews and the world-domineering Christian church; against its usurpation of Jewish primal-possession we shall maintain unswervingly our eternal claim to be the true *ecclesia*, the community of God.

To Franz Werfel, who in the course of his lifetime came closer and closer to Catholicism without giving up being a Jew, Buber in 1917 shared his own deepest feelings about Christianity:

God reveals himself in your wanting to become, not in your waiting for grace. . . . And how can I grasp, what the Christians can grasp so easily, that God does not need me! That I am made for sport and not for completion! It is not I who wait, God waits that he can say to me, to you, to *every single person* what, according to the report of the Hebrew gospel the spirit spoke to Jesus when he raised him in baptism to sonship: My son, I have awaited you in all the prophets, that you should come and I should find peace in you. You are indeed my peace. No, dear friend, nothing is imposed upon us by God, everything is expected. And you rightly say: it is up to us whether we want to live the true life in order to perfect in it our uniqueness. But according to the Christian teaching, which has perverted the meaning and ground of Jesus, it is not up to us but depends on whether we are chosen. But our teaching is: what counts is not whether He has chosen me but that I choose Him. For it is really not his affair to choose or reject. In so far as it refers the person to grace, that teaching, which calls itself Christian, hinders him from decision, the *metanoia* proclaimed by Jesus and which we once talked about in the streets of the city of Leipzig (at a time when I had not yet come to understand it out of bitter experience). Therefore I will and shall fight for Jesus and against Christianity.

Another important expression of Buber's attitude toward Christianity at this time was a response that he made to a letter from the counselor of a provincial court. Of particular significance is not only Buber's denial of Christian exclusiveness but also the war-born emphasis upon the unredeemedness of the world that was central to the Jewish understanding of messianism that he was to unfold in his translation and interpretation of the Hebrew Bible during the last forty years of his life:

You write that "nothing stands in the way of regarding Jesus as Messiah of the World. . . ." He who has liberated "the world," more exactly a part of humanity from service of idols, whether he is called Jesus or Buddha, Zarathustra or Lao-tzu, has no claim to the name of the "Messiah of the World"; that belongs only to him who redeems the world. Purification of religiousness, monotheizing, Christianizing, all that does not mean the redemption of humanity. Redemption — that is a transformation of the whole of life from the ground up, the life of all individuals and all communities. The world is unredeemed — do you not feel that as I do in every drop of blood? Do you not feel as I do that the Messianic only happens . . . as that on whose realization we can work at every hour? . . . Is it possible that this primordially Jewish feeling, that is the root of Jewish religiousness, the belief in the fulfillment at the end of days, which nothing past can anticipate yet everything past may and shall prepare, has escaped from your heart?

In a letter to his friend Hugo Bergmann at the end of 1917 Buber gave a clear statement of his messianic faith as the ancient Jewish one in which God will redeem creation. This could never be regarded as the ascent of a man to God or the rebirth of a man as a messianic event, but only as the redeeming deed of messianic men in which the absolute future is prepared in the present, in every present. Its completion is beyond the reach of our consciousness — like God; its execution is accessible to our consciousness — like the experience of God in man. "I believe in the fulfillment at the end of days that nothing past can anticipate but everything past may and shall prepare for. . . . But just from this it follows that the fulfillment cannot be anything that has happened, that can be localized in a conscious stretch of the historical past." Still less, added Buber, could it be made from a world event into an event within the I. The incessant experience of the unredeemed world has forced the Christian community to split Christ into the Messiah Come and the One Who Is to Come and to await the Paraclete as the true completer that will make redemption visible. Through this, time is also split in its temporal manifestation into an inner and an outer. The Jewish messianic faith stands opposed to this cleavage; for to Judaism the inner and the outer, the "raising of the sparks" and the lifting of mankind are inseparably united.

Thus Buber fought *for* Jesus and *against* Christianity, for the decision and turning which Jesus called for and *against* faith in Christ as the prerequisite to man's moving to meet and respond to God. In *The Holy Way* (1918), Buber fought against the split between religion and ethics, the I-Thou relationship with God and that with man, that two nineteenth-century Protestants had proclaimed, each in opposite ways — Kierkegaard and Feuerbach: "In genuine Judaism ethics and faith are not separate spheres; its ideal, holiness, is true community with God and true community with human beings, both in one." This original Jewish spirit of true community was concentrated in Jesus, Buber asserted.

> What he calls the kingdom of God — no matter how tinged with a sense of the world's end and of miraculous transformation it may be — is no other-world consolation, no vague heavenly bliss. Nor is it an ecclesiastical or cultic association, a church. It is the perfect life of man with man, true community, and as such, God's immediate realm, His *basiliea*, His earthly kingdom.

Jesus wished to build the temple of true community out of Judaism. But two millennia of Western history are filled with such massive misinterpretations of his teaching that the Jewish consciousness of a world that man can help reunite with God is replaced by an unbridgeable dualism between human will and divine grace. True community is no longer to be realized in the totality of man's life with one another — in the hallowing of the everyday — but in the Church, a community of the spirit separated from the community of the world. In this atmosphere, said Buber, Christianity gave so much to Caesar that there was nothing left to give. Paul expressed the great disappointments suffered in Judaism's reaching for realization as well as the duality within himself. He transformed Jesus's teachings, Buber added, into the dualism between faith and works, spirit and action. Thus he handed to the peoples "the sweet poison of faith, a faith that was to disdain works, exempt the faithful from realization, and establish dualism in the world. It is the Pauline era whose death agonies we today are watching with transfixed eyes."

In December 1922 Buber admitted to the Swiss Protestant theologian Friedrich Gogarten that much that he wrote was uncommonly close to Buber's own thought and that did him good. But other things that Gogarten wrote, especially the Christology, were so different from his own that at times, in pauses in the reading, he was seized with melancholy because of the abysses that separated them. "It was the same for me with Ebner's book that I only recently came to know." In another letter to Gogarten, Buber suggested that the issue between them was one that was already expressed by Dostoevsky in *The Devils* in the character of Shatov, who only *really* believed in Christ and not in God.

One evening toward the end of 1923 Buber was asked whether Christ had not overcome death. His response was that something significant had happened in the event that Christianity calls the Resurrection; yet the world was not redeemed from death nor was death done away with. "It is as if since then we had first come to taste death, which penetrates the whole of life . . . this life that really means nothing other than a lifelong dying."

"But by this this dying is not the highest meant?" one of the group pursued.

"Jesus's dying is rooted somewhere in a self-sacrificing, in a being sacrificed, in a being-denied," Buber replied. "In the dogmatic interpretation of the death of Christ there is a narrowing-down. Jesus's last words contain sacrifice, but they also contain the humanity of *not* sacrificing oneself." Buber was perhaps thinking of Jesus's prayer, "Father, if it be thy will may this cup be taken from me."

This insistence on the biblical "over-againstness" of God and man in dialogue, through which Buber recaptured the Jewish Jesus, is repeated in *I and Thou*. "God needs you — for that which is the meaning of your life," Buber said in Part III. In the same subsection, using a sentence from the Lord's Prayer as his springboard, Buber added that he "who offers his little will to God and encounters him in a great will" says only, "Let your will be done." "But truth goes on to say for him: 'through me whom you need.' "

CREATION, REVELATION, AND REDEMPTION

The only gate which leads to the Bible as a reality, wrote Buber in 1930, is the faithful distinction between creation, revelation, and redemption, not as "manifestations of God, but as stages, actions, and events in the course of His intercourse with the world." Franz Rosenzweig in his *Star of Redemption*, Buber declared, "has the great merit of having shown this to our era in a new light." These "stages, actions, and events" were already fully present and explicit in *I and Thou*.

Nothing is more central to *I and Thou* than Buber's understanding of creation. It is creation in the biblical sense that underlies Buber's assertion that man is given a ground on which to stand and that he is able to go out to meet God, man, and world from that ground. It is perhaps this that Buber hinted at in speaking of Jesus's humanity of *not* sacrificing himself. It is creation which informs Buber's belief in man's spontaneity and freedom that cannot be modified by any original sin and in man's responsibility that cannot be abridged by any fate. "The only thing that can become fate for a man is belief in fate," wrote Buber in *I and Thou*; "for this suppresses the movement of turning." This approach to creation is also inherent in Buber's understanding of God as the "absolute Person," who *is* not a person but becomes one, so to speak, to love and be loved, to know and be known by us.

> You know always in your heart that you need God more than everything; but do you not know too that God needs you — in the fulness of his eternity needs you? How would man be, how would you be, if God did not need him, did not need you? You need God, in order to be — and God needs you, for the very meaning of your life. In instruction and in poems men are at pains to say more, and they say too much — *what turgid and presumptuous talk that is about the "God who becomes"; but we know unshakably in our hearts that there is a becoming of the God that is.* The world is not divine sport, it is divine destiny. There is divine meaning in the life of the world, of man, of human persons, of you and of me.
>
> Creation happens to us, burns itself into us, recasts us in burning — we tremble and are faint, we submit. *We take part in creation, meet the Creator, reach out to Him, helpers and companions.*

With these words Buber reached decisively and forever beyond the God realized in man to the God met in present being, and he reached it without exchanging process and becoming for the absolute, unmovable Being of the metaphysicians. The paradox of the "becoming of the God that is" sets Buber against traditional metaphysics which demands the choice between an absolute that is not in relation to the world and a God who is in relation and therefore less than absolute.

In *I and Thou* Buber criticized Kierkegaard unmistakably though not by name, because of his depreciation of man's relation to creation. Speaking of the assertion that the "religious" man stands as a single, isolated being before God and has therefore gone beyond the responsibility and the ought of the "moral man," Buber passionately protested:

> But that is to suppose that God has created His world as an illusion and man for frenzied being. . . . The world, lit by eternity, becomes fully present to him who approaches the Face, and to the Being of

beings he can in a single response say *Thou*. Then there is no more ten-sion between the world and God, but only the one reality. The man is not freed from responsibility; . . . he has got the mighty responsibility of love for the whole untraceable world-event, for the profound belong-ing to the world before the Face of God. He has, to be sure, abolished moral judgments for ever; the "evil" man is simply one who is com-mended to him for greater responsibility, one more needy of love; but *he will have to practice, till death itself, decision in the depths of spontaneity, unruffled decision, made ever anew, to right action.* Then action is not empty, but purposive, enjoined, *needed, part of creation.*

The paradox of creation is that God sets the world and man at a distance and yet remains in relationship with them, that he gives man ground on which to stand and yet that the very meaning of man's free standing on this ground is that he can go forth to meet the Creator who addresses him in every aspect of his cre-ation. This paradox carried over for Buber into that of revelation; for revelation, to Buber, was neither fixed objective truth nor free subjective inspiration but hearing and responding to the voice that speaks to man out of creation and history. Hence, "all revela-tion is summons and sending." Knowledge, from this point of view, means mutual contact and communication rather than a de-tached observation of an object. Thus the knowing within the or-dinary I-Thou relationship and the knowing of revelation are not different in nature, however different they may be in intensity or historical impact.

Revelation as Buber portrayed it in *I and Thou* is neither ob-jective knowledge content nor subjective experience but an event, a happening — at times as light as a breath, at times like a wrestling bout. We do not come from the meeting the person we were when we went to it. This revelation is not past, but eternally present, here and now. "The eternal source of strength streams, the eternal contact persists, the eternal voice sounds forth, and nothing more."

"The mighty revelations at the base of the great religions are the same as the quiet ones that happen at all times," wrote Buber in *I and Thou*. This does not mean that man's desire for continuity is illegitimate, only the ways in which he tries to assure it through making God into the object of a cult. The only authentic assurance of continuity is if man realizes God anew in the world according to his strength and to the measure of each day. Religious form itself is a mixture of Thou and It. "In belief and in a cult form can harden into an object; but in virtue of the essential quality of relation that lives on in it, it continually becomes present again," as long as the power to enter into relation is not so buried under increasing objectification that the movement of turning is suppressed.

Redemption too is an event of the "between" and cannot be relegated simply to God's side or to man's, to divine grace or to human will, to apocalypse or historical process. We have seen that when Buber was fourteen, Kant's *Prolegomena to Any Future Metaphysics* saved him from suicide by showing him that time and space, which we cannot imagine either as finite or infinite, are categories of the human mind, ways in which we must think that do not reflect reality itself. But when the mature Buber, who had broken through to the life of dialogue, looked at Kant's similar attempt to dispose of the antinomy of freedom and necessity as categories of the mind, he found it of no help whatsoever. Kant might relativize the philosophical conflict between necessity and freedom by assigning one to the world of appearances and the other to the world of being. But I cannot do that, testified Buber in *I and Thou*: "If I consider necessity and freedom . . . in the reality of my standing before God, if I know that 'I am given over for disposal' and know at the same time that 'It depends on myself,' then . . . I am compelled to take both to myself, to be lived together, and in being lived they are one."

> According to the logical conception of truth only one of two contraries can be true, but in the reality of life as one lives it they are inseparable. The person who makes a decision knows that his deciding is no self-delusion; the person who has acted knows that he was and is in the hand of God. The unity of the contraries is the mystery at the innermost core of the dialogue.

The completion of creation and the response to revelation are the beginning of redemption. Redemption means the bringing of ever-new layers of the world of It into the immediacy of the Thou. The partnership of man with God in creation, the rising of a human cosmos built out of genuine community and a redemptive life of relationship, the shining, streaming constancy that the Thou may win in the It, are all hints of redemption. The true beginning, if not the completion of redemption, again and again comes from man's side as the event of turning, turning back to God — in joy, in thanksgiving, in wonder, but also in despair, in crisis, in insecurity. The collapse of the spiritually apprehended cosmos and the destruction of the *form* of spiritual life may nonetheless be the breakthrough to a renewal of genuine relationship. At the end of *I and Thou* Buber affirmed an existential trust in history in which the very turning away from reality prepares the ground for a fuller and deeper redemption. In this redemption the alien, the exiled, the problematic, the "evil" are brought — unreduced and undenied, yet transformed and transmuted — into the renewed reality of relationship. Here creation, revelation, and redemption show themselves as three aspects of a single event.

NOTES AND
SOURCES

SOURCES FOR PREFACE

Maurice Friedman, *Martin Buber: The Life of Dialogue,* 1st ed. (London: Routledge & Kegan Paul; Chicago: The University of Chicago Press, 1955), 2nd rev. paperback ed. (New York: Harper Torchbooks, 1960), 3rd rev. ed. with long new Preface and enlarged Bibliography (The University of Chicago Press Phoenix Books [paperback], 1976).

Martin Buber, *Tales of the Hasidim. The Early Masters,* trans. by Olga Marx (New York: Schocken Books [paperback], 1961), pp. 107, 169.

Martin Buber, "Autobiographical Fragments," trans. by Maurice Friedman, in Paul Arthur Schilpp and Maurice Friedman, eds., *The Philosophy of Martin Buber* volume of *The Library of Living Philosophers* (La Salle, Ill.: Open Court Publishing Co., 1967), and in Martin Buber, *Meetings,* ed. with an Introduction and Bibliography by Maurice Friedman (La Salle, Ill.: Open Court Publishing Co., 1973), "A Lecture," pp. 14 f., 32 f., respectively.

Martin Buber, *I and Thou,* trans. by Ronald Gregor Smith, rev. ed. with a Postscript by the Author Added (New York: Charles Scribner's, 1958, 1960).

Martin Buber, *I and Thou,* trans. with a Prologue and notes by Walter Kaufmann (New York: Charles Scribner's, 1970).

Martin Buber. Briefwechsel aus sieben Jahrzehnten, Vol. I: *1897-1918,* with a Preface by Ernst Simon and a Biographical Sketch as Introduction by Grete Schaeder, ed. by Grete Schaeder in consultation with Ernst Simon and with the cooperation of Rafael Buber, Margot Cohn, and Gabriel Stern (Heidelberg: Verlag Lamber Schneider, 1972). Vol. II: *1918-1938* (Heidelberg: Verlag Lamber Schneider, 1973). Vol. III: *1938-1965* (Heidelberg: Verlag Lamber Schneider, 1975).

Arnold Jacob Wolf, "The Agenda of Mordecai Martin Buber." Address given at the Buber Centennial Conference on "Humanizing Society," sponsored by Fordham University and Hebrew Union College-Jewish Institute of Religion, New York City, February 9, 1978.

SOURCES FOR CHAPTER 1:
Meeting and "Mismeeting": Buber's Childhood and Youth

Stefan Zweig, *The World of Yesterday* (London: Cassel & Co., 1943, 1953), pp. 12-24.

Paul Arthur Schilpp and Maurice Friedman, eds., *The Philosophy of Martin Buber* volume of *The Library of Living Philosophers* (LaSalle, Ill.: Open Court Publishing Co.; London: Cambridge University Press, 1967), "Autobiographical Fragments," trans. by Maurice Friedman, "My Mother," "My Grandmother," "My Father," "The School," "The Horse," "Vienna," pp. 3-8, 10, 13 f.

Martin Buber, *Meetings,* ed. and trans. with an Introduction and Bibliography by Maurice Friedman, pp. 17-20, 22-24, 26 f., 30-32.

Hans Kohn, *Martin Buber. Sein Werk und seine Zeit. Ein Beitrag zur Geistes-geschichte Mitteleuropas 1880-1930.* "Nachwort: 1930-1960" by Robert Weltsch (Cologne: Joseph Melzer Verlag, 1961), p. 19.

Ahron Eliasberg, "Aus Martin Bubers Jugendzeit: Erinnerungen," *Blätter des Heine-Bundes,* Berlin, Vol. I, No. 1 (April 1, 1928), pp. 1-3.

The translation of "The Horse" is by Ronald Gregor Smith and was originally published in Martin Buber, *Between Man and Man.*

Martin Buber, *A Believing Humanism: Gleanings,* trans. with an Introduction and Explanatory Notes by Maurice Friedman (New York: Simon & Schuster, 1969), "Reminiscence," p. 29; "Authentic Bilingualism," p. 81; "The Disciple" and "The Magicians" (plus the German originals), pp. 40-43.

Buber, "Autobiographical Fragments," 2. "My Grandmother," 3. "Languages," 8. "Philosophers," 9. "Vienna" in Paul Arthur Schilpp and Maurice Friedman, eds., *The Philosophy of Martin Buber, loc. cit.,* pp. 4-6, 11, and in Buber, *Meetings,* pp. 9-11, 27.

Hans Fischer-Barnicol, " '. . . und Poet dazu.' Die Einheit von Denken und Dichten bei Martin Buber," *Bulletin des Leo Baeck Instituts,* Vol. IX, No. 33, 1966 (Tel Aviv: Verlag Bitaon Ltd.), pp. 4 f., 11.

Schalom Ben-Chorin, *Zwiesprache mit Martin Buber. Ein Erinnerungsbuch* (Munich: List Verlag, 1966), pp. 63 f., 68, 80 f.

Martin Buber, "Geleitwort" to David Pinski, *Eisik Scheftel. Ein jüdisches Ar-beiterdrama in drei Akten,* authorized translation from the Yiddish manuscript by Martin Buber (Berlin: Jüdischer Verlag, 1904), pp. 7-9.

Trunken von Gedichten. Eine Anthologie geliebter deutscher Verse, selections and commentaries by Mann, Hesse, etc., ed. by Georg Gerster (Zurich: Im Verlag der Arche, 1953), pp. 143-55.

Grete Schaeder, *Martin Buber: Hebräischer Humanismus* (Göttingen: Vanden-hoeck und Ruprecht, 1966), p. 13. Schaeder's book has been translated by Noah J. Jacobs under the title *The Hebrew Humanism of Martin Buber* (Detroit: Wayne State University Press, 1973).

Werner Kraft, *Gespräche mit Martin Buber* (Munich: Kösel Verlag, 1966), pp. 42, 128.

Martin Buber, "Ein Wort über Stefan George" (1928) in Manfred Schlosser, *Kein Ding Sei wo das Wort Gebricht,* 2nd essentially improved ed. (Darmstadt: Agora, 1961), *Eine Humanistische Schriftenreihe,* Vol. XI, p. 123. For the German original and English translation of "Shepherd's Day" and "The Tapestry of Life" see Stefan George, *Poems,* trans. by Carol North Valhope and Ernst Morwitz (New York: Pantheon Books, 1943), pp. 54 f., 90-119. Perhaps the most damning thing that Buber said about George by implication was that it was he who disgusted Hof-mannsthal with the writing of poetry and caused him finally to renounce it. Werner Kraft, *Gespräche mit Martin Buber,* pp. 55, 73 f., 80, 86. Hofmannsthal was close to the George Circle from 1898 or earlier until 1905 or 1906 but was by then definitely rejected by it because of his connection with "mass art," such as his own dramas and the libretti that he wrote for the operas of Richard Strauss. Cf. Michael Hamburger, "Introduction" to Hugo von Hofmannsthal, *Selected Plays and Libretti,*

Bollingen Series XXXIII–3 (New York: Pantheon Books, 1963), pp. X f.
Buber, *I and Thou*, trans. by Walter Kaufmann, p. 116. Speaking of this
paragraph, Kaufmann says in n. 2 to p. 116: "Buber alludes to three
Goethe poems: 'Blessed eye' echoes *Faust*, line 11300, the song of
Lynceus. Then, one of Goethe's late *Xenien* (1823: Book III): 'Were
not the eye so like the sun, / It never could behold the sun: / If the god's
own power did not lie in us, / How could that which is godlike delight
us?' And the final stanza of 'Blessed Yearning' in Goethe's *Divan:* 'And
until you have possessed / dying and rebirth, / you are but a sullen guest
/ on the gloomy earth.' "
Martin Buber, *Pointing the Way*, ed. and trans. by Maurice Friedman (New
York: Schocken Books, 1974), "Goethe's Concept of Humanity" (1949),
pp. 79 f. I have changed the next to last word of the quotation from my
own earlier translation of "exemplary" to "exemplarily."

SOURCES FOR CHAPTER 2:
The Threat of Infinity and the Promise of Time

•————————————————————————————•

Ahron Eliasberg, "Aus Martin Bubers Jugendzeit: Erinnerungen," *loc. cit.*
Martin Buber, *Between Man and Man*, with an Introduction by Maurice
Friedman, trans. by Ronald Gregor Smith (New York: Macmillan Books,
1965), p. 136.
Schilpp and Friedman, eds., *The Philosophy of Martin Buber*, "Autobio-
graphical Fragments," 8. 'Philosophers," pp. 11–13; see also *Meetings*,
pp. 27–30.
Buber Briefwechsel III, #478. Witold O. to MB, July 29, 1962, p. 551.
Martin Buber, "Ein Wort über Nietzsche und die Lebenswerte," *Die Kunst
im Leben*, December 1900, p. 13.
Martin Buber, "Kultur und Zivilisation," *Der Kunstwart*, Vol. XIV, No. 14
(Erstes Maiheft, 1901), pp. 81–83.
Martin Buber, *Die Jüdische Bewegung. Gesammelte Aufsätze und Ansprachen.
Erste Folge, 1900-1914* (Berlin: Jüdischer Verlag, 1916), "Jüdische
Renaissance" (1900), p. 12; "Die Schaffenden, das Volk und die Bewe-
gung" (1902), pp. 67–71; "Was ist zu Tun?" (1904), p. 135; "Zweifache
Zukunft" (1912), pp. 216–20.
Martin Buber, *Der Jude und sein Judentum. Gesammelte Aufsätze und Reden*,
with an Introduction by Robert Weltsch (Cologne: Joseph Melzer Verlag,
1963), "Das Gestaltende," pp. 239–41.
Werner Kraft, *Gespräche mit Martin Buber* (Munich: Kösel-Verlag, 1966), p.
76.

SOURCES FOR CHAPTER 3:
Zionism and the "Jewish Renaissance"

•————————————————————————————•

Martin Buber, *Hasidism and Modern Man*, ed. and trans. with an Introduction by Maurice Friedman (New York: Horizon Books, 1973), "My Way to Hasidism," pp. 55-58.

Buber, *I and Thou*, trans. by Ronald Gregor Smith, pp. 51 f.

Martin Buber, *Good and Evil. Two Interpretations* (New York: Scribner Paperbacks, 1962), "Images of Good and Evil," trans. by Michael Bullock, pp. 125-27.

Martin Buber, "An Narcissus," *Jahres-Bericht der Lese- und Redehalle jüdischer Hochschüler in Wien über das Vereinsjahr 1901*, pp. 17 f.

Ahron Eliasberg, "Aus Martin Bubers Jugendzeit: Erinnerungen," pp. 3-5.

Buber Briefwechsel I, #3. MB to Theodor Herzl, Leipzig, January 6, 1899, pp. 146 f.; #7. MB to Adele Buber, Charlottenburg, December 27, 1899, p. 152; #8. MB to Solomon and Adele Buber, Charlottenburg, January 31, 1900, pp. 153 f.; #11. MB to Paula Buber-Winkler, Berlin, May 14, 1900, pp. 155 f.; #4. Paula Buber-Winkler to MB, Zurich, August 14, 1899, p. 147; #5. MB to Paula Buber-Winkler, Basel, August 15, 1899, p. 148; #6. Paula Buber-Winkler to MB, August 16/17, 1899, pp. 148-51; #10. MB to Paula Buber-Winkler, Berlin, April 24, 1900, p. 155; #12. MB to Paula Buber-Winkler, Berlin, August 4, 1900, pp. 156 f.; #13. MB to Max Nordau, Vienna, April 25, 1901, p. 159; #26. Paula Buber-Winkler to MB, October 18, pp. 167 f.; #28. MB to Paula Buber-Winkler, Vienna, October 25, 1901, p. 169; #40. MB to Paula Buber-Winkler, Lemberg, October 3, 1902, p. 177.

Grete Schaeder, "Martin Buber. Ein biographischer Abriss" in *Buber Briefwechsel* I, pp. 34-37.

Robert Weltsch, Introduction to Martin Buber, *Der Jude und sein Judentum*, pp. xiv-xvii.

Hans Kohn, *Martin Buber. Sein Werk und seine Zeit*, pp. 23-25.

Schilpp and Friedman, eds., *The Philosophy of Martin Buber*, "Autobiographical Fragments," 14. "Question and Answer," pp. 23 f. See also Buber, *Meetings*, pp. 42 f.

Martin Buber, "Unseres Volkes Erwachen," *Die Welt*, Vol. III, No. 46 (November 17, 1899). Most of Buber's poems of this period are rhymed pentameter.

Martin Buber, "Gebet," *Die Welt*, Vol. V, No. 26 (June 28, 1901), p. 13.

Martin Buber, "Zwei Taenze" (Aus dem Cyklus "Elischa ben Abuya, Genannt Acher"), einer Hellenin zugeeignet, in Berthold Feiwel, ed., *Junge Harfen. Eine Sammlung jungjüdischer Gedichte* (Berlin: Jüdischer Verlag, 1903), pp. 31-33.

Martin Buber, "Ein Purim Prolog," *Die Welt*, Vol. V, No. 10 (March 8, 1901), p. 10.

Buber, *Die jüdische Bewegung* I, "Jüdische Renaissance" (1900), pp. 10-15; "Feste des Lebens" (1901), pp. 23-27; "Gegenwartsarbeit" (1901), p. 29; "Das Zion der jüdischen Frau" (1901), pp. 36-38.

Martin Buber, "Weltzionistentag," *Die Welt*, Vol. V (1901), No. 36 (September 20), signed Baruch, p. 1.

Martin Buber, "Zwei Sprüche vom Juden-Mai," *ibid.*, No. 20, signed Baruch ben Nerijahu, pp. 9 f.

Buber, *Der Jude und sein Judentum,* "Renaissance und Bewegung," I (1903), II (1910), pp. 273-79.

Conversations with Ernst Simon and Robert Weltsch in Jerusalem, Spring 1966.

Paula Winkler, "Betrachtung einer Philozionistin" in *München Ehrt Martin Buber* (Munich: Ner-Tamid Verlag, 1961), pp. 13-19, reprinted from *Die Welt,* Vol. V, No. 36 (September 1901).

Paula Winkler, "Die jüdische Frau," *Die Welt,* Vol. V (1901), No. 45 (November 8), pp. 2-4; No. 46 (November 15), pp. 6 f.

SOURCES FOR CHAPTER 4:
Political versus Cultural Zionism: Herzl versus Ahad Ha'am

Hans Kohn, *Martin Buber,* pp. 38, 44 f., 296-300.

Martin Buber, "Referat," *Stenographisches Protokoll der Verhandlungen des III. Zionistenkongresses,* Basel, August 15-18, 1899 (Vienna: Verlag des Vereins "Erez Israel," 1901), pp. 191-93.

Buber Briefwechsel I, #9. MB to Theodor Herzl, Berlin, February 25, 1900, p. 154; #7. Theodor Herzl to MB, August 7, 1901, p. 160; #18. MB to Theodor Herzl, Semmering, August 11, 1901, pp. 161 f.; #22. MB to Theodor Herzl, Semmering, August 22, 1901, p. 165; #31 MB to Paula Buber-Winkler, Basel, December 26, 1901, p. 171; #35. MB to Theodor Herzl, Vienna, February 27, 1902, pp. 172 f.; #38. Berthold Feiwel to MB, July 28, 1902, p. 176; #41. Chaim Weizmann to MB, December 10, 1902, pp. 177 f.; #42. MB to Chaim Weizmann, December 12, 1902, pp. 179-81; #46. MB to Theodor Herzl, Vienna, January 15, 1903, pp. 184 f.; #47. MB to Chaim Weizmann, Vienna, January 23, 1903, pp. 185 f.; #49. Markus Ehrenpreis to MB, March 12, 1903, pp. 186 f.; #50. MB to the Action Committee, Vienna, March 21, 1903, pp. 187 f.; #51. Theodor Herzl to MB, April 14, 1903, p. 189; #53. Israel Zangwill to MB, May 1, 1903, p. 190; #54. Markus Ehrenpreis to MB, May 11, 1903, pp. 191 f.; #55. Theodor Herzl to MB, May 14, 1903, p. 192; #56. MB to Theodor Herzl, Berlin, May 18, 1903, pp. 193-95; #57. Theodor Herzl to MB, May 20, 1903, p. 195; #58. MB to Theodor Herzl, Vienna, May 21, 1903, pp. 195 f.; #59. Theodor Herzl to MB, May 23, 1903, pp. 196 f.; #60. MB to Theodor Herzl, Vienna, May 26, 1903, pp. 197-99; #61. Theodor Herzl to MB, May 28, 1903, pp. 199 f.; #62. MB to Theodor Herzl, Vienna, May 29, 1903, pp. 200 f.; #63. MB to Chaim Weizmann and Berthold Feiwel, Vienna, June 12, 1903, pp. 201 f.; #65. Asher Ginsberg (Ahad Ha'am) to MB, June 25 (July 8), 1903, p. 203; #66. Berthold Feiwel to MB, July 17, 1903, pp. 204-06; #68. MB to Paula Buber-Winkler, Basel, August 25, 1903, p. 207; #69. MB to Paula Buber-Winkler, Geneva, September 5, 1903, p. 208; #70. Chaim Weizmann to MB and Berthold Feiwel, September 25, 1903, p. 209; #71. Chaim Weizmann to MB, October 8, 1903, pp. 209-11; #72. MB to Chaim Weizmann, Lemberg, October 10, 1903, pp. 211-14; #73. Chaim Weizmann to MB, October 13, 1903, pp. 214-16; #74. Chaim Weizmann to MB, October 16, 1903, pp. 216 f.; #75. Chaim Weizmann to MB and Berthold Feiwel, October 23, 1903, pp. 218-21; #77. MB to Chaim Weizmann, Lemberg, December 9, 1903, p. 222; #78. Chaim Weizmann to MB, December 13, 1903, pp. 223 f.; #79. MB to Chaim Weizmann, Berlin, December 27, 1903, p. 225; #81. MB to Paula Buber-Winkler, July 6, 1904, p. 227; #331. MB to Siegmund Kaznelson, Heppenheim, January 15, 1917, p. 461.

Martin Buber, "Eine Section für jüdische Kunst und Wissenschaft," *Die Welt*, Vol. V, No. 13 (March 29, 1901), p. 9.

Marvin Lowenthal, ed., *The Diaries of Theodor Herzl* (New York: The Dial Press, 1956), "Introduction," quoted in Jay Y. Gonen, *A Psycho-History of Zionism* (New York: New American Library, 1975).

Letter from Martin Buber to Theodor Herzl, September 13, 1901.

Martin Buber, "Bergfeuer" (Zum fünften Congress), *Die Welt*, Vol. V, No. 35 (August 30, 1901), pp. 2 f., signed B.; "Die Congresstribune" (September 6), pp. 1 f., signed Baruch.

Martin Buber, "Referat" on Jewish Art, *Stenographisches Protokoll des Verhandlungen der V. Zionisten-Congresses in Basel*, December 26-30, 1901 (Vienna: Verlag des Vereines "Erez Israel," 1901), pp. 20, 30 f., 114 f., 151-69, 389-92, 399-402.

Buber, *Die Jüdische Bewegung* I, "Zionistische Politik" (1903), pp. 109-13; "Was ist zu tun?" (1904), pp. 124 f.

Joseph Klausner, "Chaim Weizmann: Early Memories" in Paul Goodman, ed., *Chaim Weizmann: A Tribute on his Seventieth Birthday* (London: Victor Gollancz Ltd., 1945), pp. 39-41.

Martin Buber, "Ein Wort zum fünften Congress," *Jüdische Volkstimme*, Vol. II (1902), Nos. 24, 25 (January 15, February 15).

Chaim Weizmann, *Trial and Error: The Autobiography of Chaim Weizmann* (New York: Harper & Bros., 1949), pp. 71, 86 f.

Letters from Martin Buber to Chaim Weizmann and Berthold Feiwel, addressed to "Liebe Freunde," February 20, 1903; June 16, 1903; Lemberg, October 18, 1903; November 18, 1903, Weizmann Archives, Weizmann Institute Library, Rehovoth, Israel.

Martin Buber (Vienna), Berthold Feiwel (Berlin), Dr. Chaim Weizmann (Genf), *Eine jüdische Hochschule* (Berlin: Jüdischer Verlag, 1902), 36 pages.

Alex Bein, *Theodor Herzl. A Biography of Modern Zionism*, trans. from the German by Maurice Samuel (Meridian Books and the Jewish Publication Society of America, 1962; first published 1942).

Alex Bein, *Theodor Herzl. Biographie* (Vienna: Fiba-Verlag, 1934), p. 569.

NOTE A TO CHAPTER 4

In the light of these facts, it is strange indeed that a half a century later Weizmann should have so far forgotten the content of his and Buber's common struggles as to set Zionism in opposition to the "aesthetic" and to suggest that Buber used the former for the sake of the latter! Speaking of the people he knew during his Geneva years at the turn of the century, Weizmann wrote: "Martin Buber and Berthold Feiwel, inseparable friends, were of the Geneva colony for a time. Martin Buber is now a professor at the Hebrew University in Jerusalem; fifty years ago he was a young aesthete, the son of a rich father, a rather odd and exotic figure in our midst. In spite of his handsome allowance from home, he was usually in debt; for he was a connoisseur of the arts and a collector of expensive items. We were good friends, though I was often irritated by his stilted talk, which was full of forced expressions and elaborate similes, without, it seemed to me, much clarity or great beauty. My· own inclinations were to simplicity, and what I admired most was the ability to reduce a statement to its essential elements. Buber was only beginning to develop the incomparable German style which, many years later, produced his remarkable translation of the Bible. Berthold Feiwel, his friend, who died in Palestine a few years ago, was also a writer, but natural, simple, sensitive and realistic. In his case particularly the style was the man; for Feiwel rendered far greater service to Zionism than his more colourful friend. In a sense, it may be said that Feiwel gave to Zionism, losing himself in it, and Buber took from it, using it as his aesthetic material." Weizmann, *Trial and Error*, pp. 86 f.

There is no reason to doubt the accuracy of Weizmann's portrayal of Buber's aesthetic tastes, his overly rich allusiveness, and his complex and affected speech, which must have been particularly irritating to a scientist. Weizmann provides us, indeed, with an invaluable picture of how Buber must have appeared to some of those with whom he worked at that time, particularly those who did not look up to him, like Eliasberg, and were not his close friends, like Feiwel. On the other hand, the facts, including Weizmann's own letters, do not bear out his depreciation of Buber's role during those early years of the movement nor his disparagement of his dedication to Zionism.

In addition to the letters already adduced, the Weizmann Archives at Rehovot, Israel, contain the following letters of Weizmann either to or about Buber: January 4, 1902, to M. Rothstein — Buber is preparing ground for committees on behalf of the university; February 17, 1902, to his wife Vera Weizmann — telegram from Buber about Herzl's negotiations with the Sultan, including "chances of concessions"; April 13, 1902, to Leo Motzkin — Buber is proposed as candidate for the Fraction cultural committee; November 6, 1902, to Buber — participation of Buber, Feiwel, and Birnbaum in *Jewish Encyclopedia*, various complaints that Buber does not write; December 1, 1902, to Buber — foundation in Vienna of committee to work for the university; December 12, 1902, to Buber — complains of an incorrect approach on Buber's part concerning the university; December 30, 1902, to Hugo Schachtel — tells of article by Buber on university in *Ost und West;* January 5, 1903, to Dr. H. Chissin (Russia) — Buber's publicity tour of Switzerland; January 7, 1903, to Davis Trietsch — Buber making every effort to create committee in Vienna on behalf of the university; January 21, 1903, to Buber — fears hostility of Action Committee toward university; February 4, 1903, to Buber — Buber's success in interesting Professor Ehrman in the university; February 4, 1903, to J. Pokrassa — Buber to be subeditor of *Der Jude;* February 13, 1903, to Buber — stipulation by Vienna professors of their participation: emphasis on university's non-Zionist character, change of name, small chance of committee in Vienna in behalf of university; February 13 and 14, 1903 — Buber will lecture in Munich; Weizmann doubts that he will be satisfied; February 27, 1903 — Buber and Feiwel will be editors of *Der Jude;* April 16, 1903, to Buber — detailed plans for first number of periodical; June 1, 1903, to Buber — financial straits of *Der Jude,* Fraction delegates to the 6th Congress, and university plan for division into Judaica and scientific faculties; June 3, 1903, to Dr. M. B. Kroll — Buber will lecture at Fraction conference; June 9, 1903, to Buber — asks him to prepare program for Judaica faculty of university; June 17, 1903 — circular to Fraction members: Buber will be Fraction candidate at 6th Congress elections and will lecture at the Fraction conference on cultural question; June 26, 1903, to V. Tiomkin — suggests Buber as Congress candidate in Tiomkin's area; July 7, 1903, to J. Pokrassa — enumerates activities of quartet (Weizmann, Buber, Feiwel, Nossig) since 5th Congress: publicity tours, university, Jüdischer Verlag, Rosenfeld Almanac, collection of poems by young Jewish poets; September 18, 1903, to Buber — Weizmann calls Herzl's *Die Welt* a "black" paper; November 2, 1903, to Buber — trouble caused by Buber's delay in composing memorandum for Johnston; Feiwel complains that Buber pays no heed to him in editing *Der Jude;* November 2, 1903, to Feiwel — Weizmann assures him that Buber has no intention of displacing him as editor of *Der Jude;* November 27, 1903, to Buber — material for *Der Jude,* must postpone his trip to London because memorandum on Zionism not ready; December 17, 1903, to Feiwel — Buber's memorandum on Zionism is too short and is in need of elaboration; December 13, 1903, to Buber — every effort being made to guarantee publication of *Der Jude;* Weizmann rebukes Buber for issuing ultimatum, will not go to London because Buber's memorandum is not satisfactory and because he has been ill; January 2, 1904, to Dr. M. B. Kroll and A. Idelson — forthcoming discussions in Berlin between Weizmann, Buber, and Feiwel; June 6, 1904, to Buber — thanks Buber for his efforts to make possible Weizmann's journey to Palestine.

Buber's own retrospective evaluation of their common work in those days is very different. On the occasion of Weizmann's seventieth birthday, Buber wrote Weizmann:

"At that time, forty-three years ago, in the 'heroic' period of Zionism, when you, friend of my youth, and I jointly fought against Theodor Herzl, the man we yet recognized and revered as our leader, and against the bulk of the Movement, what was our impulse then? Was it not our inability to put up any longer with those fascinating slogans, since Reality had revealed itself to us — the hard reality of the hour, with its task both difficult and unpretentious? And, later on, what was it raised you, Chaim Weizmann, to the position of leader but this sense of, and will to, Reality, originally common only to us, to our small group. . . .

"During the long time since those days of our common struggle I have re-examined some of the opinions I once advocated and I have found them too easy. But this one insight grew stronger and stronger within myself: the supreme command approaches us out of Reality's depth. Always slogans are powerful and Reality's core is hidden; just for this reason it is essential for us, sons of the crisis and destined to begin to overcome it, to keep, every now and again, our covenant with Reality, in the depths of which the future is being molded." Goodman, ed., *Chaim Weizmann. A Tribute*, pp. 34 f.

Buber, *Der Jude und sein Judentum*, "Die drängende Stunde" (Über Leo Pinsker und Theodor Herzl), pp. 420–41; "Die Lehre vom Zentrum (Über Achad-Haam)," pp. 442–47; "Vertrauen (Zu Achad-Haams siebzigstem Geburtstag (1926)," pp. 755 f.; "Der Wägende (Zum 60. Geburtstag Achad Haams [August 1916])," pp. 757 f.; "Achad-Haam-Gedenkrede in Berlin" (January 9, 1927), pp. 759–61; "Achad-Haam-Gedenkrede in Basel" (delivered at a public session of the XV. Zionist Congress on August 30, 1927), pp. 762–70; "Theodor Herzl" (1904), pp. 777–82; "Herzl und die Historie" (1904), pp. 783–94; "Er und Wir. Zu Herzls 50. Geburtstag" (1910), pp. 795–99; "Sache und Person. Eine Erinnerung (1929), pp. 800–04 ("The Cause and the Person" is translated in the "Autobiographical Fragments" and printed in *The Philosophy of Margin Buber* and *Meetings*; "Herzl vor der Palästina-Karte (Aus meinen Erinnerungen, 1944)," pp. 804–07.

Benjamin Segal (unsigned), "Die Juden von Gestern (Eine Erwiderung)," *Ost und West*, Vol. III, No. 4 (April 1903), columns 217–22, 225.

Ahad Ha-am, "Altneuland," *ibid.*, columns 227–44.

Max Nordau, "Achad-Haam über 'Altneuland,' " *Die Welt*, Vol. VII, No. 2 (March 13, 1903), pp. 1–5.

NOTE B TO CHAPTER 4

Buber's own interest in Davis Trietsch's colonizing activity is suggested by a letter from him of February 19, 1900, to the Zionist Action Committee forwarding a resolution passed by the Berlin Zionist Union after hearing a lecture by Trietsch: "Considering that the settlement of Cyprus by Jews in no way contradicts the Zionist program but rather, in case that country proves usable and practical, would be suited to further Zionism, the Berlin Zionist Union expects that the Action Committee turn its closest attention to this matter. It recommends sending an investigating commission to Cyprus . . . and that this question be placed in the order of the day of the next Congress." Central Zionist Archives, Jerusalem, Israel.

Martin Buber, *Israel and Palestine. The History of an Idea*, trans. by Stanley Godman (London: East & West Library; New York: The Macmillan Co., 1952); reprinted by Schocken Books as *On Zion* (1972), pp. 123–47.

SOURCES FOR CHAPTER 5:
Encounter with Mysticism

Buber, *Hasidism and Modern Man*, "My Way to Hasidism," p. 58.

Gustav Landauer. Sein Lebensgang in Briefen, ed. by Martin Buber in cooperation with Ina Britschgi-Schimmer (Frankfurt am Main: Rütten & Loening, 1929), Vol. I, "Vorwort" by Martin Buber, pp. vi f.

Hans Kohn, *Martin Buber*, pp. 29-31, 110, 117, 293 f.

The Worlds of Existentialism, ed. with Introductions and Conclusions by Maurice Friedman (New York: Random House, 1964; Chicago and London: The University of Chicago Press and Phoenix Books, 1973), Meister Eckhart (selections), pp. 29-33; Ludwig Feuerbach, "Basic Principles of Philosophy of the Future" (selections), pp. 50-54.

Martin Buber, "Ueber Jakob Böhme," *Wiener Rundschau*, Vol. V, No. 12 (June 15, 1901), pp. 251-53.

Maurice Friedman, *Martin Buber: The Life of Dialogue*, 3rd rev. ed. with new Preface and expanded Bibliography (Chicago and London: The University of Chicago Press and Phoenix Books, 1976), pp. 27-30, 40-42.

Martin Buber, "Aus Geschichte des Individuationsproblem (Nicolaus von Cues und Jakob Böhme), Ph.D. dissertation at the University of Vienna, 1904, typewritten manuscript in the Buber Archives of the Jewish National and University Library at the Hebrew University, Jerusalem, Israel. "Vorwort" and 38 pages.

Franz Rosenzweig, "Aus Bubers Dissertation" in *Unbekannten Schriften. Festgabe für Martin Buber zum 50. Geburtstag* (Berlin: Verlag Lambert Schneider, 1928), pp. 240-43.

Martin Buber, *The Origin and Meaning of Hasidism*, ed and trans. with an Introduction by Maurice Friedman (New York: Horizon Press [paperback], 1972), "Spirit and Body of the Hasidic Movement," p. 130.

Martin Buber, "Gustav Landauer," *Die Zeit* (Vienna), Vol. XXXIX, No. 506 (June 11, 1904), pp. 127 f.

Buber Briefwechsel I, #48. MB to Gustav Landauer, Vienna, February 10, 1903, p. 186; #119. MB to Eugen Diederichs, Berlin-Zehlendorf, June 16, 1907, p. 256; #120. MB to Eugen Diederichs, June 20, 1907, p. 257; #158. Georg Simmel to MB, November 14, 1910, p. 287.

Martin Buber, *Ekstatische Konfessionen* (Jena: Eugen Diederichs Verlag, 1909), "Ekstase und Bekenntnis" (Ecstasy and Confession), pp. xi-xxvi. In the Introduction to *Die Rede, die Lehre, und das Lied* (Leipzig: Insel Verlag, 1917), in which "Ecstasy and Confession" is included, Buber repudiated this essay in favor of the treatment of unity in the fifth dialogue of *Daniel*, just as he later repudiated *Daniel* in favor of *I and Thou*.

Letters from Martin Buber to Maurice Friedman (unprinted, in my personal possession and in the Martin Buber Archives at the Jewish National and University Library, The Hebrew University, Jerusalem, Israel), Tübingen, Germany, August 15, 1954; August 23, 1954.

Maurice Friedman, *Touchstones of Reality: Existential Trust and the Covenant of Peace* (New York: E. P. Dutton, 1972; Dutton Books, 1974).

Schriften der Deutschen Gesellschaft für Soziologie. I Series: *Verhandlungen der Deutschen Soziologentage*, Band I—*Verhandlungen des ersten Deutschen Soziologentages vom 19-22 Oktober 1910 in Frankfurt a. M.* (Tübingen: Verlag von J. C. B. Mohr [Paul Sibeck], 1911), pp. 206 f.

Martin Buber, "The Teaching of the Tao," in *Pointing the Way*, ed. and trans.

by Maurice Friedman (New York: Schocken Books, 1974), pp. 31-58. "The Teaching of the Tao" was originally published as an "Afterword" to an edition of the sayings and parables of the great Taoist mystic Chuang-tzu: Martin Buber, *Reden und Gleichnisse des Tschuang-Tse* (Leipzig: Insel-Verlag, 1914). Later it was republished, along with "Ecstasy and Confession" and Buber's long introductory essay to the Finnish epic *Kalevala* in Martin Buber, *Die Rede, die Lehre, und das Lied* (Leipzig: Insel-Verlag, 1917), pp. 40-94.
Buber Briefwechsel II, #113. MB to Franz Rosenzweig, Heppenheim, November 14, 1922. p. 142.
Martin Buber, *Daniel. Dialogues on Realization,* trans. with an Introduction by Maurice Friedman (New York: McGraw-Hill Paperbacks, 1965); Translator's Introduction, p. 40; text, pp. 137-40.

NOTE TO CHAPTER 5

Martin Buber, *Pointing the Way (loc. cit.* above), "The Altar," pp. 16-19; "With a Monist," pp. 25-30. It was "The Altar" to which Dag Hammarskjøld referred when he spoke in his first letter to Buber of how strongly he responded, in reading *Pointing the Way,* "to what you write about our age of distrust and to the background of your observations which I find in your general philosophy of unity created 'out of the manifold.' " See Vol. II, *Later Years,* Chapter 29, "Dag Hammarskjøld and Buber."
Martin Buber, *Between Man and Man,* "Dialogue," pp. 13, 24 f.; "What Is Man?" pp. 184 f.

SOURCES FOR CHAPTER 6:
The Discovery of Hasidism

Maurice Friedman, *Touchstones of Reality,* Chap. 8, "Hasidism and Contemporary Man."
Gershom Scholem, *The Messianic Idea in Judaism* (New York: Schocken Books, 1971), pp. 228 f.
Buber, *Hasidism and Modern Man,* Book I—"Hasidism and Modern Man," pp. 22 f.; Book II—"My Way to Hasidism," pp. 53, 59-63; Book III —"The Life of the Hasidim," pp. 85, 104-06, 110 f., 121 f.
Letter from Martin Buber to Franz Rosenzweig, October 1, 1922, quoted in Franz Rosenzweig, *On Jewish Learning,* ed. by N. N. Glatzer (New York: Schocken Books, 1955), pp. 110 f. Also found in *Buber Briefwechsel* II, #112, Heppenheim, pp. 141 f.
Buber Briefwechsel I, #93. MB to Hugo von Hofmannsthal, Florence, February 24, 1906, p. 235; #94. Hugo von Hofmannsthal to MB, March 11, 1906, pp. 235 f.; #95. MB to Hugo von Hofmannsthal, Florence, March 15, 1906, pp. 237 f.; #105. MB to Samuel Horodesky, Hail in Tirol, July 20, 1906, pp. 244 f.; #110. MB to Paula Buber-Winkler, Berlin, beginning December 1906, p. 251; #112. MB to Paula Buber-Winkler,

December 1906, p. 252; #113. Simon Dubnow to MB, January 17, 1907, pp. 252 f.; #134. Ellen Key to MB, September 23, 1908, p. 265; #135. MB to Ellen Key, Vahr bei Brixen in Tirol, September 27, 1908, p. 266.

NOTE A TO CHAPTER 6

Buber's father did not at all like Buber's description of his development in "My Way to Hasidism" and said that in the statement that he was summoned to proclaim Hasidism to the world, he was proclaiming himself formally as the Messiah! "This will create enemies for you everywhere into whose hands you yourself give a weapon." In all, he did not find this essay up to Buber's other writings. *Buber Briefwechsel* I, #380. Carl Buber to MB, end of 1917, pp. 520 f.

Hans Kohn, *Martin Buber*, pp. 47, 68; p. 306 footnote #3 to p. 71; p. 309, footnote #1 to p. 87; p. 310.

Martin Buber, *The Tales of Rabbi Nachman*, trans. by Maurice Friedman (New York: Horizon Press, 1968; Avon Books — Discussion Books, 1970; London: Souvenir Press, 1974), pp. 12-14, 20-41, 49-58. Many Kafka scholars agree that Buber's Hasidic writings, including *The Tales of Rabbi Nachman*, had an important impact on Franz Kafka.

Conversation with Professor David Flusser, Jerusalem, Israel, March 1966.

Martin Buber, *The Legend of the Baal-Shem*, trans. by Maurice Friedman (New York: Schocken Books, 1969; London: East & West Library, 1956), pp. xi-xiii, 17-50, 198 f., 207 f., *passim*.

Martin Buber, *Tales of the Hasidim. The Early Masters*, trans. by Olga Marx (New York: Schocken Books [paperback], 1961, 1971), "Sound the Great Horn!" pp. 79 f.

Martin Buber, *Die Legende des Baal-Schem* (Frankfurt am Main: Literarische Anstalt, Rütten & Loening, 1908), "Die Predigt des neuen Jahres," pp. 190-97.

NOTE B TO CHAPTER 6

Martin Buber, "Die Duse in Florenz," *Die Schaubühne*, Vol. I, No. 15 (December 14, 1905), pp. 422-24. In *Martin Buber: The Life of Dialogue*, p. 51, n. 1, and in a "Translator's Note" to my translation of Buber's Afterword on "The History of the Dialogical Principle" in *Between Man and Man* (Macmillan Paperbacks edition), p. 214, I state: "In 1905 Buber uses the term 'I and Thou' in a discussion of the drama and of the tension of the isolated individual (Buber, 'Die Duse in Florenz' . . .)." While working with the material from the Buber Archives at the Jewish National and University Library in Jerusalem in 1966 I twice read through carefully "Die Duse in Florenz" and could find no use of the language of I and Thou or even of Thou. On looking again at Hans Kohn, *Martin Buber*, I discovered later the following sentence on p. 72: "Aus diesem Volkhaften löst sich bei der Duse plötzlich die 'Untiefe des schlechthin Einmaligen das der aus Gemeinsamkeiten geborenen Erdensprache ewig widersteht: das ist der Mensch, der einsam ist von Geburt, der sich nach dem Wort verzehrt und dessen schamvoll ist.' So handelt es sich im Theater um die ewige Spannung von Ich und Du, um das Problem der Individuation, das in volkhafter Verbundenheit sich entspannt und in dem letzten Abgrund des Individuums wieder in voller Tragik ersteht." I believe I must have taken the second sentence as an indirect quotation or paraphrase of Buber's essay, just as the first sentence is a direct quote. Actually, the phrase "die ewige Spannung von Ich und Du" (the eternal tension of I and Thou) is Kohn's own interpolation. I was not able to get hold of the essay itself in America in 1950.

Martin Buber, "Drei Rollen Novellis," *Die Schaubühne*, Vol. II, No. 2 (January 11, 1906), pp. 42-48.

NOTE C TO CHAPTER 6

The French Catholic existentialist Gabriel Marcel comes very close to the view of the legend "The Return" when he talks of personal immortality not in terms of the salvation of the individual soul but of the continuance of the bond with just those persons to whom we have been closest on earth.

NOTE D TO CHAPTER 6

In the repeated emphasis on uniqueness in the "Shiflut," or Humility, section of "The Life of the Hasidim" the Welsh scholar B. J. Morse finds a striking parallel between *The Legend of the Baal-Shem* and Rainer Maria Rilke's "Ninth Duino Elegy" and the clearest evidence of the influence of the one on the other. The lines from the "Ninth Duino Elegy" that he quotes are:

> Not because happiness really
> exists, that premature profit of imminent loss,
> Not out of curiosity, not just to practise the heart,
> that could still be there in laurel. . . .
> But because being here amounts to so much, because all
> this Here and Now, so fleeting, seems to require us and strangely
> concerns us. Us the most fleeting of all. Just once,
> everything, only for once. Once and no more. And we, too,
> once. And never again. But this
> having been once, though only once,
> having been once on earth — can it ever be cancelled?

In the original German Rilke italicizes six times the word *einmal*. Buber does not italicize, but he uses the same technique of repetition to gain insistence: "*Einzig* und *einmal* ist das Seiende. . . . Die *Einmaligkeit* ist eine Ewigkeit des *Einzelnen.* . . . Jedermann soll wissen und bedenken, dass er in der Welt *einzig* ist in seiner Beschaffenheit. . . . Nur aus seiner *eigenen* Art, aus keiner fremden kann sich der Strebende vollenden. . . . Der *Einzige* schaut Gott und umschlingt ihn." (Italics added.) Benjamin Joseph Morse, "Rainer Maria Rilke and Martin Buber," in Irmgard Buck and Georg Kurt Schauer, eds., *Alles Legendige meinet den Menschen. Gedenkbuch für Max Niehans* (Bern: Francke Verlag, 1972), pp. 102-28.

Buber, *A Believing Humanism: Gleanings,* "Do You Still Know It?" p. 51. For the German original see p. 50.

Buber, *Between Man and Man* (Macmillan Paperback ed.), "Afterword: The History of the Dialogical Principle," trans. by Maurice Friedman, p. 214.

Martin Buber, "Die Mythen des Chassidismus" (from the introduction to a selection of Hasidic legends) in *Heimkehr*, ed. by Juedischer National Akademie Verein "Emunah" Czernowitz with a Foreword by Leon Kellner (Berlin: Verlag Louis Lamm, 6572, Czernowitz, 1912), pp. 187 f.

Martin Buber, *Hinweise. Gesammelte Essays* (Zürich: Manesse Verlag, 1953), "Das Epos des Zauberers," pp. 84–103.

NOTE E TO CHAPTER 6

Martin Buber, *On Judaism*, ed. by Nahum N. Glatzer (New York: Schocken Books, 1967), "Myth in Judaism" (1916), trans. by Eva Jospe, pp. 95–107. I have made my own translation from the German original in a few cases where I could not go along with Eva Jospe's translation. In *Martin Buber: The Life of Dialogue*, I pointed out the influence of Buber on H. and H. A. Frankfort in their use of the "I-Thou" and "I-It" relations to bring out the contrast between mythical and discursive thinking in their essay "Myth and Reality" in *Before Philosophy* (ed. by them). Here we can see that Buber developed this understanding of mythical thinking explicitly in terms of myth *before* and *on the road to* the language of *I and Thou*.

Martin Buber, *The Origin and Meaning of Hasidism*, ed. and trans. with an Introduction by Maurice Friedman (New York: Horizon Press [paperback], 1972), "Spirit and Body of the Hasidic Movement" (1921), pp. 122 f., 129–49.

Shmuel Agnon, "A True Story" (in Hebrew), *Ha'aretz*, February 8, 1963.

SOURCES FOR CHAPTER 7:
The Prague Bar Kochbans and the "Speeches on Judaism"

Buber Briefwechsel I, #155. Ernst Elijahu Rappeport to MB, June 4, 1910, p. 284; #156. MB to Ernst Elijahu Rappeport, June 12, 1910, pp. 285 f.; #159. MB to Ernst Elijahu Rappeport, November 21, 1910, pp. 287 f.; #160. Ernst Elijahu Rappeport to MB, November 23, 1910, pp. 288 f.; #167. MB to Ernst Elijahu Rappeport, May 25, 1911, pp. 294 f.; #173. Hans Kohn to MB, September 22, 1911, pp. 299 f.; #175. MB to Ernst Elijahu Rappeport, Seis in Tirol, September 28, 1911, pp. 301 f.; #176. MB to Ernst Elijahu Rappeport, Zehlendorf, October 8, 1911, pp. 302 f.; #190. Hans Kohn to MB, October 20, 1912, pp. 314 f.; #191. MB to Hans Kohn, October 23, 1912, p. 315; #193. Hans Kohn to MB, November 10, 1912, p. 316; #194. MB to Hans Kohn, November 12, 1912, p. 318; #195. Hans Kohn to MB, November 14, 1912, p. 319; #196. MB to Hans Kohn, November 19, 1912, p. 320; #199. Arnold Zweig to MB, December 16, 1912, pp. 321 f.; #204. Richard Beer-Hofmann to MB, April 3, 1913, pp. 327 f.; #208. MB to Hugo Bergmann, May 7, 1913, p. 331; #209. MB to Richard Beer-Hofmann, May 16, 1923, p. 332; #213.

Max Brod to MB, June 5, 1913, p. 336; #216. Ludwig Strauss to MB, August 6, 1913, p. 339; #224. Arnold Zweig to MB, November 17, 1913, p. 347; #234. Salman Schocken to MB, February 4, 1914, p. 356; #297. Ludwig Strauss to MB, March 20, 1916, p. 422.

Victor Freund, "A. H. Verband des Vereines Jüdischer Hochschüler 'Bar-Kochba,' Prag and Spolek Zidovskych Studentu 'Theodor Herzl' V Parze, In Israel" (Tel Aviv, undated, in honor of Hugo Bergmann's 50th birthday), pp. 5-13.

Robert Weltsch, "Zu Bubers Erstem Jahrzeittag," *Israelitisches Wochenblatt. Journal Israeli Suisse*, Zurich, Vol. LXVI, No. 23, June 10, 1966, p. 5.

Martin Buber, *Die Vorurteile der Jugend* (Berlin: Schocken Bücher, 1938), p. 1.

Der Jude. Sonderheft zu Martin Bubers 50. Geburtstag, 1928, Marcus Reiner, "Die Biologies des Zionismus," pp. 22-32; Leo Hermann, "Aus Tagebuchblättern. I. Erinnerungen an Bubers 'Drei Reden' in Prag, II. Berlin," pp. 158-63; Alfons Paquet, "Über Buber," p. 166.

Buber, *Der Jude und Sein Judentum*, "Das Judentum und die Juden," pp. 9-18; "Das Judentum und die Menschheit," pp. 18-27; "Die Erneuerung des Judentums," pp. 28-46; "Der Geist des Orients und das Judentum," pp. 46-65; "Jüdische Religiosität," pp. 65-78; "Der Mythos des Juden," p. 79.

Martin Buber, *Drei Reden über das Judentum* (Frankfurt am Main: Literarische Anstalt, Rütten & Loening, 1911. Gustav Landauer's copy of this book is inscribed: "Gustav Landauer, im ewig neuen Gefühl der Gemeinsamkeit, Martin Buber, 20. VII. 11." Mrs. Marianne Blum of Scarsdale, New York, kindly let me see this and many other books and papers of her grandfather's.

Gustav Landauer, *Skepsis und Mystik. Versuche im Anschluss an Mauthners Sprachkritik* (Berlin: Egon Fleischel & Co., 1903), pp. 37 f. The identical passage is found in the second number of a publication of "The New Community": *Das Reich der Erfüllung. Flugschriften zur Begründung einer neuen Weltanschauung*, ed. by Heinrich Julius Hart, Gustav Landauer, "Durch Absonderung zur Gemeinschaft," pp. 62 f.

Buber, *A Believing Humanism: Gleanings*, "On Richard Beer-Hofmann," pp. 62 f.

Jacob Agus, *Modern Philosophies of Judaism* (New York: Behrman's Jewish Book House, 1941), pp. 219, 229 f.

George L. Mosse, *The Crisis of German Ideology. Intellectual Origins of the Third Reich* (New York: The Universal Library, Grosset & Dunlap, a paperback original, 1964), pp. 41, 64-66, 182 f.

Monumenta Judaica. 2000 Jahre Geschichte und Kultur der Juden am Rhein. Eine Ausstellung im Kölnischen Stadtmuseum 15. Oktober 1963-15. Februar, 1964. Handbuch. Im Auftrage der Stadt Köln. Ed. by Konrad Schilling (Cologne: Druckerei J. P. Bachem KG, 1963), pp. 356 f., 526.

The Trial of the Major War Criminals before the International Military Tribunal, Nuremberg, November, 1945-October, 1946. Published at Nuremberg, Germany, 1947, in accordance with the direction of the International Military Tribunal by the Secretariat of the Tribunal, under the jurisdiction of the Allied Control Authority for Germany. *Official Text in the English Language*, Vol. XI, Proceedings 8 April 1946-17 April 1946.

Maurice Friedman, *To Deny Our Nothingness: Contemporary Images of Man*, 3rd ed. with new Preface and Appendix (Chicago: The University of Chicago Press and Phoenix Books [paperback], 1978), p. 72, points to the link between biological vitalism and the Nazi philosophy.

Sydney and Beatrice Rome, eds., *Philosophical Interrogations* (New York: Harper Torchbooks, 1970), "Martin Buber" section conducted and ed. and Buber's replies trans. by Maurice Friedman, pp. 76-78.

"Aus Erster Hand." Ein *Gespräch mit Prof. Dr. Martin Buber, Jerusalem*, Interviewer: Thilo Koch; Lokstedt, Germany, 11 pages mimeographed.

Hans Kohn, *Martin Buber*, p. 315.

Franz Kafka, *Briefe an Felice und andere Korrespondenz aus der Verlobungszeit*, ed. by Erich Heller and Jürgen Born with an Introduction by Erich Heller (Berlin: S. Fischer Verlag, 1967), January 16, 1913, pp. 252 f.; January 19, 1913, p. 257; January 20-21, 1913, p. 258. Kafka's *Letters to Felice* are now available in English, trans. by James and Elizabeth Duckworth (New York: Schocken Books, 1973).

Franz Rosenzweig, *On Jewish Learning*, ed. by N. N. Glatzer (New York: Schocken Books, 1955), "The Builders," p. 72.

Gershom Scholem, "Martin Buber," *Ha'aretz* (in Hebrew, Tel Aviv), February 6, 1953, trans by Uri Margolin, revised and paraphrased by me.

Gershom Scholem, "Martin Bubers Auffassung des Judentums" in Adolf Portmann, ed., *Schöpfung und Gestaltung. Eranos-Jahrbuch 1966* (Zurich: Rhein-Verlag, 1967), pp. 14, 16 f., 21, 29.

Hugo Bergmann, "Die Zeit der 'Drei Reden über das Judentum,'" *Mitteilungsblatt der Hitachduth olej Germania (M. B.)* (Tel Aviv), February 11 (1938), pp. 3-5.

Ernst Simon, "Bridgebuilder: The Problem of Buber's Influence" (in Hebrew), *Molad*, No. 115 (February or March 1958), trans. by Uri Margolin, revised and paraphrased by me, Section I.

Grete Schaeder, *Martin Buber: Hebräischer Humanismus* (Göttingen: Vandenhoeck und Ruprecht, 1966), pp. 96-98, 107.

NOTE TO CHAPTER 8:
Realization: The Kingdom of Holy Insecurity

The lyrical and ecstatic style of much of *Daniel* might lead the reader to assume that Buber had written it as an unrestrained outpouring of the spirit, as Nietzsche wrote the first three parts of *Thus Spake Zarathustra*. The hand manuscript of *Daniel* that is to be found in the Buber Archives in Jerusalem proves the exact opposite. Before any of the actual text of *Daniel* is recorded in the notebook, there are several pages outlining possible topics and combinations of themes, and these too are clearly not written all at once, for each page represents a further crystallization and selection of possibilities. The first page is dated 1909 and lists a number of topics, such as the act of creation, bound and free polarity, creation, redemption, unity, mysticism, myth and magic. The first of these topics is "Von Erlebnis und Erfahrung." In *Daniel,* as in *I and Thou,* Buber was already concerned about the uniqueness of what one meets and about the difference between a merely external, manipulative relationship to it and one that one enters with one's whole being. But in *I and Thou* Buber characterized all types of experience as I-It; whereas in *Daniel* Buber distinguished between *Erfahrung* (the word for experience in the German original of *I and Thou*) and *Erlebnis,* a "life-experience" that demands a personal participation and involvement that is not demanded by the more mechanical and external experience that Buber later consigned to the world of *It.*

On the second page Buber equated bound polarity with orienting and free polarity with realization and listed as a separate topic the problem which concerned him throughout his "Speeches on Judaism": life in the conditioned and life in the unconditioned. He also listed three stages of duality: freedom, madness, death, a combination repeated on succeeding pages but never treated as such in *Daniel.* And he had a whole topic "On Holy Insecurity" under which he listed as problems: truth and life-experience, religiousness and religion, doubt and insecurity, and the heroic life.

By the ninth page of notes, after a number of tentative outlines interspersed with a list of thirty topics, a plan had emerged for a two-volume book with twelve chapters: (1) On Direction, (2) On Reality and Realization, (3) On Decision, Inclusion, Transformation and on Composing Poetry ("Dialogue on the Theater"), (4) On Holy Insecurity and the Heroic Life, (5) On Choice, (6) On Unity and Duality, (7) On the Conditional and the Unconditional; Second Book: (1) Myth, Magic, Mystery (about the primal forms of realization), (2) Cosmos, Son of Chaos (about the teaching of Bachofen), (3) *Requies mea* (about early Christianity), (4) Deed and History (about the formative and "evolution"), (5) On Immediacy and Tradition (about the meaning of community). Of these chapters 1, 2, 3, 4, and 6 of the first book are marked and none of the second book. It is precisely those that are marked that appear in the finished book. The next two pages concern plans for Buber's 1917 book *Events and Meetings,* clearly germinating in his mind at the same time, and the page that follows contains a list of miscellaneous jottings, ranging from the German and the Romance character, the angel of Cimabue, and Italian cloisters to immediacy and the Agora, theosophy, the Jewish cemetery at Worms, and analysis and psychosynthesis. Particularly of interest, in the light of our discussion of sexual love as the original source for Buber's insight into "inclusion," are the topics "Some Women and Love" and "Panlibertinism and Panlibidism." This notebook is to be found in the Martin Buber Archives in the Jewish National and University Library at the Hebrew University, Jerusalem, Israel. The first four pages of notes are loose. The rest are bound.

SOURCES FOR CHAPTER 8:
Realization: The Kingdom of Holy Insecurity

Robert Weltsch, "Zu Bubers Erstem Jahrzeittag," *loc. cit.,* p. 5.

Ernst Simon, "Bridgebuilder: The Problem of Buber's Influence," *loc. cit.*, pp. 96-98.

Martin Buber, "Autobiographical Fragments," 6. "The Two Boys," in Schilpp and Friedman, eds., *The Philosophy of Martin Buber*, pp. 8-10, and Buber, *Meetings*, pp. 24-26.

Buber, *Daniel*, "Author's Preface," p. 47; pp. 50-54, 57-59, 67, 69, 75, 82 f., 86, 93, 98, 102-25, 128-42.

Martin Buber, *Eclipse of God. Studies in the Relation between Religion and Philosophy* (New York: Harper Torchbooks, 1957), "Religion and Philosophy," trans. by Maurice Friedman, p. 36.

Grete Schaeder, *Martin Buber: Hebräischer Humanismus*, pp. 14 f., 91-95.

Buber Briefwechsel III. #422. MB to Maurice Friedman, Jerusalem, September 7, 1959, and n. 1 to #422, both on p. 487.

NOTE A TO CHAPTER 8

Buber's coupling of danger and God in *Daniel*, p. 98, was probably influenced by Hölderlin's verse: "Nah ist / Und schwer zu fassen der Gott. / Wo aber Gefahr ist, wächst / Das Rettend auch." Cf. Werner Kraft, *Gespräche mit Martin Buber* (Munich: Kösel Verlag, 1966), p. 102. Shortly before this passage, Daniel says: " 'God and the dreams,' so goes a song, Reinold, the song of the happy early ones. But your motto will be: God and danger." The quotation, with a slight change of punctuation, Buber took from a poem of the German poet Alfred Mombert. Mombert wrote Buber expressing his complete identification with *Daniel* and later himself took up the theme of danger in *Ataïr*, where he has the poet of "Heroes of the Earth" suspect that the figure of the "bride of the world" says to him: "I am your eternal comrade, I am *danger*," words which the poet himself echoes. *Alfred Mombert, Briefe 1893-1942*, selected and ed. by B. J. Morse (Heidelberg / Darmstadt: Verlag Lambert Schneider, 1961), pp. 34 and 219, n. 3.

Letter from Martin Buber to Maurice Friedman, March 2, 1962.

Buber, *Pointing the Way*, "With a Monist," pp. 26-30; "The Space Problem of the Stage," pp. 67-73.

Gustav Landauer, "Martin Buber" in *Neue Blätter, Buberheft*, Series 3, Nos. 1, 2 (Hellerau/Berlin: Verlag der Neuen Blätter, 1913), pp. 90-107. Landauer's essay was reprinted in Gustav Landauer, *Der Werdende Mensch, Aufsätze über Leben und Schrifttum*, ed. by Martin Buber (Potsdam: Gustav Kiepenheuer Verlag, 1921).

Gustav Landauer. Sein Lebensgang in Briefen, Vol. I, #255, #256. Letters of Gustav Landauer to Martin Buber, pp. 434-36, and footnotes.

Buber Briefwechsel I, #103. MB to Hugo von Hofmannsthal, Innsbruck, June 26, 1906, p. 244; #146. MB to Lou Andreas-Salomé, Zehlendorf, February 10, 1910, pp. 276 f.; #180. Gustav Landauer to MB, July 25, 1912, pp. 306 f.; #181. MB to Gustav Landauer, Riccione (Forli), July 30, 1912, p. 307; #182. MB to Gustav Landauer, Riccione, August 7, 1912, pp. 307 f.; #183. Gustav Landauer to MB, August 10, 1912, pp. 308 f.; #185. Gustav Landauer to MB, September 9, 1912, p. 311; #192. MB to Ernst Elijahu Rappeport, October 23, 1912, pp. 315-

17; #205. MB to Karl Wolfskehl, April 29, 1913, p. 328; #206. Hugo Bergmann to MB, May 2, 1913, pp. 329 f.; #214. Lou Andreas-Salomé to MB, June 6, 1913, p. 337; #215. Carl Buber to MB, June 7, 1913, pp. 337 f.; #200. MB to Gustav Landauer, March 16, 1913, p. 323; #201. Gustav Landauer to MB, March 17, 1913, pp. 323 f.; #203. Gustav Landauer to MB, March 19, 1913, pp. 325 f.; #217. MB to Gustav Landauer, Bad Tölz, August 9, 1913, p. 340; #218. Gustav Landauer to MB, August 16, 1913, pp. 341 f.

Rudolph Binion, *Frau Lou. Nietzsche's Wayward Disciple* (Princeton, N.J.: Princeton University Press, 1968), pp. 237, 327 (letters cited and quoted are from Buber to Lou, March 28, 1906, and February 10, 1910. The latter is reprinted in *Buber Briefwechsel,* I, as #146, pp. 276 f., and is followed by #147. Lou Andreas-Salomé to MB, February 13, 1910, p. 277), 328 f., 446.

Jochanan Bloch, *Die Aporie des Du. Probleme der Dialogik Martin Bubers,* Vol. II of *Phronesis. Eine Schriftenreihe* (Heidelberg: Verlag Lambert Schneider, 1977), note to p. 300, pp. 300–02.

Werner Kraft, *Gespräche mit Martin Buber* (Munich: Kösel Verlag, 1966), entry of April 23, 1965, pp. 140; 41 f., 150 note to 28.1.1959, 1st paragraph.

Conversation with Dr. Lea Goldberg, distinguished Hebrew poetess and professor of comparative literature at the Hebrew University, Jerusalem, Spring 1966.

Buber, *I and Thou,* trans. by Ronald Gregor Smith, p. 98.

Martin Buber, "Drei Rollen Novellis," *Die Schaubühne,* Vol. II, No. 2 (January 11, 1906), pp. 42–48.

Hans Kohn, *Martin Buber,* pp. 71, 306, notes 4 and 5 to p. 71.

Briefe an Auguste Hauschner, Louise Dumont, Düsseldorf, April 30, 1919, pp. 189–91.

See Landauer's letters from October 1918 on for material on his own relationship to the summons by the Düsseldorf Playhouse in *Gustav Landauer. Sein Lebensgang in Briefen,* ed. by Martin Buber, Vol. II.

SOURCES FOR CHAPTER 9:
The First World War and the Breakthrough to Dialogue

•─────────────────────────────•

Buber, *I and Thou,* pp. 110 f., 123.

Paul Schilpp and Maurice Friedman, eds., *The Philosophy of Martin Buber,* Buber, "Replies to My Critics," trans. by Maurice Friedman, "Personal Determination," pp. 689 f.

Buber, *Hasidism and Modern Man,* pp. 23 f., 38 f.

Buber Briefwechsel I, #233. MB to Arnold Zweig, January 28, 1914, p. 355; #243. Margarete von Bendemann-Susman to MB, August 9, 1914, pp. 362 f.; #244. MB to Ernst Elijahu Rappeport, Pescara, August 10, 1914, p. 364; #245. MB to Ludwig Strauss, Zehlendorf, September 8, 1914, p. 364; #246. MB to Ernst Elijahu Rappeport, Zehlendorf, September

10, 1914, p. 365; #250. MB to Hans Kohn, September 30, 1914, pp. 370 f.; #253. MB to Frederik Van Eeden, October 16, 1914, pp. 373 f. and pp. 374-80; #255. MB to Gustav Landauer, October 18, 1914, p. 381; #257. Gustav Landauer and MB to the Forte Kreis, Hermsdorf/ Zehlendorf, end of November 1914, pp. 382-84; #269. MB to Gustav Landauer, Lindenfels im Odenwald, September 4, 1915, p. 396; #271. MB to Paula Buber-Winkler, Lindenfels, September 8, 1915, p. 397; #273. MB to Paula Buber-Winkler, Lindenfels, September 10, 1915, pp. 399 f.; #295. Gustav Landauer to MB, March 3, 1916, pp. 419 f.; #306. Gustav Landauer to MB, May 12, 1916, pp. 433-38; #321. Gustav Landauer to MB, August 22, 1916, p. 451; #381. MB to Ernst Elijahu Rappeport, January 6, 1918, pp. 521 f.; #382. MB to Ernst Elijahu Rappeport, January 28, 1918, p. 522; #399. Ernst Elijahu Rappeport to MB, October 16, 1918, p. 539.

Letters from Frederik Van Eeden to Martin Buber, March 1, 1910, May 5, 1914, Martin Buber Archives, Jewish National and University Library, The Hebrew University, Jerusalem.

Martin Buber, "Aus einem Rundschreiben von Ostern 1914," *Almanach der neuen Jugend auf das Jahr 1917* (Berlin).

Buber, *Between Man and Man,* "Dialogue" — "Opinions and the Factual," pp. 5 f.; "A Conversion," pp. 13 f.

Martin Buber, *The Knowledge of Man. A Philosophy of the Interhuman,* ed. with an Introductory Essay (Chap. 1) by Maurice Friedman, "Elements of the Interhuman," trans. by Ronald Gregor Smith, pp. 86 f.

The diary of Frederik Van Eeden, quoted in *Praemium Erasmianum,* MCM-LXIII, Inveniemus Viam Aut Faciemus (Amsterdam, 1963), p. 60.

Margarete Susman, *Ich Habe Viele Leben Gelebt. Erinnerungen* (Stuttgart: Deutsche Verlags-Anstalt, 1964), p. 78.

Liber Amicorum. Dr. Frederik Van Eeden aangeboden ter Gelegenheid van zijn zeventigsten Verjaardag 3 April 1930 (Amsterdam: N.V. Maatschappij Tot Verspreiding van Goede en Goedkoope Lectur [Wereldbibliotheek], 1930), pp. 34 f.

NOTE A TO CHAPTER 9

Looking back from the same distance, Eric Gutkind, the German-Jewish philosopher of religion and philosopher of science who was to spend his last years in America, gave a testimony strikingly similar to Buber's. "Friendship was not founded upon common opinions or common goals," Gutkind wrote Van Eeden, "but upon a glorious splendid immediacy from man to man. Just this — one man with another man — was the wonderful thing so that Van Eeden's friendship belonged to the most precious of the things that we possessed. We called our union, proudly, the original cell (*Urzelle*). For, indeed, there proceeded from this cell again and again something magnetic, like the building structure of an organism. A fullness of meeting, of friendships, and finally that circle, in which a group of serious men came together for the most sublime and intense utterances. This circle, to which a number of very well known men belonged, was for each person there a turning point in his life. And even when this circle had disintegrated, the high harmony of this being-together has continued to re-sound, and has never entirely left any of us." *Liber Amicorum*, p. 69. Gut-kind, whom I came to know in New York toward the end of his life, com-bined his interest in science and his interest in the philosophical implications of Judaism in an unusual book, *Choose Life. The Biblical Call to Revolt* (New York: Henry Schuman, 1952).

A more concrete and immediate reaction is that which Poul Bjerre wrote to Van Eeden six months after the Potsdam meeting. Once again the testi-mony was in particular directed to Van Eeden and then to the Forte Circle. "Dear friend and splendid man," Bjerre replied to a letter of Van Eeden's concerning the difficulties the group was having in continuing. "You are the only one who understands this matter as deeply as it must be understood. It is indeed wonderful how this Circle lives and works despite all. Even if we all wanted to kill it, we could not do so. You know how I strove against this Circle in Potsdam when I discovered how it came over me like a monstrous force whose life-determining significance I would not be able to deny once I had been overpowered by it. I strove as one instinctively strives against all with whose power one comes in contact. It was a crisis for me. But when I had lived through it, I was *for ever wholly committed to the cause.* . . .

"Norlind was at my country house the day before yesterday," Bjerre continued, "and I asked him: 'Have you thought about the fact that we have drawn much closer to each other through the Circle?'

" 'Naturally,' he replied, 'we have known each other for ten years, and all our common interests have not contributed so much to this drawing near-er as the Circle.' " (Copy of a letter from Poul Bjerre to Frederik Van Eeden, Tumba, September .23, 1915, in Buber Archives, Jewish and National Uni-versity Library, The Hebrew University, Jerusalem.)

NOTE B TO CHAPTER 9

Potsdam was not the only last-minute effort to preserve the peace that Buber took part in. Even after the war had begun, Buber and some of his friends clung to the idea of some possibility of peace mediation. One of these friends was Max Brod, who tells in his biography of a meeting that took place in the simple Berlin dwelling of the philosopher Max Scheler. Brod him-self was at that meeting, as were Buber and Landauer, whom Brod had met through that remarkable salon-mistress Auguste Hauschner. The grand old lady supported and sponsored the anarchist Landauer, so different from her in his basic views. At this meeting, Buber, Scheler, Landauer, and Brod sat together and strenuously discussed the fearful misfortune of the outbreak of war. The discussion in Scheler's home was without result; it *could not* lead to any result. In vain did the four men strive for formulations of their hearts' desire; they could find no common language. The reason for this be-came clear only some weeks later, all too clear, "bloodred." There appeared then a book of Scheler's fully in line with the nationalist views that prevailed among the leaders of the German nation at that time. The excellence of war was praised in the spirit of Nietzsche, and every pacifist received a verbal box on the ear. "How Scheler, who at that time had already finished his bellicose piece of writing and must already have known it to be in press, could take part in our debate without any protests has always remained a riddle to me," comments Brod. Brod, *Streitbares Leben* (Munich: Kindler Verlag, 1960), pp. 89 f.

Buber, "Autobiographical Fragments," 14. "Question and Answer," in Schilpp and Friedman, eds., *The Philosophy of Martin Buber*, pp. 23 f., and Buber, *Meetings*, pp. 42–44.

Rivka Horwitz, *Buber's Way to I and Thou. An Historical Analysis and the First Publication of Martin Buber's Lectures "Religion als Gegenwart,"* Vol. VII of *Phronesis. Eine Schriftenreihe* (Heidelberg: Verlag Lambert Schneider, 1978), pp. 128–30, 174–77. In note 25, p. 176, Horwitz writes: "A detailed article on Hechler, including a bibliography and photograph, can be found in *Encyclopedia Judaica*, vol. 8, pp. 237–239."

NOTE C TO CHAPTER 9

In his article on Buber, "Sage Who Inspired Hammerskjøld," the *New York Times Magazine*, December 3, 1961, p. 60, Meyer Levin asserts that the young man in Buber's story "The Conversation" committed suicide. Aubrey Hodes extends this fiction even further: "I asked Buber at our next meeting, 'What happened to the young man?'

"Buber closed his eyes for a moment, as if in pain. Then he said quietly, 'He went. And shortly afterward he took his own life.' " There follow two paragraphs in which Hodes pictures Buber as saying to him directly what in fact is only a paraphrase of what he wrote in the section on "Conversion" in "Dialogue." Aubrey Hodes, *Martin Buber: An Intimate Portrait* (New York: The Viking Press, 1971), pp. 10 f. This is not the only case in which, in a journalistic attempt to make his portrait of Buber "intimate," Hodes claimed as a direct dialogue between him and Buber what was, in fact, written elsewhere. Only in this case a false impression is perpetuated in the minds of many readers who have no way of checking on the truth of what Hodes said!

Letter from Martin Buber to Maurice Friedman, Jerusalem, August 6, 1961.
Grete Schaeder, *Martin Buber*, pp. 114 f.
Buber, *Pointing the Way*, "To the Contemporary," pp. 59 f.; "Hope for This Hour," p. 222.

NOTE D TO CHAPTER 9

Werner Kraft, in a diary entry of September 11, 1959, records that he pointed out to Buber that the noted German-Jewish poet Karl Wolfskehl was among the signers of the notorious proclamation of the ninety-nine German intellectuals who issued a statement declaring the support of the German intellectuals for the Kaiser. Buber no longer seemed to know just what that was, Kraft adds. Kraft, *Gespräche mit Martin Buber*, p. 56.

Martin Buber, "Pescara, an einem Augustmorgen," "Berlin nach der Heim-

kehr," *Zeit-Echo. Ein Kriegs-Tagebuch der Künstler,* Vol. I, No. 3 (1914)
(Munich: Graphik Verlag, 1914/15), pp. 38 f.

Martin Buber, "Bewegung. Aus eienm Brief an einen Holländer" (written the
middle of September), *Der neue Merkur,* Vol. I, Nos. 10/11 (January/
February, 1915), pp. 489-92.

Martin Buber, "Dem Fähnreich W. St. ins Stammbuch," *Zeit-Echo. Ein
Kriegs Tagebuch der Künstler* (Munich), Vol. II, No. 13 (1915), p. 186.

Martin Buber, "Die Engel und die Weltherrschaft: Ein altjüdisches Märchen.
Den Freunden in Feld gewidmet," *Jüdische Rundschau,* February 19,
1915, p. 62.

Martin Buber, *Die Jüdische Bewegung. Gesammelte Aufsätze und Ansprachen,
1916-1920,* Zweite Folge (Berlin: Jüdischer Verlag, 1920), "Vorwort,"
p. 5.

Martin Buber, ed., *Gustav Landauer. Sein Lebensgang in Briefen,* Vol. II
(Frankfurt a. M.: Rütten & Loening, 1929), #278. To Frederik Van
Eeden, August 18, 1914; #280. To Frederik Van Eeden, September 22,
1914, pp. 3-4; #281. To Frederik Van Eeden, September 24, 1914, pp.
4-5; #288. To Frederik Van Eeden, November 27, 1914, pp. 13-14;
#289. Letter of Landauer and Buber to the Forte Kreis, the end of
November, 1914, pp. 14-16; #323. To Hedwig Lachmann, August 3,
1915, pp. 63 f.; To Poul Bjerre, Tumba (Sweden), E. Norlind, Borgeby
(Sweden), Frederik Van Eeden, Bussum (Holland), Henri Borel, Holland;
communicated for his information to Martin Buber; request to Van
Eeden to communicate it to Romain Rolland in Genf, August 22, 1915,
pp. 71-82; #340. To Rudolf Leonhard, October 22, 1915, p. 100; #359.
To Ernst Joel, February 8, 1916, pp. 127 f.; #350. To Martin Buber,
December 10, 1915, p. 112; #361. To Martin Buber, March 3, 1916,
pp. 132-34.

NOTE E TO CHAPTER 9

Landauer declared himself unwilling to contribute to Buber's new journal *Der Jude.* "A journal that says what the Hapsburgs, Hohenzollern, and the
interest groups bound up with them would gladly hear and does not say what
is opposed to that, cannot be my journal." To speak of the Jewish stake in
German victory was to ignore all the Jewish blood spilled by the murder of
Germans, Slavs, Rumanians, Italians, Austrians, and Russians. "A pity for the
Jewish blood, indeed a pity for every drop of blood that is spilt in this war;
. . . a pity for the men; a pity also that you have gone astray in this war!'"

No answer to this bitter condemnation is extant; Buber may have taken a
train to Berlin and replied to Landauer in person. In any case, after they met
for several days in Berlin in July 1916 Landauer sent Buber a note expressing his satisfaction with *Der Jude* and his readiness to contribute to it. "The
level of your periodical is so high and the whole attitude of the recent
issues pleases me so much and, above all, my desire to work up the essay on
Judaism and Socialism is so great that I consider it best to write a formal
assent." It is unthinkable that Landauer could have thus reversed himself
had Buber not satisfied him not only by explanation but by change of atti-

tude! Paul Flohr has pointed out that Buber omitted Landauer's long letter of May 12, 1916, from the two-volume collection of Landauer's correspondence that he edited and has advanced evidence that suggests that Buber may have pressured Hans Kohn to revise the part of his 1930 intellectual-historical study of Buber that dealt with his attitude to the war. In the second edition of "Der Geist des Orients und das Judentum," Buber omitted the passages that offended Landauer.

That Landauer's letter inevitably had a powerful effect in bringing Buber to face up to the implications of his enthusiasm about the war is certain. In the light of the total picture that we have presented, however, it is impossible to hold with Flohr that "this letter, *ex hypothesi*, was a pivotal factor in Buber's turn from . . . *Erlebnis*-mysticism to the philosophy of dialogue." On the other hand, we shall find in the next chapters ample evidence for Flohr's assertion that in Buber's writings subsequent to the spring of 1916 three new elements appear: "an explicit opposition to the war and chauvinistic nationalism; a reevaluation of the function and meaning of *Erlebnis*," and a shift in the axis of *Gemeinschaft* (community) from an emphasis on subjective-cosmic consciousness (*Erlebnis*) to the relations between men. Paul R. Flohr, "The Road to *I and Thou*. An Inquiry in Buber's Transition from Mysticism to Dialogue," in Michael A. Fishbane and Paul R. Flohr, eds., *Texts and Responses. Studies Presented to Nahum N. Glatzer on the Occasion of His Seventieth Birthday by His Students* (Leiden: E. J. Brill, 1975), pp. 201-18.

SOURCES FOR CHAPTER 10:
Der Jude

•————————————————————————————————•

Buber, *A Believing Humanism: Gleanings*, "In Heidelberg," p. 34.
Franz Rosenzweig, *Kleinere Schriften* (Berlin: Schocken Verlag/Jüdischer Buchverlag, 1937), "Atheistische Theologie" (1914), pp. 283, 286 f., 289 f.

NOTE A TO CHAPTER 10

In the first letter we have from Rosenzweig to Buber, he recalls how five years earlier, in the spring of 1914, he paid a visit to Buber. Buber at that time invited him to contribute to the projected second volume of the almanac *Vom Judentum*, a book which never, in fact, saw the light of day. Rosenzweig responded to Buber's invitation by sending in the essay "Atheistic Theology." (Franz Rosenzweig, *Briefe*, selected and ed. by Edith Rosenzweig in cooperation with Ernst Simon [Berlin: Schocken Verlag, 1935], #278. To Martin Buber, pp. 370 and 370 n. 2.) The volume itself failed to appear, but even before that, this essay was returned to Rosenzweig by the editors.

On the basis of the fact that the essay was in part a criticism of Buber's own thought and that Buber was an editor of *Vom Judentum*, Herberg, Bergmann, and Simon have attributed the change in Buber's thought at this period to Rosenzweig's influence. When I told Buber what Herberg had said, he replied that the volume was edited in Prague (by Hans Kohn, Robert Weltsch, and the Bar Kochba Society), that he was only an honorary editor in Berlin, and had not even read Rosenzweig's essay. Leo Hermann tells, to be sure, of the painstaking, downright jealous concern for details that Buber exercised in working with him on the first volume while at the same time taking care never to encroach on the responsibility of the Bar Kochbans. (Leo Hermann, "Aus Tagebuchblättern. II. Berlin" in *Sonderheft zu Martin Bubers 50. Geburtstag, loc. cit.*, p. 162.) Even if this recollection suggests that Buber's participation in the preparation of the second volume may have been more direct than Buber recollected, there is no evidence that he even read Rosenzweig's essay, much less was influenced by it. If Rosenzweig sent it to the Prague editors, they might have returned it without showing it to Buber precisely because it *was* a critique of his thought. In any case, it would have been surprising indeed had Buber set aside that carefully constructed thought through which he had influenced a generation of Jewish youth at the first hint from an unknown young writer eight years his junior, who criticized his thought from a point of view that Buber did not yet share!

Anyone who imagines that Buber at this time would meekly accept criticism of his "Speeches on Judaism" should read his devastating reply to the anonymous writer who accused him of having taken the central ideas of his "Speeches" from the popular German-Jewish philosopher Constantin Brunner. Beginning with a caustic comment on those second-rate disciples to whom the whole spiritual creation of the age seems a plagiarism of their master that must be tracked down piece by piece, Buber proceeded to one merciless paragraph after another under the headings: 1. The anonymous writer had no notion of the book about which he wrote; 2. He had no notion of the man about whom he wrote; 3. He had no notion of the language of thought and its distinctions; 4. He had no notion of the history of thought; 5. He had "no notion finally of Constantin Brunner's own position in relation to my thought." Buber's concluding statement showed the extent to which he had followed the admonition of his own poem ten years earlier: "If you can be your own, never be another's." "Constantin Brunner knows what A. M. does not suspect," Buber wrote: "who I am . . . that I am independent of him as he of me . . . that I do not think something to which I have not come of myself, that I do not proclaim something that I have not thought of out of myself." In the midst of his rejoinder, lamenting the impossibility of real dialogue, Buber added: "How shall I begin with this nameless, faceless writer?" Martin Buber, "A. M. und Constantin Brunner," *Ost und West*, Vol. XII, No. 4 (April 1912), columns 333-338.

When I wrote Buber about Will Herberg's original assertion that it was Rosenzweig's "Atheistic Theology" that caused Buber decisively to change his philosophy, Buber replied: "Herberg is wrong in assuming that the change expressed in the *Vorwort* [The Foreword to the 1923 collected edition of the *Speeches on Judaism*] is due to Rosenzweig's influence. I have been influenced decisively not by men but by events, particularly in the years 1916-1919. I am somewhat astonished that H. thinks *such* a change can be effected by other persons instead of life itself. By-the-by, the change had found already some expression in the first draft of *Ich und Du,* of 1916." Letter from Martin Buber to Maurice Friedman, Amsterdam, September 9, 1953.

Leo Hermann, *op. cit.,* pp. 163 f.

Ernst Simon, "Martin Buber's Political Way," *loc. cit.*

Buber Briefwechsel I, #280. MB to Franz Rosenzweig, November 22, 1915, p. 404; #281. Robert Weltsch to MB, November 23, 1915, p. 405; #283. MB to Hugo Bergmann, November 25, 1915, p. 408; #284. Franz Kafka to MB, November 29, 1915, p. 409; #287. Kurt Singer to MB, December 8, 1915, p. 411; #290. MB to Gustav Landauer, December 24, 1915, p. 404; #293. Kurt Singer to MB, February 5, 1916, p. 417.

NOTE B TO CHAPTER 10

Buber, *Die jüdische Bewegung,* I, *1900-1914, loc. cit.,* "Die Tempelweihe," speech given at Maccabee celebration of the Berlin Zionist Union, December 19, 1914, pp. 230–241. This speech, part of which Buber later reprinted in his opening editorial to the first issue of *Der Jude,* so alienated Dr. Judah Magnes, Buber's future friend and co-worker in the cause of Jewish-Arab rapprochement, that by his own testimony he ceased to read Buber. Magnes, an American rabbi and pacifist during the First World War and founder of the famous Joint Distribution Committee for the relief of Jews in need everywhere, was greatly disappointed by Buber's Hanukkah speech. "I listened over the ocean in order to hear a real religious word from a teacher of Judaism, a word that even during the spilling of blood turned unambiguously against the spilling of blood and was *au dessus de la mêlee."* (Here Magnes uses the famous title of the controversial essay by Romain Rolland, whose presence the Forte Kreis just missed having and whose spirit it could not sustain.) After this, Magnes resolved to read no more of Buber, as of all those teachers who fell short of his expectations during the war. Even Buber's position on the Arab question, though it coincided with Magnes's, did not lead him to reverse his judgment. (Judah L. Magnes, "Al Har Hazophim," *Sonderheft zu Martin Bubers 50th Geburtstag, loc. cit.,* p. 50.) It was only their personal meeting in Jerusalem much later that altered the relationship between these two eminent men who thereafter worked in close harmony for the betterment of Israel.

NOTE C TO CHAPTER 10

In this last letter Singer wrote that the knowledge grew stronger in him daily "that no person embodies the divine more purely and creatively than [Stefan] George, . . . that the knots of time and of renewal are tied together in George. His work, understood not as the sum of individual volumes of poetry but as the totality of his effect, is for me the radiation of the new aeon, the coming kingdom of God."

#276. Siegfried Lehmann to MB, October 18, 1915, pp. 40 f.; #294. Siegfried Lehmann to MB, February 19, 1916, pp. 417-19; #303. Max

Brod to MB, May 2, 1916, p. 421; #304. Stefan Zweig to MB, May 8, 1916, pp. 432 f.; #305. Max Brod to MB, May 9, 1916, pp. 432 f.; #307. Viktor Jacobson to MB, May 25, 1916, pp. 438 f.; #311. Gerhard Scholem to MB, June 25, 1916, p. 441; #312. MB to Ernst Elijahu Rappeport, June 26, 1916, p. 442; #313. MB to Gerhard Scholem, June 28, 1916, p. 442; #314. Ludwig Strauss to MB, June 30, 1916, p. 443; #317. Gerhard Scholem to MB, July 10, 1916, pp. 446 f.; #320. MB to Julius Bab, August 7, 1916, p. 451; #322. MB to Ernst Elijahu Rappeport, August 30, 1916, p. 452; #325. Gustav Landauer to MB, October 12, 1916, pp. 454 f.; #326. MB to Gustav Landauer, October 15, 1916, pp. 455 f.; #328. Leonhard Ragaz to MB, November 6, 1916, p. 457; #240. Franz Werfel to MB, May 6, 1914, p. 361; #241. MB to Franz Werfel, undated, pp. 361 f.; #336. Franz Werfel to MB, January 31, 1917, pp. 468 f.; #338. MB to Max Brod, February 7, 1917, pp. 470 f.; #340. Max Brod to MB, February 13, 1917, pp. 472 f.; #344. Werner Kraft to MB, March 11, 1917, pp. 475-77; #345. MB to Werner Kraft, March 15, 1917, pp. 477 f.; #346. Werner Kraft to MB, March 17, 1917, pp. 478-81; #348. MB to Franz Werfel, March 17, 1917, p. 484; #357. Franz Werfel to MB, May 1917, p. 492; #359. Franz Kafka to MB, May 12, 1917, p. 494; #360. Viktor Jacobson to MB, May 14, 1917, pp. 494-96; #361. MB to Viktor Jacobson, May 19, 1917, pp. 497-98; #365. MB to Siegmund Kaznelson, July 9, 1917, p. 502; #373. MB to Ernst Elijahu Rappeport, November 28, 1917, p. 514; #366. MB to Hans Kohn, August 5, 1917, pp. 503 f.; #367. Siegfried Bernfeld to MB, September 14, 1917, pp. 305 f.; #385. MB to Stefan Zweig, February 4, 1918, pp. 525 f.; #386. MB to Hugo Bergmann, February 3-4, 1918, pp. 526 f.; #387. MB to Franz Oppenheimer, February 4, 1918, p. 527; #388. Gustav Landauer to MB, February 5, 1918, p. 528.

"Aus frühen Briefen," *loc cit.*, letter of Buber to Hugo Bergmann, May 22, 1916.

Ernst Simon, "Bridgebuilder: The Problem of Buber's Influence," *loc. cit.*

NOTE D TO CHAPTER 10

Among the prominent writers who contributed to *Der Jude* during the first three years of its existence were Ahad Ha'am, Elias Auerbach, Hugo Bergmann, Siegfried Bernfeld, Micha Josef bin Gorion (Berdycewski), Kurt Blumenfeld, Adolf Böhm, Max Brod, Martin Buber, Moses Calvary, Hermann Cohen, Simon Dubnow, Marcus Ehrenpreis, A. D. Gordon, S. A. Horodezky, Yeheskiel Kaufmann, Gustav Landauer, Ernst Müller, Alfonse Paquet, Gershom Scholem, Davis Trietsch, Robert Weltsch, Hillel Zeitlin, Julius Bab, Oskar Baum, Markus Reiner, Ludwig Strauss, Arnold Zweig, S. J. Agnon, Eduard Bernstein, Georg Brandes, Constantin Brunner, Leo Hermann, Franz Kafka ("So now I shall at last appear in *Der Jude!*" Kafka jubilantly wrote to Buber), Berl Kaznelson, Hedwig Lachmann (Landauer's second wife), Siegfried Lehmann, Margarete Susman, Franz Werfel, Nahum Goldmann (later the head of the World Jewish Agency), Harry Torczyner, and Felix Weltsch.

Franz Kafka, *Briefe an Felice*, September 23, 1916, pp. 704 f.

Walter Z. Laqueur, *Young Germany. A History of the German Youth Movement* (London: Routledge & Kegan Paul, 1962), pp. 81, 87, 115-21.

Buber, *Der Jude und Sein Judentum*, "Völker, Staaten und Zion, I. Begriffe und Wirklichkeit [Letter to Hermann Cohen (July 1916)], II. Der Staat und die Menschheit. Bemerkungen zu Hermann Cohens 'Antwort' [September 1916]," pp. 288-92, 294-304; "An die Prager Freunde (September 1916)," pp. 661 f.; "Ein politischer Faktor (August 1917)," pp. 501-04; " 'Kulturarbeit.' Zu den Delegiertentagen der deutschen und der holländischen Zionisten (Februar 1917)," pp. 671-73; "Die Eroberung Palästinas (Januar 1918)," pp. 505-07; "Zion und die Jugend. Eine Ansprache (Mai 1918)," pp. 700-10.

Buber, *Die jüdische Bewegung*, II, "Die Losung" (March 1916), pp. 14 f.; "Ein Heldenbuch" (December 1916), pp. 77-81; "Unser Nationalismus. Zum zweiten Jahrgang des 'Juden' " (April 1917), pp. 100-03; "Der Preis" (October 1917), pp. 121-31.

NOTE E TO CHAPTER 10

Ernst Simon says on the debate more than forty years later: "Cohen was caught in a fatal error when he identified the idea of the Messiah with the spirit of one concrete nation as if the Messiah had already appeared historically on earth and precisely in the spirit of the German nation of that time which in his opinion was the bearer of universal humanism. Buber, in contrast, was right when he said that every single real Zionist is on the way even as regards his inmost being, not, as Cohen thought, being at home wherever he was in the Diaspora. (Today every real Zionist knows that even here in Israel we are on the way and there is no historical guarantee once and for all for the eternal sacredness of our existence. Cohen's question to Buber, what has prophecy to do with the existence of nationality, is today a question of life and death that we think of every day.)" Simon, "The Political Way and the National View of Martin Buber," *loc. cit.*

Gershom Scholem, *On Jews and Judaism in Crisis. Selected Essays*, ed. by Werner J. Dannhauser (New York: Schocken Books, 1976), "With Gershom Scholem: An Interview," pp. 13-15.

Martin Buber, *Briefwechsel*, Vol. II, *1918-1938* (Heidelberg: Verlag Lambert Schneider, 1973), #10. MB to Fritz Mauthner, December 12, 1918, pp. 18 f.

NOTE F TO CHAPTER 10

The issue concerning the Eastern Jews that plagued Germany in the First World War was one of the real origins perhaps of the Nazis' infamous "final solution" of the Jewish question. Although Alfred Rosenberg may have cited Buber's Zionism as a support for Nazi policy at the Nuremberg trials, it is clear that the assimilatory, "liberal" German Jews contributed to the final solution precisely through *their* contempt for the *Ostjuden*. Those Jews really alien to German *Kultur* — the East European Jews — were exterminated in far greater number and proportion than the German Jews. At Yad Vashem, "the tent of remembrance" in Jerusalem, the number of German Jews listed killed is fewer than 200,000 whereas 2,800,000 Polish Jews were exterminated!

Letter from Viktor Jacobson to Salman Schocken, Jr., April 17, 1916, Central Zionist Archives, Jerusalem, Israel.

Martin Buber, "Referat aus den ausserordentlichen Delegiertentag der Zionistischen Vereinigung für Deutschland (25 & 26 December 1916)," *Jüdische Rundschau*, Vol. XXII, No. 9, January 5, 1917, pp. 4 f.

Martin Buber, "Geleitwort" to *Jiskor. Ein Buch des Gedenkens an Gefallene Wächter und Arbeiter im Lande Israel.* Deutsche Ausgabe (Berlin: Jüdischer Verlag, 1918), pp. 1 f.

Martin Buber, "Rede bei der Tagung der jüdische Jugendorganisationen Deutschlands," Berlin, March 5, 1918, *Mitteilungen des Verbandes des jüdischen Jugendvereine Deutschlands*, Vol. IX, No. 2/3 (April/May 1918), pp. 79-82.

Letter from Martin Buber to Viktor Jacobson, May 28, 1916; letter from Viktor Jacobson to Martin Buber, October 2, 1916; letter from Martin Buber to Viktor Jacobson, October 4, 1916. Central Zionist Archives, Jerusalem, Israel.

SOURCES FOR CHAPTER 11:
Communal Socialism and Revolution: The Murder of Landauer

Martin Buber, *Israel and Palestine. The History of an Idea*, trans. by Stanley Godman (London: East and West Library, 1952), "The First of the Last: Moses Hess," pp. 111-122. *Israel and Palestine* has been republished by Schocken Books under the title *On Zion*.

Maurice Friedman, *Martin Buber: The Life of Dialogue*, pp. 45-47.

Martin Buber, *Paths in Utopia*, trans. by R. F. C. Hull with an Introduction by Ephraim Fischoff (Boston: Beacon Paperbacks, 1958), chapters on Proudhon, Kropotkin, Landauer.

Martin Buber, *Kingship of God*, 3rd newly enlarged ed., trans. by Richard Scheimann (New York: Harper & Row, 1967), p. 20.

Buber, *A Believing Humanism: Gleanings*, "In Heidelberg," p. 34.

Martin Buber, "Geleitwort zur Sammlung," in Werner Sombart, *Das Proletariat*, Vol. I of *Die Gesellschaft*, ed. by Martin Buber (Frankfurt am Main: Rütten & Loening, 1906), pp. ix-xiii.

Buber Briefwechsel I, #86. MB to Hermann Stehr, Hermsdorf (Mark), May 20, 1905, pp. 230 f.; #105. MB to Gustav Landauer, Hall in Tirol, Volderwald, July 26, 1906, pp. 245 f.; #115. Gustav Landauer to MB, April 9, 1907, p. 255; #117. MB to Gustav Landauer, Zehlendorf, June 5, 1907, p. 255; #118. Gustav Landauer to MB, June 6, 1907, pp. 255 f.; #358. MB to Siegmund Kaznelson, May 8, 1917, p. 494; #389. MB to Ernst Elijahu Rappeport, February 11, 1918, p. 530; #390. MB to Siegmund Kaznelson, March 11, 1918, p. 530; #392. Gustav Landauer to MB, May 10, 1918, pp. 531 f.

Grete Schaeder, *Martin Buber*, pp. 212 f.

Martin Buber, "Gedenkworte an Charlotte Kronstein geb. Landauer," spoken in Karlsruhe im Breslau am 16. August 1927, written down by her husband Max Kronstein, December 3, 1927, Martin Buber Archives, The Jewish and National Library, The Hebrew University, Jerusalem, Israel.

Martin Buber, "Vorwort" to Gustav Landauer, *Beginnen. Aufsätze über Sozialismus*, ed. by Martin Buber in accordance with Landauer's last will (Köln: Marcan-Block-Verlag, 1924), p. viii.

Martin Buber, "Vorwort" to *Gustav Landauer. Sein Lebensgang in Briefen*, I, pp. v f.

Gustav Landauer, *Die Revolution*, Vol. XIII of *Die Gesellschaft*, ed. by Martin Buber (Frankfurt am Main: Literarische Anstalt, Rütten & Loening, 1907, 1919), pp. 12, 14, 26, 28.

Julius Bab, *Gustav Landauer*, 2nd ed. (Nürnberg & Würzburg: Verlag "Der Bund," 1924), pp. 23–27; 32–34.

Hans Kohn, *Martin Buber*, pp. 195 f., 236 f. (quotation from the dialogue on religion between Martin Buber and Theodor Bäuerle in the spring of 1929 in the Stuttgart Jüdischen Lehrhaus), 349.

Landauer issue of *Masken. Halbmonatschrift des Düsseldorfer Schauspielhauses*, Vol. XXIV (1919), Nos. 18/19, Fritz Mauthner, "Zum Gedächtnis," May 18, 1919, pp. 300, 302 f.; Eduard von Bendemann, "Erinnerung," pp. 306 f.; Martin Buber, "Landauer und die Revolution," pp. 282 ff.; Auguste Hauschner, "Gustav Landauer," p. 305.

Buber, *Hasidism and Modern Man*, "My Way to Hasidism," pp. 52 f.

Buber, *On Judaism*, "The Holy Way," trans. by Eva Jospe, pp. 108–13, 130 (italics added), 131, 134; "Herut," trans. by Eva Jospe, pp. 158 f., 170.

Buber Briefwechsel II, #22. Gustav Landauer to MB, March 20, 1919, p. 401; #23. Arnold Zweig to MB, April 3, 1919, pp. 34 f.; #47. Arnold Zweig to MB, September 25, 1919, p. 60; #14. MB to Ludwig Strauss, January 7, 1919, pp. 22 f.; #38. Arnold Zweig to MB, June 6, 1919, p. 50; #41. Louise Dumont-Lindemann to MB, August 5, 1919, p. 52; #42. MB to Louise Dumont-Lindemann, August 19, 1919, p. 53; #18. MB to Ludwig Strauss, February 22, 1919, p. 29; #24. Fritz Mauthner to MB, Easter Sunday, 1919, pp. 36, 36, n. 1. See also #26. MB to Fritz Mauthner, April 22, 1919, p. 37; #28. MB to Siegmund Kaznelson, April 28, 1919, p. 38; #32. MB to Fritz Mauthner, May 7, 1919, pp. 41 f.; #78. MB to Fritz Mauthner, April 8, 1922, pp. 97 f.; #39. Ernst Joël to MB, July 1, 1919, p. 50. (These letters are in the order in which they are cited in the chapter rather than in chronological order as in the Sources for other chapters.)

Sydney and Beatrice Rome, eds., *Philosophical Interrogations*, "Martin Buber" section, p. 70.

Buber, *Pointing the Way*, "What Is to Be Done?" (1919), pp. 109–11; "Recollection of a Death" (1929), pp. 115 f., 118–20.

Martin Buber, *Grundsätze*, Vol. I of *Worte an die Zeit* (Munich: Dreiländerverlag, 1919), pp. 5–11.

Martin Buber, *Gemeinschaft*, Vol. II of *Worte an die Zeit* (Munich: Drei-länderverlag, 1919), pp. 7-26.

Martin Buber, ed., *Gustav Landauer. Sein Lebengang in Briefen*, II. #491, p. 298; #492, pp. 299 f.; #515, pp. 336 f.; #524, Munich, December 30, 1918, p. 343; Martin Buber, Account (in German) of Landauer's Last Days and Death, pp. 421-25.

Martin Buber, Reden und Aufsätze zum 80. Geburtstag. Schriften des Zentralrats der Juden in Deutschland, No. 2 (Düsseldorf, 1958), "Professor Martin Buber schreibt der 'Basler National-Zeitung' " (April 15, 1958), pp. 54 f.

For an important study from within of the fight between the Bolsheviks and the Left Social Revolutionaries see I. N. Steinberg, *The Workshop of Revolution* (New York: Rinehart & Co., 1953). I. N. Steinberg was the first attorney general in Lenin's cabinet, but was imprisoned after two months when the Bolsheviks found themselves strong enough to dispense with the cooperation of the Left Social Revolutionaries (the so-called Norodniki).

Margarete Susman, *Ich Habe Viele Leben Gelebt*, p. 76.

Martin Beradt and Lotte Bloch-Zavriel, eds., *Briefe an Auguste Hauschner* (Berlin: Ernst Rowohlt Verlag, 1929), Stefan Grossman, Ebenhausen, April 13, 1919; Martin Buber, Heppenheim, April 15, 1919; Louise Dumont, Düsseldorf, May 7, 1919, pp. 185-92.

Conversation with Naemah Beer-Hofmann, New York City, 1967.

Buber, *The Knowledge of Man*, "Dialogue between Martin Buber and Carl R. Rogers," moderated by Maurice Friedman, The University of Michigan, Ann Arbor, Michigan, April 18, 1957, pp. 166-68.

SOURCES FOR CHAPTER 12:
Zionist Socialism and the Arab Question

Conversation with the noted Hebrew writer Shmuel Y. Agnon at his home in Talpiyoth, Jerusalem, Israel, on July 15, 1966. Agnon attributed the phrase "the last chance for the salvation of the Jewish people" in connection with the Balfour Declaration to Ahad Ha'am.

NOTE A TO CHAPTER 12

Weizmann did not confine his diplomacy to the British but established contacts with the Emir Abdullah and his brother Feisal, the latter of whom went so far as to accept the Balfour Doctrine under the condition of the independence of the Arab states (which did not materialize at that time) and even wrote to Felix Frankfurter in 1919 that the Jewish and Arab movements complemented each other, since both were nationalist, neither was imperialist, and there was room enough in Syria for both. Cf. Ernst Simon, "Nationalismus, Zionismus und der jüdisch-arabische Konflikt in Martin Bubers Theorie und Wirksamkeit," *Bulletin des Leo Baeck Instituts* (Tel Aviv), Vol. IX, No. 33, 1966, pp. 46-50, for a helpful résumé of the political and diplomatic activity of this period culminating in the Allies' acceptance of the politics of the Balfour Declaration at San Remo in April 1920.

Buber Briefwechsel II, #16. MB to Moritz Spitzer, January 19, 1919, pp. 25 f.; #17. MB to Hugo Bergmann, January 21, 1919, pp. 27 f.; #44. MB to Hugo Bergmann, September 9, 1919, p. 57; #45. Hugo Bergmann to MB, September 19, 1919, pp. 58 f.; #49. MB to Hugo Bergmann, October 21, 1919, pp. 61 f.; #50. MB to Hugo Bergmann, January 6, 1920, pp. 62 f.; #51. MB to Hugo Bergmann, January 24, 1920, p. 64; #56. Paula and MB to Ernst Elijahu Rappeport, January 2, 1921, p. 71; #63. MB to Louise Dumont-Lindemann, June 12, 1921, pp. 78 f.; #65. MB to Robert Weltsch, August 6, 1921, pp. 87 f.; #70. Carl Buber to Martin and Paula Buber, December 5, 1921, p. 91.

Buber, *Der Jude und Sein Judentum,* "Vor der Entscheidung" (middle of March 1919), pp. 508-14; "Zwei hebräische Bücher. Antwort auf eine Rundfrage (1928)," p. 771; "Der wahre Lehrer. Zum Gedächtnis A. D. Gordons (1923)," p. 772; "Der Acker und die Sterne. Den Genossen in Deganja zur Erinnerung an den Besuch von Gordons Grab (1928)," pp. 773 f. (The river to which Buber referred is the Jordan, the mouth of which, issuing from the Sea of Galilee [Kinneret], is very close to Kibbutz Degania. Gordon's house with its mounted birds and animals is still there, open as a museum to the public); "Rede auf dem XII. Zionistenkongress in Karlsbad," pp. 467-75 (the Resolution is from p. 474 f.); "Kongressnotizen zur Zionistischen Politik" (October 1929), pp. 480-87. (This article was first published in *Der Jude,* hence the reference to "these pages." The quotation is from p. 487.)

Buber Briefwechsel I, #207. Chaim Weizmann to MB, Manchester, England, May 4, 1913, pp. 330 f.; #210. Chaim Weizmann to MB, May 16, 1913, p. 333.

Ernst Simon, "The Political Way and the National View of Martin Buber," *loc. cit.*

Buber, *On Judaism,* "The Holy Way," pp. 135, 138-47.

Schilpp and Friedman, eds., *The Philosophy of Martin Buber,* Robert Weltsch, "Buber's Political Philosophy," p. 439.

Hans Kohn, *Martin Buber,* pp. 173-77, 342 f.

Buber, *Israel and Palestine [On Zion],* pp. 154-57.

Die Arbeit. Organ der zionistischen Volkssozialistischen Partei, Hapoël Hazaïr, Vol. II, No. 5/6 (April 1920), Rudolf Samuel, "Die Bedeutung der Prager Konferenz," p. 58; Robert Weltsch, "Unsere Prager Konferenz," pp. 62 f.

Martin Buber, "Der heimliche Führer," *Die Arbeit,* Vol. II, June 1920.

Martin Buber, *Israel and the World. Essays in a Time of Crisis,* 2nd ed. (New York: Schocken Books [paperback], 1963), "Nationalism," trans. by Olga Marx, pp. 214-26.

Ernst Simon, "Nationalismus, Zionismus und der jüdisch-arabische Konflikt in Martin Bubers Theorie und Wirksamkeit," *loc. cit.,* p. 59.

NOTE B TO CHAPTER 12

Buber's concern with establishing good neighborly relations with the Arabs did not begin with the Karlsbad Congress in 1921 or even with the Prague Conference in 1920. It was already present in 1918 in some of Buber's writings in *Der Jude*. In 1919 Buber coupled his attack on economic and political imperialism with the demand to build a lasting friendly understanding with the Arabs in all spheres of public life, to bring about and maintain an inclusive brotherly solidarity with them. "We are a Semitic stem, and Palestine is a Near-Eastern land." Again in 1920 Buber complained that no effort was made by anyone at the time of the Balfour Declaration to explain the situation to the Palestinian Arabs, to show them the economic and cultural gains that they might hope for from a systematic Jewish immigration. From Europe nothing took place that would consolidate the understanding between Arabs and Jews in the interests of a future national home. From Palestine itself, however, out of the circles of established authority, everything happened to disturb it; for the authorities wanted to secure the present situation, not to prepare for a future one. From this situation there developed the unrest of the last few months, Buber said, and finally the pogrom of Jerusalem. (*Der Jude und Sein Judentum*, "Vor der Entscheidung," p. 513, "In später Stunde," pp. 515 f.) (The Arabs fell upon the Jewish inhabitants of Jerusalem, and the Jews, under the leadership of Jabotinsky, undertook to defend themselves, for which Jabotinsky and the other leaders were imprisoned by the British for a number of years.)

Ernst Simon, "The Problem of Buber's Influence," *loc. cit.*

Robert Weltsch, "Nachwort: Martin Buber 1930-1960" in Kohn, *Martin Buber*, pp. 434-37. My version of Buber's letter to Magnes is based upon two texts: the translation from the Hebrew into the German in Robert Weltsch's "Nachwort," Kohn, pp. 436 f., and Uri Margolin's rough translation of the original Hebrew into English. The original is published under the title "The Truth and the Redemption" (1947) in Mordechai Martin Buber, *Am v'Olam* (Hebrew), Vol. II of *Te'udah v've'ud* (Jerusalem: Sifriah Hazionit, 1964), pp. 341 f.

For a comparison that places Buber's original version and the Congress resolution in parallel columns and makes detailed comments on the differences, see Ernst Simon, "Nationalismus, Zionismus und der jüdisch-arabische Konflikt in Martin Bubers Theorie und Wirksamkeit," *loc. cit.*, pp. 55-57.

SOURCES FOR CHAPTER 13:
Education and Politics

Address by Buber to the Zionistischen Delegiertentag Deutschlands, the end of 1916, *Jüdische Rundschau*, Berlin, January 5, 1917, quoted in Kohn, *Martin Buber*, pp. 149 f.

Buber, *The Knowledge of Man*, "Elements of the Interhuman," fourth section, "Imposition and Unfolding," pp. 82-85.

Buber, *Grundsätze*, Vol. I of *Worte an die Zeit*, pp. 5-8.

Doch das Zeugnis Lebt Fort. Der jüdische Beitrag zu unserem Leben (Berlin-Frankfurt am Main: Verlag Annedore Leber, 1965), "Erwachsenenbildung," pp. 162, 164.

Franz Kafka, *Briefe an Felice* in *Franz Kafka. Gesammelte Werke*, ed. by Max Brod, Prague, July 30, 1916, p. 673; October 14, 1916, p. 725 and n. 1, p. 725.

Hans Kohn, *Martin Buber*, p. 238 f. and n. 2 to p. 238 on p. 362.

Alfonse Paquet, "Florens," *Die Kreatur*. A quarterly, ed. by Martin Buber, Joseph Wittig, and Viktor von Zweizsäcker, Vol. I, No. 1 (Spring 1926), pp. 131-34.

Florens Christian Rang, "Glaube, Liebe und Arbeitsamkeit. Ein Brief an Walter Rathenau" (Koblenz, May 1914), *Die Kreatur*, Vol. II, No. 1 (Spring 1927), pp. 34-70.

"Ein Brief von Florens Christian Rang" (Braunfels, August 10, 1921), *Die Kreatur*, Vol. III, No. 3 (1929), pp. 279-89.

Elizabeth Rotten, "Erziehung als Begegnung," *Pädagogische Blätter*, ed. by Heinrich Sesemann, Vol. VI, No. 19/20, Berlin, October 1955, pp. 245 f., 249 f.

Buber, *A Believing Humanism: Gleanings*, "The Task" (1922), pp. 99-101; "Religion and God's Rule" (1923), p. 111.

Buber, *Rede über der Erzieherische* (Berlin: Lambert Schneider, 1926), "Vorwort."

Buber, *Between Man and Man*, "Education," pp. 83-103.

MB to Franz Rosenzweig, undated #671, Archives of the Leo Baeck Institute, New York City.

Karl Wilker, "Religion, Politik, Erziehung," in *Das werdende Zeitalter*, Vol. VII, No. 2 (February 1928), pp. 35-38.

Buber Briefwechsel II, #306. MB to Paula Buber-Winkler, Pontigny, September 2, 1929, pp. 345-47; #308. MB to Paula Buber-Winkler, Abbaye de Pontigny, September 8, 1929, pp. 348 f.; #139. MB to Leopold Marx, August 8, 1925, pp. 233 f. and n. 1; #204. MB to Leopold Marx, February 9, 1926, pp. 245 f.; #207. MB to Leopold Marx, March 21, 1926, pp. 247 f.

NOTE TO CHAPTER 14:

Franz Rosenzweig and the Frankfurt Lehrhaus

On the basis of her analysis of Buber's Lehrhaus lectures on "Religion as Presence," Rivka Horwitz asserts that Ferdinand Ebner's "pneumatological fragments" *Das Wort und die geistigen Realitäten* (The Word and the Spiritual Realities, 1921) had an important influence on Buber's way to *I and Thou*, an influence which Buber himself explicitly denied. Ebner himself was struck by the close affinity of Buber's thought and his own when he read *I and Thou*: "The line of thought which this book develops, in a lyrical-mystical order which may be characteristic of Buber, is nothing else than the basic thought of the Fragments: the essential relation of the I to the Thou, and the roots of this being in the Word." Certainly when Ebner speaks of belief in the name of God as belief in the addressed person and when he says that the man who believes in the "Thou coming to meet him" no longer asks about the meaning of life, he is uncannily close to Buber. On the other hand, Horwitz is radically wrong when she says, "It has already become clear that on a cardinal point — the idea of God as the true Thou of the human I — Buber follows Ebner closely." That would imply that other Thou's are not true for Buber, and nothing could be further from the case. Buber certainly read Ebner before finishing *I and Thou* and, once at least in the lectures, followed him in saying that designating God as He or It is an anthropomorphism. But the fact that he spoke of God only once as "the Thou in itself" in *Herut* (1919) and did not consistently use Thou for God before his lectures on "Religion as Presence" in the winter of 1921–22 did not mean that it was Ebner's book that led him to do so, as Horwitz speculates. She herself is puzzled by the fact that Buber did not stress language or speech in *I and Thou* to the extent that Ebner did. More important, as Buber himself wrote in reply to a reader of a journal who claimed that Buber was concealing the "notorious fact of his dependency on Ebner," "Ebner's basic idea is the solitary relationship of the human I to the Thou of God, mine that of the fundamental connection between it and his relationship to the Thou of his fellowman."

Horwitz suggests that the answer Buber found on the train was "very likely the sudden, responding resonance to the spiritual chord struck by Ebner's Fragments," and though this is and must remain speculation, it seems to me possible — not in the sense of cause and effect influence or *post hoc ergo propter hoc* (Horwitz's notion of "influence" is more mechanistic than dialogical) but of the clarification of something that had been struggling to the light within Buber for many years. Nor does it follow that Buber's "sudden awareness that God must *always be addressed in the second person,* as the Confronted — as Thou" — means, as Horwitz claims, that "The force and the vitality of his future book and philosophy rests on the new name for God that he had discovered." "Thou" was not a new name for God for Buber: for God to Buber was also I and man Thou, and man, nature, and art were also Thou, as they were not to Ebner. What was new for Buber was not a name but the clarification of the I-Thou relationship as the source of all real living, and this, as we have seen, was the product of an organic development over twenty years to which Ebner's Fragments might have come at best only as a clarifying period. Put another way, one cannot separate Buber's understanding of the I-Thou relationship with the world from his understanding of man's relationship to God. Precisely the significance of the encounter with Hechler, as we have seen, lay in the fact that it occurred at the beginning of the First World War, the impact of which, more than any reading, brought Buber to his breakthrough to dialogue.

In her lecture at the Centenary Conference on Buber's Thought in Israel in 1978 Horwitz suggested that the Lehrhaus lectures show a temporary but highly significant influence of Ebner in the fact that the It-world is seen there as evil in the way that it is not in *I and Thou.* Her notion of a gnostic dualism present in the lectures is an almost total misreading. Although Ebner never uses the language of the It-World or I-It, he rejects the world and with it mathematics and science in a way that Buber would never do. If in *I and Thou*, Buber was to say that the will to profit and the will to be powerful are not evil in themselves but only as they become ends rather than means, in the Lehrhaus lectures he repeated his earlier insistence that the world of orientation has a relative justification and a positive value. What Buber *did* say in the Fifth Lecture was that if we consider the two basic positions next to each other, "then we might certainly *at first* (zunächst) feel that the construction of an It-World means somehow a betrayal, a defection, a withdrawal from a task that is given to us to build up the world out of the Thou" (italics added). He also spoke of a creation that has run away from God, of a "flight before the Thou," and of having "to live ever again the disappointment of becoming It." But it is not at all true, as Horwitz says, that "it remains highly doubtful whether there exists even the possibility of a relation between the Absolute Thou and the It-world." The dialectic which informed Buber's later understanding of the I-Thou and the I-It is present here too.

The discontinuity of the moments of Thou is only an apparent one, Buber asserted in the Sixth Lecture, because of the Absolute Thou. In this same lecture he spoke of not allowing the world only to become an It-world, but to take it with one, "to use a Hasidic word to uplift it, that means to uplift it to its roots, to leave nothing outside, to affirm all, but all not as finite or infinite number of things or of events, but all in the All-Thou."

> And again, not to step out of the individual Thou-relationships, not say to renounce them, as it were suppress them, but to let them all stream into the absolute relationship, into the relationship that does not arise out of their collection but also not out of separation from them, but out of their Becoming-All.

SOURCES FOR CHAPTER 14:
Franz Rosenzweig and the Frankfurt Lehrhaus

Franz Rosenzweig, *Briefe*, #101. To his parents, October 10, 1916, 125; #109. To his parents, November 3, 1916, p. 134; #113. To his parents, November 24, 1916, p. 141; #139. To his parents, March 10, 1917, p. 172; #211. To Hedwig Cohn-Vohssen, March 7, 1918, pp. 285 f.; #266. To Mawrik Kahn, Kassel, February 26, 1919, p. 357; #278. To Martin Buber (undated, probably the end of August 1919), p. 371; #484. To Hans Trüb, March 16, 1927 (For this last letter I use the translation in Nahum N. Glatzer, *Franz Rosenzweig: His Life and Thought* [New York: Schocken Books, 1953], p. 156); #360. To Rudolf Hallo, beginning of December 1922, pp. 460–63; #364. To Rudolf Hallo, end of January 1923, p. 473; #351. To Martin Buber, August 19, 1922, p. 441; #345. To Hugo Sonnenfeld, May 10, 1922, p. 433; #349. To Gertrud Oppenheim, latter half of

June 1922, p. 437; #355. To Martin Buber, September 20, 1922, pp. 443-45.

Nahum N. Glatzer, *Franz Rosenzweig: His Life and Thought* (New York: Schocken Books, 1953), pp. 156, 198-206; "Remote and Near. A Note on a Poem by Judah Ha-Levi," pp. 278-81; "Divine and Human," p. 243.

Martin Buber, *Pointing the Way*, "Franz Rosenzweig," pp. 87-92.

Franz Rosenzweig, *Understanding the Sick and the Healthy; A View of World, Man, and God*, ed. with an Introduction by N. N. Glatzer (New York: The Noonday Press, 1953), p. 80, *passim*.

Franz Rosenzweig, *The Star of Redemption*, trans. by William Hallo with an Introduction by Nahum Glatzer (New York: Holt, Rinehart, & Winston, 1970; N.Y.: Beacon Press [paper], 1972). My presentation of *The Star* in this chapter is based on the German original, *Der Stern der Erlösung*.

Franz Rosenzweig, *On Jewish Learning*, ed. by N. N. Glatzer (New York: Schocken Books, 1955), pp. 66 f.

Nahum N. Glatzer, "The Frankfurt *Lehrhaus*," in Robert Weltsch, ed., *Year Book I*, Publication of the Leo Baeck Institute of Jews from Germany (London: East and West Library, 1956), pp. 109-18, 122.

Buber Briefwechsel II, #68. Ernst Simon to MB, October 18, 1921, pp. 89 f.; #77. Franz Rosenzweig to MB, January 25, 1922, p. 97; #71. MB to Franz Rosenzweig, December 8, 1921, p. 92; #72. Franz Rosenzweig to MB, December 9, 1921, p. 93; #102. Franz Rosenzweig to MB, undated, p. 124; #90. Franz Rosenzweig to MB, undated, pp. 108 f.; #92. Franz Rosenzweig to MB, July 30, 1922, p. 110; #93. MB to Franz Rosenzweig, August 2, 1922, pp. 109-12.

Letters from Martin Buber to Franz Rosenzweig in the Archives of the Leo Baeck Foundation, New York City: undated #491.

Martin Buber, *Werke*, Vol. I — *Schriften zur Philosophie* (Munich: Kösel Verlag, Heidelberg: Verlag Lambert Schneider, 1962), "Zur Geschichte des dialogischen Prinzips," pp. 296-99.

Buber, *Between Man and Man*, "Afterword: The History of the Dialogical Principle," trans. by Maurice Friedman, pp. 213-16.

Rivka Horwitz, *Buber's Way to I and Thou*, p. 21, n. 20; pp. 23 f., 33-37; "The Lectures *'Religion und Gegenwart,'* Fourth Lecture: February 12, 1922, pp. 83, 85, 88, 94-96; Fifth Lecture: February 19, 1922, pp. 99, 102, 106, 108 f.; Sixth Lecture: February 26, 1922, pp. 111-15, 118-25; Seventh Lecture: March 5, 1922, pp. 126-34; Eighth Lecture: March 12, 1922, pp. 138-52 (these lectures are printed in Horwitz's book only in German, so all the translations and paraphrases, here as elsewhere, are mine); pp. 172, 179.

Rivka Horwitz, *Buber's Way to I and Thou*, pp. 24, 170-82. On pp. 166-70 Horwitz conclusively dismisses Trude Weiss-Rosmarin's claim that Buber was influenced by Hermann Cohen's *Religion of Reason out of the Sources of Judaism* (1919) with its concept of "correlation."

SOURCES FOR CHAPTER 15:
From the Easy Word to the Hard Word: The World as Word

•————————————————————————————•

Letter from Martin Buber to Maurice Friedman, August 8, 1954.

Hans Kohn, *Martin Buber*, pp. 20, 26, 240 (the original poem runs: "Wir sind die Laute, die der Urmund spricht, / Und doch sind wir nur Wörter, Worte nicht. / Wann werden wir zu Worten, die sich fügen / Zu Einem Satz, dem Urspruch zu genügen?"); p. 364, n. 1 to p. 240; pp. 241 f.

Werner Kraft, "Gedenkrede auf Martin Buber," *MB (Wochenzeitung des Irgun Ole Merkas Europa)*, Tel Aviv, Vol. XXXIV, No. 24, June 17, 1966, p. 9.

Werner Kraft, *Gespräche mit Martin Buber*, pp. 26, 131.

Buber, *A Believing Humanism: Gleanings*, "Reminiscence" (1957), p. 30; "To Create New Words?" (1918), p. 31; "The Demonic Book" (1924), pp. 46 f.; "Spirits and Men" (1961), p. 53; "Hermann Hesse's Service to the Spirit" (1957), p. 70; "Style and Instruction" (1922), pp. 103-05.

NOTE A TO CHAPTER 15

Kraft, *Gespräche mit Buber*, p. 26; Letter from Buber to B. J. Morse, c. 1952 in B. J. Morse, "Buber's *Baalschem* and Rilke's *Ninth Duino Elegy*," *loc. cit.* Morse also quotes the following passage from Buber's letter: ". . . Ich bin Rilke nur einmal begegnet, in München, wo mich Karl Wolfskehl auf der Strasse mit ihm bekannt machte: das Gespräch zwischen uns war, vielleicht infolge der Art des Kennenlernens, nicht sehr ergiebig. Einen Briefwechsel mit ihm habe ich nicht gefürt . . ." (I met Rilke only once, in Munich where Karl Wolfskehl introduced us on the street; the conversation between us, perhaps because of the manner of our becoming acquainted, was not very fruitful. I did not carry on a correspondence with him . . .). Buber knew Rilke's poetry, of course, but it exercised no decisive influence on him. The influence was the other way around, especially, as B. J. Morse has demonstrated, in the impact of "The Life of the Hasidim" from *The Legend of the Baal-Shem* on Rilke's *Ninth Duino Elegy*. B. J. Morse of Cardiff, Wales, sent Buber a manuscript which is so detailed and careful in its scholarship as to be entirely convincing in its claim that "The Life of the Hasidim" specifically and significantly influenced Rilke's *Ninth Duino Elegy*. To cite only one of his conclusions: "These excerpts [from letters] . . . establish that Rilke knew and had read *Baalschem*, that he possessed the first edition of the book prior to the year 1914, when he lost his library at Paris, and that even in 1923 he could still write of it in terms that suggest that he attached a special significance to it. We know further that until 1914 he possessed practically all that Buber had written, that he had read *Daniel* in 1913, as well as *Die Rede, die Lehre und das Lied*, and *Ereignisse und Begegnungen*, both of which were issued by the Insel-Verlag in 1917" (pp. 8 f.). I cannot go here into the close textual analyses and comparisons that Morse presents, some of which I have paraphrased in Chapter 6 — "The Discovery of Hasidism." Morse's concluding sentence is an important qualification to all attempts to establish "influence": "Rilke . . . has integrated Buber's idea into his own thought sequence in such a manner that it has been dissociated from the meaning that it originally possessed in Buber. The intellectual ambient is Rilke's, not Buber's." The manuscript is now in the Buber Archives at the Jewish and National University Library in Jerusalem. I quote and refer to the above passages with permission of the author. Since Morse wrote me in 1966, the essay has been published under the title "Rainer Maria Rilke and Martin Buber" in Irmgard Buck and Georg Kurt Schauer, eds., *Alles Lebendige meinet den Menschen. Gedenkbuch für Max Niehaus* (Bern: Francke Verlag, 1972), pp. 102-28.

There are many parallels too between Buber's *Daniel*, whose beauty Rilke greatly admired, and the last Elegies. In Maurice Friedman, "Translator's Introduction" in Buber, *Daniel*, pp. 15-17, I mistakenly ascribe the influence on the *Ninth Duino Elegy* to *Daniel* but also show significant parallels. Most of all, one can say that Buber and Rilke shared a common atmosphere and a common style. Buber was critical of Rilke at times in a way that suggested a limit to this affinity. In 1963 Buber used Rilke's French poetry as an example of inauthentic bilingualism, as opposed to the "authentic bilingualism" of Buber's son-in-law the later German-Hebrew poet Ludwig Strauss. Rilke's French poems proceed, wrote Buber, "from an artistic mastery which, as is well known, Rilke only later brought under the domination of a higher power; here, in the French poems, this artistic mastery rules without opposition, manipulating the modern form of the French lyric almost as if in play." *A Believing Humanism*, "Authentic Bilingualism," p. 82. In contrast to the great German mystic Angelus Silesius, with whom Buber was much concerned at the time of writing his doctoral dissertation and, five years later, his anthology of "Ecstatic Confessions," Buber found Rilke's *Books of Hours* lacking in humility. Kraft, *Gespräche mit Buber*, pp. 116, 125.

Grete Schaeder, *Martin Buber*, pp. 29, 73.
Wilhelm Michel, *Martin Buber. Sein Gang in die Wirklichkeit* (Frankfurt am Main: Rütten & Loening, 1926), pp. 11-14.

NOTE B TO CHAPTER 15

I and Thou, pp. 42 f. "Sie aber, zum lebendigen Verkehr, dem weltauftuenden, unlustig und untauglich geworden, wissen Bescheid; sie haben die Person in der Geschichte und ihre Rede in der Bücherei eingefangen; sie haben die Erfüllung oder den Bruch, gleichviel, kodifiziert; und sie geizen auch nicht mit Verehrung und gar Anbeutung, hinlänglich mit Psychologie untermischt, wie es dem modernen Menschen geziemt. O einsames Angesicht sternhaft im Dunkel, o lebendiger Finger auf einer unempfindlichen Stirn, o verhallender Schritt!" Buber, *Werke I, Schriften zur Philosophie*, p. 106. I have revised the translation of the last phrase.

Buber, *The Origin and Meaning of Hasidism*, p. 147.
Buber, *Hasidism and Modern Man*, "Hasidism and Modern Man," p. 22.
Ibid., p. 24. Of Jiri Langer, Buber wrote me that he was an authentic man without being an authentic author. Buber was referring to Langer's book *Nine Gates to the Chassidic Mysteries*, trans. by Stephan Jolly (New York: David McKay Co., 1961).

Ibid., p. 25, where Buber himself quoted, and I translated, this passage from the Foreword to *Der Grosse Maggid und Sein Nachfolge.*

Martin Buber, *Tales of Angels, Spirits & Demons*, trans. by David Antin and Jerome Rothenberg (New York: Hawk's Well Press, 1958).

I and Thou, trans. by Ronald Gregor Smith, pp. 66, 116–19.

I and Thou, trans. by Walter Kaufmann, pp. 165–68.

Martin Buber, *Eclipse of God. Studies in the Relation between Religion and Philosophy* (New York: Harper Torchbooks, 1957), "Religion and Philosophy," trans. by Maurice Friedman, p. 36.

NOTE C TO CHAPTER 15

The "New Thinking," wrote Franz Rosenzweig, is *Sprachphilosophie*, lived speech, bound to the dimension of time. Buber himself, in his "History of the Dialogical Principle," traced the trail of this "Speech Philosophy" through Friedrich Heinrich Jacobi in the eighteenth century, Feuerbach and Kierkegaard in the nineteenth, Hermann Cohen, Franz Rosenzweig, Ferdinand Ebner, and others, including himself, in the twentieth. One could also mention the importance of Kant's great opponent Johann Georg Hamann ("Speak that I may see thee"), of the German-language philosopher Wilhelm von Humboldt, of the brothers Grimm, and of Eugen Rosenstock-Huessy. Cf. Harold Stahmer, *"Speak That I May See Thee!" The Religious Significance of Language* (studies in the works of J. G. Hamann, Eugen Rosenstock-Huessy, Franz Rosenzweig, Martin Buber, and Ferdinand Ebner) (New York: The Macmillan Co., 1968). Aside from Feuerbach and Kierkegaard, acceptance and rejection of each of whom were already a part of Buber's existence as a young man, Hamann, Humboldt, and, to a lesser extent, the brothers Grimm undoubtedly had an influence on the development of Buber's pronominal philosophy of speech (I, Thou, we, it).

Letter from Martin Buber to Ronald Gregor Smith, February 25, 1937, Martin Buber Archives, Jewish and National University Library, The Hebrew University, Jerusalem, Israel.

Buber, *Between Man and Man*, "Dialogue," "Who Speaks?" p. 15.

NOTE D TO CHAPTER 15

In his Preface to the 1923 collected edition of his *Speeches on Judaism* Buber rejected the notion of "a myth-spewing imagination" manufacturing finished products in the soul's workshop in favor of man's coming to meet God and of myth as the expression of that meeting. Myth is impressed upon that person who is alive with a burning sense of color and shape, that undivided person whose eyes can glimpse the ray of the Divine that meets it. "Divine images originate not in the depths of a lonely soul, but rather on that plane of man's being which is open to that which is other than man, though it can reflect it only in human terms." (Buber, *On Judaism*, "Preface to the 1923 Edition," pp. 7 f.) "The first myths were hymns of praise." In *I and Thou* myth is as a meeting of man with the concrete, particular Thou that confronts him, and the unconditional, divine quality of myth derives from the "between" itself. As a result, Buber's understanding of myth was later clarified and changed beyond what it was in *Daniel.* The unconditioned is no longer experienced or even "realized" *within* man but *between* man and what is over against him. Myth is the faithful report of meeting, the preservation of the meaning and intensity of the unique event responded to with one's whole being.

> The elementary impressions and emotional stirrings that waken the spirit of the "natural man" proceed from incidents — experience of a being confronting him — and from situations — life with a being confronting him — that are relational in character. He is not disquieted by the moon that he sees every night, till it comes bodily to him, sleeping or waking, draws near and charms him with silent movements, or fascinates him with the evil or sweetness of its touch. . . . he has in him only the dynamic, stirring image of the moon's effect, streaming through his body.

The occurrences to which elementary man ascribes the "mystical power" are all meetings which stir him: the encounter with the moon and the dead, the burning sun and the howling beast and the chief whose glance constrains him and the sorcerer whose singing fills him with power for the hunt. Mana is simply the effective force which has made the person of the moon into a blood-stirring Thou. Magic then becomes not something exercised by the will of man but a participation in "the grand relational events, the elemental emotional shocks." (*I and Thou,* trans. by R. G. Smith, pp. 19–21.)

NOTE TO CHAPTER 16
The Overcoming of *Erlebnis*

The undated plan which Walter Kaufmann tentatively identified as the 1916 sketch in his translation of *I and Thou* is really, Horwitz has shown, a plan composed in the summer of 1922, after *I and Thou* had been completed, and no copy of the 1919 sketch has been found. But Horwitz has found in the Buber Archives and published an outline in Buber's handwriting of February 5, 1918, entitled "The Confronted and the Between." The "Confronted" (the encountered) is envisaged in this outline in terms of forms (God, Work, Beloved, etc.) and relations (to create, to love, to command). The "Between" is seen as "Hypostatization of the *Relation*," hence as an obstructing demon rather than what Buber later was to call the "sphere of the between." It was clearly Buber's intent to reject the redemption of this demonic, hypostasized Between either through Christ or through Dionysus (Nietzsche) and to show the dualism of the Confronted and the Between in Myth, Magic, and Mystery. This hypostasized abstraction which gets in between the I and the Thou is clearly identical with what Buber later called the It (which is also no substance); hence it is not, as Horwitz suggests, "an attempt to build a philosophical system solely on the grounds of I-Thou." Nor does the absence of explicitly dialogical terminology from the plan of 1918 mean, as she suggests, that "scholars who have sought the beginnings of *I and Thou* by searching for early dialogical expressions have followed a false trail." "Dialogue" to Buber never meant mere speech, as it did to Rosenzweig and Ebner. Moreover, even if Buber found his finished terminology late, his thought developed organically and in response to events — more than to any "influence," as I have shown in this volume of *Martin Buber's Life and Work.*

In the 1907 Introduction to *The Legend of the Baal-Shem* Buber spoke of "legend as the myth of I and Thou, of caller and called, and of the finite that enters into the infinite and of the infinite that needs the finite." This was an exemplification of the dialogical relationship at its highest peak. "From this event of the exception, of the extraction, however, my thought now led me, ever more earnestly, to the common that can be experienced by all," Buber stated in "The History of the Dialogical Principle." This clarification took place, as we have seen, in "The Holy Way" (1918), "Herut" (1919), and "Community" (1919), but also in connection with Buber's interpretation of Hasidism:

> In the Preface written in September, 1919, to my book *Der Grosse Maggid und seine Nachfolge* (1921), the Jewish teaching was described as "wholly based on the two-directional relation of human I and divine Thou, on reciprocity, on the *meeting.*" Soon after, in the autumn of 1919, followed the first, still unwieldy, draft of *I and Thou.* *

In addition to the motto from Goethe, Buber had several other possible mottos for *I and Thou* which he did not use:

> Thou who readest this
> What thou willst read here is spoken to thee. . . .
> I do not know thee, how can I say Thou to thee?
> I know thee, I say Thou to thee, I address thee.

What is here called speech is the primal act of the spirit whose human consummation the spoken and all sign-languages and all the powers of expression serve as helper and instrument.

> The gods and the demons contend with one another; there the demons speak in arrogance.

> Do not give way, remain standing, do not turn over the leaves before you have decided: to leave this reading or to perceive it as a word spoken to you.**

Also preserved in the notebook for *I and Thou* is a long poetic passage on decision that was not included in *I and Thou:*

> Decision, first-born daughter of the spirit, terrestrial comrade of grace, who loves to gaze into your eyes — of your domains I have spoken time after time; of your self there is hardly anything other to say than of a song whose praise only he understands who knows it.

Toward the end of this passage is a picture of two possibilities. The first is not realizing decision and letting it flow as a poison into one's soul. The

---

*Between Man and Man, "The History of the Dialogical Principle," p. 215.
**Horwitz, p. 260, my translation.

second is realizing it, in which case too it becomes a thing among things; that which is at the beginning primordially free becomes, once the decision is made and acted upon, an external reality like any other, that which is at the beginning alone and unique becomes measurable, comparable, judgable. "This is the exalted melancholy of our fate."* This very image of exalted melancholy is used in *I and Thou* concerning the way in which every Thou must become an It. Hence we have here the connection between "With a Monist," with its understanding of the "bestowing side of things" which is unique, unmeasurable, and incomparable, and *I and Thou* with its dialectical alternation between I-Thou and I-It.

Buber also set down in this notebook a Table of Contents which can serve as a sort of skeleton key to *I and Thou:*

The Two Basic Words
The Speaking of the Basic Words
The Twofold I
It and Thou
The Relationship
Experience
World and Experience
The Three Rungs
The Creature
The Human Being
The Form
Presence and Object (*Gegenwart und Gegenstand*)
The Ideas
The Working
Love and Hate
Reciprocity
Becoming It
The Original
The Detachment of the I
Sprit and Becoming
The "Primal Paradise"
Unification and Relationship
The Inborn Thou
The Arising of the Ordered World
It-World and Thou-World
The Privileges of the It-World
The Augmentation of the It-World
Spirit and Relationship
Feelings and Institutions
Sprit and Communal Living
Freedom and Fate
The Free and the Arbitrary
(In One's Own Mouth)

*Horwitz, pp. 263 f., my translation.

Before the publication of *Ich und Du* Buber sent the page proofs to Franz Rosenzweig and received extensive criticism from him. Rosenzweig had attended Buber's lectures on "religion as Presence" as long as he was well enough to and after that had read the stenograph manuscript at his house. On January 4, 1922, just before the beginning of the Lehrhaus lectures, Buber finally finished reading for the first time *The Star of Redemption*, and Buber and Rosenzweig often discussed *The Star* and its relation to the lectures during their weekly meetings. Actually Buber seemed to be more struck by Rosenzweig's positive treatment of Christianity in the third volume than by his discussion of dialogue and speech in the second. "Where he should have agreed (II) he has not seen right," Rosenzweig wrote his wife Edith, but was "full of rejection." Even the parts on Christianity that he praised Buber "clearly rejected." "I shall rightly teach him speech in Frankfurt."* None of this or anything else that she cites bears out Rivka Horwitz's claim that "for some reason Buber felt the need to prevent his sources and the influence of contemporaries from being known." Buber's memory of the connections of events was poor, but his acknowledgment of Rosenzweig was consistent and generous despite any differences between them. As Horwitz herself testifies, "Buber was critical of the extreme systematizing [of Rosenzweig's *Star*], which runs completely against the grain of his thought," and which, in Buber's words, "fits too well." He could hardly agree either with Rosenzweig's conclusion that dialogue initially exists only between God and man and only afterward between man and man. Rosenzweig, for his

*Franz Rosenzweig, *Briefe*, #332. To Edith Rosenzweig, January 4, 1922.

part, disliked the term "relation" as too philosophical and suggested that it be replaced by "bond" or mutuality." For all this, Buber wrote Rosenzweig in August 1921 that no page of *The Star* was alien to him, no matter how far his own opinion might be from it.

That the living dialogue between Buber and Rosenzweig during this final period had a significant impact upon Buber, who was always able "to calmly and sincerely open himself to criticism," as Horwitz says, is beyond doubt. Just what that impact was is more problematic. Horwitz suggests that Rosenzweig was influential, first, in bringing Buber to a "concept of dialogue, which is central to *I and Thou* but which is almost completely absent from the manuscript of '*Religion als Gegenwart,*' " and, second, in bringing him to "the gradual elimination of the terms 'realization' and 'orientation.' " The language of *Daniel* does, in fact, appear far more often in the eight lectures than in *I and Thou*. Yet the lectures are clearly beyond *Daniel* and close to *I and Thou* in what was really decisive for Buber — the breakthrough to the meeting with the other. Rosenzweig's possible role in the process whereby Buber shed the *language* of *Daniel* is not important; for that language was left over like the cocoon from which the butterfly emerges and not an essential part of Buber's thought. "Realization" still remains, but now it is clearly the realization of meeting and of dialogue.

More important, as Horwitz recognizes, is the question of Buber's concept of dialogue. In the lectures the Thou relation does not "involve any decisive element of speech, call or dialogue," Horwitz writes.

> While one reference of man's speaking to nature exists, this thought is certainly not developed. *The dialogical basis of the I-Thou was, in fact, one of the very last additions to an already existing structure.* This fact goes far, I believe, in explaining a great deal of the problematics and inconsistencies present in the published version of *I and Thou.**

Horwitz bases this assertion on the four cardinal examples which Buber presents in "Religion as Presence" in order to explain the Thou-relation: man's relation to his beloved, to the tree (nature), to a work of art, and to a potential act upon which he decides. She cites uses of the word "realize" in the lectures ("I do not have to experience the Thou that confronts me, but to realize it") and of the change in *I and Thou* to the language of speech ("When I stand in front of a human being as my Thou and speak the basic I-Thou to him"), and she claims that the four examples really belong to the philosophy of realization rather than that of *I and Thou*.

> The examples have their source *not* in dialogical thinking, but in the philosophy expressed in *Daniel*. Three of the four do not lend themselves to real dialogue; one of them cannot even be adapted to dialogical thinking. They can be explained only in the framework of a concept of confrontation which does not include dialogue or speech.**

*Horwitz, pp. 214 f.
**Ibid., p. 215.

She recognizes, to be sure, that in the lectures Buber says Thou to nature, but dismisses this because it is inconsistent with Ebner and criticized by Rosenzweig. At the same time she gives an interesting, if inconclusive, quote from the Book of Job as the possible inspiration of Buber's idea of a work of art which confronts man as a Thou when he is conceiving it and before it has attained form:

> A spirit passed before my face. . . .
> It stood still but I could not discern the form thereof,
> An image was before mine eyes,
> There was a silence and I heard a voice.

Yet she concludes that "to identify such creative moments with I-Thou dialogue is questionable and highly problematic." In fact, she suggests that Buber himself realized how inappropriate the I-Thou relationship in art was and therefore, while retaining it in *I and Thou*, obscured it!

What is wrong with all this, aside from the fact that it is sheer speculation, is, first, that Horwitz is accepting Ebner's and Rosenzweig's use of "dialogue" as synonymous with speech as "classic" and on that basis treats Buber's use of dialogue as problematic. Dialogue does not just mean speech for Buber, as it does for Ebner and Rosenzweig. Art as dialogue, so far from being something Buber wished to obscure, recurs in all clarity in "Dialogue" (1928) and in *The Knowledge of Man* (1965). "Dialogue" already appeared in Buber's Preface to *Daniel* ("The Walking Stick") as a direct outgrowth of his relationship to nature (again a tree). Second, and equally important, it is not true that Buber was unconcerned with speech before *I and Thou* or that, as Horwitz claims, Rosenzweig clarified "For Buber the central importance of language." Chapter 16 of this book — "From the Easy Word to the Hard Word: The World as Word" — is powerful and incontestable evidence to the contrary. It *is* true that speech has a much more central place in *I and Thou* than in "Religion as Presence," and it is probably true that Buber's dialogue with Rosenzweig helped him bring into focus and integrate with his developing I-Thou philosophy the concern with speech that had been central to him too for a quarter of a century. Yet in the finished form of *I and Thou* and in the philosophy of dialogue and the philosophical anthropology that developed from it, literal speech is always only *one* of the forms of dialogue and never simply synonymous with it. In "Man and His Image Work" (*The Knowledge of Man*) the longing for perfected relation expresses itself in four potencies: knowledge, love, art, and faith. Thus more than thirty years after the publication of *I and Thou* in the most mature expression of his philosophical anthropology, something very akin to the four examples of the lectures recurs not as a leftover from the immature philosophy of realization of *Daniel* but as central and clearly thought through.

More significant for our purposes is the criticism of the galley sheets of *Ich und Du* that Rosenzweig wrote Buber in September 1922. This is a criticism that has been underscored not only by scholars such as Horwitz and Bernhard Caspar but by the one person who can claim, more than any other, to be a disciple of both Buber's and Rosenzweig's — Ernst Simon.

In a letter of September 1922 Rosenzweig sent Buber a long and brilliant critique after reading the first part of the galley proofs of *Ich und Du:*

> I shall take the bull by the horns: In the I-It you give the I-Thou a cripple as an opponent. That this cripple rules the modern world changes nothing in the fact that it is a cripple: *This* It you have, of course, easily rebuffed. But it is, in fact, the false It, the product of the great delusion, in Europe hardly three hundred years old. Only with this It is an I co- (not: spoken, but:) *thought.* No I is co-spoken with the *spoken* It. At any rate no human I. What I as human being cospeak when I rightly speak It, HE listens to. The "basic word I-It" cannot, of course, be spoken with the whole being. It is just not a basic *word,* it is at any rate a basic thought, ah no: a pointed thought, a thoughtpoint, a philosophical point. Thus when It is wholly real, it must just stand as a basic word that is precisely spoken with the whole being by him *who* speaks it. From His standpoint this basic word is called I-It (ICH-es.) From our standpoint: HE-it. If you once say, *He who kills and revives!* then you have said this basic word and have said it wholly *essentially.*
>
> From this narrowing to the I-Thou (that you at any rate share with Ebner) everything else follows, I believe. You, like Ebner, in the intoxication of the joy of discovery throw everything else (quite literally) to the dead. But *It* is not dead, although death belongs to it; It is created. But because you identify It with the certainly dead "It," you must lift everything that you do not want to see fall into this valley of death, into the kingdom of the basic word I-Thou, which thereby *must* become enormously enlarged.

Rosenzweig went on to suggest that there were two other essential basic words in addition to I-Thou, the HE-it of the Creator God over against the created world and the We-It in which lies the answers to all those problems which philosophy has sought in vain in the pseudobasic word I-It. Everything depends on being able to speak of God in the third person as the Creator. "I am a very unself-interested knight of the It," Rosenzweig concluded, "now more than ever."

> Behind my covered windows I am now truly *interested* only in I and Thou. But nonetheless. What shall become of I and Thou if it must swallow the whole world and the Creator? Religion? I dread it — and shiver before the word as always when I hear it. For *my sake* and *for thine* there must exist something else than — Me and Thee!*

Buber responded on September 14 thanking Rosenzweig for his great and splendid critique and begged him to continue doing the same when he read the rest of the proofs. In reading the Second Part, he suggested, Rosenzweig might find he had done less injustice to It and in the Third Part that HE and We existed as realities. He also confided that he had a name for each of the three parts in his own mind — Word, History, God — but hesitated to set

Buber Briefwechsel II, #103. Franz Rosenzweig to MB, undated, pp. 124–38.

them down as subtitles. Of the subsequent volumes the second would deal with the Primal Forms, the Knowledge and Law of God, the Person and Community, the Power and the Kingdom, the third with God as HE, and the fourth with We.

Of course, I have neither the sanction to speak of a decisive HE nor the authority to speak of a decisive We. Thus I must confess it — not conceal my nakedness and my loneliness, and cannot ask whether I only bear my name or perhaps may also be called human being. I would almost implore you to take me at my word that I have not been "intoxicated" for a moment; as often as I have been directed and concentrated on these things all these years, I have always had a proper sobriety that I can most easily compare to the state of mind of an only halfway informed musician who was trying to follow a difficult symphony thoroughly. It will not be especially successful, but I cannot imagine the effort to be more sober —

How much is still to say, and how little! Sometimes it seems to me that the essential difference, or as you think opposition, between us consists in the fact that we understand the Kingdom differently. Otherwise you would not have asked me "What will come of it." "Religion" certainly not.*

After Rosenzweig had read the final galley he wrote Buber on September 22 that the closeness and distance between him and Buber were heightened for him to an extreme.

How do you know that the course is not a cyclical one? Is it that it *can*not be for you? And if you know it, from where do you know it otherwise than just because — it *is*? But if there is such a being, why shall it remain invisible and inaudible to us? Why shall only the moment flame up? Why must the continuity remain *ungraspable* to us? From where then also do you believe it? That is a bundle of questions, and still really only the one first question, that of the It, transposed from the logical into the metaphysical. For I answer you thus: yes, the It in many passages receives full justice, but that is not your merit but its; the passages fall out of your course of *thought*. The created reality preceding all fictitious Its springs for you there into concept, God be thanked (really!). . . . How gladly would you accept Buddha into your paradise over which I-Thou stands written! How gladly would you accept the house cat and all pious heathen souls and Aristotle. But you cannot succeed; they only come finally to a wonderfully beautiful place in the forehell, to the It. But it does not at all need to be a fore*hell*, it would be a true fore*heaven* if you had only not let the bedeviled *I*-It of the philosophers talk you into it, but had rather the blessed HE-it of the child and Goethe and the

---

Buber Briefwechsel II, #104. MB to Franz Rosenzweig, September 14, 1922, pp. 128-30. Here as everywhere else these are my translations. Those by Rivka Horwitz are often in essential respects inaccurate.

Creator. For there has never yet been a man as long as the world existed who said: "I see the tree." Only philosophers say that.*

When Buber failed to respond to this letter, Rosenzweig wrote Buber that his expressive silence made him fear that he had been displeased by it. "I am not so timid that I cannot tolerate a sharp word, but also not so thick-skinned that I would not feel a silence more strongly than any word, even the sharpest — and that cannot be your intention." "How can you think that I am engaging in an 'expressive silence' toward you," Buber asked, "a form of speech for which I have, incidentally, neither inclination nor capacity?"

> You must have noticed that in interaction with you, from the sec-
> ond half hour of your visit to Heppenheim, I have used the pure expres-
> sion that in a somewhat messianic dream-wish one would wish to use
> with all persons. . . . That I have not answered your letter of Friday
> lay simply in the fact that at this point of the conversation I could
> presumably still have continued talking but not continued writing. . . .
> I am indeed basically, as you have probably already noticed, in general
> not a writing person; earlier I interested myself in writing, but now
> I give myself to it really when and because I am commanded to do so.
> You are one of the few persons with whom in this decade I can "ex-
> change" letters; often you pull me out of hell; at times it is stronger.**

Rosenzweig responded the next day: "The truth that is *between* us is too closely bound up with the truthfulness that is *in* us for me ever to say to you a 'naked' truth, one that I was not ready to pay for with my own life."***

Commenting on this correspondence between Rosenzweig and Buber regarding the galleys of *I and Thou*, Rivka Horwitz quite rightly says that Rosenzweig's philosophy begins with "a leap of faith," a biblical faith without which one cannot philosophize on Rosenzweig's basis. Buber, in contrast, places philosophical anthropology and not theology at the center of his philosophy. "For Rosenzweig there is no I-It, nor any basic word that cannot be spoken with the whole human being," says Horwitz. Buber is like Ebner, who states: "Of the relationship between God and the world we can literally know nothing." When I asked Buber whether God had an I-Thou relationship to man in creating him, Buber replied, "Now you are talking like the theologians. How do *we* know what relationship God had to man?" But this does not mean, as both Horwitz and Bernhard Casper claim, that Buber has no view of creation, no relation between God and nature, or that Buber "agrees with Kierkegaard in not founding his I-Thou and I-It on creation." Nothing is more central to *I and Thou* than Buber's understanding of creation, as is demonstrated in the last chapter of this volume.

Horwitz is right in seeing I and Thou as "a response to the outcry of a generation suffocated by machines, institutions, sciences and information — a generation seeking real life." But she is wrong in maintaining that I-It does not and cannot lead to God. The It is the necessary material for the

---

*Ibid, #108. Franz Rosenzweig to MB, September 22, 1922, p. 136.
**Buber Briefwechsel II, #109. Franz Rosenzweig to MB, undated, p. 138; #110. MB to Franz Rosenzweig, September 23, 1922, pp. 138 f.
***Ibid., #III. Franz Rosenzweig to me, September 29, 1922, p. 140.

becoming of the Thou, and unless it is brought again and again into the Thou, there can be no Thou. Horwitz is like those who imagine some mythically pure I-Thou unmixed with It, and it is for that reason, perhaps, that she falls into what would otherwise be an unbelievable distortion for a Buber scholar, namely the statement that "Buber's theory of I-It is in basic agreement with the Idealist's understanding of the world as dependent on human consciousness, and with his consequent denial of God's direct relation to nature." For Buber God speaks his word to man in creation. Concrete nature in its immediacy is Thou, not It, and as Thou it is really other. The impact of that otherness is exactly what Buber means by *meeting*. The It is not nature, as Horwitz occasionally remembers but more often forgets. It is man's concepts and categories about nature. Rosenzweig's real It which can be spoken with the whole being is really Buber's I-Thou relationship with nature. The It which the Thou again and again becomes is not necessarily inauthentic or any block to God, as Horwitz imagines, but neither is it, as she imagines, anything substantive. It is our subjective-objective relation to the world through the eyes of knowledge, science, and utility. The Thou breaks through all Idealism to the impact of an otherness that can never be incorporated into the I. If one does not understand this, one has not even begun to understand *I and Thou* — or one has *ceased* to understand it because one sees it only from Rosenzweig's, and not Buber's, perspective.

Because Rosenzweig uses dialogue as speech he has no actual place for the I-Thou relationship with nature. Therefore the It that he defends as prephilosophical is actually Buber's Thou (the directly comprehended, related to, concrete unique), though seen theologically through the eyes of God (HE-it) rather than man. Rosenzweig starts with a theological presupposition that enables him to speak of God's relation to creation *as if from God's point of view*. Buber starts with the existentially given I-Thou relationship from which the I-It relation necessarily derives, as the abstraction involved in our knowledge. Even where Buber later adopts Rosenzweig's triad of world-time as in "The Faith of Judaism" and "The Man of Today and the Jewish Bible," he does so not theologically but existentially, discovering creation, revelation, and redemption out of our own human experience and not from some a priori theological revelation.

We can understand this more clearly if we consider Bernhard Casper's more penetrating critique of Buber on the basis of Rosenzweig's correspondence about the galleys of *I and Thou*. Casper holds that Buber lacks both a past and a future that can be taken seriously as a reality of creation, i.e., as an irreducible given that cannot be derived from the I-Thou or already present in a concrete historical I-Thou relationship. "It is not I but *we* who first constitute the world," he says in explanation and adds that the future which is not thought but simply is there is finally the hoped-for and prayed-for future of the Kingdom of God.

> Through the clear division of the three basic words that Rosenzweig holds before Buber's eyes, the mortality of the I and of the Thou of the concrete historical event of meeting sharply emerges, but thereby also the specific timeboundness of the present happening here and at the same time the situation of the event of meeting *between*

creation (the inconceivable pre-supposition) *and* redemption (the finally valid unity that is only to be hoped for). The present which bears the concrete historical dialogue is itself only a timebound, mortal present and in no way simply eternity in time.

God is in no way merely the eternal Thou for the author of *The Star of Redemption*. This follows from Rosenzweig's taking seriously the timebound condition of thinking as speech. For talking in the second person, which can only take place in the immediacy of the present, is in no way the only real talking. Rather the speaking that takes seriously its own timebound condition, the talking *about* that takes place in the mediacy of the third person is altogether serious and in no way deficient speaking.

As soon as I witness to revelation, I must already speak *about* HIM. And this would only be deficient speaking if it no longer recognized its origin in the past event. God is for us, who perform the divine service with one another, the third, although at the same time no IT in the Buberian sense.*

Everything that Casper says makes sense in terms of Franz Rosenzweig's philosophy, or theology, but not of Buber's philosophy, which does not see either the It or the past as *mere* deficiency and does not regard speaking *about* as an evil but just the third-personal subject of the dialogue of I and Thou. This includes even the speaking about God, which is necessary, although in this latter case one must recognize that this is a metaphor and can never be other than a metaphor. Casper says that Buber must reject the naming of God as He as inauthentic in *I and Thou* and claims he fundamentally changed his position when he allowed God to be spoken of as ER (HE) in the Buber-Rosenzweig translation of the Hebrew Bible. But for Buber this ER equaled the Thou to whom we relate, hence was a metaphor and not an object of knowledge given us independently of our and past generations' dialogue with God. It is true, as Casper points out, that under Rosenzweig's influence Buber changed the "self-naming of God" from "I am that I am" in the first edition of *Ich und Du* to "I shall be there as I shall be there" in the later editions. But that was merely accepting Rosenzweig's more concrete understanding of *ehyeh asher ehyeh* and not anything which, by any stretch of the imagination, might place the Buber of the first edition "in the Platonic tradition": Buber's sense of the eternal was never a Platonic knowing above and outside of time and space and the concrete world but always in and through the historical moment in all its concreteness and uniqueness. Casper, like Horwitz, seems to have to turn Buber into an Idealist in order to justify Rosenzweig's speech-thinking, instead of recognizing, as Rosenzweig himself did in "The New Thinking," that here are two related but in some res-

---

*Bernhard Casper, "Franz Rosenzweigs Kritik an Bubers Ich und Du," paper given at the Centenary Conference on Buber's Thought, Beer-Sheva, Israel, January 3-6, 1978, to be published in German, English, and Hebrew as part of the proceedings of the conference. See also Bernhard Casper, *Das dialogische Denken. Eine Untersuchung der religionsphilosophischen Bedeutung Franz Rosenzweigs, Ferdinand Ebners und Martin Bubers* (Freiburg, Basle, and Vienna: Herder, 1967).

pects essentially different types of speech-thinking. The past and future that Casper points to are valid as seen from above, theologically, but they are no longer an *existential* past or an *existential* future, as in Buber. Rosenzweig certainly helped Buber recognize the full importance of creation, revelation, and redemption in his biblical books; yet all three are already fully present in *I and Thou*, as we shall see in Chapter 20 in the part on "Creation, Revelation, and Redemption."*

A reply which Buber made in the section of *Philosophical Interrogations* devoted to his thought sheds further light on his understanding of creation *and* of its relation to the "It." The American philosopher William Poteat asked:

> Assuming that there are two primary words which man speaks, "I-Thou" and "I-It"; assuming further that the former expresses a *religious* posture and that the latter does not; and granting that any "thing" in the world which may be addressed as an It may also be encountered as a Thou; it must follow that, the world being "twofold, in accordance with [man's] twofold attitude," no It, as It, can ever be the bearer of the divine, no being the incarnation of Being. If this is so, how can we ever say that the world is God's creature? (Cf. *"How* the world is, is completely indifferent for what is higher. God does not reveal himself *in* the world." L. Wittgenstein, *Tractatus*, VI, 432.)

To this Buber replied:

> I do not say that the world is twofold, rather, the world is twofold *to man*. I do not thereby say anything concerning anything existing independently of man. Moreover, in the biblical creation story God creates the things through the fact that he *calls* them out of their not-yet-being into being; in the third person, to be sure, but the grammatical form is not decisive here for what is meant: clearly God does not deal here with something with which he otherwise has nothing to do; he really turns to what shall come into being, the light, the water, the earth; and it is only the completion of this turning, when he

---

*Horwitz goes to extravagant lengths to try to establish Rosenzweig's influence upon Buber in the period *after* the publication of *Ich und Du*, such as her ascription of Buber's critique of Kierkegaard's denial of creation in "The Question to the Single One" (1936, not 1933 as she dates it) to the influence of Rosenzweig, or her seeing Buber's insistence on redemption as taking place "in the whole corporeal world," as being caused by Rosenzweig when it was, as we have repeatedly seen, one of Buber's earliest thoughts. Most absurd of all is her claim that "Rosenzweig's thoughts found expression in Buber's *Two Types of Faith*, a treatment of the difference between what he calls *pistis* and *emunah*. From the outset he employs Rosenzweig's distinction between the Christian as the one who believes *in* something, and the Jew, who is himself the belief." Buber's distinction is rather between faith as a knowledge proposition and faith as unconditional trust and has nothing to do with the Jew himself being the belief. What is more, Buber could never accept Rosenzweig's view of Christianity as a history religion and Judaism as simply living with the eternal outside of history. If anything, Buber saw Judaism as far more really historical than Christianity. See Horwitz, *Buber's Way to I and Thou*, pp. 234–35, 238, and Maurice Friedman, *Martin Buber's Life and Work: The Later Years – 1923-1965* (New York, E.P. Dutton, 1982), Chapter 20 – "Two Types of Faith: Jesus and Paul."

finally says to man who has come into being, "you." Wittgenstein is right: God does not reveal himself in the world; he is wrong: God addresses the world thus existing, thus created as his own.*

SOURCES FOR CHAPTER 16:
The Overcoming of *Erlebnis*

• ———————————————————————— •

Paul Schilpp and Maurice Friedman, eds., *The Philosophy of Martin Buber*, Hugo Bergmann, "Martin Buber and Mysticism," pp. 302 f.; Martin Buber, "Replies to My Critics," pp. 693, 701 f., 706, 712.

NOTE A TO CHAPTER 16

Paul Flohr has pointed out that Buber's rejection of *Erlebnis* arose as early as March 1917 when Buber characterized the sphere of Werfel's poetry as not "Leben" but "Erleben." Werfel's world was a mere extension of his ego and his feelings, "echo-words" without any prestabilizing distance from the world, as a result of which he was abandoned to destructive melancholy and doubt. In this statement Buber also clearly anticipated *I and Thou*. Unable to accept the natural aloneness of the ego, Werfel seeks union with the world, but it "is refused him, because it is not the Thou but the I of the entity he encounters, and . . . I-ness rejects union." "The real locus of duality lies in one's inability to accept the separateness of his ego and to view the world as other than I." Martin Buber, "Vorbemerkung über Franz Werfel," *Die Jüdische Bewegung*, II, pp. 104-10, quoted in Paul R. Flohr, "The Road to I and Thou," *loc. cit.*, p. 222.

NOTE B TO CHAPTER 16

Paul Schilpp and Maurice Friedman, eds. *The Philosophy of Martin Buber*, "Replies to My Critics," pp. 711 f. This does not mean that Buber rejects entirely his earlier contrast between mere experience (*Erfahrung*) and life-experience (*Erlebnis*). "Man goes over the surfaces of things and experiences them," Walter Kaufmann translates a sentence in *I and Thou* and enlarges in a helpful footnote: "The effect of the German sentence is to make the reader suddenly aware of the possibility that *erfahren* might literally mean finding out by going or driving, or possibly by traveling. But by further linking *erfahren* with *befahren* Buber manages to suggest that experience stays on the surface. In the original manuscript this point was elaborated further . . . 'Thus the fisherman gets his catch, but the find is for the diver.' " *I and Thou*, trans. by Walter Kaufmann, pp. 55, 64.

*Sydney and Beatrice Rome, eds. *Philosophical Interrogations* (New York, Harper Torchbooks, 1970), "Martin Buber" section conducted and Buber's replies trans. by Maurice Friedman, p. 85.

Rivka Horwitz, *Buber's Way to I and Thou,* Part One — "The Lectures *'Religion und Gegenwart,'* " Second Lecture: January 22, 1922, p. 60; Third Lecture: February 5, 1922, pp. 76 f., 79 f.

Buber, *On Judaism,* "Preface to the 1923 Edition," pp. 4-10.

Maurice Friedman, *Martin Buber: The Life of Dialogue,* pp. 52 f.

Buber Briefwechsel II, #17. MB to Hugo Bergmann, January 21, 1919, pp. 27 f.

Sydney and Beatrice Rome, eds., *Philosophical Interrogations,* "Martin Buber" section, trans. by Maurice Friedman, pp. 99 f.

Werner Kraft, "Gedenkrede für Martin Buber," *loc. cit.,* p. 9.

I and Thou, trans. by Ronald Gregor Smith, pp. 9, 55 f., 123. I have changed the quotation from Hölderlin to conform to my own translation in *Daniel.*

Grete Schaeder, *Martin Buber,* pp. 115, 117, 123, 138.

NOTE TO CHAPTER 17
Spirit as Response: Knowledge and Art

In 1970 I received a new translation of *I and Thou* by Walter Kaufmann. Since Kaufmann is a translator of Nietzsche and Goethe and a poet in his own right and since he knows German better than Ronald Gregor Smith, who translated the original English edition that was published in 1937 and issued in a second revised edition in 1958, I expected that he might capture even more faithfully the concise, poetic quality of the original. I was disappointed. His forty-page introduction and the elaborate scholarly footnotes, for all their service to the scholar, get in between the reader and the text. The text itself is heavy and Germanic and in most cases altogether lacking the poetic quality that the young English theologian Ronald Gregor Smith captured after he spent weeks with Buber and his friends in 1937. Some inaccuracies, to be sure, are remedied, and for this we can be grateful. But Kaufmann's rendering of key terms as well as of many crucial passages seems to me unfortunate.

Kaufmann has rendered *Umkehr* as "return," thereby losing the whole dynamic of *teshuva* or the turning, a central concept and call of the biblical prophets. Although Buber's term *Begegnung* was introduced into English as "encounter" through Emil Brunner's *Divine-Human Encounter* (Wahrheit als Begegnung), Buber and I always strongly preferred "meeting," and it is thus that Smith translated this central term in his *I and Thou.*

One of the more difficult terms to translate is the verb *verwirklichen* and the accompanying adjective *wirklich* and noun *Verwirklichung.* Smith translated them as "to realize," "real," and "realization," and I have followed this in my translation of Buber's early book *Daniel,* his philosophy of "realization." Kaufmann translates them as "actualize," "actual," and "actualization." I realize, as Ernst Simon pointed out in Jerusalem in January 1978, that in English the *usual* meaning of "realization" is to become aware that something is the case. On the other hand, the terms "actual," "actualize," and "actualization" stand in the philosophical tradition of Aristotle's contrast between the "potential" and the "actual" — a tradition that is quite foreign to the Buber of *I and Thou*, however much it may have informed his doctoral dissertation of 1904. Literally, *verwirklichen* means to make real or to become real and *Verwirklichung* the act of making real. If that resembles Goethe's "Werde was du bist" (Become what you are), it has nothing to do with that single-minded emphasis upon the realization of potentialities that informs the human potential movement in America and elsewhere, nor with Abraham Maslow's "self-actualization," which, even when it refers us outward to work and to creative relationship with others, is marred by that psychologism which makes self-actualization the measure, touchstone, and goal and our relationship to what is not ourselves the means to that goal.

The sad result of all this is that the central sentence of *I and Thou*, instead of reading, "All real living is meeting" (Smith), reads "All actual life is encounter" (Kaufmann). Kaufmann's translation of *Du* as "You" instead of "Thou," as Smith and Kaufmann's *title* both have it, is, I would grant, a moot point. Kaufmann has done a real service in trying to correct the tendency to regard the "I-Thou relationship" as exclusively or mainly between man and God — the result of its being introduced into the English-speaking world first through Neo-Orthodox Protestant theologians — and restoring the primordially Jewish recognition (and that of Jesus) that the love of God cannot be separated from the love of one's neighbor. Asked as to what he would regard as the central portion of his lifework, Buber responded that the one basic insight that led him to the study of the Bible and Hasidism, as well as to his independent philosophy, was "that the I-Thou relation to God and the I-Thou relation to one's fellow man are at bottom related to each other. ... All my work on the Bible has ultimately served this insight." Since there is no "Thou" in English, except as it is found in the Bible or among "plain-speaking" Quakers, it is natural that many regard the I-Thou as something rarefied and fall into that way of thinking which led the Old Testament scholar C. H. Dodd to say that most people imagine that everything in the Bible happened on Sunday!

On the other hand, there are two considerations that weigh heavily against Kaufmann's translation of *Du* as "You." The first is that by 1970 there was an already-established usage of thirty-three years and a whole literature in which the "I-Thou" is employed. The second is that in English "you" is all too often impersonal and means not much other than "one," thus missing entirely the directness, mutuality, openness, and presentness that Buber wished to convey by using the distinction which does exist in German (as in Spanish and French) between the *Du* and the *Sie*, the "Thou" and the "You." All things considered, I still prefer "Thou." If Ronald Gregor Smith's translation had not been taken off the market entirely, then even the reader who knows no German might have compared the two translations and come somewhat closer to the original. As it is, except for libraries, the reader has no access except to Kaufmann's translation. In *Martin Buber's Life and Work* I have mostly used Smith's translation, on a number of occasions Kaufmann's, and sometimes my own.

SOURCES FOR CHAPTER 17:
Spirit as Response: Knowledge and Art

Buber, *I and Thou*, trans. by Ronald Gregor Smith, pp. 9 f., 14, 25 f., 33, 41
f., 86 (I have revised the final sentence for the sake of clarity), 97, 129.
I and Thou, trans. by Walter Kaufmann, pp. 137 (for the sake of clarity I
have substituted Ronald Gregor Smith's translation for Kaufmann's
in the last half of the first sentence quoted: see *I and Thou*, trans.
by R. G. Smith, p. 89 f.), 141, 145 f.; "Afterword," p. 175.
Sydney and Beatrice Rome, eds., *Philosophical Interrogations*, "Martin
Buber" section, p. 36.

NOTE A TO CHAPTER 17

In 1955 I placed the distinction between I-Thou knowing and I-It knowledge at the center of my chapter on "Theory of Knowledge" in *Martin Buber:
The Life of Dialogue*, only to discover in 1978 that Buber had made that
identical distinction between the direct knowing of relationship and indirect
knowledge in his 1922 lectures on "Religion as Presence." (Rivka Horwitz,
Buber's Way to I and Thou, "Religion als Gegenwart," Eighth Lecture: March
12, 1922, p. 141.) In the 1922 unpublished manuscript of *Ich und Du* Buber
further emphasized the particularity of knowing in relationship. The creature
announces itself not in abstraction or law but in itself. Only the one who
contemplates this fulfills the meaning of the act of knowledge as one that is
real and living between men. (Horwitz, p. 265, my translation.)

Schaeder, *Martin Buber*, p. 145.
Buber, *A Believing Humanism: Gleanings*, "Philosophical and Religious World
View" (1928), p. 130.
Martin Buber, "Lesser Ury," in Martin Buber, ed., *Juedische Kuenstler* (Ber-
lin: Juedischer Verlag, 1903), pp. 45 f.

NOTE B TO CHAPTER 17

Buber, *Pointing the Way*, "Productivity and Existence," pp. 8-10. The professor in this essay was the great German sociologist Georg Simmel, and
the friend whom Simmel wished the I of the essay to persuade of the
effectiveness of writing books was Buber himself. See *Buber Briefwechsel*
II, #336. MB to Hermann Gerson, Marina di Massa, September 4, 1930,
p. 382.
Rivka Horwitz, *Buber's Way to I and Thou*, "Religion als Gegenwart," Fifth
Lecture: February 19, 1922, pp. 100 f.
Martin Buber, "Autobiographical Fragments," 10. "A Lecture," in Schilpp
and Friedman, eds., *The Philosophy of Martin Buber*, pp. 14 f., and
Buber, *Meetings*, pp. 32 f.
Buber, *The Knowledge of Man*, "Man and His Image-Work," trans. by Maurice
Friedman.

SOURCES FOR CHAPTER 18:
Love and Marriage, Politics and Community

• ――――――――――――――――――――――――― •

Buber, *I and Thou*, trans. by Walter Kaufmann, pp. 67, 108 f., 155.

NOTE A TO CHAPTER 18

In 1921, Schaeder points out in her introduction to the first volume of Buber's correspondence, Paula Buber had published a book in which the elements, which had been pagan in her previous work, were full of God. Thus it is probable that she was the person whom Buber had in mind as the "you" from whom he obtained, by waiting, God's presence in all elements. Kaufmann strengthens Schaeder's interpretation by observing that "the two lines in the *Divan* that follow upon Buber's epigraph support her reading: *Wie du mir das so lieblich gibst! / Am lieblichsten aber dass du liebst:* 'How you give this to me in such a lovely way! But what is loveliest is that you love.' "

Grete Schaeder, "Martin Buber. Ein biographischer Abriss," *Buber Briefwechsel* I, p. 39.

Walter Kaufmann, "I and You. A Prologue" in Buber, *I and Thou*, trans. by Walter Kaufmann, pp. 26 f.

Buber, *Daniel*, pp. 58 f.

Buber, *A Believing Humanism: Gleanings*, "Power and Love" (1926), p. 45, see p. 44 for the German original; "On the Day of Looking Back" (1928), p. 49, see p. 48 for the German original; "Do You Still Know It . . . ?" (1949), p. 51, see p. 50 for the German original; "A Conversation with Tagore" (1950), pp. 183 f.; "China and Us" (1928), pp. 186 f.

Hugo Bergmann, "Paula Buber," *M B (Mitteilungsblatt von irgun olej merkas Europa*, Tel Aviv), Vol. XXVI, No. 34 (August 22, 1958), p. 4.

Buber, *I and Thou*, trans. by Ronald Gregor Smith, pp. 47-52, 59 f. When Ronald Gregor Smith was translating *I and Thou*, Buber wrote to him that he used "the way" (*die Bahn*) in *I and Thou* with Lao-tzu's Tao in mind. Letter from Buber to Ronald Gregor Smith, February 25, 1937, Martin Buber Archives, Jewish and National University Library, the Hebrew University, Jerusalem, Israel.

Schalom Ben-Chorin, *Zwiesprache mit Martin Buber*, pp. 188 f.

NOTE B TO CHAPTER 18

Harvey Cox, *The Secular City* (New York: The Macmillan Co., 1965), pp. 41-49. Harvey Cox admitted the justice of these two criticisms at a dialogue we held before two hundred ministers at Union Theological Seminary in New York City in the summer of 1967 when we were both on the faculty of Union Theological Seminary.

SOURCES FOR CHAPTER 19:
The Self and the World: Psychologism and Psychotherapy

Buber, *I and Thou*, trans. by Ronald Gregor Smith, pp. 68 (I have revised the last sentence for the sake of clarity), 70-72, 43-45, 93-95.
Buber, *I and Thou*, trans. by Walter Kaufmann, pp. 120, 141.

NOTE TO CHAPTER 19

Walter Kaufmann uses "ego," not "individual," as the "self-willed man" that Buber sets in contrast to "person." Kaufmann writes, in explanation: "*Eigenwesen*, literally own-being, or self-being, is a highly unusual word. In the first English version of the book it has been rendered as 'individuality' although Buber had expressly protested on seeing page proofs that this bothered him a great deal (*'stört mich doch sehr'*): But I cannot think of anything better. In French there is the word *égotiste* (cf. Stendahl) which comes close to what I mean. . . . In a covering letter, dated March 8, 1937, Buber . . . insisted that he had nothing against individualities and added: '*Eigenwesen*, on the other hand, refers to a man's relation to himself. I do hope that you will find it possible to translate it differently. . . .' 'Ego' works perfectly in all the many passages in which Buber speaks of *Eigenwesen*. . . ."

Maurice Friedman, *Martin Buber: The Life of Dialogue*, pp. 185 f.
Maurice Friedman, *Problematic Rebel: Melville, Dostoievsky, Kafka, Camus,* 2nd radically revised and enlarged ed. (Chicago and London: The University of Chicago Press, Phoenix Books, 1970), pp. 95-128, 182-216, 446-69.
Rivka Horwitz, *Buber's Way to I and Thou*, "Religion als Gegenwart," Third Lecture, February 5, 1922, p. 72, my translation.
Buber, *A Believing Humanism: Gleanings*, "On the Psychologizing of the World" (1923), pp. 144-52.
Buber, *Between Man and Man*, "Dialogue" (1928), pp. 19-24; "Afterword: The History of the Dialogical Principle," p. 215.
Buber, *The Knowledge of Man*, "Dialogue between Martin Buber and Carl R. Rogers," p. 167.
Buber, *The Origin and Meaning of Hasidism*, "Spirit and Body of the Hasidic Movement," pp. 142 f.

SOURCES FOR CHAPTER 20:
The "Eternal Thou"

Buber, *I and Thou*, trans. by Walter Kaufmann, pp. 128-31, 156, 166 f., 182.
In his translation of *I and Thou*, p. 156, n. 9, Walter Kaufmann writes: "*Kammerfensters*. Buber explained in March 1937 that he was thinking of a *Dachkammer* and proposed the English words, 'of his garret win-

dow,' adding (in German): 'it is a poor student who lives in a garret;
  at night he opens the window and looks out into the infinite dark.' "
Buber, *I and Thou*, trans. by Ronald Gregor Smith, pp. 66 f., 79, 82 (italics
  added), 85, 96, 99, 107–09 (italics added), 115; "Postscript" (1958),
  p. 136.

NOTE TO CHAPTER 20

In contrast to Friedrich Schleiermacher and Rudolf Otto, who emphasized man's dependence on God and his "creature feeling," Buber stressed
in his "Religion as Presence" lectures and in *I and Thou* that one can with
equal justification speak of "a feeling of simple independence" and of the
spirit's becoming independent not only in personal religiousness but in great
religions. Rivka Horwitz, *Buber's Way to I and Thou*, "Religion als Gegenwart," Third Lecture, February 5, 1922), pp. 73 f.
Buber, *Eclipse of God*, "Report on Two Talks," trans. by Maurice Friedman,
  pp. 5–9. At the end of the talk with Natorp I have gone back to the
  German original, "Wir wollen uns Du sagen," rather than the rough
  English equivalent I substituted for it in my original translation, "Let
  us be friends."
Martin Buber, *Two Types of Faith*, trans. by Norman P. Goldhawk (New
  York: Harper Torchbooks, 1961), p. 12.
Buber, *On Judaism*, "Renewal of Judaism," pp. 45–49; "Jewish Religiosity,"
  pp. 90 f. (in the text I have translated the title of the essay "Jewish
  Religiousness" since "religiosity" has a pejorative connotation of affect-
  ed piety and elaborate devotionalism); "The Holy Way," all trans. by
  Eva Jospe, pp. 122 f., 125–28.
Dr. Martin Buber, Zehlendorf, "Ein Brief an den Herausgeber" in *Diskus-
  sion, Kultur-Parlament. Eine Monatschrift*, ed. by Hans Ostwald, Berlin,
  1910, No. 1, "Lebte Jesus?"
Martin Buber, "Eine Feststellung," *Die Welt*, Vol. XVIII, No. 21 (May 22,
  1914), p. 505.
Buber Briefwechsel I, #348. MB to Franz Werfel, March 17, 1917, pp. 483 f.;
  #372. MB to Landgerichtsrat S., November 26, 1917, pp. 512 f.; #375.
  MB to Hugo Bergmann, December 4, 1917, pp. 516 f.
Buber Briefwechsel II, #115. MB to Friedrich Gogarten, December 20, 1922,
  p. 145; #116. MB to Friedrich Gogarten, December 22, 1922, p. 146.
"Abende" (unpublished), *loc. cit.*, notes on Buber's fourth evening discus-
  sion with Hugo Bergmann and others on December 3, 1923.
Buber, *Israel and the World*, "The Faith of Judaism," p. 17.

Index

Buber's activities in, 55, 57–59,
141–142, 203, 276–278, 295,
297–300, 357
Buber's philosophy of, 88–89, 156,
161, 264–265, 276, 278–281
folk, 261, 276, 277, 282
Frankfurt Lehrhaus in, 282, 291–
300
Frankfurt Union in, 277–278
Jewish, 141–142, 203, 222, 224,
261, 276, 277, 279, 282, 291–300
political realities and, 279–281
religious, 281
"Education" (Buber), 257–258
Eisik Scheftel (Pinski), 10
Eisner, Kurt, 246–247, 250
"Elements of the Interhuman"
(Buber), 182, 233
Eliasberg, Ahron, 37, 38, 39, 41
friendship with Buber of, 22–26
Elijah (Buber), 18, 312
Emerson, Ralph Waldo, 79
"Epic of the Magician, The"
(Buber), 118
Erotic, The (Salomé), 172
eternity, Buber's intuition of, 29–30,
131
"Ethical Culture Society," 24
Events and Meetings (Buber), 190, 310
evil urge, 35, 97, 106, 136, 167
evolutionism, 12, 137
existentialism:
Buber's transition from mysticism
to, 82, 89, 91, 161, 168–169,
176, 329
God-world-man entities in, 286–
290
"Jewish Question" and, 130–132,
135–136
experience (*Erlebnis*), 320–322

Fackel, Die, 213
faith, reality and, 357–358, 366
fall of man, as psychologism, 350
Faust (Goethe), 48
"Feast of Life: A Confession"
(Buber), 43–44
feelings, modern man's concern for,

320, 347, 348
Feiwel, Berthold, 10, 53, 54, 56, 57,
59, 60, 61, 63, 66, 67, 68, 125,
206
Jewish university and, 57, 59, 261
feminine aspect, 170–172
Ferid-eddin-Attar, parables of, 310
Feuerbach, Ludwig, 78, 112, 366
"Fiddler, The" (Buber), 307
Fischer-Barnicol, Hans, 8, 16, 317–
318, 336
Florence, Italy, 98, 100
Flusser, David, 104, 105
form, 313
dynamism vs., 32, 111, 334, 371
as Thou, 333–334
Forte Kreis (Potsdam "group of
eight"), 172, 180–185, 195–199
as Jewish-Christian dialogue,
184–185
For the Sake of Heaven (Buber), 65,
109, 205, 312
"For You" (Buber), 52
fragmentation, creativity vs., 35–36
Frankfurt Lehrhaus (Freies Jüdisches
Lehrhaus), 141, 282, 291–300
Buber's course at, 295, 297–300
Frankfurt Union, 277–278
Frankfurt University, 203
Franzos, Karl Emil, 23–24
freedom:
Buber on, 83, 84–85, 344, 368, 369,
370
mystics and, 87, 106
necessity vs., 370
Free Jewish Club, Berlin, 143
Freud, Sigmund, 172, 180, 352
Friedman, Maurice, 86, 128, 155, 176,
298, 304, 319, 328
friendship, in Hasidic vs. Christian
hierarchy, 113
Fromm, Erich, 291
"From the History of the Problem of
Individuation (Nicholas of
Cusa and Jacob Boehme)"
(Buber), 79–82, 159
future:
as basic idea in Judaism, 139, 361

mythic nature of, 118, 161
nature and, 12, 14, 19, 159–160,
314–315, 319, 329
poet in, 162
realization and, *see* realization
response to Kant and, 29
revelation and, 288–290
Rosenzweig's understanding of,
287–290
speech in, 22, 311–318
uniqueness concept and, 80
unities in, 348
see also I; *I and Thou;* Thou
"It Is Time" (Rosenzweig), 291

Jacob's Dream, 17
Jacobson, Viktor, 215, 217, 225–226,
227, 308
Jesus, 34, 35, 301, 359–367
Buber's relationship with, 44, 184,
360–361, 363, 367
as Christ (redeemer), 365
"Jew," as term of abuse, 40
Jewish Almanac, 10, 133
Jewish Culture Committee, 277
Jewish folk culture, 261, 276, 277,
282
Jewish Movement, The (Buber), 210
"Jewish Mysticism" (Buber), 105
Jewish National Committee, 205, 206
"Jewish Religiousness" (Buber),
143, 363
Jewish Renaissance movement, 18,
31, 259
agrarian life as basis for, 263–264
Buber's Nietzschean approach to,
44–45
Buber's rejection of, 137–138, 270
Herzl's misconceptions about, 66
translations of Hebrew and Yiddish
in, 53
Zionism and, 34–52, 216, 224, 259
Jewish Socialists, Germany, 193
Jewish Society for International
Understanding, 269
Jewish state:
Balfour Declaration and, 259
cause of humanity to be fulfilled

in, 219, 223, 224, 260
Herzl and, 59, 61, 65–66, 71
Jewish nationalism and, 216–219,
222–223, 227–228
kingship of God and, 216, 218–219,
227, 230, 265
see also Israel, State of; Palestine;
Zionism
"Jewish Woman, The" (Paula
Buber), 51
Jewish youth movement (1920s),
228–230, 351
Joël, Ernst, 255–256
Judaism:
Baal Teshuvah in, 282, 296
"blood" vs. "environment" in, 84,
131–136
Buber's integration of Hasidism
into, 96–97, 101–102
as community, 134, 224, 229, 363–
364, 366
Der Jude and, 59–60
East-West oppositions and synthesis in, 46, 53, 72–73, 94–95, 126,
131, 146–147, 206, 215, 219–220
as existential choice, 130–132,
135–136
festivals as secular celebrations
in, 43–44
ghetto (Galut; exile), 39, 40, 45,
70, 136, 362
prophetic, *see* messianism
psychological duality in, 135–136,
138
relation to God in, 322
renewal concept in, 137–139
revelation in, 204, 225
three "ideas" of, 139, 361
three stages of realization in, 144–
145
Zionism and, *see* Zionism
"Judaism and Mankind" (Buber),
127, 135, 139
Jude, Der:
Buber's editorship of, after 1916,
200, 201, 206–230, 262, 283, 296
contributors to, 208–209, 214
founding of, 59–60